Monstrosity, Identity and Music

Monstrosity, Identity and Music

Mediating Uncanny Creatures from Frankenstein *to Videogames*

Edited by
Alexis Luko and James K. Wright

BLOOMSBURY ACADEMIC
NEW YORK · LONDON · OXFORD · NEW DELHI · SYDNEY

BLOOMSBURY ACADEMIC
Bloomsbury Publishing Inc
1385 Broadway, New York, NY 10018, USA
50 Bedford Square, London, WC1B 3DP, UK
29 Earlsfort Terrace, Dublin 2, Ireland

BLOOMSBURY, BLOOMSBURY ACADEMIC and the Diana logo are trademarks of Bloomsbury Publishing Plc

First published in the United States of America 2023
This paperback edition published 2024

Copyright © Alexis Luko and James K. Wright, 2023

Each chapter copyright © by the contributor, 2023

For legal purposes the Acknowledgments on p. xi constitute an extension of this copyright page.

Cover design: Federico Bebber
Cover image: Demons (2016) © Federico Bebber

All rights reserved. No part of this publication may be reproduced or transmitted in any form or by any means, electronic or mechanical, including photocopying, recording, or any information storage or retrieval system, without prior permission in writing from the publishers.

Bloomsbury Publishing Inc does not have any control over, or responsibility for, any third-party websites referred to or in this book. All internet addresses given in this book were correct at the time of going to press. The author and publisher regret any inconvenience caused if addresses have changed or sites have ceased to exist, but can accept no responsibility for any such changes.

Library of Congress Cataloguing-in-Publication Data

ISBN: HB: 978-1-5013-8004-4
PB: 978-1-5013-8008-2
ePDF: 978-1-5013-8006-8
eBook: 978-1-5013-8005-1

Typeset by Deanta Global Publishing Services, Chennai, India

To find out more about our authors and books visit www.bloomsbury.com and sign up for our newsletters.

Contents

List of Illustrations — vii
List of Contributors — viii
Acknowledgments — xi

Introduction — 1

Part I Frankenstein in Film, Theater, Music, Comics, and Visual Art

1. *Frankenstein*'s Frontispiece, the Missing Phallus, and the Pornographer: The Alchemy of Conceiving Monstrosities *Marie Mulvey-Roberts* — 9
2. Mashing the Medium: The Aesthetics of Screen Frankensteins *K. J. Donnelly* — 27
3. Frankenstein and the Media of Serial Figures *Shane Denson* — 43
4. Musical Directions, Sound, Silence, and Song in *Presumption, or the Fate of Frankenstein* (1823) *John Higney* — 64
5. Birth of a "Miserable Monster": The Alchemical Theatricality of Male Self-Procreation in Stage and Screen Adaptations of *Frankenstein* *André Loiselle* — 85
6. Excising the Repulsive: Metaphysics and Psychology in Edison's *Frankenstein* (1910) *Ethan Towns* — 98
7. *Frankenstein*'s Organ Transplant: Adaptation in Afro-Futurist and Electronic Dance Musics *Mark A. McCutcheon* — 114

Part II Monstrosity in Music, Film, and Videogames

8. Monstrosity as a Queer Aesthetic *Lloyd Whitesell* — 133
9. Twelve-tone Terror: Representing Horror and Monstrosity in Dodecaphonic Film Music *James K. Wright* — 150
10. The Horror, the Horror!: White Women are the True Monsters in Jordan Peele's *Get Out* *Frederick W. Gooding Jr.* — 172
11. Indigeneity as Monstrosity in *The Four Skulls of Jonathan Drake* *Murray Leeder* — 186
12. A "Distaste for . . . Allegory" or: In the Bowels of Horror *Daniel Humphrey* — 198

13 Tragic Wraiths, Seductive Sirens, and Man-Eating Vampires: Female
    Monstrosity in *The Witcher 3: Wild Hunt* Video Game *Sarah Stang*   213

Bibliography   233
Filmography   252
Index   257

Illustrations

Figures

1	Constantine Meglis, from the original cast of Andrew Ager's opera, *Frankenstein*	xii
1.1	Carl Lagerquist, *Frankenstein* (1922)	14
1.2	Lynd Ward, *Frankenstein* (1934)	15
1.3	Theodor von Holst, Frontispiece, *Frankenstein* (1831)	17
1.4	Theodor von Holst, *Faust in his Study* (1820–5)	19
1.5	Detail from Theodor von Holst, Frontispiece, *Frankenstein* (1831)	20
1.6	Theodor von Holst, Title page, *Frankenstein* (1831)	23
1.7	Henry Fuseli, *The Rosicrucian Cavern* (1805)	25
6.1	Frankenstein's Monster emerges from the cauldron	105
6.2	Frankenstein's Monster terrifies its creator in the parlor	109
8.1	Poster, *Heresies* (Fall 1977)	136
9.1	Image from Hanna Barbera's *Tom and Jerry* series, episode 16 (1'20"): "Puttin' on the Dog Part 2" (1944)	158
9.2	Threads of lineage, influence, and pedagogy connecting some of the leading composers (many of them film composers) of the twentieth century	161
12.1	Linked together: *The Human Centipede*	204
12.2	Linked together: *Us*	211
13.1	A screenshot of the noonwraith from the "Devil by the Well" side quest	217
13.2	A screenshot of the plague maiden challenging her former lover to prove his love by kissing her	221
13.3	A screenshot of succubi reveling at the feet of one of the main antagonists of *The Witcher 3: Wild Hunt*	224
13.4	Screenshot of the bestiary entry for sirens	225
13.5	A screenshot of the more monstrous form the siren takes when she attacks	226
13.6	Screenshot of a siren's corpse floating on the water	227
13.7	A screenshot of the bruxa card from Gwent, the card game in *The Witcher 3: Wild Hunt*	228

Table

4.1	Titles, Authors, Characters, Locations, and Function/Features of Songs in *Presumption*	79

Contributors

Shane Denson is associate professor of film and media studies in the Department of Art & Art History at Stanford University. His research and teaching interests span a variety of media and historical periods, including phenomenological and media-philosophical approaches to film, digital media, comics, games, and serialized popular forms. He is the author of *Discorrelated Images* (2020) and *Postnaturalism: Frankenstein, Film, and the Anthropotechnical Interface* (2014). He is also coeditor of several collections: *Transnational Perspectives on Graphic Narratives* (2013), *Digital Seriality* (2014), and the open-access book *Post-Cinema: Theorizing 21st-Century Film* (2016).

K. J. Donnelly is professor of film and film music at the University of Southampton. He is author of *The Shining* (2018), *Magical Musical Tour* (2016), *Occult Aesthetics: Sound and Image Synchronization* (2011), *British Film Music and Film Musicals* (2007), *The Spectre of Sound* (2005), and *Pop Music in British Cinema* (2001). He also coedited *Contemporary Musical Film* (2017), *Today's Sounds for Yesterday's Films: Making Music for Silent Cinema* (2016), *Herrmann and Hitchcock: Partners in Suspense* (2016), *Music in Video Games: Studying Play* (2014), *Tuning In: Music in Science Fiction Television* (2011), and *Film Music: Critical Approaches* (2001).

Frederick W. Gooding Jr. (PhD, Georgetown University) is an associate professor of history and is the inaugural holder of the Dr. Ronald E. Moore endowed professor of the Humanities at Texas Christian University in Fort Worth, TX. Featured in national outlets such as *New York Times*, *USA Today*, and Associated Press, Dr. Gooding is a professor of pop culture who engages audiences on subtle racial patterns "hidden in plain sight." Dr. Gooding has also provided social commentary on CNBC, CBS, and Fox News networks and has reached an international audience with messages of racial healing through the podcast "Reconcile This!" (https://podcasts.apple.com/us/podcast/reconcile-this/id1549430350?uo=4).

John Higney is an instructor in music at the School for Studies in Art and Culture at Carleton University, where he serves as supervisor of performance studies. He has presented research in Canada, the United States, and England, and has written on performance practice, Henry Purcell reception and dissemination, seventeenth- and eighteenth-century English musical aesthetics, early-nineteenth-century English musical reportage, music and Canadian cultural policy, and popular music and Canadian politics.

Daniel Humphrey received his doctorate from the University of Rochester and is professor of film studies in the School of Performance, Visualization & Fine Arts, as well as the coordinator of the Film Studies Program at Texas A&M University. He is the author of *Queer Bergman: Sexuality, Gender, and the European Art Cinema* and *Archaic Modernism: Queer Poetics in the Cinema of Pier Paolo Pasolini*. He has published articles in *Criticism, Screen, GLQ, Post Script, Invisible Culture*, and various anthologies. He specializes in European art cinema, film authorship, queer theory, and the horror genre.

Murray Leeder is an adjunct professor in the Department of English, Film, Theatre and Media at the University of Manitoba. He is the author of *Horror Film: A Critical Introduction* (2018), *The Modern Supernatural and the Beginnings of Cinema* (2017), and *Halloween* (2014) and editor of *Cinematic Ghosts: Haunting and Spectrality from Silent Cinema to the Digital Era* (2015) and *ReFocus: The Films of William Castle* (2018). He has published in journals such as *Horror Studies, The Canadian Journal of Film Studies, The Journal of Popular Culture*, and *The Journal of Popular Film and Television*.

André Loiselle is dean of the Faculty of Humanities at St. Thomas University, Fredericton, where he also teaches film studies. His main areas of research are Canadian and Québécois cinema, theatricality in cinema, and horror film. He has published almost fifty refereed articles and chapters in anthologies, as well as a dozen books, including (most recently) *Cinema of Pain: On Quebec's Nostalgic Screen* (2020, with Liz Czach) and *Theatricality in the Horror Film* (2019). Dr. Loiselle joined St. Thomas University in 2018 after twenty years at Carleton University, where he taught film and held several administrative positions, including assistant vice-president (academic).

Alexis Luko is professor of Music and the director of the School of Music at the University of Victoria. She has published widely on film music, music of the Renaissance, and early music analysis. Her articles have appeared in *The Journal of Scandinavian Cinema, The Journal of Film Music, TVNM,* the *Cambridge Journal of Plainsong and Medieval Music,* and *Early Music History*. Her monograph, *Sonatas, Screams, and Silence: Music and Sound in the Films of Ingmar Bergman*, was published by Routledge in 2016.

Mark A. McCutcheon is professor of Literary Studies at Athabasca University. His book *The Medium Is the Monster: Canadian Adaptations of Frankenstein and the Discourse of Technology* won the Media Ecology Association's 2019 Marshall McLuhan Award for Outstanding Book in the Field of Media Ecology. His research on Frankenstein adaptations has appeared in scholarly periodicals, including *Continuum* (2011) and *Popular Music* (2007), and in *Popular Postcolonialisms* (2019). Mark's debut poetry book, *Shape Your Eyes by Shutting Them*, has just been published by AU Press, and his poems have appeared in literary journals, including *Grain, EVENT,* and *On Spec*.

Marie Mulvey-Roberts is professor of English literature at the University of the West of England, Bristol. She has edited many books, including *Dangerous Bodies: Historicising the Gothic Corporeal* (2016) – winner of the Allan Lloyd Smith Memorial Prize – and coedited *Global Frankenstein* (2018). She is the co-founder and editor of the quarterly journal *Women's Writing* on historical women writers, for which she has coedited a special issue on Mary Shelley. Her two short films on Frankenstein and its links to Bristol and Bath are accessible on a MOOC (Massive Open Online Course) entitled "Writing the West: Writers of the South West."

Sarah Stang is an assistant professor of Game Design in Brock University's Centre for Digital Humanities. She received her PhD from the Communication & Culture program at York University. Her research primarily focuses on gender representation in both digital and analog games. She is the secretary for the International Communication Association's Game Studies Division and the former editor-in-chief of the game studies journal *Press Start*. Her published works can be found in journals such as *Games and Culture*, *Game Studies*, *Human Technology*, and *Loading*.

Ethan Towns recently completed an MA in film studies at Carleton University, Ottawa, with a thesis titled "The Silent Horror Film, 1896–1922: Narrative, Style, Context" (2020). He is the author of several short articles on film, including "Andy Muschietti's IT: Coming-of-Age and Horror Cinema," published in the journal *Film Criticism*. He is currently a PhD candidate of cultural studies at Trent University, Peterborough. His research interests include film history, film theory, Canadian cinema, and horror film. He is a two-time recipient of the Ontario Graduate Scholarship and a recipient of a SSHRC Canada Graduate Scholarship.

Lloyd Whitesell is professor in the Schulich School of Music, McGill University. His research explores the importance of sexuality, style, form, and emotion in modern music. His book *Queer Episodes in Music and Modern Identity* (coedited with Sophie Fuller) won the Philip Brett Award for outstanding LGBT musicology. Other interpretive studies include *The Music of Joni Mitchell* and *Wonderful Design: Glamour in the Hollywood Musical*.

James K. Wright is professor of music in the School for Studies in Art and Culture and the College of the Humanities at Carleton University. A McGill University Governor General's gold medal recipient, his publications include award-winning books on Arnold Schoenberg and *They Shot, He Scored*, on the life and work of the prolific Canadian film composer Eldon Rathburn. He is also widely known as a composer of chamber and vocal works, many of which involve the integration of music with dance and visual art. In 2019, he was named University of Toronto Louis Applebaum Distinguished Visiting Professor in Composition.

Acknowledgments

As with any book of this scope, countless colleagues, collaborators, students, and friends have contributed substantively to its preparation. To begin, profound thanks are due to the outstanding Bloomsbury Academic Press editorial and production team: Leah Babb-Rosenfeld (commissioning editor), Rebecca Morofsky and Joanna McDowall (marketing), Elizabeth Kellingley (production editor), Vishnu Prasad (project manager), Louise Dugdale (designer), and Rachel Moore (editorial assistant). Indexer Siusan Moffat has also been extraordinarily generous with her time and expertise. It has been a luxury to work with editorial collaborators with this level of skill, experience, and professionalism.

In part, this collection of chapters grew out of an international symposium, "The Gothic, the Abject, and the Supernatural: Two Hundred Years of Mary Shelley's *Frankenstein*," that we hosted on a memorable Halloween weekend in 2019. It was our special honor to welcome two outstanding scholars from the UK to deliver keynote addresses at the symposium: Marie Mulvey-Roberts (professor of English literature, University of Western England) and Kevin Donnelly (professor of film and film music, University of Southampton), whose contributions are featured herein as the first two chapters of this book.

We are indebted to many colleagues, students, and staff members at Carleton University who supported and encouraged this research, including Benoit-Antoine Bacon (President and Vice-Chancellor), Pauline Rankin (Dean, Faculty of Arts & Social Sciences), Brian Foss (Director, School for Studies in Art and Culture), Peter Coffman (School for Studies in Art and Culture: Art and Architectural History), Kristin Guth (Administrator, School for Studies in Art and Culture), Paul Jasen (Multimedia Technician, School for Studies in Art & Culture), John Rosefield (Carleton University Event Services), Andrew Riddles (Carleton University Web Services), Allen Scott (Carleton University Graphics Services), Barbara Leckie (Department of English Language and Literature), Mara Brown (Director, Carleton Dominion-Chalmers Arts Centre), and graduate students River Doucette, Ethan Towns, and Adrian Matte. We are particularly grateful to Jack Hui Litster, our ever-reliable research assistant, for lending considerable editorial skill to the project, and for his patient engagement and dialog with us and with our authors. We also wish to acknowledge the important collaboration of colleague James Deaville, who was a key contributor and interlocutor during the preparatory stages of both our symposium and this volume, and who initiated our conversation with Bloomsbury.

In conjunction with the symposium, we hosted the Ottawa première performance of Canadian composer Andrew Ager's opera, *Frankenstein*, at the Carleton Dominion-Chalmers Centre. We wish to single out two cast members for special mention: operatic bass Constantine Meglis (pictured in Figure 14.1 as Frankenstein's creature, in the original cast) and soprano Bronwyn Thies-Thompson (in the role of Elizabeth Lavenza,

Figure 1 Constantine Meglis, from the original cast of Andrew Ager's opera *Frankenstein* (photo courtesy of Chris Roussakis, Phantom Productions, Ottawa, Canada).

Victor Frankenstein's fiancée) were both outstanding performers and kind supporters of our symposium.

In addition to the symposium participants whose work is published in this book, we wish to thank Evangelia Mitsopoulou (Aristotle University of Thessaloniki, Greece), John Tibbetts (University of Kansas), Shoshannah Bryn Jones Square (Kwantlen Polytechnic University), Martin McCallum (McGill University), Michael Saffle (Virginia Tech), André Caron (Université du Québec à Montréal), Ashley Caranto Morford (University of Toronto), Sean Moreland (University of Ottawa), Stefan Honisch (University of British Columbia), and Derek Newman-Stille (Trent University) for their important contributions to our dialog. We also wish to thank our friend Dianne Parsonage, who encouraged this project from the outset in innumerable ways, providing invaluable perspective, level-headed counsel, and kind logistical support during the symposium. The British High Commission in Canada provided generous support, and we especially wish to thank Susan le Jeune d'Allegeershecque (British High Commissioner to Canada, 2017–21) and her staff members Samuel J. Jeremy (first secretary) and Samuel P. Kelly (second secretary) for their generosity with their time and resources.

We wish to extend our most heartfelt thanks to digital artist extraordinaire Federico Bebber, of Udine, Italy, for kindly granting permission to allow his phantasmagoric masterpiece, *Demons* (2016), to grace the cover of this book. In Federico's words, the images that constitute his work "are literally ripped out of everyday life, combined and merged with agonizing shapes, exposed to a fantastic metamorphosis, within a dream-like and surreal environment." He hopes that viewers of his work "will stop to listen, as if waiting for some sound, without knowing whether it will be music, words or screaming." It seems impossible to imagine a work of art better suited for our cover, and we are deeply grateful to Federico for his kind collaboration.

This research has been generously supported by the Carleton University Office for Research Initiatives and Services, and the Social Sciences and Humanities Research Council of Canada.

Introduction

Alexis Luko and James K. Wright

Monstrosity, Identity and Music: Mediating Uncanny Creatures from Frankenstein to Videogames assembles the work of a multidisciplinary team of researchers who share a common interest in the exploration of monstrosity—that which is deficient, horrifying, deformed, grotesque, and somehow "contrary to nature" (in Aristotle's problematic conception).[1] The book's initial inspiration grew out of a desire to reflect on the impact of Mary Shelley's proto-gothic novel, *Frankenstein; or, The Modern Prometheus*, two centuries after the publication of its first edition in 1818. Like the physical body of Victor Frankenstein's creature, it brings together a range of seemingly disparate discourses, threading together a conversation that illustrates the continuing importance and resonance of Shelley's nightmarish vision.

In studying abject creatures torn from the deepest and darkest imaginings of the human psyche, our thirteen authors deploy the latest analytical approaches drawn from such diverse fields as literary studies, musicology, gender studies, queer studies, technology studies, identity politics, critical race theory, psychoanalysis, film studies, and film music studies. The result is a book that weaves the manifold sounds, sights, and stories of monstrosity into a rich discursive tapestry that sheds light on some of the major social issues of our day.

Part I, "Frankenstein in Film, Theater, Music, Comics, and Visual Art," looks at a wide range of cultural "offspring" of Shelley's novel, as presented in film, theater, music, serialized comic books, and the visual arts. For readers and audiences from the early nineteenth century through to the present day, the figure of Shelley's Monster has evoked complex emotional responses of horror, awe, and new and confusing feelings of sympathy for the inhuman, while also inviting reflections on hubristic folly and the potential threat to humanity that unenlightened scientific exploration might represent. Part I sets out to explore how posterity has sustained, amplified, and elaborated on these manifold responses to Frankenstein's creature.

Marie Mulvey-Roberts (Chapter 1) focuses her attention on Theodor von Holst's hitherto overlooked frontispiece in the third edition (1831). Mulvey-Roberts traces the visually encoded semiotics of sexuality in artworks by Holst and his contemporaries and illustrates ways in which they both align and conflict with the novel in the context of the sexual mores of Shelley's social circle, including the notorious Lord Byron. Kevin

---

[1] See Joanna Sowa, "When Does a Man Beget a Monster? (Aristotle's *De generatione animalium*)," *Collectanea Philologica* 19, no. 1 (2016): 5–13.

Donnelly (Chapter 2) invites the reader into the bizarre realm of Monster Mash films, a curious subgenre that thrived around mid-century among the innumerable cinematic adaptations that followed the film that firmly situated the filmic identity of Frankenstein's Monster in the popular imagination: James Whale's *Bride of Frankenstein* (1935). For Donnelly, film form supplants elements of the original Frankenstein story over time, as a growing appetite for violence progressively disjoints the monster from its relationship to its creator. Shane Denson (Chapter 3) argues that Marvel's Frankenstein comics of the 1960s and 1970s offer a useful case study in the dynamics of serial narration, as it pertains both to comics in particular and to the larger plurimedial domain of popular culture in general. Denson interrogates the comics' storytelling techniques, arguing that Marvel's staging of the Frankenstein Monster mixes both linear and nonlinear modes of narrative seriality, forms that are correlated with two distinct types of series-inhabiting characters. This process sheds light on the medial dynamics of serial figures—characters including not only the monster but also serialized pop culture icons including Batman, Superman, Tarzan, and Sherlock Holmes—that are adapted again and again in a wide variety of forms, contexts, and media.

John Higney (Chapter 4) examines *Presumption, or the Fate of Frankenstein* (1823), Richard Brinsley Peake's early-stage adaptation of Shelley's novel, aligning it with contemporary Gothic English dramatic and comedic strategies. He argues that Peake's detailed stage instructions regarding sound and accompanying music, and the Romantic melodramatic effects obtained thereby, prefigure modern cinematic adaptations of *Frankenstein*. André Loiselle (Chapter 5) attends to gender-based perceptual and representational modes in *Frankenstein*, contrasting the thematic anxiety around childbirth and mothering in Shelley's novel with the misogynistic focus on male procreation through "science" that is manifest in later theatrical and film adaptations. What was originally a philosophical literary examination is transformed by the theatricality of stage and film into dramatic symptoms of a patriarchal phobia.

Ethan Towns (Chapter 6) focuses on Edison Studios' silent film, *Frankenstein* (1910), the first cinematic adaptation of Shelley's novel, written and directed by J. Searle Dawley. Noting that the Edison team specifically adapted the film to cater to early-twentieth-century American moral and religious norms and strictures, Towns decodes the filmic techniques, characterizations, and visual imagery through which these moral precepts are reinforced. Mark McCutcheon (Chapter 7) offers a close reading of Maestro Fresh Wes's "Let Your Backbone Slide." In a chapter replete with *Frankenstein* references, McCutcheon expands the scope of Adaptation Studies through his unique examination of the Maestro's classic track, Toronto's hip-hop scene, Afro-Futurism, and discourses characterizing technology as "manufactured monstrosity."

Part II, "Monstrosity in Music, Film, and Videogames," expands beyond Shelley's *Frankenstein* to explore other representations of monstrosity in music, film, and videogames. From the Latin *monstrare* (to "demonstrate") and *monere* (to "warn"), the monster can teach us lessons about our time, our culture, and our society. *Where* monsters live, *what* they represent, and *how* they are represented in different media change with time. Since monsters warn us about ourselves and about the societies in which we live, the messages in these warnings fluctuate in relation to our own shifting fears. In the chapters of Part II, "demonstrations" and "warnings" come in the form of what Jeffrey J. Cohen would identify as *monsters* that "dwell at the gates of difference," with "externally incoherent bodies," that resist categorization and rarely participate in socially constructed conceptions of "the order of things."[2] The monsters that inhabit these chapters challenge definitions and binary classifications, forcing a rethink of our understandings of the categorical boundaries of gender, sexuality, race, and aesthetic practice.

Lloyd Whitesell (Chapter 8) examines queer counter-discourses of monstrosity across different media and the significance of monstrous archetypes among queer artists: filmmaker John Waters; writers Tristan Alice Nieto, Bertha Harris, and Oscar Wilde; scholar Susan Stryker; visual artist Allyson Mitchell; and musicians Mykki Blanco and the Pet Shop Boys. Whitesell asks, "what is going on psychologically?" when queer artists draw upon the aesthetic imagery of monstrosity or adopt monsters as icons of queer counter-discourse? He draws upon examples by artists working in media outside of the horror genre—such as literature, opera, film, popular music, and visual arts—to illustrate the impact of queer subjectivity and "disidentification" through the representation of monstrosity in their aesthetic practice. James K. Wright (Chapter 9) considers the use of Arnold Schoenberg's twelve-tone method of composition in twentieth-century horror and monster film soundtracks. While Schoenberg viewed his method as "emancipating" dissonance, contemporaneous critics deemed it monstrous, deviant, and aberrant—subversively ignoring the boundaries of the tonal system. Wright's wide-ranging survey of significant composers and their scores—for feature films, sponsored shorts, and animation—charts the historic rise and fall of this compositional style among composers scoring for horror and monster films. Wright concludes that this music's limited emotional range and the attendant cessation of its usage in film scores of the twenty-first century now relegate it to a brief and clearly defined temporal period.

Frederick Gooding Jr. (Chapter 10) re-evaluates the characters of Rose and Missy Armitage in Jordan Peele's *Get Out* (2017) prompting an unpacking of the film's and Hollywood's racialized themes, and the history of slavery and racism in America. Gooding Jr. provides a rich context for the film, examining the cinematic history of interracial mixing, Hollywood's Third Rail, and the depiction of Black males on screen. He argues that Rose and Missy Armitage, who "appear to be nice," are the most monstrous of all the characters as they "anesthetize, sanitize, and rationalize the horror of dastardly destructive racist behavior and beliefs," and ultimately parallel the roles of white women of society who actively support institutionalized discriminatory practice within the framework of the white racial frame. Murray Leeder (Chapter 11) provides a close reading of Edward L. Cahn's obscure film, *Four Sculls of Jonathan Drake* (1959), and brings to our attention the lacuna that is the critical discussion of Indigenous peoples in horror. Leeder examines the role that Indigeneity has played in horror literature and horror theory in general, and argues that a "reverse colonialism" is often at play in race-themed horror films, where indigenous "subjects, artifacts, and forces . . . leave their exotic confines and make themselves known in the core of civilization." Embodied in

---

[2] Jeffrey Jerome Cohen, ed. *Monster Theory: Reading Culture* (Minneapolis: University of Minnesota Press, 1996), 7–9.

the racially mixed villain of the film, Dr. Emil Zurich, are settler anxieties rooted in Indigenous South America. As the othering of indigeneity is fundamental to the colonial project, so it is with its representation in horror films, where it is continuously leveraged to assuage settlers' anxieties about their own self-construction of "innocence" and purity.

In Chapter 12, Daniel Humphrey examines allegory, confronts its limitations, and critiques its multivalent relationship with discourses of violence and the contemporary constructions of race. Though, on the one hand, allegorical subtexts can validate horror films in the eyes of critics, allegory's subversive power to say one thing and mean another can simultaneously incite suspicion and even confusion, on the other hand. Films such as Passolini's *Salò* (1975) convey the "horror of a dysfunctional allegorical text" where, Humphrey argues, allegory itself has become monstrous. While Jordan Peele's *Us* "provides knotted allegories," Tom Six's *The Human Centipede* (2009) might be interpreted as a difficult to stomach "allegory about allegory," as well as a warning about meaning. Sarah Stang's contribution (Chapter 13) continues the feminist project of critical analysis in film and brings it to media studies by focusing on a selection of female monsters from the dark fantasy roleplaying videogame *The Witcher 3: Wild Hunt* (2015). While the female monster embodied in game characters—such as the wraiths, the sirens, the succubi, and the bruxae—draws on the image of a powerful, willfully monstrous woman, ultimately, Stang argues that they are misogynistic constructs, designed by men to be killed by male protagonists and male players. Stang calls for pushing back against misogynist tropes that have been remediated in mainstream videogames and suggests that monstrosity should instead be formulated as transgressive and empowering.

Within these chapters, various subtopics emerge. Some of our researchers employ transhistorical, intertextual, and intermedial perspectives, examining common monster tropes that resurface within and across genres and, in "translation," across media. Others examine the mediated social and cultural identities and the public reception of monster archetypes through the ages—Frankensteins, vampires, werewolves, and goblins—that live on in recombinant forms through comic books, theater, visual arts, opera, song, rap, film, music videos, television, and videogames. A number of chapters yield insights into how the concept of monstrosity underpins intersecting formations of race, gender, and sexual orientation as established by sights and sounds across a variety of different media.

What we have set out to accomplish in *Monstrosity, Identity, and Music* is captured well by Mary Shelley in her introduction to the third edition of *Frankenstein* (1831), where she reflects on the nature of creativity and discovery and raises troubling questions about both science and social responsibility:

> Invention does not consist in creating out of void. ... In all matters of discovery, even of those that appertain to the imagination, we are continually reminded [that] invention consists in the capacity of seizing on the capabilities of a subject, and in the power of moulding and fashioning ideas suggested by it.[3]

---

[3] Mary Wollstonecraft Shelley, *Frankenstein; or, The Modern Prometheus* (Oxford: Oxford University Press, 2008), 8.

Our authors have sought to seize upon various mediated representations of monstrosity that have emerged during the two centuries that have elapsed since Mary Shelley penned her groundbreaking novel. In their work presented together here, this chorus of commentary and reflection amply confirms that, within a wide range of contemporary scholarly discourses, "it's alive!"

Part I

Frankenstein in Film, Theater, Music, Comics, and Visual Art

1

Frankenstein's Frontispiece, the Missing Phallus, and the Pornographer

The Alchemy of Conceiving Monstrosities[1]

Marie Mulvey-Roberts

Mary Shelley's novel has been interpreted as encoding various sexual taboos, including those relating to illegitimate births and homoerotic tensions within her circle. Illustrated editions of *Frankenstein* that have brought out queer readings include the work of artists Carl Lagerquist and Lynd Ward. This chapter will argue for the first time that the 1831 edition of the novel contains obscure erotic iconography that has been previously overlooked and never before received critical attention. The artist is Theodor von Holst (1810–44), who gained notoriety for his erotic drawings and whose mentor was Henry Fuseli (1741–1825). This analysis proposes that the virility of the monster created by Victor Frankenstein is encrypted in the novel's frontispiece as a joke, which plays with the semiotics of sexual difference, homosexual panic, and the horrors of dissection and monstrous reproduction. My argument that the frontispiece contains sexual symbolism will also be tied to the esoteric traditions of alchemy and Rosicrucianism through the work of Fuseli. Whether or not Mary Shelley was aware of Holst's eroticized iconography or his unsavory reputation as a pornographer remains a tantalizing question.

In 1991, rock star Alice Cooper released a song entitled "Feed My Frankenstein," the sexual connotations of which were matched by a predictably raunchy stage performance. The title is a metaphor for the monstrous phallus, demanding erotic sustenance. In regard to Mary Shelley's novel, the hunger for love expressed in these lyrics chimes with the monster's desire for a mate to compensate for his deprivation of parental love and nurturing. At a pivotal meeting with Victor Frankenstein on the Mer de Glace in the French Alps, he manages to persuade his maker into agreeing to make him a mate. After embarking on this second act of creation, Victor reneges on his

---

[1] My thanks go to Nora Crook, James K. Wright, Marion Glastonbury, Tom Willard, Nigel Biggs, Christopher Frayling, and Grant F. Scott for their invaluable advice.

promise for fear of the two monsters spawning a "hideous progeny"[2] that could harm the human race. Horrified by this prospect, he rips the female monster into pieces, a brutal act of dismemberment, witnessed by her prospective bridegroom. As I shall argue in the section on *Frankenstein*'s illustrators, body parts, relating to reproduction and nurture, can be seen in the iconography of the frontispiece of the 1831 third edition of the novel, which also reminds us of how Victor's male and female creations were assembled from atomized human remains. The aggrieved and grieving monster takes revenge on his maker and mate's un-maker by killing his bride on her wedding night. Significantly, she is found dead on her bridal bed. Returning to the words of Alice Cooper, did the "psycho" monster "feed" his "libido" by combining murder with rape? What is latent in the novel was actualized through a rape scene in Danny Boyle's 2011 theatrical adaptation, performed at the National Theatre, London. As these instances of monstrous sexuality demonstrate, the novel addresses the consequences of conceiving horror, manifested in the birth of monstrosity through Frankenstein's creation.

Conceiving Monstrosities: Mary Shelley and Her Circle

The idea for the narrative was triggered by Mary Shelley's waking dream or nightmare, in which she describes, "the pale student of unhallowed arts kneeling beside the thing he had put together. I saw the hideous phantasm of a man stretched out, and then, on the working of some powerful engine, show signs of life, and stir with an uneasy, half vital motion. Frightful must it be."[3]

The pale student may well be a reference to Dr. John Polidori, whose training as a medical student would have involved him, like Victor Frankenstein, in the "unhallowed arts" of dissecting cadavers. Dr. Polidori was Lord Byron's physician and both men were spending the summer of 1816 at Villa Diodati on the shore of Lake Geneva in Switzerland. Along with Percy and Mary Shelley (known then as Mary Godwin), Mary's stepsister Claire Clairmont, and Lord Byron, Polidori participated in the same ghost story entertainment, which was the catalyst for *Frankenstein*. Mary Shelley had spent a fair amount of time conversing with him and in view of her protagonist's role as an anatomist, who had assembled his creation from various body parts, they might have discussed anatomy and dissection. Polidori had a less congenial friendship with Byron, who mockingly called him "Polly-Dolly."[4] The friction between the two is thought to have been exacerbated by a homoerotic tension that has informed queer interpretations of Polidori's short story, "The Vampyre" (1819), whose eponymous

---

[2] Mary Shelley, *Frankenstein*, ed. Johanna M. Smith (Boston: Bedford, 1992 [1831]), 23.
[3] Ibid., 22–3.
[4] Elma Dangerfield, *Byron and the Romantics in Switzerland 1816* (London: Ascent Books, 1978), 26.

protagonist is based on Byron, and which saw the birth of another literary monster arising from the same ghost story entertainment.[5]

Illicit sexual couplings and illegitimate procreations were not uncommon in this proto-Bohemian enclave. Mary Shelley had given birth out of wedlock twice,[6] and Claire Clairmont was associated with two illegitimate births, one fathered by Byron and the other, allegedly, by Percy Shelley.[7] In her journal, Clairmont recorded that Thomas Jefferson Hogg was amused by Shelley and his *"two Wives."*[8] In a recently discovered memoir, Clairmont equates the excesses of free love with monstrosity, by revealing, "Under the influence of the doctrine and belief of free love . . . the two first poets of England," Percy Shelley and Byron, had turned "their existence into a perfect hell" and "become monsters of lying, meanness [sic] cruelty and treachery."[9] Byron was notorious for pederasty and an incestuous infatuation with his half-sister, Augusta Leigh. It was this relationship, as well as reports of his sexual depravity, which had prompted him to leave England, a few months before he would be entertaining Percy Shelley and his companions at Villa Diodati in 1816. Over two years earlier, Augusta gave birth to a daughter, Elizabeth Medora Leigh, and it was widely speculated that Byron was the father. He had visited the baby three days after her birth and later declared to Lady Melbourne, in what sounds tantamount to a confession of paternity, "Oh! but it is 'worth while'—I can't tell you why—and it is *not* an '*Ape*' and if it is—that must be my fault."[10] This alludes to the folkloric belief that the child of an incestuous relationship would be born an ape. Rumors of Byron's consanguineous union with his sister may have contributed toward Mary Shelley's invention of Victor's incestuous Oedipal and necrophiliac dream in her novel, which describes him kissing his fiancée, Elizabeth, who then turns into his dead mother for, as Ellen Moers has pointed out, Victor already had a "semi-incestuous love for an abandoned, orphan girl [Elizabeth] brought up as his sister."[11] The subject of Mary Shelley's second novel *Mathilda*, written in 1819-20, was also incest, only this time involving father and daughter. She sent the manuscript to her father William Godwin, who condemned it as "disgusting and detestable"[12] and prevented its publication in her lifetime.

Besides incest, feminist critics have explored *Frankenstein* as a site of monstrous birthing, whose offspring is destruction and death. Moers points out how Mary Shelley transforms "the standard Romantic matter of incest, infanticide, and patricide into a

---

[5] Byron's contribution to the entertainment laid the groundwork for Polidori's short novel.
[6] Clara was born on February 22, 1815, and William was born on January 24, 1816, preceding the marriage of Mary Shelley on December 30, 1816.
[7] Benita Eisler, *Byron: Child of Passion, Fool of Fame* (New York: Vintage Books, 2000), 679-80.
[8] Deirdre Coleman, "Claire Clairmont and Mary Shelley: Identification and Rivalry Within the Tribe of the Otaheite Philosophers," *Women's Writing* 6, no. 3 (1999): 312.
[9] Daisy Hill, *Young Romantics: The Shelleys, Byron and Other Tangled Lives* (London: Bloomsbury, 2010), 307-8.
[10] Eisler, *Byron*, 423.
[11] Ellen Moers, *Literary Women* (London: The Women's Press, 1978), 99.
[12] Mary Wollstonecraft Shelley and Elizabeth Nitchie, "Mathilda," *Studies in Philology* 56, no. 3 (1959): xi.

phantasmagoria of the nursery."[13] As recorded in her journal, the dream she had of her dead baby coming back to life, the year before she started working on her story, has been related to the monster's birth. The novel has also been seen as an outlet for another bereavement, that of her mother, Mary Wollstonecraft, whose death from postpartum infection took place ten days after giving birth to her daughter. Yet there is another less well-known pregnancy and birth, which was more immediate and links topographically to the genesis of the story in Switzerland and its transformation into a novel in the Georgian city of Bath. This relates to Claire Clairmont, who was expecting Lord Byron's baby and—significantly—the letters written from Captain Walton to his sister, which frame *Frankenstein*, span the gestation period of nine months. Accompanied by Mary and Percy, Claire had gone to Villa Diodati presumably to try and secure Byron's paternal support. On their return the following September, they were resolute on keeping her pregnancy secret from William Godwin, the father of Mary and stepfather of Claire, who would have disapproved, even though he and Mary Wollstonecraft had conceived Mary out of wedlock. In fact, Godwin had secretly enumerated in a diary the number of times they engaged in sexual intercourse, presumably as a guide to birth control.[14] It provides a parallel with how the monster reads about his own creation on finding Victor's laboratory notes, represented in the frontispiece by the open book lying on the floor. Distancing themselves from Godwin, who was living in London, the three took up residence in the West Country city of Bath, over a hundred miles away. While Mary and Percy resided at 5 Abbey Churchyard, Claire stayed a short walk away at 12 New Bond Street. It was where Mary cared for her and, in January 1817, reported back to Byron that she had given birth to his daughter. As Mary toiled away on turning her story into a novel, while caring for Claire and reminding Byron of his obligations, it is perhaps not surprising to find that her fictional monster has much in common with an abandoned and neglected child. Indeed Byron, who neglected all of his children, can be seen as a model for Victor's abdication of his parental responsibilities, though ironically it was Claire, through financial necessity, who reluctantly gave up her child, Allegra, into the "care" of her father. The result was that Byron packed Allegra off to a convent; despite Claire's misgivings and anxieties about her daughter's increasingly fragile health, she was powerless to save her from dying of typhus at the age of five.

In *Frankenstein*, Mary Shelley's fears and anxieties around birth are transferred to those of monstrous reproduction. As mentioned earlier, Victor's motivation in destroying the mate he was building for his male creature was to prevent the hybrid couple from generating a monstrous species. As Victor's anxiety demonstrates, the monster's sexual potency was never in question. This has given rise to ribald humor, as in Mel Brooks's film, *Young Frankenstein* (1974), a parodic reversal of the parenting text, in which Dr. Frederick Frankenstein loves and cherishes his monster, while Elizabeth actually falls in love with him. This is due to the enormity of his male member or *Schwanstücker* in pseudo-German, which, by the end of the film, has been

---

[13] Moers, *Literary Women*, 99.
[14] William St Clair decoded Godwin's secret record in *The Godwins and the Shelleys: The Biography of a Family* (London: Faber and Faber, 1990), 497–503.

transplanted onto Dr. Frankenstein. The word "Frankenstein" has entered the lexis as a metaphor for the gargantuan, from Frankenstein food to a Frankenstein penis, a term for artificial enlargement, and has been applied to recent groundbreaking transplant surgery. Queer readings of the novel have not neglected this part of the creature's anatomy. Even though it is never identified as such in the novel, the monster's phallus occupies a projected imaginary space that has been made more explicit through the work of certain book illustrators.

The Frankenstein Illustrators: Lagerquist, Ward, and Holst

These three artists have represented the sexuality of the monster through a desirable body, as opposed to the hideous monster described in the novel. There, Victor's reaction on first observing his creation, whom he had designed to be beautiful, is to exclaim: "Beautiful!—Great God! [. . .] Oh! no mortal could support the horror of that countenance. A mummy again endued with animation could not be so hideous as that wretch."[15] The creature registers Victor's disappointment in having fallen short of creating a new "Adam,"[16] but in a 1922 illustrated edition of *Frankenstein* published in Boston, the artist Carl Lagerquist portrays him with a handsome bodybuilder's physique that barely equates to his description in the novel, in which his "skin scarcely covered the work of muscles and arteries beneath."[17] The curtain he stretches across his body to hide his genital area is a token gesture toward an Adamite fig leaf and his attempt at modesty is belied by his leering grin. With the back of his hand pressed against his forehead, Victor looks quite dazed as he is fixed with the piercing gaze of his animated handiwork who approaches him as he reclines on his four-poster bed. There is ambiguity in Victor's body language, as he is half in and half out of the bed, which raises the question—is he planning to escape, or would he really rather remain? Ostensibly, this sets up expectations of either a rape scene or an act of homosexual seduction. In the novel, Victor has just awoken from the necrophiliac incestuous dream mentioned earlier. A queer reading of the illustration depicts this as a homoerotic awakening or dream-like fantasy of a largely built muscular naked man, bearing a few manly scars on his face and across his broad chest, approaching his bed (Figure 1.1).

The woodcut illustrations of the American artist Lynd Ward for a 1934 edition of *Frankenstein* also support a queer reading. In contrast to Lagerquist's print of the same scene, which portrays both creator and creation, Ward depicts only the monster, as seen through Victor's eyes, approaching his bed. His gait is one of increasing closeness, while his knee is positioned as if ready to kneel on the mattress. He is framed by the bed curtains, which he pushes aside. The sensual folds of the drapes snake around his left arm, mirroring the rippling bulging muscles in his thigh. The lower part of his

---

[15] Shelley, *Frankenstein*, 58–9.
[16] Ibid., 90.
[17] Ibid., 58.

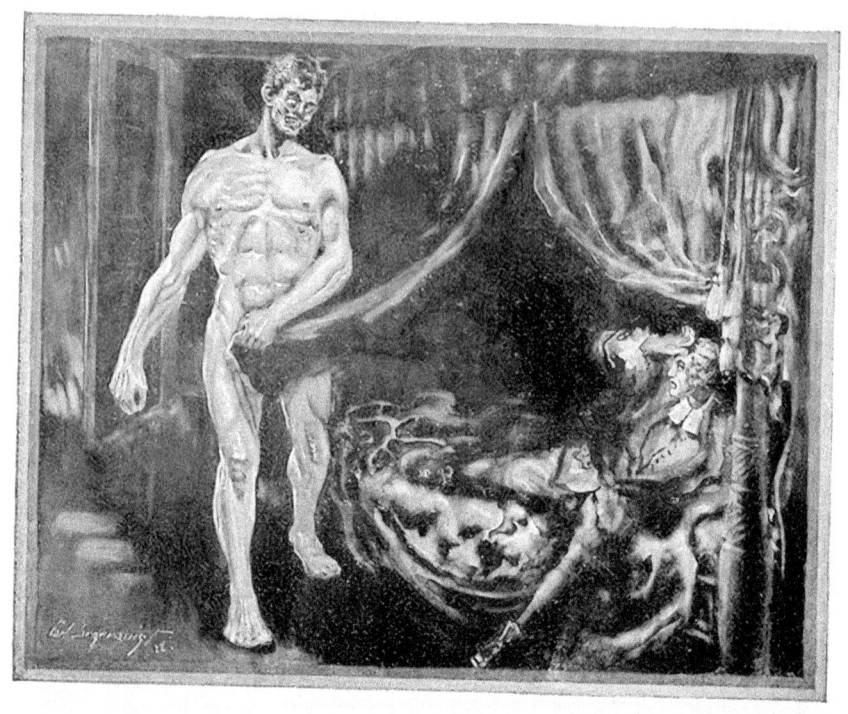

I BEHELD THE WRETCH, THE MISERABLE MONSTER WHOM I HAD CREATED

Figure 1.1 Carl Lagerquist, *Frankenstein* (1922), opposite p. 44 (used by kind permission of Grant F. Scott).

body is more prominent than his head and torso, and as Grant F. Scott aptly observes: "The creature's overture to Victor is most eloquently expressed in the rich darkness and mystery that surrounds the genital area and the illuminated curve of his penis"[18] (Figure 1.3).

Mary Shelley's novel can be read as encoding the forbidden sexuality of homoerotic desire. According to Mair Rigby, it is "a tale of dangerous queer desire,"[19] which in terms of a Foucauldian reading participates "in the discursive *production* and even *dissemination* of cultural 'knowledge' about sexual nonconformity."[20] Homosexual readings of the novel have focused on Victor's repressed desire for his creature and

---

[18] Grant F. Scott, "Victor's Secret: Queer Gothic in Lynd Ward's Illustrations to *Frankenstein* (1934)," *Word & Image* 28, no. 2 (2012): 208–9. Scott notes that Ward's first version of this woodcut contained more prominent and larger genitals, 232. See Lynd Ward, *Storyteller Without Words: The Wood Engravings of Lynd Ward* (New York: Harry N. Abrams, 1974), 288.

[19] Mair Rigby, "'Do You Share My Madness?': *Frankenstein*'s Queer Gothic," in *Queering the Gothic*, ed. William Hughes and Andrew Smith (Manchester: Manchester University Press, 2009), 36.

[20] Ibid., 38.

Figure 1.2 Lynd Ward, *Frankenstein* (1934), opposite p. 54 (used by kind permission of Grant F. Scott).

vice versa. The creature's declaration, "I shall be with you on your wedding-night,"[21] was a threat that Victor mistakenly assumed to be leveled at *him* and not at his bride. Her murder is revenge for Victor's destruction of the monster's own bride, sealing their fates as a conduit for the homoerotic flow of the novel. As Rigby indicates, "in *Frankenstein* the monster of desire with its terrifying power of disclosure is always a haunting presence in the 'bedchamber' of paranoid male subjectivity."[22]

Eve Kosofsky Sedgwick writes about paranoid male Gothic in regard to homosexual panic and homophobia,[23] which was especially rife at the time Mary Shelley was writing. Between 1805 and 1818, there had been twenty-eight trials for sodomy, a crime that could incur a capital penalty until 1835, when the last execution took place.[24] Rigby's argument, that the novel "creates an impression of deviant and

---

[21] Shelley, *Frankenstein*, 143.
[22] Rigby, "Do You Share My Madness?" 42.
[23] See Eve Kosofsky Sedgwick, *The Epistemology of the Closet* (Berkeley: University of California Press, 1990).
[24] See Rigby, "Do You Share My Madness?" 42.

dangerous sexual possibility,"[25] can be applied to the sobering fact that homosexual acts could be deadly by leading to a death sentence. Indeed, Victor does die as a result of pursuing the possibilities of dangerous and forbidden knowledge. He breaks with the surreptitiousness that he has maintained around his experiment by divulging his terrible secret to Captain Walton, who colludes with him in sharing the "unspeakable," and this has given rise to speculation about their relationship. Rigby sees the latter's "homoerotic energy" as couched in the language of erotic desire for the acquisition of Victor's "forbidden knowledge."[26] As Victor agonizes with Walton, there is danger in too much knowing, and he rebukes him with the rhetorical question: "Unhappy man! Do you share my madness?"[27] This could constitute a warning not to succumb to dangerous sexual temptation at a time when it was condemned by society, for as Victor puts it, "How they would, each and all, abhor me, and hunt me from the world, did they know my unhallowed acts."[28] Mary Shelley's nineteenth-century readers are likely to have associated this confession with the blasphemy of Victor's God-like ambition. Blasphemy and sexual deviancy converge through sodomy, as a crime against the divine, nature, and the state. Through his nefarious activities in bringing a monster to life out of secret places, Victor, like the sodomite, becomes a bringer of death.

The first stage adaptation of the novel in 1823, entitled *Presumption, or the Fate of Frankenstein*, was described in a hoax notice as having been "publicly exposed by the Society for the Suppression of Vice and Immorality." Declaring that "The Wages of Sin are Death," it denounced the play as "impious" and "horrid and unnatural," adjectives that correlate to the language used against sexual deviancy.[29] The success of the stage version drew attention back to the book, helping generate further editions which reinforced Shelley's valediction made in her 1831 preface to the novel, in which she bids her hideous progeny to go forth and prosper.

For this revised edition of Frankenstein, illustrations were included for the first time, a title-page vignette, and a frontispiece made from a steel engraving by the French engraver William Chevalier (1804–66). He employs the same cross-hatched technique for light and shade in other engravings on literary themes, including scenes from Shakespeare's *Richard II* and *Richard III*. An extract from the novel is bolted onto the bottom of the frontispiece, providing the following context: "By the glimmer of the half-extinguished light, I saw the dull, yellow eye of the creature open; it breathed hard, and a convulsive motion agitated its limbs . . . I rushed out of the room." The artist Theodor von Holst is generally regarded as the bridge between Henry Fuseli and William Blake and the later Pre-Raphaelites, including Dante Gabriel Rossetti, who referred to him as, "in some sort the Edgar Poe of painting."[30] Holst, like Fuseli

---

[25] Ibid., 36.
[26] Rigby, "Do You Share My Madness?" 38.
[27] Shelley, *Frankenstein*, 35.
[28] Ibid., 155.
[29] Rigby, "Do You Share My Madness?" 50–1.
[30] Max Browne, *The Romantic Art of Theodor Von Holst 1810–44* (London: Lund Humphries, 1944), 43.

Figure 1.3 Theodor von Holst, Frontispiece, *Frankenstein* (1831).

and Blake, was a literary artist who had produced illustrations for Fouqué's *Undine*, Schiller's *The Ghost Seer*, and Dante's *Inferno*.

Frankenstein's infernal "workshop of filthy creation"[31] is the setting for Holst's frontispiece. A contemporary description of the artist's studio around 1826 bears an uncanny resemblance to the laboratory recreated in his artwork. It is described as "quaint," containing items that share some gothic characteristics with the artist's: "would have made an antiquarian's teeth water to look upon; ponderous volumes iron clasped and iron bound."[32] The anonymous observer notes that these weighty tomes would have been envied by the Scottish medieval wizard Michael Scott, who was a court astrologer to Emperor Frederick II. This astrological association, reflecting the occult ambience of Holst's studio, connects to the horoscope in Holst's depiction of Victor's laboratory, a detail that does not appear in Mary Shelley's original (Figure 1.3). Holst's gothic paraphernalia in his studio includes:

> [a] skull the bony forehead of which was decked with a wreath of faded flowers.... The youth himself, too, seemed to belong to a by-gone age, being clad in a kirtle of grey cloth reaching to the knee, confined at the waist by a leathern girdle, his

---

[31] Shelley, *Frankenstein*, 56.
[32] Browne, *The Romantic Art of Theodor Von Holst 1810–44*, 11.

dark waving hair falling low on his shoulders. . . . His features were regular and well developed; his forehead high and marked; his eyes large, dark and bright as a gazelle's; his form slight but graceful . . . the works that surrounded him . . . possessed the wildness of a poetic imagination . . . he delighted in the vague and the terrible. *The Wild Huntsman careering on the Storm Blast, The Demon Lover and his Mistress, A Sabbath of Witches,* or a *Fiendish Dance round the Gallowstree,* were among his favourite subjects.[33]

There are unmistakable parallels between Holst's studio and his recreation of Victor's laboratory in his frontispiece to the novel. The skull in the studio has quadrupled in the engraving and the iron-clasped volumes transformed into a half-opened book. Holst was fond of self-portraiture and, as his 1827 sketch of himself reveals, he shares with the creature long dark hair, heavy brows, high forehead, and a Grecian nose, in stark contrast to the creature's hideous visage, described in the novel. As the artist was of slender build, the monster's muscularity may have been modeled upon that of the actor, Thomas Cooke, who played the monster in the first stage version and whose powerful physique was visible through his tight shirt. Both figures in the frontispiece have "eyes large, dark and bright as a gazelle's" in common with the description of Holst above, whose knee-length kirtle of gray cloth bears some resemblance to Victor's cloak in the frontispiece.

Holst's love of medievalism and Satanic Romantic art was out of step with the transition toward pictorial art during the 1830s.[34] His attraction to gothic themes was shared by his mentor Fuseli, with whom he studied at the Royal Academy. Indeed, the similarity in the subject matter and style of both artists proved detrimental to Holst, who was regarded, until relatively recently, as a mere pale imitator or copyist of his master. Indeed, artwork created by Holst has been wrongly attributed to Fuseli and disentangling one from the other is an ongoing process.[35] Holst's own practice was certainly inspired by Fuseli, not least as a practitioner of pornography. Apart from his frontispiece for *Frankenstein*, Holst is most well known for his Faust drawings, though for many years it was assumed that they too had been the work of Fuseli.[36]

In common with his mentor, Holst's main inspiration was literature. Goethe's *Faust* (1828–9) was his favorite dramatic text, which he could read in the original German. His drawings were probably influenced by a London theater adaptation at the Theatre Royal Drury Lane in 1825, which prompted his fellow artist Eugene Delacroix to declare, "theatre can go no further" in dramatizing "the most diabolical thing imaginable."[37] Holst never completed his drawings, but he had certainly done enough

---

[33] Ibid., 11.
[34] Holst was brought back into the public eye by the groundbreaking *Gothic Nightmares* exhibition of 2006 at the Tate Gallery in London. See Martin Myrone, ed., *Gothic Nightmares: Fuseli, Blake and The Romantic Tradition* (London: Tate Publishing, 2006).
[35] See Browne, *The Romantic Art of Theodor Von Holst 1810–44*, 11, 14–16.
[36] Gert Schiff challenged Fuseli attributions in favor of Holst, see "Theodore Matthias Von Holst," *The Burlington Magazine* 105, no. 718 (1963): 24.
[37] Browne, *The Romantic Art of Theodor Von Holst 1810–44*, 17.

Figure 1.4 Theodor von Holst, *Faust in his Study* (1820–5) (The Trustees of the British Museum).

to equip him for creating the frontispiece of *Frankenstein* into which he incorporated details of his first Faust drawing (Figure 1.4).

In comparing the two prints, both contain a skull and an alchemist's alembic, which consists of two vessels connected by a tube, used by alchemists for distilling chemicals. The bookcases are in the same position, as are the windows, both of which are framed by a Romanesque arch, with the glass arranged in circles in most of the panes. However, at the top of the window in the Faust etching, there are three trefoil designs divided by stone tracery. In the *Frankenstein* frontispiece there is a more elaborate pattern. Here these sets of three rounded lobes in the corresponding windowpanes have become distorted and irregular so as to resemble the contours of male genitalia, specifically a scrotum and phallus. Directly beneath appear four outlines, of the head and breasts of women, symbolic of the nurturing which the creature never received (Figure 1.5). These male and female representations illustrate how generation and death, in the form of the creature propped up against a quasi-tombstone, with a skeleton lying beneath him,

Figure 1.5 Detail from Theodor von Holst, Frontispiece, *Frankenstein* (1831).

meet in Victor's "workshop of filthy creation."[38] This interpretation of the engraving has some commonality with the queer readings of Lagerquist and Ward. Instead of depicting the creature's body as repellent, in keeping with Victor's reaction to his creation in the novel, all three artists have portrayed an attractive muscular masculine figure, capable of provoking erotic desire.[39] In *Frankenstein*, the line of vision for both maker and monster can be traced to a point located between the creature's legs. What they might be seeing there could account for their startled expression, bearing in mind that the creature's parts were constructed in proportion to the whole (Figure 1.3).

For the creature, this could amount to a double shock, first, from the life-giving electrification, and secondly, in seeing his erection for the first time. In the light of the enormity of this spectacle, Victor's fleeing from the scene can be seen as an act of homoerotic panic. The suggestion here too is that, even though the monstrous phallus is concealed from the viewer between the creature's legs, it is now hidden in plain sight and multiplied in the windowpanes as a clandestine joke. According to Max Browne, the artist's work sometimes displayed a "bizarre and eccentric sense of humor."[40] A similar shape recurs in Holst's watercolor, *A Seated Courtesan Holding a Phallic Object* (1824–30) and elsewhere in his work. Compared to the symmetrical shapes in the window of the Faust etching, their irregularity in the corresponding part of the

---

[38] Shelley, *Frankenstein*, 56.
[39] Only the bones on his left foot are clearly visible, whereas the novel refers to the skin barely covering the network of muscles and arteries.
[40] Browne, *The Romantic Art of Theodor Von Holst 1810–44*, 85.

Frankenstein illustration could only have been intentional for such a precise draftsman as Holst. The subversive iconography in the background of his frontispiece to Mary Shelley's novel could also point to the monster's fertility in potentially fathering a new "race of devils,"[41] which had so alarmed Victor Frankenstein. Additionally, it could serve as an ironically priapic celebration of Victor's solitary male propagation, while the outlines of maternal female breasts are a reminder of Victor's attempt to make a female monster and how the male monster was deprived of mothering.

Both Holst and Fuseli had a keen interest in the erotic female body. Their friend, the artist and notorious poisoner Thomas Wainewright (1794–1847), was in possession of a private portfolio of "exquisite delineations of the female human form,"[42] which prompted all three artists to produce similar works. Erotic material was restricted to private collections since the Society for the Suppression of Vice (founded in 1802) was actively engaged in convicting purveyors and publishers of pornography. It might have amused Holst that his sexually significant windowpanes were, in all innocence, being mass-produced, because the lewd joke they embedded was passing by unnoticed.

Holst was certainly no ingénue when it came to pornographic art. Early in his career, he was commissioned by his patron Sir Thomas Lawrence to produce erotic drawings, some of which were commissioned for King George IV, whose taste for erotica was insatiable. The Regency Court had previously satisfied itself with the bawdy humorous drawings of Rowlandson but was now requiring more refined erotic stimulation.[43] Examples of Holst's erotic artwork include sketches of a whip-wielding flimsily clad woman riding on the back of a bridled man and a pencil and watercolor painting of two nude female figures being intimate with an ithyphallic man.[44]

Most of Holst's erotic drawings have disappeared, probably consigned to the flames by his wife, though one reckoning estimates around forty-four being sold in a private sale. Holst took the royal pornographic commission from his patron probably because he was in need of money since his gothic style of painting was no longer popular. In his obituary in the *Art-Union* monthly magazine, it was noted that this artwork was "of a class which a youth with very limited means may have been tempted to execute; but the subjects were little to the credit of the President [Holst's patron] and his royal employer. Who shall say how far the after-career of Holst may have been influenced by this ill-directed patronage?"[45] Holst would have been too young and not sufficiently well established to escape damage to his reputation, but that did not prevent him from being commissioned by the publisher Henry Colburn to create the frontispiece for the revised 1831 edition of *Frankenstein*. Holst had already been commissioned

---

[41] Shelley, *Frankenstein*, 140.
[42] Browne, *The Romantic Art of Theodor Von Holst 1810–44*, 66.
[43] See ibid., 14.
[44] See Theodor Matthias Von Holst, *Aristotle and Phyllis* (studies of woman riding on back of philosopher, brandishing whip) before 1844. Available online: http://spenceralley.blogspot.com/2018/04/theodor-von-holst-follower-of-fuseli.html (accessed October 10, 2020) and *Ithyphallic Man and Two Women with Elaborate Hairstyles* (c. 1822–30), see Browne, *The Romantic Art of Theodor Von Holst 1810–44*, 67.
[45] Browne, *The Romantic Art of Theodor Von Holst 1810–44*, 13.

by Colburn to illustrate some early volumes of his series and given his taste for the Gothic, most especially through his work on Faust, he would have seemed an obvious choice. There is no record of Mary Shelley ever having met the artist but, she would have known of him through her parents' connections with Fuseli, and her friendship with Edward Bulwer Lytton, who purchased some of Holst's work on Faust and commissioned him to paint his portrait. In the late 1820s, Mary Shelley was acquainted with Holst's patron, Sir Thomas Lawrence, who died in 1830. Would she have been aware of his role in commissioning Holst's erotic drawings for the king? Holst was also known to the painter of her 1841 portrait, Richard Rothwell, who complained that he had introduced him to a disreputable woman, probably a prostitute.[46] Furthermore, Percy Shelley went out of his way to see Holst's paintings, whose watercolor *Les Adieux* (1827) had been inspired by his own poem *Ginevra* (1824).[47] It tells of how a bride is found dead on her bridal bed after the wedding ceremony, in a scene redolent of *Frankenstein*.

We can only speculate as to whether or not Mary Shelley approved of Holst's engraving. If she had deciphered the shapes along the lines I have suggested, might she have been offended or would she have shared in the joke over monstrous sexualities? Certainly, she was used to perusing book illustrations such as those accompanying the stories she wrote for the *Keepsake* magazine. Most were styled in the manner of the illustration on *Frankenstein*'s title page, depicting Frankenstein's farewell to Elizabeth, a type of domestic sentimental art that had little affinity with Holst's demonic Romanticism (Figure 1.6). The illustrations were intended to boost book sales and were a feature of Colburn and Bentley's Standard Novels series, which turned expensive three-volume editions into cheaper octavo-sized single-volume works. *Frankenstein* appeared as number seven in the series and had been selected because of its popularity.

It had been a very different story when Mary Shelley was trying to get the novel published initially, as it had been rejected by several publishers, including Byron's, John Murray, forcing her to go down-market to Lackington, Hughes, Hardy, and Mavor, who specialized in esoteric publications. They had brought out Francis Barrett's *The Magus; or Celestial Intelligences; a Complete System of Occult Philosophy, Being a Summary of all the Best Writers on the Subjects of Magic, Alchymy, Magnetism, the Cabala &c . . .* [1801]; and also Barrett's *Lives of the Alchemystical Philosophers, with a Critical Catalogue of Books on Occult Chemistry . . .* [1815]. So in many respects, *Frankenstein* found itself in the right company, since its scientist hero started off as a devotee of the alchemists. Occultist titles relating to prophecy, apparitions, ghosts, hobgoblins, and haunted houses were advertised across two pages accompanying this very first publication of *Frankenstein* in 1818, in a commercial bid to appeal to the novel's readership.

---

[46] Holst's interest in prostitutes is evident from his pencil and watercolor, *Young Courtesan Exposing Herself* (c. 1825–30). See Browne, *The Romantic Art of Theodor Von Holst 1810–44*, 19.
[47] See Browne, *The Romantic Art of Theodor Von Holst 1810–44*, 22.

Figure 1.6 Theodor von Holst, Title page, *Frankenstein* (1831).

Alchemy and *The Rosicrucian Cavern*

In the frontispiece, Holst takes further liberties with Mary Shelley's original by depicting alchemical equipment in Victor's laboratory not mentioned in the novel. The best-known alchemist in literature is Faust, with whom Holst identified in several self-portraits.[48] Victor Frankenstein is another Faustian figure and, like Faust, was a student at the University of Ingolstadt which provided him with a conducive environment for his enthusiasm for the teachings of alchemists, most notably Paracelsus and Cornelius Agrippa. His tutor, Professor Waldman, acknowledges the debt that modern scientists owed to these men whom he regards as geniuses in a passage evidently derived from Mary Shelley's reading of the introduction to Humphrey Davy's lectures on chemistry of 1802, while she was living in Bath. Victor's father dismisses his son's interests in the alchemists as "sad trash."[49] By contrast, Mary Shelley's father, William Godwin,

---

[48] See ibid., 55.
[49] Shelley, *Frankenstein*, 44.

chose an alchemist for the hero of his novel *St Leon* (1799) and wrote the non-fictional *Lives of the Necromancers* (1834), which has entries on Faustus, Cornelius Agrippa, and Paracelsus. Agrippa is also the subject of Mary Shelley's short story, "The Mortal Immortal" (1833), about a sorcerer's apprentice.[50] James Rieger acknowledges the importance of the alchemists for the success of Victor's scientific discovery when he refers to "Frankenstein's chemistry" as "switched-on magic, souped-up alchemy, the electrification of Agrippa and Paracelsus."[51] Even though the use of electricity to animate the monster is not mentioned in the actual novel, Holst introduces a pair of horned galvanic electrodes in his frontispiece, for imparting the vital spark or shock. The presence of electrodes, as well as an alembic in the *Frankenstein* illustration, testifies to Victor's pursuit of both science and the occult in his creation of life.

As he would have been aware, alchemists claimed to have created life through homunculi. The earliest mention of these miniature humans is in *De Natura Rerum* (1537) (Latin for *The Nature of Things*), a text attributed to Paracelsus that provides a recipe for the creation of homunculi. The instructions involve incubating semen in horse dung for forty days until a little man is born. Menstrual blood offered an alternative bodily fluid, only it carried the risk of producing a monster whose looks could kill, like the basilisk. Faust's assistant in Goethe's play, Wagner, creates a homunculus in his laboratory and in James Whale's 1935 film *The Bride of Frankenstein*, Dr. Pretorius shows off his homunculi to his colleague, Dr. Henry Frankenstein, admitting, "normal size has been my difficulty, I need to work that out with you." Herein may lie the solution to Victor's dilemma in having created an eight-foot monster with the capability to murder, for had he not abandoned the alchemists, he might have produced a pint-sized monster, which would have been far easier to contain and control.

One of Victor's other mistakes is to have dispensed with female nature through male science, as opposed to the hermetic tradition of alchemy, which maintained a harmonious balance between the sexes. However, this harmony is retained within the frontispiece through the iconography of the male sexual organs and nurturing female breasts. Alchemists believed that the *materia prima* of alchemy could grow into gold when impregnated by a vital fluid that included semen and that could serve as a sexual force. The chemical wedding or marriage, sometimes called coniunctio, is the joining of the male elements (fire and air as represented by sulfur) with the female elements (water and earth that equate to argent vive or quicksilver) in philosophical mercury. These oppositions are brought together through the union of gold and silver symbolizing respectively the sun, personified as King Sol, and the moon as Queen Luna. This is the final fusion in the alchemical process to produce the philosopher's stone, a mythic object believed to be capable of transmuting base metal into gold and from which the elixir of immortal life could be derived. Victor took this very seriously early on in the novel when he admits, "I entered with the greatest diligence into the

---

[50] See Marie [Mulvey-] Roberts, *Gothic Immortals: The Fiction of the Brotherhood of the Rosy Cross* (London: Routledge, 1990), 87–92.
[51] Mary Wollstonecraft Shelley, *Frankenstein or the Modern Prometheus the 1818 Text*, ed. James Rieger (Chicago: The University of Chicago Press), 3.

Figure 1.7 Henry Fuseli, *The Rosicrucian Cavern* (1805).

search of the philosopher's stone and the elixir of life."[52] The merging of the male and female has been represented within alchemy as a marriage (Figure 1.7).

An alchemical romance, whose title is pertinent to this imagery, is *The Chemical Wedding of Christian Rosencreutz* (1616). Divided into seven days, or seven journeys, it recounts how Christian Rosencreutz is invited to a fantastical castle full of miracles, in order to assist with the chemical wedding of the king and the queen. In the castle, the dead are brought back to life and decapitated heads restored. It concludes with the creation of a male and female form—the homunculus duo for, as the text reveals, the goal of alchemy is not chrysopoeia, the transmutation of base metal into gold, but the artificial generation of humans. Christian Rosencreutz was the mythical founder of the mystical alchemical Rosicrucians or Brotherhood of the Rose Cross and, according to legend, his body was found in a cave in a state of perfect preservation by his disciples 120 years after his death. In one version, his body is guarded by a

---

[52] Shelley, *Frankenstein*, 47.

mechanical statue, which is depicted in Fuseli's *The Rosicrucian Cavern* (1803). Comparisons can be made between this drawing and the *Frankenstein* frontispiece which both draw on the hermetic tradition. Both compositions have a source of light emanating from around or across the center. In each, there is a rounded arch and the figures in flight are both to the right of the respective pictures. Even though the figure in the Fuseli engraving is supposed to be that of a mechanical man, his body does not resemble clockwork and has more in common with the muscularity of the monster in the frontispiece. The author of *The Chemical Wedding*, Johann Valentin Andreae, famously declared that the treatise was a hoax or ludibrium, which is often seen as the third manifesto of the Rosicrucians, whose symbol of the rose cross encompasses the sexually nuanced female rose and male cross. The Brotherhood of the Rose Cross was closely associated with alchemy, at the heart of which lies the union between the male and the female, resulting in the Great Hermaphrodite or androgyne.

The concept of the rebis, or the being that is two in one, may be extended to the gender ambivalence of the creature in the *Frankenstein* frontispiece, whose male body has a head resembling that of a woman. This feminization can be seen in how he functions, rather like the alembic, as a receiving vessel into which Victor Frankenstein's ambitions and desires have been distilled. In the novel, Victor who, in certain respects, becomes the creature's double, is also subject to being feminized. An instance of this lies in the nervous agitation he experiences during the latter stages of his creature's gestation, almost if he is about to give birth himself. The mirroring of the two characters in the novel is a twinship, indicated in the square astrological chart on the wall of Victor's laboratory in Holst's frontispiece, which appears to contain the symbol of Gemini, or the twins. This merging of the masculine and the feminine lends itself to the Great Hermaphrodite or androgyne, which is the point of synthesis within the alchemical process. To return to Holst, he makes use of the figure of the androgyne in a self-portrait entitled *Girl in Renaissance Student's Disguise* (c. 1825–35),[53] and it can be no coincidence that Mephistopheles first appears in Faust's study wearing a student's disguise.

Transvestitism and androgyny are no strangers to Holst's artwork. His play with sexual difference is evident from his self-portraiture in his Faust illustrations in various combinations of cat-like eye-makeup, arched manicured eyebrows, a mustache, and naked female breasts.[54] This preoccupation of self and gender ambiguity appears to be replicated in his depiction of the creature in the *Frankenstein* frontispiece. Furthermore, the pornographic iconography seemingly encrypted in the window may be a mischievous reference to Victor's apprehensions concerning his creations' monstrous reproduction. In turn, this can be seen as a nightmarish dramatization of the illicit births and transgressive sexual relationships taking place within Mary Shelley's circle. Through his frontispiece which, as I have argued, encodes a hidden monstrous sexuality, Holst entered into a multilayered visual dialog with the words of Mary Shelley which reaches out to her readers from across the centuries.

---

[53] See Browne, *The Romantic Art of Theodor Von Holst 1810–44*, 57.
[54] See ibid., 22, 57, 85.

2

Mashing the Medium
The Aesthetics of Screen Frankensteins

K. J. Donnelly

Film versions of her novel have transformed Mary Shelley's original ideas, hastening "Frankenstein" coming to mean the Monster rather than the scientific aristocrat. As the twentieth century progressed, "Frankenstein" increasingly got mashed up in a number of films, meeting a selection of gothic monsters (and others) who partially defined his character and against whom he is measured. These are not highly valued films and have been regularly ignored by scholars.[1] While it is extremely tempting to regard these rarely registered multi-monster films as simply the diminishing returns of a fading cinematic idea, I contend that they are more interesting. They not only chart a broad trajectory of development for the Monster, from novel to overly familiar, but also provide him with a situated identity, in relation to other monsters. Indeed, psychologists often understand identity as contextual and relational rather than absolute.[2] So, the Monster might change in relation to who he meets and become redefined in different situations. Moving above a level of simple character and narrative, the context defining the Monster is structural-aesthetic and emanates from aspects of film's format. Through cinematic history, Frankenstein's Monster is perhaps less a thing in himself and more defined by other characters surrounding him and other aspects of varying contexts. These aspects are sometimes considered little more than "backdrop," and a determining factor in these is the film medium itself. Marshall McLuhan's famous adage of "the medium is the message" referred simultaneously to both the "invisible" channel and the background context (the "ground") to what is taken to be the important "figure" in the foreground. As he noted, following the

---

[1] For example, Rebecca Baumann only includes one sentence about Universal's Frankenstein films after *Bride of Frankenstein* (1935). See Rebecca Baumann, *Frankenstein 200: The Birth, Life, and Resurrection of Mary Shelley's Monster* (Indianapolis: Indiana University Press, 2018), 90.
[2] Jeffrey Jensen Arnett, "The Psychology of Emerging Adulthood: What is Known, and What Remains to be Known," in *Emerging Adults in America: Coming of Age in the 21st Century*, ed. Jeffrey Jensen Arnett and Jennifer Lynn Tanner (Washington: American Psychological Association, 2006), 303–30.

insights of Gestalt psychology, in all patterns, when the ground changes, the figure too is altered by the new interface.[3]

In Frankenstein films, the Monster's fragmented origin is projected onto his surroundings. Further, the fragmented nature of film aesthetics is particularly well suited to the Monster. Both are stitched together from disparate fragments. They offer us something of his experience, as a phenomenological analog. As Picart notes, "the Frankenstein narrative cast in film leads one to the conclusion that the production/evolution of a film is itself a Frankensteinian exercise. It entails the serendipitous sewing together of numerous elements."[4] I argue that the form of these Monster Mash films, and the Monster himself, emanate from a sense of the fragmented and tessellated, even to the point where the Monster may lose a sense of being fragmented himself but the film format surrounding him retains that attribute, appearing chaotic and incoherent. Indeed, the underlying and primary characteristics of the film medium itself determine much of the Monster and his surrounding and defining terrain.

Adaptation or Reconfiguration

While the story of Baron Frankenstein and his creation have origins in Mary Shelley's novel, increasingly they (and particularly the Monster) have been made into something else. Indeed, Shelley's creation has strayed far from his creator. I live near the location of Mary Shelley's grave in Bournemouth on the English south coast. Opposite the graveyard is a pub called "The Mary Shelley." While many of the drinkers might well know who she is, I would be surprised if many have read her novel. The pub appears unaware of subtle differences, as its sign sports the iconic image of Universal Studios' Monster.[5]

The film versions utterly transformed Shelley's original ideas, almost beyond recognition.[6] As is universally accepted, increasingly "Frankenstein" came to mean the monster created by Frankenstein rather than the adventurous scientific aristocrat. A series of encrustations and gradual additions took place in the theater in the

---

[3] Marshall McLuhan, *Understanding Me: Lectures and Interviews*, ed. Stephanie McLuhan and David Staines (Cambridge, MA: MIT Press, 2004), 180; Izabella Pruska Oldenhof and Robert K. Logan, "The Spiral Structure of Marshall McLuhan's Thinking," *Philosophies* 2, no. 9 (2017): 2.

[4] Caroline Joan S. Picart, "Visualizing the Monstrous in Frankenstein Films," *Pacific Coast Philology* 35, no. 1 (2000): 17.

[5] The image is in fact based on Glenn Strange's face rather than Karloff's. While Universal owned the image rights to the Frankenstein Monster's face, Karloff's daughter's company, Karloff Enterprises, owned the copyright to her father's face.

[6] This is registered in surveys of Frankenstein on film: Albert J. Lavalley, "The Stage and Film Children of Frankenstein: A Survey," in *The Endurance of Frankenstein: Essays on Mary Shelley's Novel*, ed. George Levine and U. C. Knoepflmacher (Berkeley: University of California Press, 1979), 243–89; Carolyn Joan Picart, Frank Smoot and Jayne Blodgett, *The Frankenstein Film Sourcebook* (Westport: Greenwood Press, 2001); Carolyn Joan Picart, *Remaking the Frankenstein Myth on Film* (New York: SUNY Press, 2003); and Mark Jancovich, "Frankenstein and Film," in *The Cambridge Companion to Frankenstein*, ed. Andrew Smith (Cambridge: Cambridge University Press, 2016), 190–204.

century following the novel's publication,[7] meaning that by the time Frankenstein was transposed to film it had already acquired a number of new elements and emphases. The Edison version of *Frankenstein* (1910), now digitally restored but long thought of as lost, crystallized an emphasis on visual horror, centering the creature and pushing the Baron to the margins. This took decisive steps further with the extremely successful Universal film *Frankenstein* (1931) featuring Boris Karloff. However, Radu Florescu states that

> the book as it was written does not transfer well to film. It is a book that allows the reader's imagination to take control. . . . *Mary Shelley left much unsaid and Hollywood has been trying to fill in the blanks ever since. Perhaps one day someone will realize that the blanks are not what is important* [my italics]. Surely Shelley did not think so or she would have filled them in herself. What is important is the root of the story, the core itself. The moral that Frankenstein gives us is what counts.[8]

He thus dismisses all adaptations and developments, some of which have proven remarkably successful, as being derivative and worth little next to Shelley's novel and original ideas. This denies the complex, but crucial, relationship between the book (and its stage adaptations) and films. Take, for instance, the Creature's bride. In the novel, at the creature's behest, Baron Frankenstein starts making a mate for him but halts, fearing creating an even larger threat to humankind. Films finish what Shelley started, bringing the bride to full fruition in a number of films, including *The Bride of Frankenstein* (1935) and *The Bride* (1985).[9] I, therefore, disagree with Florescu's conclusion, as films develop subtext and undertones, while adding, updating and refining. This is precisely what has given some of Shelley's core ideas more prominence and longevity than her novel could have achieved on its own.

Moreover, films exploit what the novel lacks. Many of them retell the Frankenstein story and change it, sometimes utterly beyond recognition. The succession of films, with their different manifestations of the Frankenstein Monster, illustrates the principles of history, cultural evolution, and aesthetic development.[10] A remarkable trajectory exists across the century of film, from the terror of Karloff's first appearance in Universal's 1931 version to the "tamed" notion of the Monster in films such as the animated *Monster Family* (2017). I would suggest that all the screen Frankensteins are not

---

[7] For instance, Richard Brinsley Peake's *Presumption; or, the Fate of Frankenstein* (premiered in 1823 in London) added the assistant Fritz who appeared in the Universal Frankenstein films, later being renamed Igor.
[8] Radu Florescu, *In Search of Frankenstein: Exploring the Myths behind Mary Shelley's Monster* (London: Robson Books, 1999), 217.
[9] Although the Monster meets his bride a number of times in films, I wish to focus on the Monster Mash films and their multiple meetings, where he meets notorious and canonical "equals."
[10] And in all other media, too. See Megen de Bruin-Molé, *Gothic Remixed: Monster Mashups and Frankenfictions in 21st-Century Culture* (New York: Bloomsbury, 2019); Eddy Von Mueller, "The Face of the Fiend: Media, Industry, and the Evolving Image of Frankenstein's Monster," in *Frankenstein - How A Monster Became an Icon - The Science and Enduring Allure of Mary Shelley's Creation*, ed. Sidney Perkowitz and Eddy Von Mueller (New York: Pegasus, 2018), 136–61.

versions of Shelley's Frankenstein, but in almost every case a derivative of Universal's, where the Monster was forged completely anew by Boris Karloff's landmark portrayal.

Discussing film adaptations of Stevenson's *Strange Case of Dr. Jekyll and Mr. Hyde* (1886), James Twitchell notes that rather than doing injustice to the story, they actually play out some implications missing in the novella. He writes: "The more derivative and exploitative the version, the more revealing it may be."[11] I concur with Twitchell's assertion that in less reverent adaptations remarkable subtext can float to the surface. The boldness of adaptation and extremity of inspiration can take a startling idea far from its origin, and this seems particularly apt with respect to screen Frankensteins. Many of these were exploitative and perhaps even degenerate, and the most extreme of these were the so-called "Monster Mashes" or "Monster Rally" films, which featured multiple monsters.

Among Frankenstein films, the Mashes constitute an unregistered subgenre of their own. As the twentieth century progressed, Frankenstein increasingly got mashed up in films, meeting a selection of gothic monsters and others. These Monster Mashes typically follow a particular line of development in their encounters. The creature is often not the lonely figure of Shelley's novel; indeed, people seem to want to meet him (following the assumption that audiences want other monsters to meet him). He not only meets other monsters but also dinosaurs, cartoon and comedy figures, and adventurous children. These films sometimes are signposted by being titled as "Frankenstein meets . . ." or "Frankenstein vs . . .," established by the first such film, *Frankenstein Meets the Wolf Man* (1943), and with a connotation of a boxing match or perhaps a marriage of sorts. The combatants are often from the pantheon of canonical monsters, and they often simply fulfill well-rehearsed character appearances and repetitive outcomes.

In discussing *Frankenstein*'s appearances in Marvel Comics, Shane Denson notes the "serially self-reflexive monster" always in dialog with older and different versions. These new versions probe the medium of the comic itself.[12] This seems a fair assessment of developments of the Frankenstein story; however, I would suggest that with the Monster Mash films it is the other way round: the film format probes and often determines the form of the elements of the original Frankenstein story.

The sense of longer narratives of the series/sequels might allow for the chance to develop the Monster's character, the chance to change the context and illuminate the Monster in a different light and amend or remove the Monster's relationship with his creator/father Baron Frankenstein. On the other hand, it might allow the Monster to appear ready formed, as an unchanging stock entity about whom audiences already know everything worth knowing. Indeed, there was something of a family in

---

[11] James B. Twitchell, *Dreadful Pleasures: An Anatomy of Modern Horror* (Oxford: Oxford University Press, 1985), 84.

[12] Shane Denson, "Marvel Comics' *Frankenstein*: A Case Study in the Media of Serial Figures," *Amerikastudien / American Studies* 56, no. 4, Issue: "American Comic Books and Graphic Novels" (2011): 532.

Universal's canonical monsters, and something reassuringly familiar about them from the late 1930s.

In *The Medium Is the Monster*, Mark McCutcheon argues for an intimate connection between technology (in the widest sense) and the notion of Frankenstein and his Monster offspring. Indeed, he suggests that our whole understanding of technology has been redefined by the Frankenstein scenario.[13] Yet the novel's failure to depict or discuss the technology of the Monster's birth is more than made up for by film. The covert technological basis of film found a particular expression of itself and manifestation in the Frankenstein films. These films are about fragmented multimodality, and the Monster Mashes are the epitome of collage culture, encouraged by the qualities of film as a medium (and, indeed, other subsequent audiovisual culture).

While discussions have focused on representation and narrative, they have been less interested in format translation. Shelley's epistolary novel paid attention to the format of literature, and since Frankenstein was converted to film, the Creature's developments regularly have shown a partially concealed concern with film as technology and the potential of film as a medium to achieve novel things. As a technological creation, Frankenstein's Monster is about construction from fragments, very much like film itself, while also highlighting issues of audiovisual culture, such as the fetishizing of vision (with spectacles of violence and innovative makeup and special effects) and the potentially ambiguous relationship between sound and image.[14] If Frankenstein's creation was a new man for a new world, film was about seeing the world anew and in fresh ways, most clearly in its early years but also intermittently since. The Frankenstein films often appeared fragmented, as rough patchworks in formal and stylistic terms, as much as they were fragmented compounds in terms of theme, narrative, and representation. The principle of the Monster Mash films was to take the process of fragmented collage further. For instance, the Universal films comprise not only a succession of monsters but also alternation of smaller narrative strands and succession of atomized incidents. Furthermore, they reuse characters and archetypes, settings and actual sets, special-effects designs, and music recordings.[15] Aesthetic aspects and preexisting ready-mades determine the Monster Mash films more than any desire to adapt Shelley's book or to develop related conceptual imperatives.

---

[13] Mark McCutcheon, *The Medium is the Monster: Canadian Adaptations of Frankenstein and the Discourse of Technology* (Edmonton: Athabasca University Press, 2018), 2–3.

[14] The iconic 1931 *Frankenstein*, a few years after the adoption of synchronized recorded sound, embodies something of the uncertain relationship between sound and image. See Robert Spadoni, *Uncanny Bodies: The Coming of Sound Film and the Origins of the Horror Genre* (Berkeley: University of California Press, 2007), 98–9.

[15] While *Frankenstein* (1931) reused some of the sets from *Dracula* (1931), the Universal Frankenstein films all used the "German Town" set built for *All Quiet on the Western Front* (1930). Similarly, *Frankenstein Meets the Wolfman* (1943) includes some musical cues from *Son of Frankenstein* (1939), while the title music from *Son of Frankenstein* was re-recorded as the title music for *House of Frankenstein* (1944) and *House of Dracula* (1945), among other instances.

Universal Studio's Monster Mashes

Universal's cycle of horror films is now widely considered emblematic of the 1930s and 1940s heyday of the Hollywood studio system. Universal was one of the Big Five studios that effectively ran a cartel, keeping out competitors and making accommodations with other major studios. As part of this, studios often specialized to some degree, and the horror film became largely Universal's domain. Added to this, a Taylorist factory production line was a defining characteristic of Hollywood, leading to a tendency toward sequelization and a canonical group of monster figures becoming the roster of stars. In 1931, Universal released in succession *Dracula* with Bela Lugosi and *Frankenstein* with Boris Karloff, both of which were remarkably successful and led to a series of sequels. After the initial adaptation of Shelley's novel, the Frankenstein films became adventurous. The first sequel, *Bride of Frankenstein* (1935), develops ideas from the novel and transfers the focus firmly to the monster at the expense of his maker. Reprising the monster, Karloff meets scientist Praetorius (Ernest Thesiger), a collaborator with and partial surrogate for Baron Frankenstein, and then briefly meets and is rejected by the reanimated "Bride" (Elsa Lanchester) in a lengthy, camp, and histrionic set-piece sequence, capped with Franz Waxman's score using wedding bells for the bride's unveiling. Universal had a clear policy of producing sequels for its monster films. The next decade saw a regular run of not only Frankenstein films but many others, including five sequels to *The Mummy* (1932).

In 1936, when the horror-obsessed Carl Laemmle Jr. stepped down as head of production, Universal stopped producing horror films, but in 1938 *Frankenstein* and *Dracula* were re-released on a double bill, again to notable success, leading to immediate plans for more Frankenstein films with a substantial budget.[16] This double bill in effect mashed together the two best-known monsters and set the logic for later films. Indeed, *The Black Cat* (1934) had also inaugurated something of the mash logic, bringing together the two lead actors of the 1931 films (Karloff and Bela Lugosi), although in different roles. The ensuing Frankenstein films retained the two actors, with *Son of Frankenstein* (1939) having Karloff's monster-friendly with Lugosi's hunchback Igor. Indeed, their friendship becomes remarkably physically close. In the following film, *The Ghost of Frankenstein* (1942), at the end, Igor's (Lugosi's) brain is inserted into the Monster (Lon Chaney Jr.). Aptly, the succeeding film, *Frankenstein Meets the Wolf Man* (1943), has Lugosi playing the Monster.

As the films progress, they are marked by a line of development through actors too: after his debut, Karloff played the monster in two more Universal films, *Bride of Frankenstein* and *Son of Frankenstein*; Lon Chaney, Jr. took over the part from Karloff in *The Ghost of Frankenstein*; Bela Lugosi portrayed the role in *Frankenstein Meets the Wolf Man*; and Glenn Strange played the monster in the last three Universal Studios films to feature the character—*House of Frankenstein* (1944), *House of Dracula* (1945), and *Abbott and Costello Meet Frankenstein* (1948). On the surface, there appears to be

---

[16] Murray Leeder, *Horror Film: A Critical Introduction* (New York: Bloomsbury, 2018), 28–9.

a law of diminishing returns, which becomes apparent certainly by the last films of the cycle.

Universal's Monster Mash films appear late in their horror cycle, in the wake of *The Ghost of Frankenstein* being the first of the Monster's continued career as a B picture star. They were the trilogy *Frankenstein Meets the Wolf Man* (1943), *House of Frankenstein* (1944), and *House of Dracula* (1945), and as something of an appendix, the Monster went on to *Abbott and Costello Meet Frankenstein* (1948).

As the title suggests, the Monster meets another canonical monster in *Frankenstein Meets the Wolf Man*. The pair has a short, but spirited, battle at the film's conclusion. Chaney's wolf man has a good heart and endeavors to remain at least partly human, despite his animalistic and uncontrolled violence. In contradistinction, Frankenstein's Monster (played by Lugosi) appears less than human, destructive at heart and lacking much sense of humanity. One might have expected more from him, as he now is driven by a new brain, originally belonging to hunchback Igor and inserted at the conclusion of *The Ghost of Frankenstein*. So, it is apt that he's played by Lugosi, who had portrayed the hunchback sidekick who often had more of a mind of his own than being a simple helper to the Frankenstein family. Lugosi certainly brings something to the role, with his disturbing leering mouth movements. While these are most uncanny, their origins are more mundane. *Frankenstein Meets the Wolf Man* was made with a talking Monster, as had been the case in *The Ghost of Frankenstein*, but the film was recut after test screenings and he was rendered mute. So, his quivering mouth movements are the ghostly remains of his dialog. These make the strongest impression in a few eerie close-up shots. As another legacy from *The Ghost of Frankenstein*, the Monster is blind, and the recurrent image of the Monster lurching around with arms outstretched comes directly from this moment. He is one-dimensional and utterly destructive. The Wolf Man appears almost as a double of archetypal scientist Dr. Mannering and defends the couple (Mannering and Elsa Frankenstein) from the Monster at the conclusion. He may be corrupted, but he retains a sense of humanity (despite being part animal), whereas the Frankenstein Monster, on the other hand, is human meat but with no soul.

This is a strange development from previous films, particularly as Lon Chaney Jr. meets himself, as it were. Chaney was the Monster in *The Ghost of Frankenstein*, and here, as the Wolf Man, he meets the Monster he was. That Monster is now Lugosi, who had been Igor in the previous film and had his brain transplanted to allow him to take up the Monster role. This underlying logic is not apparent to the casual viewer, who probably was more taken by wondering who would win the contest between the two monsters, yet this added a crucial level of interest to the cinephilic devotee. As it turns out, neither wins nor loses, as the film concludes with the dam breaking and a massive flood wave engulfing the battling monsters. *Frankenstein Meets the Wolf Man* is the first of the canonical Monster Mash films, and as such has been referenced in films that see themselves a continuation of that genealogy, with the film appearing on television sets in the films *King Kong vs Godzilla* (1962) and *Alien vs Predator* (2004).

The ensuing pair of Monster Mashes have distinct similarities and could easily be edited together into a feature-length single film. *House of Frankenstein* (1944) and *House of Dracula* (1945) were both directed by Erle C. Kenton and merely make a few minor changes to scenarios and situations. After *Frankenstein Meets the Wolf Man*, Universal clearly thought that continued movement in the same direction was the best policy. Instead of simply two monsters, in *House of Frankenstein* we have four: the Monster, Dracula, the Wolf Man, Boris Karloff as Dr. Niemann, which sounds similar to *niemand* (nobody). Niemann is a clear mad scientist successor to Baron Frankenstein. The poster also lists "Hunchback" and although the character could hardly be called monstrous, his physique is enough to corral him as an attraction with the others.

House of Frankenstein is episodic, starting with Niemann and Hunchback assistant Daniel escaping from prison and taking over a traveling sideshow. They subsequently reanimate Dracula (played by John Carradine), who causes trouble until he is vanquished after a horse carriage chase. Next, a love triangle story begins between Daniel, gypsy Ilonka and Laurence Talbot (Lon Chaney Jr. as the Wolf Man). Then, Niemann's revenge on former associates involves putting the brain of one into the Frankenstein Monster, who revives and then flees a mob of villagers with burning torches, carrying Niemann into quicksand.

Each narrative line appears minimal, to the point where each monster has their own. However, the Monster's is smaller than the other two. He is revived briefly at the film's conclusion despite being discovered earlier, frozen in an ice cave along with the Wolf Man. Disappointingly, no battle ensues between monsters here. The hapless hunchback conflicts with the Wolf Man and is thrown out a window by the Monster before the rapid self-destructive conclusion.

In this example, temporal format is clear and stands proud of the surface, with the brisk episodic character probably appearing to audiences at the time much like the sort of serials that would have been presented as short films alongside this very film. Indeed, the famous *Flash Gordon* serial (1936–40) was also made by Universal and used some of the recorded music scores that had appeared in Universal's series of horror films. To add to the sense of fragmentation, there appears to be some anachronistic confusion, where the seemingly nineteenth-century setting includes a modern American woman. The episodic character of *House of Frankenstein* also fits the self-conscious approach of having a traveling horror show at the film's center. Indeed, the film's isolated succession of attractions are much like such a show, with Karloff having progressed from being the lumbering Monster in earlier films to being the ringmaster (of "Professor Lampini's Chamber of Horrors").

Frankenstein's Monster is played by Glenn Strange, who retains some of Lugosi's snarling mouth movements from *Frankenstein Meets the Wolf Man*. The Monster is given a brain transplant from Niemann's old assistant, Ullman, to revive him, and perhaps the mouth movements are somewhere on the way to words. However, there is little sense of the Monster's behavior being decided by the new brain; indeed, his destructive character appears almost unconnected, and his self-destruction alongside Niemann is ambiguous rather than seeming to be exacting revenge. His behavior seems motivated more by escaping the mob rather than being suicidal. Perhaps it is no surprise that the Monster is to a degree reduced. Niemann runs a traveling phantasmagoria and the Monster is like one of its sideshow attractions. Indeed, like the traveling show, *House of Frankenstein* appears less as a coherent linear object and more like Tom Gunning's description of the "Cinema of Attractions" as a grab bag of different attractions and effects, which was at the heart of early cinema and sustained into areas of later cinema.[17] There is a direct line of ascendancy from *House of Frankenstein* to the following film.

Its close sister film, *House of Dracula* (1945), was made with the working title *Dracula vs the Wolfman*, featuring the same three monsters and their respective actors: Frankenstein's Monster (Glenn Strange), Dracula (John Carradine), and the Wolf Man (Lon Chaney Jr.), with Onslow Stevens now occupying the role of the mad scientist (named Edelmann). Initially, he seems reasonable, aiming to cure both vampirism and lycanthropy but later loses his sanity through an infected blood transfusion. Again, a hunchback assistant appears and is noted as an attraction on the film's poster. This time it is Nina, and like Daniel in the previous film, she hopes the Doctor will remedy her spinal curvature.

Again, the Monster is reduced to little more than an appearance at the film's conclusion.[18] While this might be understood as the cherry on the cake for the film, it also suggests a notion that the Monster lacked dramatic narrative possibilities. Each other character in the film has some sort of narrative built around them, no matter how small. The Monster really is only present to explode into violence once revived, for a brief, but torrid, rampage before being caught under the collapsing and burning building as the end title materializes. The Monster's rampage is built around a duel with the Wolf Man, or rather Talbot, who has been cured of his lycanthropy. This is a near repeat of the conclusion of the film in the series, two before this, except that rather than finishing with a cleansing tide of water, we have fire. Talbot escapes, leaving a startling final shot of the Monster trapped under a flaming wooden beam.

While Edelmann's initial intentions are to cure monsters, it is unclear what he aims to do with the Frankenstein Monster. Edelmann seems intent on doing good but proves that the road to hell is paved with good intentions. His collecting of the Monster is a disaster waiting to happen. While the supernatural is scientized (Dracula has a blood parasite and the Wolf Man has pressure on his brain), the Frankenstein Monster's evil is not explained away. An interesting point is that he contains the brain of Ullman, Niemann's old assistant, and yet his minimal motivations and activities remain constant to when he had Igor's brain or the abnormal brain in a few films before that. This seems an intriguing premise, that the brains retain little or no character from their original person and that dead meat is evacuated of human aspects, rendering the Monster a void of humanity occupied merely by a nihilistic death drive. His duel with Talbot and faceoff with the Wolf Man in *Frankenstein Meets the Wolf Man* underline this. Talbot's humanity and desire to save are in contrast with the Monster's innate

---

[17] Tom Gunning, "Cinema of Attractions: Early Film, Its Spectator and the Avant-Garde," in *Early Cinema: Space-Frame-Narrative*, ed. Thomas Elsaesser and Adam Barker (London: British Film Institute, 1990), 63.

[18] Almost in acknowledgment of this, a daydream sequence includes reused footage of the Monster from *The Ghost of Frankenstein* and *Bride of Frankenstein*.

desire for destruction.[19] As in *House of Frankenstein*, the Monster has no interaction with Dracula. The emphasis is upon his interaction with mad scientist Edelmann and particularly the Wolf Man/Lawrence Talbot. The Monster's aggression is absolute, and his only relationship with other entities is one of animosity. He appears as a locus of violence, indeed as a signifier of undiluted, undirected aggression. While these films appear based on the awe of the freakshow they also have the broad structure of the morality play, or at least a simple sense of moral structure.

Robert Horton aptly describes the Universal Frankenstein films as "a series of increasingly berserk vehicles for its marquee monsters."[20] Overall, the Universal Monster Mashes trade very much in already known characters, needing no introduction or development. Baron Frankenstein transforms into either relations or other mad scientist figures, and almost always has a more proletarian assistant (who is sometimes hunchbacked). The Monster does not develop as a character. If anything, he becomes more streamlined. He is more simple, losing the more complex aspects of the character, or indeed the surrounding questions. His sense of consciousness and motivations are pretty much forgotten and he appears as a cipher, representing an epicenter of destruction and nihilism more than a confused unity of fragments. Even swapping brains seems to have little effect on his behavior.

The narrative situations in *Frankenstein Meets the Wolf Man*, *House of Frankenstein*, and *House of Dracula* are such that they are built around a confrontation scene between the Monster and the Wolf Man, and the episodic format develops shorter sections only around other characters, such as Dracula and the Mad Doctor. These sections are merely of interest along the way to the final battle. As such, the Monster has no need to develop merely to be himself. That self is less a fragmentary figure and more like a golem, or like the tradition of stage Calibans that Richard Hand notes influenced stage versions of Shelley's novel.[21]

As part of Universal's establishment of a monster franchise, these Monster Mash films appear to take place in parallel universes. While the Monster is indestructible, Talbot/the Wolf Man is not. He was likely killed at the conclusion of *Frankenstein Meets the Wolf Man*. He reappears in *House of Frankenstein* and dies at the end, only to be alive in *House of Dracula* and end up cured of his lycanthropy. Indeed, the Wolf Man appears more connected to life and death than the Monster, which, although he was made of separate human parts, has set over the years and become a coherent single being. His connections with the dead are remote, and he is defined more by his unremitting appetite for violence and destruction.

Although it marks an appendix to the Universal Frankenstein films, *Abbott and Costello Meet Frankenstein* (1948) appears as a curious ending to the successful cycle

---

[19] In *House of Dracula*, the Wolf Man/Talbot even has his own associated musical theme music, perhaps underlining that he has a soul after all.

[20] Robert Horton, *Frankenstein* (New York: Columbia University Press/Wallflower, 2014), 34.

[21] Richard J. Hand, "Paradigms of Metamorphosis and Transmutation: Thomas Edison's *Frankenstein* and John Barrymore's *Dr Jekyll and Mr Hyde*," in *Monstrous Adaptations: Generic and Thematic Mutations in Horror Film*, ed. Richard J. Hand and Jay McRoy (Manchester: Manchester University Press, 2007), 12.

of films by drifting into farce.[22] A remarkably serious monster cast of Strange as the Frankenstein Monster, Lugosi as Dracula, and Chaney as the Wolf Man are made into bit-part players for the comedic double-act. We should be careful not to characterize this as a massive fall from grace, as Abbott and Costello were extremely successful comedians at this point. Indeed, *Abbott and Costello Meet Frankenstein* was one of Hollywood's highest-grossing films of the year.[23] So, it was also something of a reinvention for the Monster. Here, all three monsters are lampooned, which militates against the Frankenstein Monster being particularly scary or representative of much beyond a simple, threatening thug. Furthermore, he even refers to Dracula as his "master" and, like a golem, can be controlled. This is a significant transposition. It points the Monster in the direction of the children's film Monster that has become prevalent in recent decades. Meeting child-like comedians made him less scary and more of a familiar, indeed perhaps even a reassuring, friendly figure.

The Road to the *Dracula vs Frankenstein* Trilogy

A bizarre appendix to the Universal Monster Mashes, and a direct continuity with the last, was an unlicensed remake in the Mexican film *Frankenstein, el vampiro y compañía* (Frankenstein, the Vampire and Company, 1962), where Paco (Manuel "El Loco" Valdés) and Agapito (José Jasso) are the comic act engaging the monsters.[24] While humor was now part of the Monster on film, his world could also still be serious. In the late 1950s, British company Hammer rebooted the canonical Universal monsters, such as Dracula, the Mummy, the Wolf Man, and Frankenstein and his Monster. Again, making them scary, Hammer shifted the focus onto Victor Frankenstein and emphasized the Monster less. They also declined to continue mashing the monsters. Around the same time, American independent productions had successes with cheaply made films that were aimed primarily at drive-in cinemas. Examples include *I was a Teenage Frankenstein* (1957), *Frankenstein 1970* (1958), *Frankenstein's Daughter* (1958) and *Jesse James Meets Frankenstein's Daughter* (1966). The Monster and the process of creating a being from dead parts remained perennial cinematic attractions, although often rendered cheaply and with little consideration. Indeed, the Monster often simply embodied a negative force in these films, building directly upon the later years of Universal's Monster. The Monster also was appearing as an increasingly familiar figure, often in little or no need of introduction.

---

[22] The comedians went on to two films with Boris Karloff, *Abbott and Costello Meet the Killer, Boris Karloff* (1949) and *Abbott and Costello Meet Dr. Jekyll and Mr. Hyde* (1953) as well as *Abbott and Costello Meet the Mummy* (1955).
[23] "Top Grossers of 1948," *Variety*, January 5, 1949, 46.
[24] Another Mexican monster mash film was the horror comedy *El castillo de los monstrous/Castle of the Monsters* (1958), which had a mad scientist with hunchback assistant alongside a group of monsters in a castle. Although the Frankenstein Monster doesn't officially appear, the butler looks remarkably like him.

Toho, the Japanese film company that made the *Godzilla* films, had its own highly individual take on Frankenstein: *Frankenstein Conquers the World* (1965) (*Furankenshutain Tai Baragon* [*Frankenstein vs Baragon*]). It was a Japanese-American co-production directed by Ishirō Honda, who had directed *Godzilla* (1954) and the ensuing series of films. Rethinking Shelley's ideas beyond recognition, the film starts in Germany during the Second World War, where the heart of the Frankenstein Monster is stolen by the Nazis and then taken to Japan. The atom bomb dropped on Hiroshima makes a new and gigantic body grow from it, and then the new Monster fights against another behemoth Baragon, who was wrecking the Japanese countryside. There was a sequel of sorts, where the Monster's cells are grown in two gigantic brothers who fight in Tokyo (*The War of the Gargantuas* [1966]). *Frankenstein Conquers the World* is a good example of format determining the material, as the Frankenstein Monster is simply inserted to Toho's monster film setup, where men in rubber suits do battle on miniature sets. The Monster battles the destructive Baragon, which makes him something of a hero.

Around the turn of 1970, there were three films that have been assigned the title *Frankenstein vs Dracula*. Indeed, these films had a number of different titles and had divergent material. The first was *Dracula vs. Frankenstein*, also commonly known as *Assignment Terror* (also *El Hombre que vino del ummo*, *Dracula jagt Frankenstein*, and *Los Monstruos del terror*). It was released in 1969, was a Spanish, West German, and Italian co-production, directed by two Argentinian directors: Tulio Demichelli and Hugo Fregonese. Starring Michael Rennie, Karin Dor, and Paul Naschy, it is the third in the film series with Naschy as the werewolf "Count Waldemar Daninsky." This was Rennie's last film, and it is a chaotic affair. In effect, it is a remake of *House of Frankenstein*, with pretty much the same elements just mixed and in a different order. Mad scientist Rennie leads aliens on a possible invasion of the Earth. Using an Anthology of the Monsters, he assembles nosferatu, the Mummy, werewolf Daninsky, and the Frankenstein Monster (inexplicably known as "The Monster of Farancksalan"), and then watches events on a TV screen from a scientific laboratory. The Monster has almost closed eyes and a hipster polo neck jumper, which makes him fit well with some of the film's décor, including a discotheque scene. Disappointingly, the Monster does not battle Dracula. Instead, Daninsky the werewolf fights the other monsters and, wanting to die; is shot with silver bullets by a woman who loves him. This is exactly like *House of Frankenstein*, with the werewolf able to represent human positivity despite his affliction. Daninsky beats the Monster by throwing him onto electrical equipment. The Monster here is mind-controlled, quite possibly blind, and simply a slow, violent henchman figure. Structurally, he is again the antithesis of the werewolf figure, who is not beyond redemption and able to ultimately vanquish the more powerful Monster.

The second film was the American *Dracula vs. Frankenstein*, made by Independent-International Pictures and released in 1971. It was directed by Al Adamson[25] and

---

[25] Al Adamson's most famous films are probably the Blaxploitation films *Dynamite Brothers* (1974), *Black Heat* (1976) and *Black Samurai* (1977).

starred J. Carrol Naish, Lon Chaney Jr, Zandor Vorkov as Dracula, and the 7 foot 4 John Bloom as the Frankenstein Monster. The film is also known as *Blood of Frankenstein, Teenage Dracula, The Revenge of Dracula, They're Coming to Get You*, and *Draculas Bluthochzeit mit Frankenstein* (Dracula's Blood Wedding with Frankenstein). It has direct continuity with the Universal films in that it stars Naish, who played the hunchback Daniel in *House of Frankenstein*) as well as Chaney, who had appeared not only as the Wolf Man but also as the Monster in *Ghost of Frankenstein*. *Dracula vs Frankenstein* has an extremely complex narrative. In an amusement park setting, Dracula helps Naish's mad scientist revive the Monster, who then joins Dracula in exacting revenge on the scientist's enemies and strangers for his experiments. A woman searches for her missing sister and ultimately is tied up by Dracula but released by the Monster, and the two then fight. Dracula pulls the Monster apart but is killed by the sunlight. In this film, the Monster has a bloated and puckered face, making expression difficult. The film also uses very dark lighting throughout, making the images obscure and giving a distinctive cast to this bizarre film. Here, for the first time in a Monster Mash film, the Monster does battle with Dracula at the conclusion. Structurally, he has changed position. Whereas earlier the Wolf Man occupied the "good" position, having the possibility of redemption, and the Monster was the unswervingly evil function, Dracula retains the evil position. The Monster decides to save the captured woman from him, inspired by her beauty and perhaps even having a slight trace of humanity.

The third, also known as *Dracula, Prisoner of Frankenstein*, was directed by Jesús ("Jess") Franco and released in 1972. Another transnational European co-production, this time between Spain, France, Lichtenstein, and Portugal, it starred Denis Price as Victor Frankenstein, Howard Vernon as Dracula, and Fernando Bilbao as the Monster. Victor Frankenstein uses the Monster and controls Dracula to terrorize a village. Some gypsies make a werewolf appear, who then encounters and fights the Monster, who finally is electrocuted by Victor. Like many of Franco's films, the narrative is weak and fragmented, although there is plenty of interesting material along the way. It is a bold and fragmented film. The opening seventeen minutes has no dialog. This part showcases music by Bruno Nicolai, but music that was taken from his scores for two other Franco films, *Marquis de Sade's Justine* (1968) and *Count Dracula* (1970). This approach to the recycling of music is similar to that of Universal, in that music was reused from their films, and the later Frankenstein films incorporate music from other, earlier horror films. The Monster looks similar to Universal's with prominent stitching on his square forehead, bolt anodes in his neck and green skin (which was notable on Universal's posters and publicity still rather than in the black-and-white films). Indeed, he is almost a quotation of Universal's Monster, and so is very traditional. While *Dracula vs Frankenstein* contains much that is novel, in many ways it wishes to remain unmistakably connected to the Universal films. Despite not looking quite like a normal person, the Monster also does not look like an assemblage of different parts. He could almost be a road crash victim who has had some crude sutures. In a now-traditional manner, the Monster fights the Wolf Man at the film's conclusion, while Dr. Frankenstein stakes Dracula, who has mostly been his "prisoner" and doing his bidding, as one of the film's titles denotes.

There were further European developments for the Frankenstein Monster during this period that were almost of a piece with these. *Lady Frankenstein* was a 1971 Italian horror film directed by Mel Welles and written by cult writer Edward di Lorenzo. It stars Joseph Cotton as Victor Frankenstein, who makes the Monster and then is killed by him, after which the Monster goes on a rampage killing villagers in the vicinity. Frankenstein's daughter (played by Rosalba Neri) transplants the brain of her father's assistant into a young man's body, making him inhumanly powerful. The Monster and the brain-transplanted man fight at the end of the film, with the Monster vanquished by the pair at the end. The film is peppered with sex scenes and grim violence. The Monster looks gruesome and nothing like Universal's, with a distended head, a face covered in scar tissue and metal anode spikes coming from his upper head. Following a traditional pattern, the Monster is a soulless negative force, shown up by his opposed forces, who are rendered more clearly as heroes in the film for their vanquishing of the Monster.

Like the later Universal films, many films from that time and since seem to divorce the Monster from his creator. This loses the often evident sense of them being halves of a single psyche but opens the possibility of his new counterpart being something of an equal. Indeed, the concept of a death-match event in the title *Dracula vs Frankenstein* was taken literally by Mexican wrestling (*Lucha Libre*) film star Santo in *Santo y Blue Demon contra Los Monstruos* (*Santo and Blue Demon vs. the Monsters*, 1970), which had two sequels. Hollywood went on to move back closer to the Universal films,[26] although the canonical monsters appeared with a strong dose of camp and parody,[27] in children's films *The Monster Squad* (1987) and the *Hotel Transylvania* series of films (2012, 2015, 2018, 2021), among others.[28] Less juvenile attempts at reinvention included the mash of monsters in *Van Helsing* (2004), and independent productions *Frankenstein vs The Creature from Blood Cove* (2005) and *Frankenstein vs The Mummy* (2015), all of which follow directly from the tradition of Monster Mashes established by Universal.[29]

---

[26] Friedman and Kavey note the intermittent continuation of the Universal Monster Mash tradition. Lester D. Friedman and Allison B. Kavey, *Monstrous Progeny: A History of the Frankenstein Narratives* (New Brunswick: Rutgers University Press, 2016), 105.

[27] A good example is *Monster Mash* (1995) which directly parodied the Universal Monster Mash films. As an adaptation of the 1960s stage musical that was inspired by the titular song by Bobby "Boris" Pickett from 1962, the film underlined how the Frankenstein Monster and other canonical monsters became the stuff of Halloween laughter rather than terror.

[28] It is an indication of the infantilization of Universal's Monster that both the Frankenstein Monster and Dracula became mascots for children's breakfast cereal in the early 1970s. Baumann, *Frankenstein 200*, 88.

[29] As for television's take on the Frankenstein Monster, there was Universal TV's *The Munsters* (1964–6), the NBC's *Monster Squad* (1976–7), and Hanna Barbera cartoon *The Drak Pack* (1980), all of converted the canonical monsters to heroes in comic settings. The medium made a more thoughtful reimagining of the Monster in Showtime's serial *Penny Dreadful* (2014–16), where Baron Frankenstein makes two Monsters, one of whom destroys the other ("Caliban" and "Proteus").

Conclusion

Overwhelmingly, Monster Mash films have been considered as low-quality and low-status films. Murray Leeder refers to them as "enjoyably silly,"[30] while many other scholars have studiously ignored them. I understand perfectly what Leeder means, as these films appear not to *want* to be taken too seriously. However, this militates against seeing them as a notable phenomenon, worth scrutiny, and my discussion seeks to take them more seriously.

To a degree, the Monster's identity is contextual and defined by situations and antagonists, some of whom are equals in monstrosity and compete for film space. The Monster has a confused identity, being an amalgamation with no clear unified past. He is at least partially defined by who he meets (in some cases getting a long way from Mary Shelley's original). They throw him into relief, though—at times reducing him to being a simple machine of destruction, with little character definition. He regularly makes big meetings, similar to video game boss battles, at the conclusion of the Monster Mashes. The structure of the films, which often pose a climactic confrontation between the Monster and another, suggests a *mirrored* logic that, to some degree, they might be each other's double, perhaps even complementary halves of a whole. The Monster is not a fully developed character. He is like a puzzle with many missing pieces (or bits from different puzzles)—the other monsters structurally complete him—both psychologically and narratively. This makes the films parallel rather than linear and might, to a degree, account for the films being very fragmented and lacking a sense of coherent narrative development. This suggests a situation reminiscent of the dual-focus narrative characteristic of the film musical where a male and female character remain apart and have their own songs until the film's climactic "consummation."[31] Indeed, it is worth noting that Al Adamson's *Frankenstein vs Dracula* was also known as *Draculas Bluthochzeit mit Frankenstein*—Dracula's blood wedding with Frankenstein!

In many of these films, the Frankenstein Monster appears almost like a machine.[32] He is seemingly only partially human and reminiscent of E. T. A. Hoffmann's automaton in his short story "The Sandman," emblematically used by Freud to explicate the Uncanny in his essay from 1919.[33] Less a fragmentary chimera than a hulking, mindless golem, the Monster's destructive activities in these films are less his fault, and more that of his creator. His mechanical movements, lack of facial expression betray

---

[30] Leeder, *Horror Film*, 32.
[31] Rick Altman, *The American Film Musical* (London: BFI, 1987), 19.
[32] Curiously, Julia Douthwaite and Daniel Richter point to a possible origin of Shelley's story in François-Félix Nogaret's *Le Miroir des évènemens actuels, ou la belle au plus offrant: Histoire à deux visages* (*The Looking Glass of Actuality, or Beauty to the Highest Bidder: A Two-Faced Tale*, from 1790), where an inventor called "Frankenstein" makes an automaton musician. See Julia V. Douthwaite and Daniel Richter, "The Frankenstein of the French Revolution: Nogaret's Automaton Tale of 1790," *European Romantic Review* 20, no. 3 (July 2009): 381–411.
[33] Freud's use of "The Sandman" to illustrate the Uncanny is remarkable in that the story is about illusion and misguided perception. Film is in essence about perception, the chemical-mechanical assemblage giving an illusion of organic life, of the audience looking at reality. Sigmund Freud, *The Uncanny*, trans. David McLintock (New York: Penguin, 2003), 139–40.

a mindless, soulless, and partly dead character. Shelley's monologues and pathos are replaced with disturbing and graphic images and violence, as is the nature of the film medium's affordances.

While on one level, the Frankenstein story might be about the illusory unity of consciousness, and its fragmentary nature and origins, on another it is about the tension between the desired illusion of stability and the disavowed reality of fragmentation. Film and audiovisual media have proven to be central to culture for over a century. While some might argue that this has enabled the (further) fragmentation of the human psyche, it is equally possible that film's tessellated and multimodal form is an effective analog of modern experience as fragmented. The monster's genesis, as a collage of disparate elements, doubles the aesthetic process of these films, which bring together different elements into a whole that often lacks satisfactory coherence and fails to take seriously its own implications. However, if we think the key to the Monster is that he is made of disparate parts we are missing the point: he is unified despite having a body of disparate origins. This mirrors an argument in psychological approach in the Humanities: on the one hand cognitive psychology and its obsession with atomized analysis that looks to separation and different components; and on the other hand, Gestalt psychology, which habitually deals with objects as synergetic wholes. Indeed, his fragmentation is displaced onto the aesthetic whole in a fractal pattern across the whole film. Yet this is derived more from the medium of film than any originary aspect of the Frankenstein story. It appears to be the case that the Frankenstein Monster is particularly suited to film as an embodiment of film's processes, where a maximum of fragmentation is held momentarily in an armature of continuity.

3

Frankenstein and the Media of Serial Figures

Shane Denson

Introduction

"It's alive!" cries the mad scientist in any given monster movie.[1] As if in reply, a figure in Marvel Comics' *The Monster of Frankenstein* #3 (May 1973) cries, "God help us! It's still alive!" The exclamation acknowledges a series of conventionalized representations, endlessly quoted, and ups the ante by signaling both that the comic belongs to that series and that it is capable of taking ownership of it and writing its continuation. The argument of this chapter, for which this exclamation can stand as a concise example, is that Marvel Comics' appropriations of the narrative events and characters first developed in Mary Shelley's *Frankenstein* exemplify certain tendencies of serial narration that are both typical of comics in particular and informative with regard to the general dynamics of broader-based, plurimedial phenomena in the domain of popular culture. Marvel's Frankenstein comics of the 1970s, along with other appearances of the Frankenstein Monster in various Marvel series from the 1960s onward, enact an interplay between moments of repetition and variation—an interplay that constitutes the basic stuff of seriality—on a number of different levels, including both the narrative and the pictorial levels of the comic book medium. That is, these comics draw, on the one hand, on established and even stereotypical narrative patterns and iconic visual representations associated with the Frankenstein tale, thus adding another retelling to the endless series of adaptations, appropriations, and misappropriations of Shelley's hideous progeny. On the other hand, however, Marvel's appropriation attempts to go beyond mere repetition and produce something new, for which purposes the oft-told tale is expanded and continued beyond the frame of Shelley's novel or the Universal films of the 1930s. Thus, this interplay between repetition and innovation in fact involves a negotiation between two different forms of seriality that are co-present and that overlap

---

[1] This chapter has benefited greatly from discussions on the topic of seriality with fellow members of the DFG Research Unit "Popular Seriality—Aesthetics and Practice"; in particular: my collaborator Ruth Mayer, research group speaker Frank Kelleter, Andreas Jahn-Sudmann, Daniel Stein, and Jason Mittell. It is a slightly revised reprint of an article that was first published as "Marvel Comics' Frankenstein: A Case Study in the Media of Serial Figures," *Amerikastudien/American Studies* 56/4 (2011): 531–53.

in the graphic and narrative depictions of characters and events: a linear form of serial continuation and development and a nonlinear form of "concrescent" (compounding or cumulative) seriality. By blending these modes in a somewhat volatile mixture and oscillating between them, Marvel's retelling and continuation of the Frankenstein tale involves an indirect probing of the comic book medium itself, for the creature negotiates not merely his place between nature and artifice or between human society and monstrous incommensurability but also among the media that form the substrate of his narrative existence. Both his literary origins and the iconic visual representations of the cinema—the media that most centrally determine the parameters of his back-and-forth between repetition of fixed patterns and innovation—are acknowledged in Marvel's take on the monster, whose quest thus becomes an ongoing (i.e., both continuing and cyclically recurrent) struggle against, and reworking of, preconceived narratives and images. Words and images, the basic building blocks of comics as a medium, become the central concerns of a serially self-reflexive monster.

What I hope for, in mounting this argument, is to demonstrate a necessary interconnectedness among the media of popular culture's serial forms—an interconnectedness that is only approximated in prevalent theories of literary adaptation and intermediality. At stake here is a nexus where mediality and seriality inform and transform one another in the ongoing evolution of modern popular culture. To be sure, the Frankenstein comics investigated here are not in any way central to that evolution, but it is precisely my point that the popular mediality/seriality nexus is lacking such a center, that it is composed almost singularly of "marginal" phenomena: figures, themes, and stories that bleed across the margins of their medial instantiations, cross the boundaries between individual media, and institute a plurimedial field in which they promiscuously intermingle. Given this inherent "marginality" of the nexus, we cannot afford to ignore marginalized media forms, such as comics have traditionally been, or even those instantiations, like Marvel's Frankenstein comics, that must surely be judged marginal in relation to the dominant currents of cultural significance of their time. For those currents must be seen to take shape within a larger pool, in a substratal basin where chaotic flows and chance encounters give rise to the more visible, apparently central, couplings of media and cultural contents. In this broader arena of plurimedial popularity, Marvel's Frankenstein comics can be seen to probe the nexus between seriality and mediality in a particularly instructive way. The monstrous marginality that defines at once the thematic and the medial essence of these comics promises, ultimately, to illuminate the dynamics at work in popular culture's tendency toward serialization, or the recursive proliferation of contents beyond and across the margins that demarcate the media of those contents' instantiation.

Frankenstein vs. *Frankenstein*, or: Popularity and Seriality

It is not by accident that the phrase "Marvel Comics' Frankenstein" in the title of this chapter lacks the italicization that would designate *Frankenstein* as the title of a work.

Though Marvel Comics did, in 1977, produce a stand-alone comic by that title—an adaptation proper of Shelley's novel (*Marvel Classics Comics* #20)—my main concern lies elsewhere: not in a work at all but in a series of *Frankenstein*-inspired characters and narratives that span various story arcs across several comic book series and culminate in the Bronze Age[2] horror titles *The Monster of Frankenstein* (which debuted in January 1973 and was renamed *The Frankenstein Monster* from issue #6 to the final issue #18 of September 1975) and *Monsters Unleashed* (a black-and-white comic magazine which ran for eleven issues from August 1973 to April 1975 and included, beginning with issue #2 and continued in #4 through #10, an ongoing modern-day series, "Frankenstein '73"—later redubbed "Frankenstein '74" and finally just "Frankenstein's Monster").[3] The main focus of these series, as well as of the present chapter, is in fact the so-called monster, not a character named Frankenstein (though several different characters going by that name make guest appearances). This is not to say that Marvel was guilty of the common confusion of creator and creature that has lent the latter the former's

---

[2] The topic of comic book "ages" is a subject of some debate among comics fans, collectors, and scholars alike. In the present chapter, I assume quite conventionally the following progression: The Golden Age runs from 1938 (with the advent of superhero comics) to the mid-1950s (when the Comics Code went into effect, following a postwar decline in superheroes' popularity); the Silver Age witnesses a revival of superheroes and lasts until the late 1960s or early 1970s (ending around the time the Comics Code was revised and made less restrictive with regard to the depiction of horror and crime); afterward, a somewhat grittier Bronze Age lasts at least through the 1970s, perhaps into the 1980s, and may be followed by one or more additional ages—the Modern Age currently being the leading contender to the title. Despite widespread acceptance, however, this schematization is regularly challenged as too simplistic (e.g., the postwar/pre-Code era is distinguished from the Golden Age as a separate Atom Age, or the Modern Age is broken down into any number of ages: Copper, Lead, Chrome, etc.). On the other hand, a critic such as Geoff Klock is able to challenge the periodization from the opposite angle, effectively eliminating the Bronze Age altogether and reducing the ages of comics to three: Golden, Silver, and a contemporary age marked by what Klock calls "the revisionary superhero narrative" (3). Against the proliferation of ever-finer-grained historical categories, on the one hand, I maintain that the rougher cut common wisdom is a better, more wieldy tool for most purposes; but against suggestions like Klock's, which would even further simplify the scheme, I can only point out that for *my* purposes here—where I am concerned specifically with comics and themes associated with the horror genre—the notion of a Bronze Age helps to identify a significant development in the comics industry, marking out a space in which, among other things, the horror genre became possible again after a near-total absence under the original Comics Code's policing of the Silver Age.

[3] It should be noted that rival DC Comics has its own history of *Frankenstein*-inspired characters and stories which could be interrogated along the same lines as Marvel's various appropriations. DC's take on the tale begins in *Detective Comics* #135 (May 1948), in which Batman and Robin travel back in time to witness and intervene in the story, which has little in common with Mary Shelley's novel. Later, in the 1970s, a figure known as "Spawn of Frankenstein" would appear in the pages of DC's *Phantom Stranger* (first in issue #23, February 1973, and continuing for over a year—thus running concurrently with the main Marvel Frankenstein comics). This creature was an artificial being whose early history parallels more closely the events of Shelley's novel but who then went on to undertake previously untold adventures—much like Marvel's Bronze Age monster, with which DC's version may be seen in a sort of serial competition. Even more recently, two Frankensteinian characters have made appearances in DC Comics: Frankenstein's Monster (sometimes referred to simply as Frankenstein) and Young Frankenstein (who may or may not be the same character in his younger years). And these, as well, are matched by contemporaries at twenty-first-century Marvel: Frankenstein's Monster is named Adam in the miniseries *Bloodstone* (#1 to #4, December 2001–March 2002), and a certain Frank fights alongside the First Line superhero team in the series *Marvel: The Lost Generation* (numbered in reverse: #12 to #1, March 2000–February 2001).

surname, but neither did they insist too emphatically on the difference. Instead, the ambiguity of "Frankenstein," I suggest, was approached less as an error to be corrected (presumably with reference to the "original" by Mary Shelley) than as a central aspect of the popularization of "Frankenstein" as it appears in the title of my chapter: neither the title of a work nor the proper name of a character, this Frankenstein is more a locus (at once thematic, figural, and medial) of a serially staged narrative complex.

The types of seriality and serialization processes that I have in mind here are central parts, indeed, of the popularization processes that, in modern societies, work to render narratives and characters ever adaptable and thus relatively autonomous from the authors who gave birth to them and the literary or artistic works into which they were first born. Marvel's restaging in the 1970s is therefore a case study, as indicated by my title, with regard to a larger process that, in the case of Frankenstein, begins in the nineteenth century with numerous stage adaptations of Shelley's gothic novel,[4] continues in the twentieth century with further theatrical and above all filmic instantiations,[5] but also branches out into radio, television, merchandising tie-ins, breakfast cereals, video games, and so on. The proliferation of the Frankenstein tale across a variety of media has charged it with a dynamic all its own, abstracted from the novel and its author, such that Karloff and other monster-movie embodiments exert a greater force today than Mary Shelley does on any new production.[6] They provide the background against which any new figuration must appear, and this circumstance is no less true for ostensible attempts (such as Kenneth Branagh's conspicuously titled 1994 film *Mary Shelley's Frankenstein*) to provide a "faithful" adaptation or return to the "original." Though the novel *Frankenstein* is not unpopular, the popular Frankenstein is now far removed from the novel, for the overall *series* of productions has largely absorbed the novel as one more non-definitive version of a tale that continues to evolve.

In any case, it is telling that Marvel's one-off attempt at adaptation in a narrow sense of the word, the aforementioned *Frankenstein* that appeared as a self-contained story in the proto-graphic-novel series *Marvel Classics Comics*, is itself marginalized in the Marvel Universe to the benefit of the company's far-less-faithful serializations.[7] Significantly, in this regard, the fan-driven Wikipedia-style *Marvel Comics Database*[8] is able to account for every known appearance of the Frankenstein Monster in the

---

[4] See Nitchie as well as Forry.
[5] For detailed lists and facts about Frankenstein films, see Glut; Picart, Smoot, and Blodgett.
[6] Boris Karloff starred as the monster in the first three of Universal Studios' Frankenstein films: *Frankenstein* (1931), *Bride of Frankenstein* (1935), and *Son of Frankenstein* (1939). Lon Chaney, Jr. took over the role in *Ghost of Frankenstein* (1942), followed by Bela Lugosi in *Frankenstein Meets the Wolf Man* (1943), and Glenn Strange in *House of Frankenstein* (1944), *House of Dracula* (1945), and *Abbott and Costello Meet Frankenstein* (1948). Despite these changes, Karloff's image determined the appearance of his successors, and his portrayal remains iconic to this day.
[7] Indeed, the publication format in which Marvel's adaptation proper appeared is interesting in its own right, for in serializing (in terms of publication) a set of stories that are (diegetically) self-contained and offer "remakes" of literary classics, the *Marvel Classics Comics* "series" raises central questions about the interchanges between repetition and continuation, or about various types of serialization practices. In the next section, I return to these questions from a somewhat different angle.
[8] The site can be accessed at https://marvel.fandom.com/wiki/Marvel_Database.

pages of a Marvel series, no matter how marginal or apparently contradictory to the major developments in Marvel's Bronze Age appropriation, by according them all a place within the Earth-616 continuity—that is, a place in the overarching "world" in which all of Marvel's productions cohere (apart from those that explore one of the many alternate universes that, beyond our own reality, make up the larger Multiverse). The 1977 adaptation, apparently the closest thing Marvel has to the story's "original," is the *only* exception; this is what the *Database* currently has to say about it:

> This issue is the official Marvel Comics adaptation of the 1818 Mary Shelley novel, *Frankenstein, or, the Modern Prometheus*. Although the events detailed in this issue mirror those that correspond to the character of the Frankenstein Monster in the Earth-616 continuity, it represents its own singular continuity.[9]

Thus, in a dramatic inversion of the original/spinoff hierarchy, the diegetic setting of Earth-616, in which *The Monster of Frankenstein* and "Frankenstein '73" are set, provides the true account of the history of the universe, and it is thus Earth-616, and *not* Shelley's novel, that is the yardstick of faithful adaptation in letter or spirit. The monster's appearances in the pages of *The Avengers* (issues #131 and #132, as well as *Giant-Size Avengers* #3), *Iron Man* (#101 and #102), or alongside Spider-Man in *Marvel Team-Up* (#36 and #37) are thus more canonical, and closer to the truth, than a more or less straightforward adaptation, which only "mirrors" or approximates the true reality of the Marvel Universe. (Furthermore, and perhaps even more tellingly, the 1983 "Marvel Illustrated Novel" edition of Shelley's *Frankenstein*, which included the full text of the 1831 revised edition of the novel and a set of highly acclaimed illustrations by comic book artist Bernie Wrightson, is not mentioned in the *Database*.)

Go Figure: A Tale of Two Serialities

The coherence of Earth-616, particularly as regards the Frankenstein Monster's various apparitions there, is hardly obvious or unproblematic. Indeed, it is in part the problematic nature of rendering the character coherent, of constructing a continuous and non-contradictory biography that would contain and conjoin all the various appearances across the different series, that makes Marvel Comics' Frankenstein such an interesting case study.[10] For it is precisely the tension between the various individual series (and the installments of which they are composed) and the overarching synthesis

---

[9] See https://marvel.fandom.com/wiki/Marvel_Classics_Comics_Series_Featuring_Frankenstein_Vol_1_1 (accessed January 13, 2020).

[10] DC Comics' treatment of the Frankenstein tale and related characters is no less interesting in this regard. Is the Bronze Age character "Spawn of Frankenstein" the same as the more recent "Frankenstein's Monster" (or simply "Frankenstein"), and is the latter merely an older version of DC's "Young Frankenstein" figure? It is far from clear, due to the complex nature of the DC Universe (with its varied continuities of Earth One, Earth Two, etc.), how these figures all relate to one another, if at all.

of a spatiotemporally consistent diegetic world that brings us face to face with the two types of seriality mentioned in the introduction: (1) a linear form of serial progression, continuation, and development; and (2) a nonlinear form of serial "concrescence," snowballing accumulation, or compounding sedimentation. The difference between these two may perhaps be explained most accessibly by way of the types of characters that each of them involves. The first type of character may be called a "series character"; this is a figure that unfolds within a continuing narrative (e.g., in a soap opera, a novel series, or saga), tending to take on an increased psychological depth and/or ever more complex social involvements in the course of this development. On the other hand, the second type of character, the "serial figure," is apt to remain "flat" and, as Umberto Eco once wrote of Superman, to experience a repeated "virtual beginning" with each new production or installment, which is not absolutely bound by the events of the preceding one ("The Myth of Superman" 19).[11] The serial figure is a stock character of sorts, who appears again and again in significantly different adaptation forms, contexts, and in various media. The series character exists *within* a series, where he or she develops or evolves; the serial figure, on the other hand, exists *as* a series—as the concatenation of instantiations that evolves not within a homogenous diegetic space but *between* or *across* such spaces of narration. And because serial figures, in stark contrast to series characters, lead a sort of surplus existence outside of any one given telling, they are in a perfect position to reflect on the manner—and the media—of their repeated stagings.

Frankenstein's Monster, generally speaking and with a view to the discontinuous and plurimedial stagings that it has undergone over the course of its career, is—like Dracula, Sherlock Holmes, Tarzan, Superman, or Batman—a serial figure. But, as any of these instances will demonstrate, the distinction between serial figures and series characters is not absolute. Though not confined to any particular (diegetically coherent) series, the monster enters into any number of such series, for example the Universal films of the 1930s and 1940s or the Marvel Comics series *The Monster of Frankenstein*, in which he temporarily becomes a series character. But, like Batman or Superman, who are both capable of sustaining quite long-term linear serialities, the monster is also susceptible to the occasional "reboot"—a radical revision of the character's history that amounts, effectively, to rebirth. What makes these characters serial figures, though, and not just disjointed collections or remakes of themselves as series characters, is that they carry traces of their previous incarnations into their new worlds, where the strata of their previous lives accrue in a nonlinear, nondiegetic

---

[11] The series character/serial figure distinction was coined by Ruth Mayer and myself in the context of a joint research project on "Serial Figures and Media Change," part of the larger DFG-funded research group on "Popular Seriality—Aesthetics and Practice" (director Frank Kelleter, University of Göttingen); a more detailed exploration of the series character/serial figure distinction is provided in our co-authored paper, "Grenzgänger: Serielle Figuren im Medienwechsel," in *Populäre Serialität: Narration - Evolution - Distinktion*, ed. Frank Kelleter (Bielefeld: transcript Verlag, 2012), 185–203. Also relevant in this regard is Eco's later essay, "Innovation and Repetition: Between Modern and Post-Modern Aesthetics," *Daedalus* 114, no. 4 (1985): 161–84, in which Eco returns to his earlier observations about Superman and generalizes a large-scale change in narrative practice and reception.

manner. This takes place, typically, in the realm of the figures' medial or material substrates, whether they be of a linguistic, graphic, photographic, cinematic, or other nature. Indeed, it is precisely as the measure of the difference between the media of a figure's various instantiations that the serial link is sealed—the extra-diegetic link that constitutes the seriality of the serial figure as such. Thus, for example, director James Whale's classic *Frankenstein* (1931) transformed the monster (portrayed by Boris Karloff) into a mute being, in stark contrast to the novel's linguistically eloquent creature.[12] Shelley's Monster, it must be said, was already a highly self-reflexive figure, in which the ontological question of the human was cast, in part, as a question of media: the conceptual pair humanity/monstrosity was treated in the book in such a way that it was inseparable from the tale of the monster's language acquisition through a small canon of literary works. But the iconic cinematic rendition updated this self-reflexivity and endowed it with a comparative dimension. In its new form, the monster still posed questions regarding the limits of the normal and the natural; in its historical context, however, this excessively visual—that is, photographic—monster also embodied a media-technological question that was intimately tied not only to the shift from a literary to a visual culture but also more specifically connected to the transition from silent to sound film.[13] Here the mute monster foregrounded the still problematic image/sound relations of the early sound cinema, though this capacity faded quickly over the course of its development in the Universal series. On the other hand, a series like the Hammer Frankenstein films of the late 1950s to 1970s, which took the creator rather than the creature as its central figure, reactivated the self-reflexive potential of the tale by highlighting the difference between the deep reds of its Eastmancolor blood and the monochromatic world of its forebears.[14] Thus, the monster of the movies, like the monster of the printed page, has continually oscillated between diegetic and nondiegetic roles and functions, articulating variable interrelations between narrative and medial liminalities which, due to the serial nature of the figure's repeated staging, are subject to historical—and indeed media-historical—comparison.

Because the Frankenstein Monster is—and has long been—a truly serial figure, firmly established across the media of popular culture, this set of background relations did not, of course, disappear when the creature entered into the Marvel Universe. Marvel's Frankenstein had to contend with the fact, well known to Marvel's artists,

---

[12] I have dealt with Whale's Frankenstein films in "Incorporations: Melodrama and Monstrosity in James Whale's Frankenstein and Bride of Frankenstein," in *Melodrama! The Mode of Excess from Early America to Hollywood*, ed. Frank Kelleter, Barbara Krah, and Ruth Mayer (Heidelberg: Universitätsverlag Winter, 2007), 209–28, and they play a major role in my book *Postnaturalism: Frankenstein, Film, and the Anthropotechnical Interface*, (Bielefeld: Transcript-Verlag, 2014).

[13] The most detailed argument for this thesis appears in Robert Spadoni, *Uncanny Bodies: The Coming of Sound and the Origins of the Horror Genre* (Berkeley: University of California Press, 2007). I make a related argument regarding the classic Tarzan films starring Johnny Weissmuller in my "Tarzan und der Tonfilm: Verhandlungen zwischen 'science' und 'fiction.'"

[14] The British company Hammer Film Productions produced seven films documenting the continuing (mis)adventures of Baron Frankenstein: *Curse of Frankenstein* (1957), *Revenge of Frankenstein* (1958), *Evil of Frankenstein* (1964), *Frankenstein Created Woman* (1967), *Frankenstein Must Be Destroyed* (1969), *Horror of Frankenstein* (1970), and *Frankenstein and the Monster from Hell* (1974).

writers, editors, and readers alike, that the iconic representations and revisions effected in the medium of film had come to color any and all subsequent perceptions that viewers or readers might possibly have of the monster and the act of his creation. Indeed, this fact was hardly new, and it had long rendered comic book appropriations of the tale parasitic on cinema's images: hence the proliferation of bolt-necked, flat-headed, platform-shoe-wearing monsters hastily put together by mad scientists in the pages of so-called funny books. Indeed, comics' subordination to cinematic Frankensteins was capable of assuming a wide variety of forms. At one extreme of the spectrum, we find a fumetti (i.e., photo-based comic) adaptation of the third installment in Universal's film series, *Son of Frankenstein*, released concurrently with the film in *Movie Comics* #1 from April 1939, which due to the comic's technical means of production is not only beholden to the film's narrative conventions (which were quickly becoming clichés) but also directly reproduces its raw images.[15] On the other hand, a more diffuse influence was present in Dick Briefer's famous pre–Comics Code adaptations,[16] which between 1940 and 1954 put filmic stereotypes to work for the purposes of both horror and humor.[17] Now Marvel's one-world policy (only later to be dubbed Earth-616) provided an ingenious solution to this problem of influence. For under this policy, all aspects of "our" world, that is, the real or nondiegetic world in which the reader consumes Marvel's comics, are absorbed into the diegetic world of the Marvel Universe, which is complete with its own Marvel Comics Group printing comics presumably identical to those we read, with the singular difference that they chronicle non-fiction adventures of really existing superheroes. With this narrative mechanism in place, the real-world influence of real-world media on real-world readers remains, without a doubt, a real problem, but it is one now capable of quite novel solutions—solutions that allow the comics to acknowledge the existence of serial precursors (of the nonlinear, plurimedial, serial-figure type), which are taken up and repeated, and which are overhauled through this very act of repetition in order to synthesize and mark the innovation that drives serial figures onward.

---

[15] The entire eight-page story can be viewed online, at the *Golden Age Comic Book Stories* (blog), http://goldenagecomicbookstories.blogspot.com/2009/01/son-of-frankenstein-fumetti-adaptation.html (accessed August 31, 2010).

[16] The Comics Code, based in large part on the Film Production Code, was an industry attempt at self-regulation in reaction to controversy over the allegedly negative influence of comic books, especially in their depictions of crime and horror, on youth. As a result of the code, which went into effect in 1954, a once booming horror comics market vanished overnight, until a 1971 revision of the Code allowed that "Vampires, ghouls and werewolves shall be permitted to be used when handled in the classic tradition such as Frankenstein, Dracula and other high calibre literary works written by Edgar Allen [*sic*] Poe, Saki (H. H. Munro), Conan Doyle and other respected authors whose works are read in schools throughout the world" (qtd. in Nyberg 172). For a detailed history of the Comics Code, see Nyberg.

[17] Briefer's Frankenstein comics start in *Prize Comics* #7 (December 1940), kicking off a series that would shift from horror to humor after the Second World War and continue in the pages of that comic book until 1948 (up to issue #68), in addition to spawning an independent title, *Frankenstein*, which initially ran for 17 issues from 1945 to 1949 and was later revived as a horror series from 1952 to 1954 (issue #18 to #33), when the Comics Code spelled its end.

Seriality and Mediality

Two pre-1970s Marvel takes on the Frankenstein tale hint at the range of possibilities. In *The X-Men* #40 (January 1968, in a story entitled "The Mark of the Monster!"), the young mutants are pitted against a version of the Frankenstein Monster that is clearly influenced by the Karloff/Universal depiction: a rampaging giant with flat head and electrodes in his neck who is able to shoot laser beams from his eyes. Rather than trying to conceal this monster-movie influence, the comic signals its awareness of it very clearly, thereby acknowledging that readers also know all about it. Thus, Professor Xavier summons the X-Men to tell them that "[t]he unholy creation known as Frankenstein's monster—has been found!"—to which follows the skeptical reply: "Frankenstein's monster? But he's just a myth—something you see on the late, late show!" (3). Rather than ignoring readers' incredulity, the comic thus gives it a voice in the diegesis, thereby laying the groundwork for its absorption and, ultimately, neutralization. Xavier continues, "But, I'm not speaking of a movie monster! Rather, I mean the eight-foot humanoid referred to in the novel by Mary Shelley! I've always believed the book was based on an actual occurrence—and now I'm sure of it!" (3). Xavier quickly educates his pupils (and the comic's readers) about the novel's Arctic ending, which helps to explain why the monster was now found frozen in a block of ice (a device that had also been employed in Universal's 1943 *Frankenstein Meets the Wolf Man* to explain how the monster once again survives his apparent death at the end of the last film). When a hubristic scientist thaws and revives the monster, the creature goes berserk, and the scientist can only quote the movies in surprise: "He lives! The monster lives!" (6). And while the monster is full of the aggression typical of that displayed in B-grade monster flicks, he is true to Shelley's novel in one respect: he is an articulate speaker, in command of a large vocabulary, even if he puts it to questionable use, as in this characteristic rant: "Human worms! You have served . . . your purpose! [. . .] Now stand aside . . . or I crush you like fleas!" (6). Even in the heat of battle, the creature continues to deliver a blow-by-blow commentary on the action, in response to which the X-Man known as the Beast quips, "You'll bore us to death with your salacious soliloquies, my fatuous friend! Why can't you be the strong, silent type—like Boris Karloff?" (13).

Clearly, this engagement with the Frankenstein Monster is one that is aware of the figure's extra-diegetic seriality, which the comic ingeniously puts to work for its own purposes by mobilizing visual and narrative aspects of a great variety of the figure's incarnations. In other words, the comic pits the novel's narrative and its characterization of the creature against not one but a whole range of cinematic associations, including the iconic image and melodramatic sentimentality of the Karloff creature and the killing-machine kitsch into which it devolved. The result is that the mediality of the monster is foregrounded rather than concealed, and the payoff is that the comic book is able to highlight its own superiority as a medium, one which combines literature and cinema—word and image—and is thus able to subject them to a synthesis unimaginable in either medium in isolation. Narratively, this triumph is consummated, and the to and fro between filmic and literary influences comes to an end when Professor Xavier, having probed the defeated monster's mind, reveals "the real origin of the so-called 'Frankenstein's monster,'" which both the novel and its many filmic progenies had consistently gotten wrong (15). In fact, this monster turns out to be an android, "the creation of some alien race from a far-off tropical planet—which passed near our world 150 years ago"; meant as an "interstellar ambassador," the android malfunctioned and ran amok, thus inspiring Shelley's speculative account (15).[18] With this revelation, the comic book effectively transcends both the novel and the movies by rewriting both of them into its own diegetic world.

This, then, is one way in which a self-conscious repetition of serialized tropes can be made to serve the ends of narrative and medial innovation through a sublimating absorption into the Marvel Universe. *Silver Surfer* #7 (August 1969) demonstrates another approach. The story, entitled "The Heir of Frankenstein," opens with the title character, a descendant of the original "Count" Frankenstein, lugging a corpse into his alpine castle laboratory with the help of his misshapen assistant. The latter establishes the seriality of the event right on the first page: "But, master . . . you have tried so often . . . and failed so often" (1). And despite initial signs of success, this renewed attempt at animating a corpse fails as well. Alas, the obligatory torch-wielding villagers quickly gather outside the castle, break down the gate with a makeshift battering ram, and set fire to the building. With no alternative left to him, Frankenstein vows to go through with the mysterious "Experiment X," which, his assistant tells us, is "the one experiment . . . which even you have sworn . . . never to attempt" and for which he will—gasp!— "need a living victim!" (6). Meanwhile, the Silver Surfer notices the fire, interpreting it as the mob's injustice against their fellow man; Frankenstein takes advantage of the Surfer's gullibility and demonstrates to him the supposedly benevolent nature of his work, designed to help others, but met with mistrust and fear by the ignorant villagers. When the Silver Surfer departs, Frankenstein instructs his assistant: "Borgo! The films! Quickly, you grotesque non-entity! I must view them once more!" (12). While the sinister Frankenstein muses about his plan to trap the Surfer for Experiment X, Borgo threads the film he has retrieved into a projector, commenting, "Master . . . you have seen it far more times than I can count" (13). A clearly crazed Frankenstein replies, "And I shall see it again . . . and again . . . and again . . . for I must never repeat the mistakes that my witless ancestors made!" (13). What we then see over Frankenstein's shoulder on the projection screen is a scene that we, too, have seen again and again and again: the "original" creation scene, in which (according to this version) a white-haired scientist attaches cables to the electrodes on the neck of a gray-skinned monster, who is again presented in a Universal-style rendition with a flat head, and who even dons (as we see when he stands to attack his maker) Karloff-inspired high-water trousers

---

[18] Compare DC's *Detective Comics* #135 (May 1948), which similarly usurps Mary Shelley's claim to authorial creation and integrity. Time-travel allows Batman and Robin to witness "The True Story of Frankenstein." This is the story of the scientist Frankenstein's assistant Ivan, a gentle giant, turned into a mindless killer by the combination of an electric shock compounded by adrenalin shock—a story, that is, that involves no artificial creation. According to the comic, the notion that Frankenstein stitched together a monster from corpses was an embellishment invented by Mary Shelley, who fictionalized the true story upon hearing the details from Batman.

and thick boots. After reviewing the film, Frankenstein goes on to conduct more experiments, and he eventually succeeds in convincing the Silver Surfer to help him, whereupon an evil duplicate of the doubly "duped" Surfer is produced. While the real Silver Surfer battles it out with his copy, the villagers again attack the castle, and Borgo, unable to tolerate Frankenstein's injustice any longer, pushes his master out an open window and jumps to his own death.

The interesting thing about this particular reimagining of the Frankenstein tale is the extreme way in which it countenances seriality as a basic fact of its subject matter while integrating the serial figure's mediality into the world it depicts, going so far as to insinuate that, far from being fictional productions, the films we all know and love are documents of the original act of creation. In a new twist on a self-reflexive trope that has long been employed by Frankenstein films, the monster's animation is itself a filmed and/or filmic event. In films ranging from Thomas Edison's one-reeler *Frankenstein* (1910) to CGI-heavy productions like *Van Helsing* (2004), the creation scene often serves as a showcase in which to display the cinema's own powers of creation, its ability to infuse lifeless photographs with life by means of ever-advancing techniques and special effects.[19] The result is that the monster's existence, and the viewer's attention as well, is split between diegetic and nondiegetic, that is, media-technical, levels of articulation—between the depicted spectacle of technical creation and the spectacular creation of technical depiction. Only by means of this split can the tireless repetition of the creation scene be imbued with a feeling of novelty, where the innovation resides not in the content but in the medial makeup of the scene, which strives to differ and improve upon its forerunners.[20] Again, this interplay of repetition and innovation is the very basis of the monster's continued existence as a serial figure. Significantly, when the monster appears in the pages of *Silver Surfer*, he does so *as* a filmic image—both highlighting the figure's medial constructedness (right down to the black-and-white film stock mimicked in the creature's pale gray skin and jet-black hair) *and* reframing that mediality as an element of reality (i.e., the ostensibly unmediated "real world"). The effect is less to eliminate the reader's awareness of the diegesis/medium divide as to aggravate this awareness by subjecting it to a hyperbolic compounding: a self-reflexive nesting of that divide, along with the cinema's self-reflexive awareness of it, into the diegetic side of the split—which, of course, immediately opens onto a new nondiegetic side or onto an intensified awareness of mediality as the motor of the serial figure.

In both the X-Men's and the Silver Surfer's run-ins with the Frankenstein tale, we find that repetition and conventionality are employed, and even recognized as such, in order to highlight a form of innovation that concerns the mediality of the serial figure—to the benefit, of course, of the comic book. Before going on to consider

---

[19] I explore the nature and historicity of this filmic self-reflexivity in detail in my *Postnaturalism: Frankenstein, Film, and the Anthropotechnical Interface*.

[20] As Daniel Stein reminds me, it is also characteristic of the superhero genre to repeat, recycle, and revise "origin stories" and "origin scenes." Though it is beyond the scope of the present paper, a more nuanced picture of popular serialization strategies could be attained by means of a careful comparison between the repetitions and variations of Frankensteinian and superhero *Urszenen*.

Marvel's more systematic elaboration of the monster in its Bronze Age series, it will be helpful to cast a theoretical light on the connection emerging here between mediality and seriality, and to approach this nexus with the aid of Niklas Luhmann's theory of media. Inspired by psychologist Fritz Heider's distinction of medium and thing, defined as the difference between a "loose coupling" and a "tight coupling" of elements of a given sort,[21] Luhmann approaches mediality as a *relation* between a given medial substrate and the forms that may be constituted in it.[22] Substrate and form are always composed of the same basic "stuff," the same elements, whatever they may be in a given case; the difference, then, between substrate and form lies in their respective organization of these elements: a substrate is a loose coupling, that is, a relatively unordered mass of particles, while forms are tight or strict couplings, that is, relatively ordered combinations of elements. Thus, for example, the loosely coupled molecules of the air can be temporarily ordered into forms, wave patterns, by the tone-emitting action of a radio's loudspeaker; the tones that become perceivable by such means are themselves a medium out of which specific couplings or combinations can be formed to produce music. Similarly, the letters of the alphabet constitute a medium in which specific orderings, words as forms, can be composed; and words, in turn, constitute a medium for the construction of sentence forms, sentences a medium for textual forms, and so on. As these examples show, the distinction between substrate and form is strictly relative. A medial substrate exists only in relation to the forms it enables and vice versa. Accordingly, a medium does not lead an independent, objective existence but is related to an observer or system as "the operative deployment of the *difference* of medial substrate and form" (*Die Gesellschaft der Gesellschaft* 195; my translation).

Clearly, this manner of approaching media is very different from an apparatus-based approach that restricts media to empirical devices, infrastructures, and carriers such as film strips, television sets, or books. Luhmann's approach is more flexible, but it might also seem a bit vague and slippery. Can it, for example, help us decide whether comics, composed of text + image, are best considered a bi-medial compound, or whether comic books are a singular medium in their own right? In effect, Luhmann's theory licenses both approaches, depending on the circumstances of observation. Text can be treated as an independent medium, and so can the image; their combination can also be seen this way, though, for it demarcates its own unique distinctions between substrate and form that its components do not. In this way, the text + image compound enables the construction of a syntax of sorts that would regulate the spatiotemporal and narrative progression from one illustrated panel to the next. Moreover, the collection of such progressions into the higher-level medium of the comic book allows for the development of various logics of higher-order progressions: linear continuation between one issue and the next, for example, or cyclical, episodic iterations of a basic

---

[21] See Fritz Heider, *Ding und Medium* (1926; repr., Berlin: Kulturverlag Kadmos, 2005).
[22] For a detailed treatment, see Niklas Luhmann, *Die Kunst der Gesellschaft* (Frankfurt: Suhrkamp, 1995), 165–214 (translated as *Art as a Social System*). See also Niklas Luhmann, *Die Gesellschaft der Gesellschaft* (Frankfurt: Suhrkamp, 1997), 190–412.

formula with variations on a theme. We arrive, then, at the serial modes that I have been concerned with in this essay.

In fact, however, Luhmann's theory of mediality is even more intimately tied to a theory of seriality: Luhmann notes on one occasion that one way to elaborate his distinction of medial substrate and form is "by means of the distinction between redundancy and variety."[23] He explains:

> The elements that form the medium through their loose coupling—such as letters in a certain kind of writing or words in a text—must be easily recognizable. They carry little information themselves, since the informational content of an artwork must be generated in the course of its formation. The formation of the work creates surprise and assures variety, because there are many ways in which the work can take shape and because, when observed slowly, the work invites the viewer to contemplate alternate possibilities and to experiment with formal variations.[24]

According to this redescription, the substrate/form distinction that defines mediality for Luhmann falls into line with the repetition/variation distinction that characterizes the nonlinear seriality of the serial figure. We can readily apply Luhmann's insights here to the case of the Frankenstein Monster as he appears alongside the X-Men or the Silver Surfer. In both cases, the narratives employ a figure that is iconic, conventional, and thus "easily recognizable," as Luhmann says. "Variety" or innovation arises not through the use of new materials but through the novel employment of the old, through repetition itself, but conducted in such a way as to induce "the viewer to contemplate alternate possibilities and to experiment with formal variations." What if Shelley's novel were a misinformed account of true occurrences? What if the classic Frankenstein films were actual footage of artificial creation? As the very "stuff" of the interplay between repetition and variation, the serial figure of the monster is itself the medium in which such speculation ("what if?") is generated as the endless play of an iconic or repeatable substrate and its novel graphic and narrative forms. Itself a medium in this sense—and thus itself articulating a distinction between a relatively formless (medial) substrate and the (diegetic) forms it is capable of assuming—it is no wonder that the serialized monster problematizes the mediality of those higher-level media, such as a film or comics, with which it comes into contact.

Framing the Monster, Framing the World

The foregoing examples underline the generative potential of the Frankenstein Monster as a serial-figure-cum-medium, but they also highlight a problem to which I pointed earlier. If, as I have shown, the figure of the monster lends itself to a proliferation

---

[23] Luhmann, *Die Kunst*, 105.
[24] Ibid.

of non-identical "what-if" scenarios—scenarios that draw their interest in large part from the unexpected innovation that results from a sublimating repetition of well-known elements—then it is hardly to be expected that these scenarios should converge or settle into a consistent groove. Would this not, indeed, contradict the impetus of the serial figure's dynamic tension, which demands that innovation renew the basic substrate time and again, and which guarantees such renewal by ensuring that the material substrate is never completely absorbed or eclipsed by its formal expression? I am contending, in other words, that the mediality of the serial figure is never allowed to become wholly transparent, but that a recalcitrant margin remains in any crystallization into narrative, visual, or other forms of appearance. But, if this is so, how could the various "what-if" scenarios be synthesized into a coherent "world," as the Marvel Universe's one-world policy demands?[25] Earlier, I suggested that it is here—in the domain of practices associated with what is commonly called "retcon"[26]—that the two forms of seriality, the linear and the nonlinear forms that characterize series characters and serial figures respectively, come to a head most dramatically. It is only appropriate, then, that we turn now to the monster's entry, in the 1970s, into his own linearized, continuing Marvel Comics series, and that we attend carefully to the interplay between seriality types.

The two cases I have considered thus far were one-off episodes that, though they fail to mesh overtly with one another, are capable of being integrated into the Marvel Universe through various ad-hoc explanations: perhaps the android in *X-Men* #40 was not the real monster after all, perhaps the filmstrip in *Silver Surfer* #7 was genuine, but maybe not a record of the *very first* creation scene (e.g., maybe it was the attempt of another forgotten member of the Frankenstein family). The game of "what-if" continues.[27] By way of contrast, Marvel's series *The Monster of Frankenstein*, which in

---

[25] With the appropriately titled series *What If . . . ?* (original series running from 1977 to 1984, followed by a second series from 1989 to 1998 and a variety of more recent one-shots), Marvel Comics has repeatedly tackled these issues in its own way, exploring counterfactual scenarios such as "What if Spiderman had joined the Fantastic Four?" or "What if Captain America became president?" These scenarios, packaged as a series but inherently one-off narratives, are important pieces of the puzzle in understanding the dynamic tensions at the heart of the popular serial forms I am exploring here. They attest to the contradictory tendencies at work in both the production and reception of comic books: on the one hand, the tendency of narratives to proliferate and spawn alternative views and possibilities (mirrored in fans' appropriations of stories and characters for their own "unlicensed" purposes); on the other hand, the desire for coherence and continuity expressed both in production-side practices of "retcon" and in the corresponding efforts of readers, who at their most extreme engage in an almost Leibnizian exploration of the compossibility of possible worlds in the attempt to systematize the Multiverse (see, for example, the *Marvel Comics Database*'s entry for the term "Multiverse," which includes an overwhelming list of official and unofficial universes, with names ranging from Earth-0 to Earth-989192).

[26] "Retcon," short for retrospective continuity, refers to a set of techniques for revising the history of the diegetic world, either adding, subtracting, or changing past events. This can be done for various reasons and to various effects—for example, allowing an apparently deceased character to live on, bracketing out certain narrative arcs as illusory (often explained as a dream) in order to advance the narrative in a different direction, filling in a "behind-the-scenes" view of previously narrated events, or disposing of unpopular storylines.

[27] Such ad hoc solutions remain vital well into the 1970s. For example, *The Avengers* #131 (January 1975), #132 (February 1975), and *Giant-Size Avengers* #3 (also February 1975) present a three-

its first four issues retold the monster's origin story before moving on from there to trace his continuing adventures, was committed to providing an explicit and causally coherent continuity. And because it thus combines a retelling with a continuing sequelization, this series alone provides a concise study in the dynamic interchanges between linear and nonlinear serialities. Add to it a second series, "Frankenstein '73," published concurrently but set in a completely different diegetic timeframe, and throw into the mix Marvel's assurance that all of its productions, these two not excepted, take place in the same world[28]—and someone's got some serious explaining (or retconning) to do!

Actually, it all boils down to a question of framing: a question of negotiating an overarching frame within which all of the various scenarios generated by the monster can be seen to co-exist in a single diegetic space.[29] Framing, indeed, is also what is at stake in Luhmann's theory of mediality: since a medial substrate and its forms are composed of the same basic "stuff," it is merely the degree of organization, or the manner of framing, that constitutes their difference. Luhmann's forms are merely framed patterns, the various manners of framing a given substrate. For Luhmann, then,

---

episode story arc-in which the monster is plucked out of 1898 (the initial setting of *The Monster of Frankenstein*) and teamed up with a group of dead "villains" as the "Legion of the Unliving" to fight the Avengers in a limbo realm before being returned, without consequence for the further course of history, at the end of the story.

[28] This is stated explicitly, for example, in response to a reader's letter in *The Frankenstein Monster* #16 (May 1975): "all the characters depicted in our mags—be they monster or super-hero—do indeed inhabit the same magnificent, mind-bending Marvel Universe (or cosmos; we're not picky)" (n.p.). At stake in this particular context was less the question of whether Marvel's two Frankenstein series were set in the same world (their convergence was made clear in *The Frankenstein Monster* #12), but whether the monster should be allowed to meet up with other Marvel monsters, as had already taken place in *Giant-Size Werewolf* #2 (October 1974), or even with Marvel's superheroes, as would occur in *Iron Man* #101 and #102 (August, September 1977) or with Spider-man in *Marvel Team-Up* #36 and #37 (August, September 1975). The very idea of the latter pairing had been ridiculed in a reader's letter in *The Frankenstein Monster* #12 (September 1974), to which even the editor conceded in reply: "We tend to agree that a Spidey/Monster issue of MARVEL TEAM-UP would be a tad ridiculous (we think)" (n.p.).

[29] Recent discussions of frames and framing often draw on one of two sources. The first is Derrida's discussion, in *The Truth in Painting*, of the picture frame as *parergon*, a supplement seen to stand outside the work when attention is directed at a painting, but seen to belong to it (as part of a figure) when one focuses on the wall (as ground). The other source is Bateson's metacommunicative concept of framing, developed in "A Theory of Play and Fantasy" and adapted by Goffman in his *Frame Analysis: An Essay on the Organization of Experience*. Recently, the latter has been at the center of attempts to apply cognitive theory to narratological ends; a prominent example is the collection of essays, *Framing Borders in Literature and Other Media*, edited by Wolf and Bernhart. While there are points of contact with both Derrida's deconstructive approach and Bateson's and Goffman's constructivist perspective, my own use of framing pays no special allegiance to either one of them. Like Wolf, who unites a wide range of frame concepts with the claim that "all of the different approaches to 'frames' converge in one frame function, namely to guide and even enable interpretation" ("Introduction" 3), I am interested primarily in a pragmatic, if not common-sensical, notion of framing, which is not restricted to either narrative or visual, cognitive or physical, senses of the term. It is just such a pragmatic conception of framing, I contend, that illuminates the nexus that, following the leads provided by Luhmann, unites mediality and seriality. The concept of the frame, accordingly, is for me instrumental to the task of understanding that nexus, which is the home turf of the serial figure.

mediality *is* framing. And this way of looking at things is also helpful for considering the difference between series characters (those that exist *in* a series) and serial figures (those that exist *as* a series): ideally, series characters are formed or framed in such a way as to conceal their framing, so that their mediality is transparent and does not get in the way of their diegetic (psychological, etc.) development; serial figures, on the other hand, thrive on the existence of an opaque or semi-opaque margin, a frame that is at least sometimes visible and that prevents these figures from being contained absolutely in the diegetic domain. The visible frame ensures that the medial substrate of which they are composed is never completely exhausted—and again, it is this excess of the apparent frame that allows serial figures to exist outside of a given narrative and to move between various media. The serial figure, in short, is a plurimedial and a many-worlded creature, held together only by the incomplete erasure of its nondiegetic medial framing, on the sole basis of which cross-medial comparisons, relations, and serial concrescences become possible. There is significant tension, then, between the framing strategy of Marvel's one-world policy and the many-worldedness of the serially framed monster.

With its frame-within-a-frame structure of nested narratives, Mary Shelley's gothic novel provides a natural place to explore these issues,[30] and Marvel seizes the opportunity in an ingenious way in *The Monster of Frankenstein*. Establishing the definitive (i.e., Earth-616) account of the monster's origins, the first four issues of the series repeat, in more or less faithful fashion, the tale as told in the novel—with one important embellishment: namely, the novel's frame structure (with Walton's epistolary narration at the outer frame, containing Frankenstein's account of events as related to him, which in turn includes the monster's own account at the center) is expanded by an additional frame, and this addition has both narrative and medial consequences with regard to the serial dynamics of repetition and innovation. For it is now Walton IV, the great-grandson of the novel's captain, who narrates the outermost tale, set a full century after the novel and thus ensuring that the nested repetition of the well-known tale, though agreeing in most points with the book, is already subject to a displacement that is both formal and, by laying the ground for a continuation of the tale from the fifth issue onward, diegetic as well. This reframing thus performatively combines *both* forms of serialization: a nonlinear compounding of the literary tale by means of its emplacement in a more inclusive frame, and a linearizing continuation enacted through the insertion of a century of diegetic history (with more to follow).

A closer look at the narrative structures of issues #1 through #4 reveals a deep-seated ambivalence between these serial forms. Having rediscovered the frozen monster, Captain Walton IV tells his cabin-boy (and the reader) the tale that has been passed down to him through his forefather's letters. He recounts Frankenstein's experiments, his success in animating a composite creature, his fearful realization of what he had done, the murder of his brother William at the hands of the monster, and the trial

---

[30] In his "Framing Borders in Frame Stories," Wolf provides a useful discussion of literary framing in general with specific reference to *Frankenstein*.

and hanging of the innocent Justine. As the narrative reaches Frankenstein's meeting with the monster in an alpine cave, the monster prepares to tell his famous tale, but the narration is interrupted quite abruptly and returned to the outer frame, where a storm has broken out and Walton IV's mutinous crew demands that the monster be expelled from the ship. Below deck, meanwhile, the monster thaws and his hand curls into a fist, as the first issue comes to a dramatic close. Issue #2 opens with Sean Farrell, the cabin-boy addressee of the first issue's narrative, discovering the monster; when the monster carries the unconscious boy above deck, Walton IV can just manage to prevent the mutineers from firing at the creature, subduing them and evoking pity for the monster by repeating the creation story and continuing where he left off before. Thus bridging the first issue's cliffhanger ending and repeating the story for the benefit of both the reader and the rest of the crew, the Walton IV figure proves a clever means of negotiating serial continuation and repetition, hence mirroring the historical proliferation of retellings in the comic's own ongoing serialized enactment of retelling.

Now follows the monster's tale, prefaced visually with a close-up of the monster's face, which functions as a gateway or border between external and internal narrative frames (between the cave setting in which the monster relates his tale to Frankenstein and the internal frame of the related tale) (6, panel 5). After he has told of coming to his senses, of observing a blind man and his family, of learning their language, and of being driven from human society, his narrative closes with a close-up of the creature's yellow eye in a wavy-bordered panel that exists liminally between one narrative frame and another (18, panel 3): spatially attached both to the (self-narrated) monster persecuted by a mob of angry villagers and to the (narrating) monster in the mountain cave, the eye stands between and links the two temporal frames of narration. From this intermediate position, the monster's eye mirrors the reader's eye as well, the eye that moves from one graphic frame or panel to the next in the temporal process of reading. The reflexivity established by the eye, which emerges from the page in close-up and protrudes from the narrated world as well by linking two spaces of narration, transcending both of them to enter the space of the reader, is therefore a medial self-reflexivity in a strong sense: it directs attention toward the processes of medial construction at the same time that it serves a constructive medial purpose. Back, now, in the cave, the monster demands of Frankenstein the creation of a mate, which he (unlike his counterpart in the novel) in fact carries out before brutally destroying the female monster; the enraged monster kills Frankenstein's friend Clerval in retribution. Having discovered the corpse, the traumatized Frankenstein is arrested for murder, his face foregrounded with a blank eye (similar to the monster's discussed earlier) staring at—or through—the reader in a panel that transitions between this narrative frame and Walton IV's ship in 1898 (25, panel 4). There, the ship suddenly rams an iceberg and begins to sink, bringing issue #2 to another cliffhanger close.

At the outset of the next issue, the sailors scramble into lifeboats in the belief that the monster, thrown overboard in the crash, is dead. But when the monster, whose hand juts ominously out of the water, boards their boat and begins wreaking havoc, one of the sailors exclaims, "God help us! It's still alive!" (3)—an intensification of the standard line in Frankenstein films, fully self-aware of its seriality. Sparing the captain, his cabin-boy, and his guide, the monster rows them to firm ice and a "rotting ship's wreckage" (5), which provides makeshift shelter. There, the monster insists: "The story, man! You must tell me the rest of the story!" (5). With his back turned, Walton IV prepares to continue the narrative, while the monster's face, set in profile, literally replaces the gutter between two panels and forms the border between two spatiotemporal frames as well: the "here and now" that he shares with Walton IV and the "there and then" of Walton's story, where we see Frankenstein again stabbing the female monster (6, panels 1 and 2). Once again, the monster's face and eyes mediate the threshold between narrative frames, between temporal settings, and between the act (or the fact) and the content of mediation—between the constructed "inside" of a tale and the "outside" setting of its telling. The distinction is further complicated by the fact that Walton's tale is reported in a sort of disembodied voice-over, to which the monster adds, also in textual voice-over-type comments, his own recollections. Thus, the images we see belong to the interior, the textual instances to the exterior of narration, where narration itself is executed by means of a dialog between the captain and the monster. We see, for example, the monster standing outside a window looking in at Frankenstein and Elizabeth setting their wedding date (12, panel 4); in voice-over mode, the spatially and temporally distant co-narrators engage in a dialog over Frankenstein's state of mind, the monster insisting he must have known that the vow to "be with [him] on [his] wedding night" (11) was meant in earnest, and Walton replying that he was blind with love (12). Set around the image of the monster at the window, this dialog reinforces both visually and textually the meeting of inside and out as defining the space of narrative mediality, where the monster embodies an opaque mediality that contrasts ostentatiously with the window-like transparency often demanded of narrative media. In a series of panels, Walton explains Frankenstein's plan to spend his wedding night far away from home, and we see him checking the house and making sure no one could have followed him and Elizabeth to their secluded retreat (13–14). Then Walton addresses the monster directly: "Now perhaps you can best explain the horrible minutes which followed!" (14). The monster's face again marking a threshold for shifting gears between narrative instances and frames, the creature accepts the challenge (14, panel 5).

What we see in this cooperative back-and-forth between the two narrators, each complementing the other and filling in a picture that is not quite coherent but perspectivally fractured, is an image (both a metaphorical and, with the monster's face repeatedly marking the shifts between narrative frames, a literally graphic image) of the serial process of cumulative, palimpsest-like repetition and variation that revolves around the serial figure of the monster. Here, the Frankenstein tale is repeated, but also expanded, revised, transformed, and transplanted in a manner that acknowledges and interrogates this telling's own place in the larger plurimedial series of tellings; it therefore focuses on the narrative's mediality more than its content, highlighting construction and multiplicity rather than imaging coherent origins and univocity.

When he resumes his part of the narrative, Walton IV takes us up to the end of the novel, covering the Arctic pursuit, Frankenstein's discovery by the crew of Walton I, Frankenstein's narration to the original captain, and his death on board. Pushing the serialization of the narrative further, though, Walton IV demands that the monster explain what happened after the events recorded in his great-grandfather's letters (i.e., after the novel): "There must be more . . . much more! How else can we explain your presence here?!" (27). How else indeed? But alas, a storm rises and destroys their makeshift shelter, a heavy beam falls on the monster, and the cliffhanger is complete: "Next: The end . . . or the beginning?!!!" (28).

Issue #4 brings us up to speed, detailing the monster's lone wanderings across the tundra, his encounter with a primitive tribe, where he briefly finds communal acceptance, and its tragic loss due to war with a neighboring tribe. We learn, further, of the monster's fall into the icy waters, of the century-long entombment in ice that led to his encounter with Walton IV. At the end of the story, Walton IV is dying, but he reveals to the monster an "urgent" piece of information (27): "A descendant of Victor Frankenstein—still lives—near the family birthplace—in Ingolstadt!" (28). Thus ends the story arc begun in issue #1, and thus begins the monster's quest to find the last of the Frankensteins and kill him.[31] This quest, which begins in issue #5, is more episodic in nature, bringing the creature into contact with werewolves, gypsies, a giant spider, Dracula, and eventually even a descendant of his creator, one Vincent Frankenstein, who takes the monster to turn-of-the-century London. Concurrently with issue #5, however, the modern-day series "Frankenstein '73" also kicks off in the pages of *Monsters Unleashed* (issue #2, September 1973), a black-and-white magazine regularly adorned with movie stills of Karloff, where a very movie-inspired monster encounters mad neuroscientists, undergoes brain transplants, becomes increasingly bulletproof, and just barely escapes being enlisted in a voodoo-doll wielding master's hideous corps of freaks. Meanwhile, issue #12 of the color comic, now called *The Frankenstein Monster*, brings the two series together by plunging the monster once more into icy waters, preserving him through the world wars and technological advances of the twentieth century, until he is again discovered and put on display in a Midwestern freak show. Subsequently revived, he undergoes a variety of adventures, fighting chimeric clone monsters and international crime rings, and eventually meeting not one but two female descendants of Victor Frankenstein.

Though the two series cover different episodes in the life of the monster, it is clear that they both cover the same monster, leading the same life in the same world. Thus, the first installment of "Frankenstein '73" recounts the monster's origin story in a version that is highly compressed but consistent with the version told in *The Monster of Frankenstein* #1 to #4. And issue #12 of the color comic references events told in the black-and-white comic, going so far as to explicitly refer the reader in a footnote to issues #2, #4, and #6 of *Monsters Unleashed*. Together, the comics frame an increasingly unified monster in an increasingly unified world. They work, that is,

---

[31] The four-issue story arc, though not quite self-contained, does possess a certain unity—most obviously constituted by its overarching cyclical narrative structure—that is lacking in the continuing sequelization that follows. Implicitly recognizing this, Marvel reprinted issues #1 to #4, but not further, in *Book of the Dead* #1 to #4 (December 1993–March 1994).

to frame a linearized history that charts a continuous biographical development, thus transforming the creature from a serial figure into a series character.[32]

And yet the margin of the monster's medial framing, upon which a nonlinear accrual of extra-diegetic seriality takes place, is never wholly eradicated. For example, the monster of "Frankenstein '73" is mute from the outset, and in a magazine full of Karloffian images and articles on monster movies, there can be little doubt but that this is a cross-medial nod to the classic Frankenstein films. The initially articulate monster of the color comic is also rendered mute (in issue #9, March 1974) when a vampire bites him and paralyzes his vocal cords. In issue #7 of the black-and-white series (August 1974), a different explanation is offered for his speechlessness: the fire that, in issue #2's first installment, woke the monster from suspended animation and freed him from the freak show, had damaged his throat. When, the following month, in *The Frankenstein Monster* #12 (September 1974), the continuities of the two series are brought together, this fire is depicted once more, and the vampire explanation is never mentioned again. Even if we can overlook the discrepancies in continuity, and even if we can suppress our knowledge of the mute movie monster's influence (which, after all, is absorbed and explained diegetically in an ingenious feat of framing), the point here is that the monster's muteness renders the act of framing visible by initiating a self-reflexive probing of the comic book medium. The monster's speechlessness translates into an inability to produce text on the page, a conspicuous absence that renders text all the more important, and which concomitantly highlights the importance of the monster's visuality—his grotesque patchwork appearance functions narratively to explain his immediate rejection by humans, but it also marks a specifically medial fact of his construction. In particular, this enhanced visual role recalls the monster's graphically and narratively liminal functions in *The Monster of Frankenstein* #1 to #4, the quasi-syntactic functions whereby his image marked the border between the closing and opening of narrative frames and self-reflexively highlighted the fact of the comic book's graphic framing via sequentially ordered panels.

Even on Earth-616, then, the serial framing of the monster remains apparent; its medial excess is never completely absorbed in the diegetic synthesis of a biography. And, as a result, the two central framing media of the comic book—word and image—

---

[32] The significance and contingency of these acts of framing are ironically attested to by the German publication history of Marvel's Frankenstein comics. The Williams Verlag began publishing *The Monster of Frankenstein*, under the title *Das Monster von Frankenstein*, in January 1974. Beginning with issue #12, the German publisher began splitting the tales of the American comics into two issues, thus stretching the eighteen issues of the American original into twenty-five German issues. Apparently, the German edition was more successful than the American turned out to be, for when the American series was canceled and the final issue #18 ended with an unrequited cliffhanger, the Williams Verlag commissioned its own ending to the story, with no American model to go by. Effectively, the tale told in *Das Monster von Frankenstein* #26, "Baronesse von Frankenstein," provided a means of transitioning from the ongoing saga of *The Monster of Frankenstein* (aka *The Frankenstein Monster*) to the "Frankenstein '73" series from *Monsters Unleashed*, which Williams printed—in color rather than the original black-and-white—in *Das Monster von Frankenstein* #27 to #33, thus spanning all but the very last story in that series before the German magazine was canceled. William's publication practice thus reframes the two concurrent American series as one continuous series, demonstrating the radical variability of serial narrative framings.

never quite recede from view and achieve total transparency. Constantly repeating the same old story in an unexpectedly innovative way, compounding retellings in concentric and cyclical frames while continuing along novel lines of development, the monster's negotiations of serial forms constantly pull the media of any particular articulation—such as Marvel's comics—back into a diffuse and plurimedial substrate: the slimy pool out of which the monster emerged and into which he oozes back to recollect himself as a serial figure, biding his time before he strikes again—perhaps in another age, in another medium altogether. "God help us! It's still alive!"

4

Musical Directions, Sound, Silence, and Song in *Presumption, or the Fate of Frankenstein* (1823)

John Higney

Frankenstein; or, the Modern Prometheus was published anonymously on January 1, 1818. Five years later, on August 11, 1823, it was published with authorship now attributed to Mary Shelley. Coming two weeks after the July 28, 1823, premiere of Richard Brinsley Peake's melodrama, *Presumption, or the Fate of Frankenstein*, the timing of this second publication was fortuitous. In a letter to Leigh Hunt after attending the show, Shelley remarked "but lo and behold! I found myself famous. F[rankenstein] had prodigious success as a drama & was about to be repeated for the 23rd night at the English opera house."[1] Peake's adaptation, though met with uneven reviews, ultimately ran thirty-seven performances over a three-month season and was a considerable success. Stephen C. Behrendt estimates that as many as 55,000 London theatergoers saw the original run. *Presumption* marked the beginning of a two-century-long global popular culture phenomenon.[2]

Frankenstein moved from the page to the stage within five years of its publication and the adaptation—including musical directions, references to sound and music, and songs—is of its time. Yet it and the many adaptations that followed contributed much to the modern conception of the creature and the Frankenstein narrative in popular culture. Fourteen English and French stage adaptations of Shelley's tale were produced within three years of *Presumption*,[3] and their cultural reach was extensive. The English Opera House, where *Presumption* premiered, had a capacity of approximately 1,500 people. The Coburg Theatre, where *Frankenstein, or the Demon of Switzerland* appeared within a month of *Presumption,* boasted a maximum

---

[1] Mary Shelley to Leigh Hunt, September 9, 1823, in Betty T. Bennett, ed., *Selected Letters of Mary Wollstonecraft Shelley* (Baltimore: Johns Hopkins University Press, 1995), letter 1,378.
[2] Stephen C. Behrendt, "Introduction," in *Presumption: Or, the Fate of Frankenstein* (electronic edition) ed. Stephen Behrendt (Boulder: University of Colorado, 2001), available online: https://romantic-circles.org/editions/peake/apparatus/introduction.html (accessed May 15, 2021).
[3] Steven Earl Forry, *Hideous Progenies: Dramatizations of Frankenstein from Mary Shelley to the Present* (Philadelphia: University of Pennsylvania Press, 1990), 3.

house of 3,800.⁴ In comparison, early editions of the novel were "upmarket" and expensive and were printed in comparatively small numbers. The cost of a single *Bentley's Standard Novel*, as the 1831 edition of *Frankenstein* was published, was equivalent to nearly half the weekly wages of a skilled manual laborer or a clerk.⁵ Only between 7,000 and 8,000 copies of the novel were sold during the first forty years of its life.⁶ So extensive was the reach of the theatrical adaptations that William St. Clair posits any single performance of one of the adaptations might have reached a wider audience than did the novel in "ten or twenty years."⁷ As Emma Raub notes, Peake's *Presumption* not only influenced the flood of melodramas and burlesques that rapidly followed, the stylistic features of melodrama embodied in the adaptation gave form to aspects of the creature's characterization and the Frankenstein story that persisted into the age of film.⁸ Moreover, unlike the gothic novel, whose stylistic features developed without state-mandated strictures, the late-eighteenth- and early-nineteenth-century English gothic melodrama was the product of regulations designed to protect the "legitimate drama" of the so-called major houses (patent theaters) of Drury Lane and Covent Garden. As what follows will demonstrate, these regulations also shaped *Presumption*, the creature's characterization, and the Frankenstein story.

Blocked from presenting the spoken word of legitimate drama—tragedy and comedy of manners—London's "minor houses" where gothic drama and melodrama developed resorted to an assemblage of drama, comedy, pantomime, spectacle, and music. The presence of drama and spectacle in gothic melodrama would surprise few familiar with gothic literature. However, pantomime, comedy, music, and song as important elements of gothic melodrama might appear incongruous to those unfamiliar with the theatrical genre. As Jeffrey N. Cox noted, not merely the result of regulations, comedy was integral to the gothic theater aesthetic. So much so that gothic terror and drama without comedic characters, as in Joanna Baillie's *De Monfort* (1798) and Charles Maturin's *Bertram; or, the Castle of St. Aldobrand* (1816), transformed the gothic into traditional tragedy.⁹ Peake's melodramatic adaptation was powerfully shaped by the regulatory conditions and aesthetic characteristics briefly described earlier. It was a product created for the socioeconomically diverse audience of the minor houses where drama, comedy, horror, spectacle, music, and song were all combined as producers walked a fine regulatory line in search of broad audience appeal and profit.

Many features of subsequent adaptations—both theatrical and film—can be traced to Peake's *Presumption*, London theatrical regulations, and the conventions of gothic theater. For example, the blue-painted face, long hair, tunic and physically imposing

---

4 William St. Clair, "The Impact of Frankenstein," in *Mary Shelley in Her Times*, ed. Betty T. Bennett and Stuart Curran (Baltimore: Johns Hopkins University Press, 2000), 52.
5 Ibid., 45.
6 Ibid., 48.
7 Ibid., 52.
8 Emma Raub, "Frankenstein and the Mute Figure of Melodrama," *Modern Drama* 55, no. 4 (Winter 2012): 454–5.
9 Jeffrey N. Cox, *Seven Gothic Dramas, 1789–1825* (Athens: Ohio University Press, 1992), 23.

figure of the creature as first portrayed by Thomas Potter Cooke in the adaptation are echoed in the ghostly painted face, disheveled tunic, long hair, and intimidating physicality of the creature in the 1910 Edison Studios film adaptation. Well read, thoughtful, and articulate in the novel, Cooke's pantomimic blue-faced creature informed the inarticulate green-skinned creature first depicted by Boris Karloff in James Whale's 1931 Universal Films production, *Frankenstein*. This characterization continued in Universal sequel films, including *Bride of Frankenstein* (1935), *Son of Frankenstein* (1939), and *The Ghost of Frankenstein* (1942). Variously named Karl or Igor in later films, Peake's stock comedic character (a common figure in gothic drama and melodrama), Fritz, appears in Whale's 1931 film version. The visually and sonically spectacular reanimation scene in Dr. Frankenstein's laboratory in which he proclaims the creature is alive, memorably rendered in Whale's 1931 film as "it's alive," can also be traced to a similar scene in *Presumption*.

Peake's script contains a large number of songs—another feature of gothic drama shaped by the regulation of the minor houses—and an unusual abundance of musical and sonic cues. Of course, it is impossible to trace a direct line from the soundscape of *Presumption* and the many Frankenstein adaptations that followed later film adaptations. However, scholars such as David Neumeyer[10] and Michael Pisani[11] make a strong case that techniques of early film music find precedents in nineteenth-century melodramatic music practices. At the very least, music and sound cues in melodramas such as *Presumption* likely would have borne some resemblance to the sonic landscapes in early film adaptations including those referenced above. Comedic scenes, frequently concerned with everyday subjects such as eating, drinking and, relationship concerns, as Cox writes, "offer a center of conventional domesticity with the horrors of the central Gothic action."[12] It is in such scenes that Peake placed most of the songs in *Presumption*.

Although no musical score survives, this chapter investigates the many musical directions, references to sound, and songs in *Presumption* in the contexts of the 1818 edition of Shelley's novel and the period theatrical practices and aesthetics outlined earlier. As what follows will demonstrate, Peake's *Presumption* both looked backward to musical scenes and references in the original version of the novel and looked forward to shape Shelley's story in ways recognizable to modern readers. Moreover, the product of both theatrical regulations and the gothic theatrical aesthetic, the songs, melodramatic musical cues, silence, and references to sound in *Presumption* powerfully contributed to the success of a spectacle that, Dr. Frankenstein-like, breathed life into Shelley's novel and launched her story as an enduring popular culture phenomenon.

---

[10] David Neumeyer, "Melodrama as a Compositional Resource in Early Hollywood Sound Cinema," *Current Musicology* 57 (April 1995): 61–94.
[11] Michael Pisani, "When the Music Surges: Melodrama and the Nineteenth-Century Theatrical Precedents to Film Music Style and Placement," in *The Oxford Handbook of Film Music Studies*, ed. David Neumeyer (New York: Oxford University Press, 2014), 559–82.
[12] Cox, *Seven Gothic Dramas*, 23.

Music and Sound in Shelley's Novel

References to music and sound were a common feature of the gothic novel, and they are present in *Frankenstein*, even if the work can only nominally be categorized as "Gothic." As James Wierzbicki observes, de-emphasizing the moral, scientific, and philosophical elements, early dramatists such as Peake amplified ideas that were sometimes only suggested in Shelley's novel. These include the alchemical dimension of Frankenstein's experiments, the sinister nature of his laboratory, and the demonic characterization of the creature. While references to music and sound are a feature of the novel, as Wierzbicki writes, for "gothic as well as theatrical purposes, too, these dramatists exaggerated the creature's relationship with music."[13]

Gothic novelists used references to music in several ways. Decorative music references were deployed to intensify the "awe-inspiring" affective impact of a sublime site, such as a cathedral, or to make a village scene more vivid. Narrative references were intended to animate the plot by supplying "narrative agency" where music plays a role in summoning supernatural beings or directly affecting natural or supernatural characters.[14] Shelley's use of music falls into the latter category.

Music significantly figures in theatrical and film adaptations of Shelley's novel; however, references to music in the original are limited to only a few chapters. Nonetheless, these references serve as a means of illuminating the creature's inner world, its sense of self, and its desire for the familial love exemplified by the DeLacey family. In short, Shelley used music and sound to show us the creature's humanity. As Wierzbicki noted, most musical references appear in the five chapters that comprise chapter 11 to chapter 15 of the 1831 edition.[15] All subsequent references to music in the novel are to the corresponding chapters in volume two of the 1818 version (chapter 2 to chapter 6), as Peake would have used that edition.

Chapter 2 presents a lengthy and traumatic dialog between creature and creator on Glacier Montanvert, but chapter 3 provides the reader with the first detailed insight into its mind.[16] Here the creature emerges from the fog of his early reanimation. His senses intensely present themselves such that he states, "a strange multiplicity of sensations seized me, and I saw, felt, heard, and smelt at the same time."[17] Initially, he describes a synesthetic difficulty in distinguishing between his inchoate senses but slowly learns to distinguish one from the other. Written in the first person, the opening paragraphs of chapter 3 present an inventory of senses beginning with sight, followed by temperature, fatigue, hunger, thirst, sound, and smell.[18] Investigating the sense of

---

[13] James Wierzbicki, "How Frankenstein's Monster Became a Music Lover," *Journal of the Fantastic in the Arts* 24, no. 2 (2013): 256.
[14] Ibid.
[15] Ibid., 248.
[16] M. Wollstonecraft Shelley, *Frankenstein, or, The Modern Prometheus*, ed. Dorothy K. Scherf and D. Lorne Macdonald, 2nd ed. (Peterborough: Broadview Press, 1999). All subsequent references are to this edition.
[17] Ibid., 128.
[18] Ibid., 129.

sound via birdsong represents the creature's first solitary conscious engagement with the world.[19]

The creature's discovery of birdsong provides the reader with perhaps the earliest glimpse into its essential goodness and its inquisitive, gentle interiority which Shelley gradually unfolds. Lauren Shohet argues that the novel presents "different kinds of Miltonic readers in its characters" and notes that the creature is an "Edenic" figure. As such, the creature, who delights in the sights and sounds of the natural world (as opposed to the frequently inhospitable spaces his creator inhabits),[20] enjoys "precisely" what the prelapsarian Adam and Eve enjoyed.[21] The music and sound references in these five chapters inform many of the musical scenes in subsequent stage and film adaptations.[22]

Chapter 3 also contains the scene in which the creature makes his first contact with humans other than Frankenstein. Hiding in a hovel attached to the cottage and peering through the chinks in the boards, he sees and hears DeLacey and his grown children, Agatha and Felix.[23] The creature first hears actual music in this scene and Shelley has him directly connect it with the "Edenic" birdsong he experienced previously:

> and she sat down beside the old man, who, taking up an instrument, began to play, and to produce sounds sweeter than the voice of the thrush or the nightingale. It was a lovely sight, even to me, poor wretch who had never beheld aught beautiful before. The silver hair and benevolent countenance of the aged cottager won my reverence, while the gentle manners of the girl enticed my love.[24]

This vignette in the cottage serves to further illuminate the creature's inner life and stands as an inversion of the trauma of his encounter with his "father" at Glacier Montanvert in chapter 2. After a fiery exchange, the creature expresses to Frankenstein its goodness and humanity which is rejected.[25] The musical scene between DeLacey and his daughter in chapter 3 continues with the old man's "mournful air":

> He played a sweet mournful air which I perceived drew tears from the eyes of his amiable companion, of which the old man took no notice, until she sobbed

---

[19] Ibid., 130.
[20] Tang Soo Ping, "Frankenstein, 'Paradise Lost,' and 'The Majesty of Goodness,'" *College Literature* 16, no. 3 (Fall 1989): 258.
[21] Lauren Shohet, "Reading Milton in Mary Shelley's *Frankenstein*," *Milton Studies* 60, nos. 1–2 (2018): 161.
[22] These include H. M. Milner's *Frankenstein; or, The Man and the Monster* (1826), Jean-Toussaint Merle and Beraud Antony's *Le monstre et le magicien* (1826), and James Whale's film adaptation, *The Bride of Frankenstein* (1935).
[23] The name, Agatha, translates as "good" and, Felix, as "happy." This is surely intentional as both are attributes of the DeLacey family and are what the creature desires in his own life.
[24] Shelley, *Frankenstein, or, The Modern Prometheus*, 134.
[25] "Believe me, Frankenstein, I was benevolent; my soul glowed with love and humanity; but am I not alone, miserably alone? You, my creator, abhor me; what hope can I gather from your fellow creatures, who owe me nothing? They spurn and hate me." Shelley, *Frankenstein, or, The Modern Prometheus*, 126.

audibly; he then pronounced a few sounds, and the fair creature, leaving her work, knelt at his feet. He raised her, and smiled with such kindness and affection, that I felt sensations of a peculiar and overpowering nature: they were a mixture of pain and pleasure, such as I had never before experienced, either from hunger or cold, warmth or food; and I withdrew from the window, unable to bear these emotions.[26]

Shelley continues her exploration of the aforementioned relationship inversions, this time presenting the loving and tender relationship between DeLacey and his son, Felix. Whereas the creature is met with disgust, regret, and revulsion from his "father,"[27] he sees beauty in the contrast between the old man and the "slight and graceful" youth.[28] The beauty and grace of the DeLacey children and their loving relationship with their father represent all the creature can neither have nor share with his "father."

Hitherto only implied, chapter 4 makes explicit DeLacey's blindness and presents two further references to music. The first, in which the creature learns DeLacey spends his "leisure hours on his instrument or in contemplation,"[29] and the second, in which he describes the harshness of his own voice compared with the "soft music of their tones."[30] Chapter 5 presents several further significant musical scenes and social interactions between the DeLaceys who are now joined by Felix's beloved, Safie.

The first musical scene in chapter 5 presents DeLacey playing the guitar to Agatha and a melancholy Felix.[31] The playing is interrupted by a knock at the door and Safie's arrival.[32] The scene in which Safie is welcomed into the cottage is followed by a musical interlude, again featuring DeLacey and his guitar. This instrument is taken up by Safie, whose song deeply moves both the old man and the creature:

> the Arabian sat at the feet of the old man, and taking his guitar, played some airs so entrancingly beautiful, that they at once drew tears of sorrow and delight from my eyes. She sang, and her voice flowed in a rich cadence, swelling or dying away, like a nightingale of the woods.[33]

Safie's performance is followed by Agatha's:

---

[26] Shelley, *Frankenstein, or, The Modern Prometheus*, 134.
[27] Frankenstein: "Why do you call to my remembrance circumstances of which I shudder to reflect, that I have been the miserable origin and author? Cursed be the day, abhorred devil, in which you first saw light! Cursed (although I curse myself) be the hands that formed you! You have made me wretched beyond expression. You have left me no power to consider whether I am just to you or not. Begone! Relieve me from the sight of your detested form." Shelley, *Frankenstein, or, The Modern Prometheus*, 127.
[28] Shelley, *Frankenstein, or, The Modern Prometheus*, 135.
[29] Ibid., 136.
[30] Ibid., 141.
[31] Ibid.
[32] Ibid., 142.
[33] Ibid., 143.

> She played a simple air, and her voice accompanied it in sweet accents, but unlike the wondrous strain of the stranger. The old man appeared enraptured, and said some words, which Agatha endeavoured to explain to Safie, and by which he appeared to wish to express that she bestowed on him the greatest delight by her music.[34]

The remainder of chapter 5 moves from overheard music to overheard books which Felix reads aloud to Safie. Continuing this focus on literature, volume two, chapter 7 is largely devoted to the creature's encounter with Milton's *Paradise Lost*, a volume of *Plutarch's Lives*, and Goethe's *The Sorrows of Werther*. Like music in the previous chapters, this autodidactic education serves to further humanize the creature.

The final significant musical scene in these chapters comes toward the end of chapter 6 and is sometimes rendered in film adaptations:

> When his children had departed, he took up his guitar, and played several mournful, but sweet airs, more sweet and mournful than I had ever heard him play before. At first his countenance was illuminated with pleasure, but, as he continued, thoughtfulness and sadness succeeded; at length, laying aside the instrument, he sat absorbed in reflection.[35]

Here the creature notes that the blind DeLacey is alone and approaches him hoping that, through the sound of his voice, he might establish a rapport and acceptance from the family and society at large. This does not happen and the chapter concludes with violence and rejection.

Music and Songs in Peake's Adaptation

The playbill for opening night describes *Presumption* as "an entirely new Romance of a peculiar interest." However, as Michael Pisani noted, nineteenth-century English theatrical productions with music were created under a "dizzying variety" of interchangeable genre designations.[36] Pisani reports that the music for *Presumption* was "generally praised" but acclaim was not universal for it was poorly regarded by the anonymous *Harmonicon* reviewer:[37]

> There are two or three agreeable duets in this *melodrame*; but as a whole, the music is heavy and common. The overture we presume it is called, is a very humble affair indeed.[38]

---

[34] Ibid.
[35] Ibid., 157.
[36] Michael V. Pisani, *Music for the Melodramatic Theatre in Nineteenth-Century London and New York* (Iowa City: University of Iowa Press, 2014), 73.
[37] Ibid., 82.
[38] *The Harmonicon* 1, no. 9 (September 1823): 126.

Much of the music for English melodrama of the period was drawn from stock material that was circulated in manuscript. Indeed, an early review in the *Times of London* noted that "there were at least thirteen movements which we have heard in every melodrama for the last five-and-twenty years, not to speak of their occasional performance in operas, overtures, and between the acts."[39] In this context, it is likely that the composer, "Mr. Watson" (or John Watson, the resident leader at the English Opera House), composed only the "overture" and the music for the songs. Watson was an important figure in early nineteenth-century London and, later, in New York theatrical music scenes. If he is remembered at all today, it is likely as the impresario who brought Paganini to London and father of the celebrated singer Charlotte Watson. Infamously, Charlotte Watson ran away to France with the violinist in a scandal some historians regard as manufactured.[40] This episode provides the plot line for the 2013 film *The Devil's Violinist*. Unfortunately, neither Watson's nor any of the other original music for *Presumption* appears to have survived.

Peake greatly expanded the infrequent and localized references to singing and playing in Shelley's original. The genres that could be presented in specific London theaters were highly regulated, and Peake's adaptation, with its profusion of songs and choruses, indicates that it was likely thus presented for licensing reasons.[41] Music and sound in *Presumption* are of several varieties: melodramatic music (accompanying dialog or action), solo songs, duets, a *sestetto*, choruses (sung by large groups of "exotic" characters such as "gipsies"), onstage and offstage diegetic music, and references to music and sounds in the spoken dialog and stage directions.

Melodramatic Music Directions and Sounds in *Presumption*

The most common terms used to describe theatrical music in the early nineteenth century were "appropriate," "characteristic," "incidental," and "melodramatic."[42] "Appropriate" music follows the arc of the spoken word or a dramatic scene. "Characteristic" music is like the modern term "programme music" in that it was intended to evoke extra-musical events, places, national or ethnic identities, or even an actor's physical comportment or personal traits. Used as in the modern sense, the term "incidental" music refers to music added to a preexisting theatrical work. "Melodramatic" music refers to "any music required to accompany any necessary action in the play."[43] *Presumption* makes use of all these sometimes overlapping varieties.

---

[39] In Pisani, *Music for the Melodramatic Theatre in Nineteenth-Century London and New York*, 82.
[40] Andrew Clarke, "Loder and Sons, Bath: A Band of Musicians," in *Musicians of Bath and Beyond: Edward Loder and his Family (1809–1865)*, ed. Nicholas Temperley (Woodbridge, Suffolk: The Boydell Press, 2016), 92.
[41] Pisani, *Music for the Melodramatic Theatre in Nineteenth-Century London and New York*, 82.
[42] Ibid., xv.
[43] Ibid.

As mentioned earlier, Peake's text contains an unusual number of melodramatic music instructions which can come in rapid succession and are often extremely specific. For example, melodramatic music frequently accompanies actions, such as Safie's arrival toward the end of 1.2,[44] and serves to establish the atmosphere of a new scene, such as Frankenstein's "sleeping apartment" at the opening of 1.3.[45] As there are too many examples to discuss in this space, sections from 1.3, 2.2, 2.3, and 3.1 will serve as an introduction to Peake's extensive use of melodramatic music and sound in *Presumption*.

The directions for 1.3 are particularly specific with reference to characteristic "storm music" and the sound of "distant thunder":

SCENE III:

The sleeping Apartment of Frankenstein. Dark. The Bed is within a recess between the wings, enclosed by dark green curtains. A Sword (to break) hanging. A Large French Window; between the wings a staircase leading to a Gallery across the stage, on which is the Door of the Laboratory above. A small high Lattice in centre of scene, next the Laboratory Door. A Gothic Table on stage, screwed. A Gothic Chair in centre, and Footstool. *Music expressive of the rising of a storm.* Enter Frankenstein, with a Lighted Lamp, which he places on the table. *Distant thunder heard.*[46]

Melodramatic music and sound are crucial in setting tone and creating dramatic tension in the opening of 1.3 and, toward the close of the scene, they also telegraph gothic horror. Here a trembling Fritz peeks into his master's laboratory accompanied by storm sounds and melodramatic music.[47] In this scene, Fritz, originally played by popular comedic actor, Robert Keeley,[48] beholds Frankenstein's reanimation of the creature in what was surely among the most memorable moments of the adaptation. The comedic is rapidly followed by the spectacular and the terrifying and, as will be argued later, this is a recurring dramatic strategy in *Presumption,* as it is in gothic drama in general.

The opening paragraph of chapter 5 of the 1818 edition, where the monster comes to life, is a subdued affair compared to the corresponding scene in *Presumption* and later dramatic and cinematic versions. In *Presumption*, melodramatic music underscores a scene moving from Fritz's soon to be extinguished candle light, to an eerie blue flame which transforms into a demonic "reddish hue" accompanying

---

[44] Richard Brinsley Peake, "Presumption, or the Fate of Frankenstein," in *Seven Gothic Dramas*, ed. Jeffrey N. Cox (Athens: Ohio University Press, 1992), 395. All subsequent references are to this edition.
[45] Ibid., 397.
[46] Ibid. Note that italics in all remaining long quotations indicate my emphasis.
[47] The reader is reminded that Fritz, Frankenstein's comedic sidekick of Peake's invention, is the model for similar comedic characters in later dramatic and cinematic adaptations.
[48] Amnon Kabatchnik, *Blood on the Stage, 1800-1900: Milestone Plays of Murder, Mystery, and Mayhem* (Washington: Rowman and Littlefield, 2017), 72.

Frankenstein's proclamation "It lives! It lives!"[49] With music and sound directions occurring as frequently as every few lines, this closing scene of 1.3 was encrusted with melodramatic and appropriate music. Along with music and sounds, Peake artfully builds tension by enlisting the affective powers of lighting and acting directions. The playwright utilizes physical tension in Fritz's body to amplify dramatic tension as the actor is instructed to precariously stand tiptoe on a stool to glimpse the creature. Fritz's nervous comedic anticipation is followed by terror at the sight of the monstrous revelation, and Frankenstein's shock upon looking at the horror of his own creation. This scene was recognized as a highlight of the entire production:[50]

> *Music.*—Fritz takes up footstool, he ascends the stairs, when on the gallery landing place, he stands on the footstool tiptoe to look through the small high lattice window of the laboratory, *a sudden combustion is heard within.* The blue flame changes to one of a reddish hue.
>
> FRANK. (Within.) It lives! It lives!
>
> FRITZ. (*Speaks through music.*) Oh, dear! oh, dear! oh, dear!
>
> Fritz, greatly alarmed, jumps down hastily, totters tremblingly down the stairs in vast hurry; when in front of stage, having fallen flat in fright, with difficulty speaks.
>
> FRITZ. There's a hob—hob-goblin, 20 feet high! wrapp'd in a mantle—mercy—mercy—
>
> [Falls down.]
>
> *Music.*—Frankenstein rushes from the laboratory, without lamp, fastens the door in apparent dread, and hastens down the stairs, watching the entrance of the laboratory.
>
> FRANK. It lives! [It lives.] I saw the dull yellow eye of the creature open, it breathed hard, and a convulsive motion agitated its limbs. What a wretch have I formed, [his legs are in proportion and] I had selected his features as beautiful—"beautiful"! Ah, horror! his cadaverous skin scarcely covers the work of muscles and arteries beneath, his hair lustrous, black, and flowing—his teeth of pearly whiteness—but these luxuriances only form more horrible contrasts with the deformities of the Demon.[51]

---

[49] Peake, "Presumption, or the Fate of Frankenstein," 398.

[50] "The description of the first dawn—the first tremulous motion of life, is in the novel frightfully given:—and on recurring to it, we are only surprised (*sic*) that any Melo-dramatist (the wildest going) should ever have thought of bringing it out of the charmed book to the stage—and that we are astounded that such an attempt should have been attended with success. The management of this part of the novel in the drama is really the most perfect masterpiece of Melo-dramatic ingenuity that we have ever in any piece or on any stage witnessed. We say this unreservedly and decidedly," *The London Magazine* 8 (September 1823): 322.

[51] Peake, "Presumption, or the Fate of Frankenstein," 398-9.

Dramatic tension is heightened in this scene not only through the sonic and visual elements described earlier but, significantly, by the use of silence and sounds. As Frankenstein waits at the foot of the staircase, immediately following the chilling description of the yellow-eyed monster directly adapted from Shelley's text, Peake explicitly calls for silence. He directs, "yet it is quiet" and "he listens still," followed by Frankenstein's words "all is still."[52] Here Frankenstein moves from a vivid outward and physical description of the creature to an equally vivid inward description of his own mental state where he describes the toll of his quest upon his health and sanity. Peake has him state "it will be fatal to my peace for ever."[53] Additionally, Peake has Frankenstein describe his actions as "impious" twice in this speech which concludes with the cry, "I am! [– lost—lost] Elizabeth! brother! Agatha!—faithful Agatha! never more dare I look upon your virtuous faces. Lost! lost! lost!"[54] As music intensified the dialog and action in the preceding scene, so silence does here. The soliloquy and silence serve a dual function in this scene: to draw focus to Frankenstein's anguish, ethical struggles, and isolation, and to prepare the audience for the climatic conclusion of the first act.

After a brief silence, when Fritz returns to see "his master" sleeping in a chair, he plans his escape. This plan and Frankenstein's slumber are interrupted by the sounds of "sudden combustion," smoke, and the return of the eerie "red fire within."[55] Melodramatic musical directions precede each of the three remaining action directions and three lines of dialog in which Frankenstein challenges the silent creature. This tension-laden closing scene would have been arresting. Here the creature, played by the physically commanding, yet pantomimically subtle, Thomas Potter Cooke,[56] snaps Frankenstein's sword and throws it—and him—to the floor. The act concludes with the stage direction "Thunder and lightning until the drop falls."[57] These dramatic actions, dialog, visuals, jarring sounds, and eerie lighting effects were further intensified by melodramatic music. While Peake used only the general term "music" in the stage directions for this scene in the laboratory, the opening stage direction of act 2 provides us with some sense of its affective features. Set at Elizabeth's house at Belrive, the scene directs the "hurried music from the close of the First Act to play in continuance until this scene is discovered."[58] Features of this closing scene with its dramatic blending of music, sound, visuals, and foreboding pathetic fallacy through thunder and lightning, were to become common in later cinematic settings of the story.

---

[52] Ibid., 398.
[53] Ibid.
[54] Ibid., 398–9.
[55] Ibid., 399.
[56] "Mr. T. P. Cooke as (-----) for he is so described,—and we see no reason for foregoing our parenthesis because its palings touch those of Mr. Peake's) has proved himself to be the very best pantomime actor on the stage. He never speaks but his action and his looks are more than eloquent. The effect of the music upon him is affecting and beautiful in the extreme." *The London Magazine* 8 (September 1823): 323.
[57] Peake, "Presumption, or the Fate of Frankenstein," 399.
[58] Ibid., 400.

The second act introduces diegetic flute (absent in the novel) and guitar music. The flute first appears in 2.2 and is played onstage and offstage by DeLacey's son, Felix.[59] In the same scene, DeLacey's guitar in the novel is transformed variously into a harp and lute.[60] Set in a wood "in the neighbourhood of Geneva," the scene also features a group of nameless "gipsies" and two named males with the racist appellations, Tanskin and Hammerpan.[61] Gathered around a fire and cooking caldron, this scene is ostensibly meant to represent a kind of comedic pastoral set piece. The scene begins with the chorus "Urge the Slow Rising Smoke" (the text of which is as racist as the aforementioned names) sung by the "gipsies," and is followed by Tanskin and Hammerpan's comedic discussion of creature sightings.[62] This is followed by the equally pastoral entrance of Felix telegraphed by offstage strains of his flute. The pastoral calm of the group enjoying a meal in the wood is obliterated by the fleeting appearance of the monster at the periphery. The "gipsies" flee at the sight of the monster to the accompaniment of melodramatic music as the creature occupies their camp:[63]

> *Music.* Throws bowl away. Hammerpan and all the Gipsies shriek and run off. The Demon descends, portrays by action his sensitiveness of light and air, perceives the gipsies's fire, which excites his admiration—thrusts his hand into the flame, withdraws it hastily in pain. Takes out a lighted piece of stick, compares it with another faggot which has not been ignited. Takes the food expressive of surprise and pleasure. *A flute is heard, without. The Demon, breathless with delight, eagerly listens. It ceases—he expresses disappointment.* Footsteps heard and the Demon retreats behind the rock.
>
> Enter Agatha, *followed by Felix, his flute slung at his back.*[64]

At Agatha and Felix's entrance, by means of visual gestures and sound, Peake, like Shelley, uses music to flesh out the creature's humanity. Following Agatha and Felix's duet ("Of All the Knots which Nature Ties"), as a means of further humanizing the creature, Peake has him emerge out of hiding and commence watching them as Felix plays his flute. The creature reacts to music as in the corresponding scene in the original, discussed earlier. However, rather than using music to demonstrate his sensitivity, Peake's creature "stands amazed and pleased" snatching at the empty air and placing clenched hands to each side of his head as if to seize the sound and deposit it in his ears.[65] As the following directions demonstrate, although rendered as pantomime—and to considerable acclaim by, leading London actor, Thomas Potter (T. P.)

---

[59] 2.2 refers to Act 2, scene 2. Peake, "Presumption, or the Fate of Frankenstein," 402–3, and 405.
[60] Peake, "Presumption, or the Fate of Frankenstein," 402–5.
[61] Ibid., 405. The name "Hammerpan" likely refers to the once common Roma and Traveler profession of metal working.
[62] Ibid., 402.
[63] Peake, "Presumption, or the Fate of Frankenstein," 402–3.
[64] Ibid., 403.
[65] Ibid., 405.

Cooke—little of the psychological subtlety of the corresponding scene in Shelley's novel is preserved:

> *Music.*—The Demon cautiously ventures out—his mantle having been caught by the bush, he disrobes himself leaving the mantle attached to the rock; he watches Felix and Agatha with wonder and rapture, appears irresolute whether he dares to follow them; *he hears the flute of Felix,* stands amazed and pleased, looks around him, *snatches at the empty air, and with clenched hands puts them to each ear— appears vexed at his disappointment in not possessing the sound; rushes forward afterwards, again listens, and, delighted with the sound, steals off catching at it with his hands.*[66]

2.3 begins with the creature observing the blind DeLacey as he proclaims his joy of "lute" playing. In what follows, the creature experiences his most intimate and human interaction of the entire adaptation. As in the novel, this occurs only because the blind DeLacey does not perceive the creature's hideousness:

> Music.—DeLacey returns to his seat and *plays several chords.* The Demon enters, *attracted by the lute,* suddenly perceives DeLacey, and approaches towards him— expresses surprise by action that DeLacey does not avoid him—discovers his loss of sight, which the Demon appears to understand by placing his hand over his own eyes, and feeling his way. *At the conclusion of the music on the lute—occasioned, as it were, by the Demon having placed his hand on the instrument—a short pause, and during which the Demon, having lost the sound, appears to be looking for it, when the lute music is again resumed. In the midst of the music (without ceasing) a voice is heard.*
>
> FELIX. (Within.) This way, Agatha.
>
> The Demon, alarmed, observes the little door of hovel, which he pushes open, signifies that he wishes for shelter, and *retreats into this hovel or wood-house by the ending of the lute music by DeLacey,* when Enter Felix and Agatha.[67]

This scene and its pathos clearly echo Shelley's novel and prefigure a similar scene with the creature and a blind violin-playing hermit in James Whale's classic 1935 horror film, *Bride of Frankenstein.* As depicted in volume two, chapters 2 to 6 of the 1818 edition of the novel, Shelley's creature is an intelligent, sensitive, and thoughtful creature who delights in nature and music, who reads Milton, Plutarch, and Goethe. Peake's creature is brutish, silent, and psychologically simplistic by comparison. It is in scenes such as those discussed above that Peake, T. P. Cooke, and the conventional demands of melodrama in the minor houses transformed the subtle interiority of Shelley's creature

---

[66] Ibid., 405–6.
[67] Ibid., 405.

into pantomime and gave rise to the silent and psychologically simplified creature so frequently depicted in modern film adaptations.

As illustrated in the selected examples earlier, *Presumption* is littered with sonic and musical directions. However, "*Music, the Harmonica,*" appearing at the beginning of 3.1, is perhaps the most tantalizing of all.[68] Almost certainly this is a reference to the glass *armonica* as the earliest predecessor of the modern free reed wind instrument of that name was only patented at Vienna in 1824.[69] Invented by Benjamin Franklin in 1761, the glass *armonica* enjoyed a brief, if not controversial, period of popularity in Europe and America from the late eighteenth century to the mid-nineteenth century. From its inception, its ethereal, pure sonority evoked the occult, the supernatural, spiritual liminality, madness, and feminine eros.[70] One wonders if a fleeting appearance of the glass harmonica was intended to evoke the strange practices of roughly contemporary "scientists" such as Luigi Galvani and Giovanni Aldini, who electrified corpses to grotesque effect in London. Such figures were part of the cultural fabric of the day.[71] In the fall of 1818, natural philosopher Andrew Ure, of Glasgow's Andersonian Institute, famously conducted electrical experiments on a corpse which appeared to laboriously "breathe" and twitch its fingers.[72] This was only months after *Frankenstein* was first published. If not Peake, Shelley was certainly aware of such strange scientific experimentation, as she discussed galvanism and the potential for reanimating corpses in the introduction to the 1831 edition of her novel.[73] While speculative, the otherworldly sounds of the glass harmonica might have been an effective means of sonically evoking the strangeness of Frankenstein's scientific work. At the very least, it demonstrates Peake's extraordinary attention to musical and sonic detail in his adaptation.

Music and sound in the novel play a small but significant role in providing insight into the creature's interior life and serve as a conduit into the world into which he was thrown. As a melodrama, music, sound, and song naturally play a more significant role in the adaptation than in the novel. Indeed, early theatrical adaptations by dramatists such as Peake and Milner actually concentrated and emphasized gothic elements in the original.[74] As mentioned earlier, gothic theatrical adaptations of the

---

[68] Ibid., 416.
[69] Alec Hyatt King, "Musical Glasses," *Grove Music Online. Oxford Music Online*. Oxford University Press, available online: https://www-oxfordmusiconline-com.proxy.library.carleton.ca/grovemusic/view/10.1093/gmo/9781561592630.001.0001/omo-9781561592630-e-0000019422 (accessed June 12, 2021).
[70] Heather Hadlock, "Sonorous Bodies: Women and the Glass Harmonica," *Journal of the American Musicological Society* 53, no. 3 (Autumn 2000): 507–8.
[71] Elizabeth Stephens, "'Dead Eyes Open:' The Role of Experiments in Galvanic Reanimation in Nineteenth-Century Popular Culture," *Leonardo* 48, no. 3 (2015): 276–7.
[72] Kathryn Harkup, "The Science behind the Fiction: Frankenstein in Historical Context," *Natural History* 126, no. 4 (April 2018), available online: https://link.gale.com/apps/doc/A536255858/CPI?u=ocul_carleton&sid=bookmark-CPI&xid=6c45b27c (accessed June 11, 2021).
[73] Mary Shelley, *Frankenstein: Complete, Authoritative Text with Biographical, Historical, and Cultural Contexts, Critical History, and Essays from Critical Perspectives*, ed. Johanna M. Smith, 2nd ed. (Boston: Bedford/St. Martin's, 2000), 23.
[74] Forry, *Hideous Progenies*, 14.

novel also amplified the role of music and sound found in the original text. This went beyond merely satisfying theater regulations or entertaining audiences. While left to the reader's imagination in the novel, music and sound on the stage were audible to actors and audiences alike and served purposes specific to melodramatic presentation. Mostly used to illuminate the monster's inner life in the novel, music and sound in the adaptation powerfully shaped mood, characterizations, and dramatic pacing. As an example of gothic melodrama, *Presumption*'s musical directions, sound, and songs (in different ways, as examined later) contributed much to the modern popular conception of the creature and the Frankenstein story.[75]

The Songs

Peake took considerable liberties in terms of plot simplification, characters, and relationships. Whereas only two characters sing in Shelley's novel, Safie and Agatha, Peake's adaptation presents thirteen vocal numbers performed by nine named characters, an unnamed "bass," and a chorus of "gipsies." *Presumption* features four romantic relationships: Safie and Felix, Elizabeth and Clerval, Agatha and Frankenstein, and the invented comedic stock characters, Ninon and Fritz. Of these couplings, only the first is present in Shelley's novel. With only a few exceptions, the majority of the songs are romantically themed and reflect or amplify aspects of the relationships listed earlier. Several of these musical interludes make glancing reference to the novel, but most of the scenes in which they were placed were partly or entirely invented by Peake. The songs typically appear in transitional or climactic locations and, as Stephen C. Behrendt has noted, they are used both to "decorate" and advance the story.[76] Titles, authors, characters, locations, and function/features are presented in Table 4.1. In the interests of space, only a few songs will be considered herein.

In the novel, the songs of Agatha and Safie, so important to illuminating the creature's inner life and desire for belonging, human connection, and acceptance, are only peripherally related to these sentiments in Peake's adaptation. Agatha and Felix's duet, "Of all the knots which nature ties," briefly mentioned earlier, follows Agatha's declaration that she henceforth will dedicate herself to caring for her "poor dark father."[77] This song text is one of the few that closely mirrors the novel, as it serves to communicate the sense of Agatha and Felix's familial devotion depicted in the original. It is also one of the few songs that is not romantically themed.

Fritz is the first to sing with "Oh, dear me! what's the matter" and this song is an exception in that it is also not romantically themed.[78] Located at the top of 1.1,

---

[75] Wierzbicki, "How Frankenstein's Monster Became a Music Lover," 256.
[76] Stephen C. Behrendt, "Novel into Drama," in *Presumption: or, the Fate of Frankenstein* (electronic edition), ed. Stephen Behrendt (Boulder: University of Colorado, August 1, 2001), available online: https://romantic-circles.org/editions/peake/apparatus/drama.html (accessed May 15, 2021).
[77] Peake, "Presumption, or the Fate of Frankenstein," 404.
[78] Ibid., 387.

Table 4.1 Titles, Authors, Characters, Locations, and Function/Features of Songs in *Presumption*

Title	Author	Character(s)	Location: Act and Scene	Function/Features
1. AIR: "Oh, dear me! what's the matter?"	R. B. Peake	Fritz	1.1	Introduces the invented comedic character, Fritz. Establishes comedic/gothic juxtaposition which is repeated throughout the adaptation.
2. SONG: "Ere witching love my heart possest"	Peter Pindar	Clerval	1.1	Introduces Clerval's love for Elizabeth.
3. SONG: "The summer sun shining on tree and on tower"	Henrique	Elizabeth	1.2	Introduces Elizabeth and the boy, William Frankenstein. Along with dialog and lighting directions, foreshadows the creature's later abduction of the boy.
4. DUETT: "Hark how it floats upon the dewy air"	William Cowper	Elizabeth and Safie	1.2	Concludes 1.2. Song text refers to a nightingale's song in the preceding dialog between Elizabeth and Sadie. Possible oblique reference to birdsong references discussed above. "Pastoral" duet contrasts with the gothic 1.3 which introduces a "rising storm," the laboratory, the creature, and its emergence into life with Frankenstein's famous words "It lives! It lives!"
5. SONG: "When evening breezes mildly blow"	M. H. ("Miss Harries" aka Margaret Harries Baron-Wilson	Elizabeth	2.1	Concludes 2.1. Romantically themed song (Elizabeth and Clerval). Follows Elizabeth's dialog with an agitated Frankenstein who sets off for "the Valley of the Lake" in search of his estranged beloved, Agatha. Leads into the "gipsie" chorus which opens 2.2.
6. CHORUS: "Urge the slow rising smoke"	R. B. Peake	Tanskin and Hammerpan with others	2.2	Opens 2.2. Chorus is set in a wood near Geneva. The text is rife with racist language and introduces the only two named "gipsy" characters, Tanskin and Hammerpan. Song and comedic scene precede a terrifying interaction between the "gipsies" and the creature.

(*Continued*)

Table 4.1 (Continued)

Title	Author	Character(s)	Location: Act and Scene	Function/Features
7. DUET: "Of all the knots which Nature ties"	John William Cunningham	Felix and Agatha	2.2	Closes 2.2. Stresses familial love and mirrors scenes from chapter 3 to chapter 6 of the novel where the creature observes the DeLaceys from afar. The scene following this song features the creature listening to Felix and Agatha from behind a rock. This is a compression of the musical scenes, and scenes depicting the creature's emerging senses found in chapters 3 to 6. Felix's flute replaces the songs and guitar as the object of the creature's fascination in the novel.
8. SONG: "In vain I view the landscapes round" (Flute accompaniment, behind the scenes)	R. B. Peake	Agatha	2.3	Concludes 2.3. Romantically themed on the topic of Agatha's love for her "former love," Frankenstein.
9. SONG: "Thy youthful charms, bright maid, inspire"	Arley (Miles Peter Andrews)	Felix	2.4	Opens 2.4. Romantically themed on the topic of Felix's love for the recently returned Safie.
10. CHORUS: "Beware, Beware"	R. B. Peake	Undetermined chorus followed by a "Full Chorus of Gypsies"	2.5	Designated as the "finale" of act 2. Likely intoned rather than sung, the chorus accompanies the creature hanging from the rafters and, "with malignant joy," setting fire to the DeLacey's cottage.
11. DUET: "Come with me, dear"	R. B. Peake	Safie and Felix	3.1	Romantically themed. Marks the transition from Frankenstein and Agatha's reunion and the comedic scene between Fritz and Ninon. This culminates in Clerval and Elizabeth's wedding, the abduction of William, and the climax/transition to 3.2.
12. DUET: "Oh! I'll hail the wedding day"	R. B. Peake	Ninon and Fritz	3.1	Romantically themed. Comedic parallel to Safie and Felix's song heard in the previous section of the scene. Comedic duet and dialog intensify the abduction that concludes 3.1.
13. Congratulatory Sestetto: "Since to all beauty's rip'ning bloom"	Arley (Miles Peter Andrews)	Agatha, Safie, Elizabeth, Felix, Clerval, and unnamed bass	3.1	Romantically themed. Set in the country (and far from the abduction) with a "rustic church in the distance," the sestetto opens 3.2. Serves to contrast/mitigate the abduction scene horror.

and set in a "Gothic Chamber in the house of Frankenstein,"[79] the scene serves to establish both the comedic and the Gothic early in the adaptation. This comedic/gothic juxtaposition will serve to intensify the elements of terror and horror in several pivotal and climactic scenes. Here Peake has Fritz seated in slumber in a "Gothic chair," rubbing his eyes, coming to consciousness, and gradually moving downstage during the "symphony of the song."[80] The text, with rhymes such as matter/clatter, marrow/harrow, sneezes/wheezes, fret/sweat, and preserve us/nervous, would doubtlessly have provided Watson, as a composer, and Keeley, as an actor, with plenty of opportunities for musical and physical comedy.[81]

Gothic dramatists, including Peake, frequently juxtaposed comedic and gothic scenes to open up affective and psychological distance which maximized the impact of terror. Fritz's second song, "Oh, I'll Hail the Wedding Day," a comedic duet with Nanon which precedes the marriage scene of Clerval and Elizabeth, does exactly this. First, it presents a comedic burlesque of the themes of love and domesticity found in the wedding scene that follows in 3.2. Second, preceding the conclusion of 3.1, it sets up one of the most horrifying scenes of the adaptation where the creature seizes the boy, William, covers the child's mouth with his hand, flings him over his shoulder, and flees.[82]

As Jeffrey N. Cox notes, comedic characters such as Fritz and Nanon and scenes of comedic domesticity were a common feature of gothic drama and, for reasons discussed earlier, the comedic and Gothic are closely linked in gothic melodrama.[83] The structure of gothic drama frequently oscillates between scenes of spatial enclosure and open spaces[84] as well as comedic scenes and scenes of shock and terror.[85] If mishandled, scenes of terror, as Cox argues, can easily descend into the ridiculous as "there are few things as funny as a botched attempt to evoke horror."[86] Furthermore, comedic scenes and songs such as in 1.1 where Fritz delivers, "Oh, dear me! what's the matter" frequently play upon gothic tropes and to some degree serve to "insulate" the performance from ridicule, should the gothic terror which follows somehow fail.[87]

As the score appears not to have survived, little can be said of the musical settings of the songs.[88] The British Library Catalogue lists some twenty-three scores by John Watson, "Composer to Covent Garden Theatre," but none appear in modern editions.

---

[79] Ibid.
[80] "Symphony" is used here in the pre-classical sense and indicates an instrumental section or composition. This stage direction provides one of very few insights into the musical features of the songs and suggests that the "symphony" must have been substantial enough to set the mood for the scene. Peake, "Presumption, or the Fate of Frankenstein," 387.
[81] Peake, "Presumption, or the Fate of Frankenstein," 387.
[82] Ibid., 418–19.
[83] Cox, *Seven Gothic Dramas*, 24.
[84] Ibid., 20.
[85] Ibid., 24.
[86] Ibid.
[87] Ibid.
[88] While it is not known if the same tune was used in the adaptation, the published version of "When evening breezes mildly blow" states it was sung to the air "Sul margine dun rio," *The Theatrical Inquisitor, Or, Monthly Mirror* 14 (1819): 289.

Watson's songs, though sometimes disparaged in printed reviews of *Presumption*,[89] clearly had some popular appeal, as they were printed in collections such as *The Universal Songster, or Museum of Mirth* (1825), *Tegg's Social Songster and Everlasting Melodist* (1828), and even as late as *Clarke's Orphanic Warbler* (1850) and *The Crotchet; Or, The Songster and Toast-master's Companion* (1854). Such collections of popular and theatrical songs printed the texts without music as the tunes were well known.

The Origins of the Song Texts

Other than the two incorrect attributions in the text submitted to Lord Chamberlain's Examiner of Plays (John Larpent) reported in Jeffrey N. Cox's edition, *Presumption* scholarship has not engaged the provenance of the song texts.[90] Once assumed to be written by Peake, research for this chapter reveals that more than half of the song texts, like the melodramatic music used in the 1823 production, were assembled from preexisting materials. Of the thirteen songs in *Presumption*, only those with texts that reference specific characters and/or actions were written by Peake. The remaining texts not of Peake's composition came from popular printed poetic miscellany from as early as the 1780s, which were aimed for general middle-class consumption. These collections compile some of the most popular and widely read poets of the age, as well as a few obscure ones. Peake drew from six poets for song texts: Peter Pindar (aka John Wolcot), Henrique, John William Cunningham, M. H., William Cowper, and Arley.

Two of these, Henrique and M. H., are minor poets. Henrique is an obscure poet and essayist whose work was published in the *Pocket Magazine of Classic and Polite Literature* (1819). Research for this chapter determined that M. H. is the poet, playwright, and composer, Margaret Harries Baron-Wilson (1797–1846). She is referred to as both M. H. and "Miss Harries" in a passage in *The Theatrical Inquisitor, Or, Monthly Mirror, Vol. 14* (1819), which laments her temporary retreat from poetry due to her "sacrifice at the shrine of Hymen" (marriage).[91] Harries was a regular in the poetry columns of *La Belle Assemblée*, a magazine to which Mary Shelley herself contributed. She later founded *La Ninon, or, Leaves for the Album* (1833), and the *Weekly La Belle Assemblee* (1833). Baron-Wilson had a comic interlude, *Venus in Arms*, produced at the Strand Theatre in 1836, and was among the first female biographers published in English.[92]

---

[89] See note 41 above.
[90] "Ere Witching Love My Heart Possest" was attributed to "Dr. Walcot." This is clearly a misspelling of Wolcot (Peter Pinder's real last name). Cox, *Seven Gothic Dramas*, 390; "Of All the Knots Which Nature Ties" was attributed to "De Rance" (*De Rance* is the title of a poem by John William Cunningham). Cox, *Seven Gothic Dramas*, 404.
[91] *The Theatrical Inquisitor, Or, Monthly Mirror* 14 (1819): 320.
[92] *Oxford Dictionary of National Biography*, s.v. "Wilson [née Harries], Margaret [known as Mrs Cornwell Baron Wilson] (1797–1846), Poet," Available online: https://www-oxforddnb-com.proxy.library.carleton.ca/view/10.1093/ref:odnb/9780198614128.001.0001/odnb-9780198614128-e-29645 (accessed June 5, 2021).

The remaining poets were well known as writers and public figures and were widely published. Arley or Miles Peter Andrews (1742–1814) was a parliamentarian, gunpowder manufacturer, and playwright.[93] Today, John Wolcot (1738–1819), or Peter Pindar, is chiefly remembered for his output of satires. He wrote in other forms, including reviews, theater, sentimental odes, and ballads, but these are widely held to be "in the main mediocre."[94] John William Cunningham (1780–1861) was an evangelical cleric and leader who published a large number of sermons and was a minor literary figure as a writer of poems and hymns. He was the target of satire in Frances Trollope's 1837 novel, *The Vicar of Wrexhall*.[95]

William Cowper (1731–1800) is remembered today as perhaps the most widely read poet of his age; he has been described as "the foremost poet of the generation between Alexander Pope and William Wordsworth." More than a hundred editions of his poems were published in Britain, and almost fifty in America.[96]

While little can be said of their musical features and how they musically contributed to the drama, the texts do offer insight into the tastes of the compiler (likely Peake) and the theater-going public of London in 1823. As collections containing works by these poets were widely available, middle- and upper-class audiences would surely have been familiar with many or most of the authors of the song texts, if not some of the poems themselves. Indeed, four of the six texts can be found in collections from as recent as 1819, and three of these are found in the *Pocket Magazine of Classic and Polite Literature Vol. 3* (1819). The poem by Henrique appears to be printed only in this volume, and, while not conclusive, this strongly suggests that this popular publication is likely the compiler's source for at least three of the poems.

Presumption is most certainly an example of gothic melodrama, but the romantic and domestically themed songs and comedic scenes, in their profusion and textual features, prefigure the rise of the domestic melodrama and the twilight of the Gothic. At face value, the presence of light, mostly romantically themed poems taken from popular poetry collections, might seem incongruous with a gothic melodrama. However, congruity is restored when we recognize that the sentimentality of the poems from popular miscellanies, like the comedic scenes and songs, was merely redeployed for gothic effect, as discussed earlier.

---

[93] *Oxford Dictionary of National Biography*, s.v. "Andrews, Miles Peter (1742–1814), Playwright and Politician," *Oxford Dictionary of National Biography*, available online: https://www-oxforddnb-com.proxy.library.carleton.ca/view/10.1093/ref:odnb/9780198614128.001.0001/odnb-9780198614128-e-528 (accessed June 5, 2021).

[94] *Oxford Dictionary of National Biography*, s.v. "Wolcot, John [pseud. Peter Pindar] (bap. 1738, d. 1819), Poet and Satirist," Available online: https://www-oxforddnb-com.proxy.library.carleton.ca/view/10.1093/ref:odnb/9780198614128.001.0001/odnb-9780198614128-e-29828 (accessed June 5, 2021).

[95] *Oxford Dictionary of National Biography*, s.v. "Cunningham, John William (1780–1861), Church of England Clergyman," Available online: https://www-oxforddnb-com.proxy.library.carleton.ca/view/10.1093/ref:odnb/9780198614128.001.0001/odnb-9780198614128-e-6927 (accessed June 5, 2021).

[96] *Gale Literature: Dictionary of Literary Biography*, s.v. "William Cowper (November 15, 1731–April 25, 1800)," Available online: https://link-gale-com.proxy.library.carleton.ca/apps/doc/LKSPVQ144724565/DLBC?u=ocul_carleton&sid=bookmark-DLBC&xid=3a4e7570 (accessed June 5, 2021).

Like Shelley's *Frankenstein*, Peake's *Presumption* was a product of an age in which gothic narrative, macabre imagery, and philosophical rumination coexisted and interacted with the sentimentality of popular poetic collections and the spectacle of melodrama. Shelley herself stated that she liked the silent creature in *Presumption* but described the story "as not well managed."[97] Little did she know that so many musical, sonic, visual, and dramaturgical elements rooted in melodramatic practice, and first seen in *Presumption*, would go on to shape adaptations of the Frankenstein story for nearly two centuries.

---

[97] Mary Shelley to Leigh Hunt, September 9, 1823, in Bennett, *Selected Letters of Mary Wollstonecraft Shelley*.

5

Birth of a "Miserable Monster"

The Alchemical Theatricality of Male Self-Procreation in Stage and Screen Adaptations of *Frankenstein*

André Loiselle

Danny Boyle's 2011 National Theatre production of Nick Dear's stage play *Frankenstein*, in which Benedict Cumberbatch and Jonny Lee Miller alternated on a nightly basis in the leading roles of the Creature and Victor Frankenstein, purposefully sought to avoid "the popular conception of the Creature based largely on 20th century movies" by making the Monster an articulate being who can speak about life, love, and the scientist's responsibility toward his creation.[1] It is true that, in its emphasis on the Creature's intelligence, Boyle's stage production, which reached a broad international audience by being broadcast simultaneously to cinemas around the world, is closer to Shelley's original than most screen adaptations. Other stage plays have also sought to emphasize the Creature's ability to reason and behave ethically, rather than showcasing the grotesque monstrosity that is generally displayed on screen. For instance, Alden Nowlan and Walter Learning's version,[2] produced at the Fredericton Playhouse by Theatre New Brunswick in 1974, includes passages borrowed directly or paraphrased from the novel in which the Creature expresses itself rationally and shares its inner turmoil, anger, and yearnings with its misguided creator:

> CREATURE: I am malicious because I am miserable. Why should I pity a man who does not pity me? You would not even call it murder if you took my life. If one human being accepted me, I would weep in gratitude. But I will not be an abject slave! I will revenge my injuries!
> VICTOR: You've already revenged yourself upon me!
> CREATURE: (Losing control): What I have done is nothing to what I can do. (Turning away and calming) But I came here to reason with you not to threaten you. (Turns to VICTOR): You (Pointing) are my creator and I have

---

[1] Lynnette Porter, "It's Alive! But What Kind of Creature is National Theatre Live's 'Frankenstein'?" *Studies in Popular Culture* 35, no. 2 (2013): 1.
[2] I am grateful to famed Alden Nowlan aficionada Kerri Froc for drawing my attention to this play.

come to you with a request. (It bows) I am alone and miserable. Humans will not associate with me. But one as deformed and horrible as myself would not refuse to be my companion. What I ask is moderate and reasonable. (Crosses left of bed) You must create a female for me.[3]

This conversation is far more coherent and lucid than anything found in typical horror movies based on Shelley's work. However, even plays that are more charitable than movies toward the Creature still tend to be as radically different from the original novel as any film version in their highly theatrical portrayal of the Monster's "birth." Shelley spends very little time relating the moment of the Creature's coming into existence. But playwrights generally describe the "nativity scene" at length so it stands out as a breathtaking and terrifying spectacle, emphasizing the grotesquely dramatic vision of the Monster being jolted out of its inanimate state into a breathing frenzy of convulsive consciousness. For instance, Nowlan and Learning's version indulges in lengthy stage directions outlining the procedures followed by the scientist and his assistant Fritz to spark the Creature's nascency:

They insert the first ring in slots right and left of the CREATURE's abdomen. VICTOR picks up the second ring and they insert it in slots right and left of the CREATURE's head. They then attach the wires to the metal rings. VICTOR puts headrest on the blood machine . . . FRITZ crosses left to the bellows and starts to pump slowly on VICTOR'S cries of "IN." The Creature's chest rises and falls with each pump of the bellows. After five intakes of breath, the body on the table twitches as if it had received a massive electric shock. . . . It steps off the table. It rips the breathing hose from its mouth and spasmodically sucks its first breath of air. It gropes at its abdomen and grasps the hose from the blood machine firmly with its two hands. With great effort it rips the umbilical cord from its stomach, emits an horrendous wail of birth, and its eyes spring open wide in wonderment and pain. As the CREATURE turns and recognizes VICTOR as its "mother," the painful wail becomes a wordless cry for help as it reaches out for VICTOR imploringly.[4]

This moment of birth, where the Creature wails and cries "imploringly," is depicted even more strikingly in Boyle's version.

Boyle's production opens on an intensely histrionic performance, with the drawn-out scene of the Creature being galvanized into existence, struggling to emerge from an artificial "womb" and painstakingly crawling and staggering its way to a precarious standing position, while moaning, wailing and howling like some abominable, two-hundred-pound baby. Sound is as important as physicality in these early moments of the show. The embryonic Monster's groaning, squealing, grunting and gurgling conjures up images of the pleasure and pain of early life—the awakening of primeval

---

[3] Alden Nowlan and Walter Learning, *Frankenstein: A Full-Length Play* (Woodstock: Dramatic Publishing, 1981), 57.
[4] Ibid., 33–6.

humanoid consciousness, energized by primitive discovery, wonder and joy—clashing with the bone-crushing pain of a flesh-tearing confrontation with a brave new world of terror, menace, fear and dread. This retching cacophony of abjection stirs up such ancient body memories that it might very well liquefy the audience's bowels.

As Jenny McDonnell puts it, this makes for an "arresting opening, and the lengthy sequence that follows is equally engrossing, as the solitary Creature (Cumberbatch) gradually becomes aware of his surroundings, his limbs, and the noises that issue from his mouth."[5] In its protracted focus on the spectacular moment of the Monster's birth, Boyle and Dear's version evokes the intense theatricality of film adaptations like James Whale's *Frankenstein* (1931) and its remarkable sequel, *The Bride of Frankenstein* (1935), Terence Fisher's *The Curse of Frankenstein* (1957), Jack Smight's *Frankenstein: The True Story* (1973), Kenneth Branagh's *Mary Shelley's Frankenstein* (1994), and Paul McGuigan's *Victor Frankenstein* (2015). All of these screen versions indulge in over-the-top representations of the Creature's genesis, through broad histrionics and flamboyant visual and musical effects. As such, they all drastically depart from Shelley's brief and rather underwhelming description of Victor's "miserable monster" coming to life, which occupies only a few paragraphs in the novel:

> It was on a dreary night of November that I beheld the accomplishment of my toils. With an anxiety that almost amounted to agony, I collected the instruments of life around me, that I might infuse a spark of being into the lifeless thing that lay at my feet. It was already one in the morning; the rain pattered dismally against the panes, and my candle was nearly burnt out, when, by the glimmer of the half-extinguished light, I saw the dull yellow eye of the creature open; it breathed hard, and a convulsive motion agitated its limbs . . . I beheld the wretch, the miserable monster whom I had created.[6]

Looking at the birth of the "miserable monster" in a few stage and screen adaptations of *Frankenstein*, I argue that this conspicuous departure from Shelley's original in some theater and film versions results from a shift in representational modes, which happens to coincide with a shift in the authors' gender. While Shelley might have written her novel as a literary examination of her own fears about the organics of childbirth, exploring her "myriad anxieties about the processes of pregnancy, giving birth, and mothering,"[7] the male dramatists and filmmakers who use her work, to fill the stage and screen with the spectacle of monstrous birth, approach procreation from a male perspective that equates life-giving with the garishness of pseudoscience, or more specifically alchemy, broadly understood. Men of the stage and the screen have relied on perceptual modes of expression, as opposed to literary abstractions, to convey the self-centered desire

---

[5] Jenny McConnell, "National Theatre Live: Frankenstein Encore Screening, October 2013," *The Irish Journal of Gothic and Horror Studies* 13 (2014): 154.
[6] Mary Shelley, *Frankenstein* (Mineola: Dover, 1994), 34–5.
[7] Anne K. Mellor, "Making a Monster," in *Mary Shelley's Frankenstein*, ed. Harold Bloom (New York: Infobase Publishing, 2007), 46.

of *men* to create life. While Shelley could rely on the conceptualizing power of the written word to delve deep into philosophical explorations of the implications of creating life and the ensuing responsibility of the creator to fulfill his parental duty,[8] stage and screen versions depend on affective performances, materials, images, and sounds to make their point. Consequently, on stage and on screen, man's misguided dream of self-procreation—his hubristic yearning to "breathe the breath of God"[9]— must adopt the *superficial* form of spectacular alchemy, using ostentatious theatricality to break with the commonplace realism of natural procreation. It is worth clarifying the meaning of the term "theatricality" in this context.

Theatricality refers to techniques that trigger a radical break from realist or "transparent" representations of the narrative. It can manifest itself through the depiction of the site of horror—the *locus horribilis*—where space, architecture and landscape operate as striking theatrical spectacles in contrast to the mundane depictions of surrounding boroughs. The artifice of the gothic castle in shadowy ruins, the foggy cemetery with broken down tombstones and twisted gnarly trees, and of course the mad scientist's laboratory full of alchemical cauldrons, flasks and tubes, Jacob's ladders, surgical apparatuses and mechanical contraptions are only the most iconic examples of how the theatricality of horror subverts the realism of the peaceful village or dreary suburb where people normally live. Even in a live performance, the strangeness of the scientist's birth-giving apparatus, as in Boyle's version, in its extreme difference from old man De Lacey's modest dwelling, which is depicted in accordance with realist stage conventions, appears as a conspicuous instance of theatricality on stage. On film, radical syntagmatic departures from realism through frantic montage also create *showy* theatrical moments of dread that disrupt the stability of the mundane and the everyday unremarkably conveyed through conventional continuity editing. Music can also partake of the theatricality of horror as discordant harmonies, chaotic rushes of notes, violent tones, and orchestral clashes played at the moment of terror can shatter the smooth flow and unremarkable anonymity of innocuous background melodies.

Through all these techniques, theatricality isolates moments of horror from the rest of the narrative, effecting a stylistic displacement away from the realism of normality toward something more extraordinary, more striking, more appealing, but also much more threatening and terrifying. In the case of the Creature's birth in stage and film adaptations of Shelley's novel, theatricality denaturalizes the natal moment, detaching it from natural processes, and purposefully estranging women from the nativity scene. But as suggested above, theatricality is also all about surface: a superficial spectacle that can amaze but cannot dig deep into notions of parenthood or human responsibility. As such, it presents an intriguing paradox for the depiction of male self-procreation through "science," for theatricality is the opposite of the sober empirical discourse that shuns flamboyant displays and embraces instead the tedious pragmatics of the

---

[8] Shelley, *Frankenstein*, 69.
[9] Nick Dear, *Frankenstein, Based on the Novel by Mary Shelley* (London: Faber & Faber, 2011), 69.

scientific method. The representation of "science" as the creator of life, therefore, is undermined by the very spectacle of the Monster's birth. Rather, theatricality reveals the fallacy behind Frankenstein's "scientific" venture, exposing it to be mere alchemical quackery rather than authentic science.

The theatricality of the Creature's nativity on stage dates back to some of the earliest dramatic versions of Shelley's novel. The fulminating laboratory filled with the mesmerizing apparatuses of modern alchemy first appeared in playwright Henry Milner's 1826 staging of *The Man and the Monster* at London's Royal Coburg Theatre (now known as "the Old Vic"). As Kris Hirschmann explains, Milner's play "took the audience into Frankenstein's laboratory to witness, for the first time ever, the moment when the scientist animates his creation. The playwright . . . included explicit instructions for the scene in his script: 'Laboratory with bottles and chemical apparatus. First sight of the monster an indistinct form with black cloth.'"[10] There had already been hints of the monster's theatrical creation in Richard Brinsley Peake's 1823 *Presumption; or, the Fate of Frankenstein*.[11] While the laboratory itself is offstage in Peake's version, a window allows both Fritz, the mad scientist's assistant, and the spectator to see the flashes of blue light, which change to a reddish hue signifying the alchemical creation of life by Dr. Frankenstein.[12] But it is only starting with Milner's stage version that the spectacle of creation became a crucial part of the Frankenstein narrative. Later-nineteenth-century stage productions, such as Richard and Barnabas Brough's "burlesque extravaganza" *Frankenstein or the Model Man* from 1849, continued to emphasize the theatricality of the birth scene through spectacular sets: "Frankenstein's laboratory a gothic chamber strewn about with chemical apparatus books & Frankenstein at work putting the finishing touches on to the monster with a paint brush. The monster as yet inanimate stands on a pedestal."[13] For the remainder of the nineteenth century, the popular image of the Creature's fiery nativity artificially galvanized by the newfound energies of modern science did not arise from "the reading of the text of the book, but seeing adaptations of the story on the stage."[14]

The early twentieth century added electricity to the mix as the powerful force that could jolt dead body parts to life. Paul Dickey and Charles Goddard's 1915 *The Last Laugh*, a loose adaptation of Shelley's classic, was among the first stage plays to include a "laboratory scene, with electrical contrivances going at full speed."[15] But it is only with James Whale's 1931 seminal film version, inspired in great part by the "electrically

---

[10] Kris Hirschmann, *Frankenstein* (San Diego: ReferencePoint Press, 2012), 38.
[11] Christopher Fraying, *Frankenstein: The First Two Hundred Years* (London: Real Art Press, 2017), 80, 87.
[12] Sarah A. Winter, "'A Mass of Unnatural and Repulsive Horrors': Staging Horror in Nineteenth-Century English Theater," in *The Palgrave Handbook of Horror Literature*, ed. Kevin Corstorphine and Laura R. Kremmel (New York: Palgrave Macmillan, 2018), 142.
[13] H. Philip Bolton, *Women Writers Dramatized: A Calendar of Performances from Narrative Works Published in English to 1900* (London and New York: Mansell, 2000), 277.
[14] Fraying, *Frankenstein*, 96.
[15] Alexander B. Magoun, "Why Frankenstein Became Electric [Scanning Our Past]," *Proceedings of the IEEE 107*, no. 2 (February 2019): 493.

sublime moment of the robot's animation" from Fritz Lang's 1927 *Metropolis*,[16] that electricity fully replaced alchemy as the magical foundation of the Creature's birth. Since then, most films versions of *Frankenstein* have offered variations of Whale's emphasis on electricity, ranging from Terence Fisher's Hammer classics *The Curse of Frankenstein* and *The Revenge of Frankenstein* (1958) to Branagh's *Mary Shelley's Frankenstein* and McGuigan's *Victor Frankenstein*. Even on stage, electricity became crucial to the laboratory setup. In Nowlan and Learning's version, the laboratory is described as such: "Exploding Light Bulb. Blood Machine and Umbilical Cord and Attachment. Bellows and Hose. Control Console. Operating Table that tips to vertical position. Headrest (Hollow). Two Sheets to cover Bodies. Brain Jar. Brain. Top of Skull. Needle Thread. Scissors. Scalpels. Medical Instruments. Towels. Two pair of Goggles. Two Electrodes with cables."[17]

There are a few exceptions that avoid the electrodes and the exploding light bulbs found in most stage and screen adaptations, and instead hark back to the alchemical origins of the spectacle. Ricardo Islas's 2011 film *Frankenstein: Day of the Beast* relies on the injection of mysterious alchemical fluids rather than electricity to bring a stitched-up corpse back to life. Older films also evoke the alchemy of self-procreation. Jesús Franco's 1973 *La maldición de Frankenstein* shows the malevolent Cagliostro, who stole Dr. Frankenstein's creature, using ancient alchemical potions made of earth, air, water, and fire to create "women" whom he intends to breed with the Monster to produce a new, superior race called "Pantos." The theme of using Frankenstein's Monster to create a "superior race" is also exploited in Paul Morrissey's lustfully campy *Flesh for Frankenstein* aka *Andy Warhol's Frankenstein* (1973).

While the fascist instrumentalization of the Frankenstein myth to analogize the siring of a "superior race" is beyond the scope of this chapter, it will prove instructive to take a very short detour to examine, however briefly, the masculinist hubristic obsession with androcentric self-procreation that was at the core of much of the late 1920s and 1930s German cinema. Beyond the famous and incomparable example of *Metropolis*, several other films of the period show German men creating artificial wombs through which they can give birth to a hyper-masculine *Übermensch*. For instance, Kurt Bernhardt's 1933 *Der Tunnel*[18] endeavors to demonstrate the superiority of the European male through a pathologically narcissistic Frankensteinian experiment in constructing a womb-like subway tunnel from the old continent to America. The entire film is an illustration of the myth of self-procreation as a masculinist ideal, where an exclusively male crew works and groans and sweats together, as they travail their way deep underground, far below the mundane lives of domesticated petit bourgeois. As Lutz Koepnick points out:

---

[16] Ibid., 495–6.
[17] Nowlan and Learning, *Frankenstein*, 30.
[18] Bernhardt also made a French version shortly after the original German film, titled *Le Tunnel* and starring France's epitome of masculinity, Jean Gabin.

the imagery of displaced intercourse (the phallic drilling devices) intersects with the desire for a regressive reunion with a self-constructed mother (the womb of the tunnel). Both moments culminate, ironically but not surprisingly, in the ultimate materialization of male self-procreation, accomplished in the final sequence when the European worker appears in the vaginal opening to welcome the American crew-a striking image of male technological self-birth, of clean and safe sex indeed.[19]

Referring to Mac Allen, the brilliant engineer hired to realize this impossible manly vision, Koepnick continues:

Machines, muscles, and marching tunes meet here to overcome phobias concerning female agency. Whereas sexuality above ground remains transmuted into cathartic rituals, Mac Allan's underground opens a space in which men may enact their desire to break free from compulsory heterosexuality as much as from any possible dependence on the female as other and as mother. Mac Allan and his working armies dig ever farther through the dirt, not to connect the two continents but to pursue their dream of male self-procreation through technology, a dream that establishes male identity as a completely autonomous system of desire and signification but that ultimately only reproduces already given structures of power. Mac Allan's enterprise, in other words, enables homoerotic desires only in order to promote a phobic erasure of difference and alterity.[20]

Victor Frankenstein would have been proud of this feat of engineering inspired by his own ambitions to self-procreate through the miracle of "science," and dispose of all the imperfect carnal procedures performed by the creatures that breed in matrimonial bedrooms across the land.

Whether it is clunky digging machines, alchemical concoctions, electrical contraptions, or any other modern technology, all of these metaphors of masculinist reproductive narcissism share the same function in man's eternal desire to create life: they are "the elixir of the World Soul, the spark of Creation."[21] Indeed, alchemy and electricity were long perceived as having similar (mysterious) powers and purposes. As Dennis Stelling observes in eighteenth-century writings "electricity, expressing both material and immaterial effects, was not divested of the ancient symbolic projections ... thus permitting the symbols carried by electricity to drive modern science toward accomplishments that strongly echo the goals of alchemy: the transmutation and spiritualization of matter."[22] Erik Davis further points out that "many of the earliest

---

[19] Lutz Koepnick, *The Dark Mirror: German Cinema Between Hitler and Hollywood* (Berkeley: University of California Press, 2002), 69.
[20] Ibid.
[21] Erik Davis, *TechGnosis: Myth, Magic, and Mysticism in the Age of Information* (Berkeley: North Atlantic Books, 2015), 36.
[22] Dennis Stilling, "Editor's Preface," in *The Theology of Electricity: On the Encounter and Explanation of Theology and Science in the 17th and 18th Centuries*, ed. Ernst Benz (Eugene: Pickwick Publications, 2009), xi–xii.

books on electricity described the force in distinctly alchemical terms, dubbing it the 'ethereal fire,' the 'quintessential fire,' or the 'desideratum,' the long-sought universal panacea."[23] The traditional discourse around alchemy, which can be extended to electricity and other technologies, saw no limit to the potential of this "scientific" endeavor.

Paracelsus, an early-sixteenth-century physician who straddled the transition from medieval quackery to modern medicine, believed in the limitless potential of alchemy. According to Lois Magner, "Paracelsus claimed that through natural magic and alchemy human beings would one day see beyond the mountains, hear across the oceans, divine the future, make gold, cure all diseases, and even create life."[24] Paracelsus's ultimate alchemical ambition was to create the *Homunculus*, a "little man ... often depicted as sitting in a test tube."[25] This vision of a small person artificially brought to life is memorably approximated in Whale's *Bride of Frankenstein*, in which Frankenstein's former mentor, Dr. Septimus Pretorius, has managed to create miniature human beings that he keeps in bottles, and that he claims to have grown from seeds, thus vaguely evoking Paracelsus's own formula. Paracelsus's "1537 recipe replaces the mother's organism with an artificial medium. The sperm is incubated in a concoction of horse dung, urine, and other ingredients, and kept warm inside a pumpkin."[26] Paracelsus's conception of the *Homunculus*, which does away with the mother altogether and replaces her with the artifice of "science," is often referred to as "patriarchal alchemy." As Immanuel Wallerstein explains, "what we see in patriarchal alchemy is an attempt at the usurpation of the female fertility, pregnancy, and birth process, not only in theory but also in reality."[27] As Seabra Ferreira and Maria Aline Salgueiro suggest,

> the male alchemist would thus become the sole progenitor of his child. The alchemical jar for its part, can be seen as a representation of an artificial womb, as a prefiguration of ectogenesis. The *homunculus*, a tiny fully formed man who would issue from the male alchemist's jar, can thus be seen as the alchemists' answer to Athena, born fully formed and fully armed from Zeus's head. As Rosi Braidotti remarks, "Alchemy is a *reductio ad absurdum* of the male fantasy of self-reproduction."[28]

Not surprisingly, the scene from *Bride of Frankenstein* where Dr. Pretorius emerges from the darkness to enlist Frankenstein in his groundbreaking research, which he

---

[23] Davis, *TechGnosis*, 36.
[24] Lois N. Magner, *A History of the Life Sciences, Revised and Expanded* (New York: Marcel Dekker, 2002), 79.
[25] Immanuel Maurice Wallerstein, *The Modern World-System in the Longue Durée* (Boulder: Paradigm Publishers, 2004), 72.
[26] Christiane Nüsslein-Volhard, *Coming to Life: How Genes Drive Development* (San Diego: Kales Press, 2006), 135.
[27] Wallerstein, *The Modern World-System in the Longue Durée*, 73.
[28] Seabra Ferreira and Maria Aline Salgueiro, *I Am the Other: Literary Negotiations of Human Cloning* (Westport: Praeger, 2005), 114.

hopes will go even beyond the *Homunculus*, takes place in the latter's nuptial bedroom. Pretorius, who is introduced in the conjugal space by the maid as a "very queer-looking old gentleman," quickly makes Frankenstein's new bride, Elizabeth, feel superfluous as he contemptuously tells her that his business with Frankenstein "is private!" Pretorius and Frankenstein's subsequent life-creating work in the film represents an instance of "patriarchal alchemy," where procreation happens without women. One of the film's many ironies is that the two male scientists create a woman in the absence of women; the process of creating a bride for the Monster excludes the literal "bride of Frankenstein."

The moment of creation in *The Bride of Frankenstein*, which is perhaps the most iconic and influential mad scientist scene in all of horror cinema, presents an amalgamation of visual and musical theatricality that emphasizes the patently unnatural artifice of birth achieved through male self-procreation. Quick editing, extreme camera angles, and off-kilter composition are used to depict in a most ostentatiously extravagant fashion Frankenstein and Pretorius operating the flamboyantly complicated apparatuses of electrical alchemy deployed to reanimate the dead body. These brazen visual techniques reject the classical Hollywood realism used through most of the film, especially in the scenes representing Frankenstein's domestic life with Elizabeth, which are usually shot following the rules of transparent continuity editing. As such, the theatricality of the birth sequence accentuates the aberrant actions that bring the bride to life through electrical machines rather than the natural organs of human reproduction. Distorted close-ups of Frankenstein and Pretorius, techniques that were rather rare in the 1930s, further identify the two men as engaging in ungodly deeds that defy the natural order of things. And yet, these are among the most exciting images of any Universal monster show of the time, and they highlight the theatrical appeal of these gestures of masculine hubris.

Similarly, Franz Waxman's remarkable musical score for *The Bride of Frankenstein* contrasts domesticity and the scientists' experiments by creating a dichotomy between the leitmotifs of romanticism and the "atonal" resonances of the collaboration between Frankenstein and Pretorius. As Joe Tompkins puts it, Waxman's score

> is often recognized as a landmark of horror film scoring and includes both late romantic styles and leitmotif structures (in the Monster and Bride themes), as well as indices of early atonal music (Dr. Pretorius's theme). Furthermore, it also contains orchestral bursts (akin to the stinger chord) which underwrite moments of dramatic spectacle: Waxman recalls using a "big dissonant chord" at the end of the film in order to underscore the Monster's destruction of the laboratory.... Music here also proves to be a source of ironic commentary, as in the church bells that accompany the Bride's creation scene.[29]

---

[29] Joe Tompkins, "Mellifluous Terror: The Discourse of Music and Horror Films," in *A Companion to the Horror Film*, ed. Harry M. Benshoff (Chichester: Wiley Blackwell, 2014), 195.

Moreover, to underline the clash between realist sounds and the dissonance of alchemical birth, the sequence includes a symphony of thunder and rain, mechanical grinding and electrical crackling that enriches and offsets the rousing effect of conventional orchestral arrangements. Didier C. Deutsch observes that

> Franz Waxman's monumental score for the 1935 *The Bride of Frankenstein* was one of the earliest fully developed film scores in a day when most films had very sparse musical accompaniment. With its blend of romantic motifs and a variety of inventive horrific passages, the most notable being the "Creation" music, wherein the composer musically depicted the chilling noises of the laboratory equipment to create an impressionistic and unique musical sequence.[30]

The music and the sound effects coalesce to create a soundscape of masculine fantasy where harmonious nature is subjected to the discordant will of the positivist phallus of Victorian industrialism. Perhaps only Bernard Herrmann, some twenty-five years later, would manage to create a more evocative score for a horror film, in Hitchcock's *Psycho* (1960).

This sequence fulfills, at least in the imaginary realm, the "dreams of male self-procreation [that] can be seen as symptomatic of fantasies of patriarchal domination and self-perpetuation, eliminating the need to have women as essential parts of the reproductive process."[31] Likewise, in *Victor Frankenstein*, the good doctor, along with his faithful but overly anxious assistant "Igor," the devious Finnegan, who finances Victor's research for his own nefarious purposes, and an army of *male* technicians vaguely reminiscent of the diggers of *Der Tunnel* bring the Monster to life in a spectacular orgy of thunder, lightning, fire, explosion, and musical excess that completely excludes women. In fact in this version, Victor has no central love interest. Rather it is Igor, a former circus performer, who is in love with a beautiful aerialist, Lorelei, with whom he reunites in a traditionally romantic happy ending after the earth-shattering birth and death of the Monster. But Victor himself remains utterly uninterested in women's ability to give life through the boringly commonplace natural means of biological procreation. Several other adaptations of the novel also dispose altogether of Elizabeth.

For instance, in Hammer Studio's *The Evil of Frankenstein* (1964), which takes place several years after Frankenstein's initial experiments, the disastrous results of which forced him to flee his hometown of Karlstaad, there is no mention of Elizabeth having ever existed. This version, which revolves around Frankenstein's return to Karlstaad and his efforts to reanimate the original Monster, makes clear that the scientist has absolutely no interest in the pleasures of the flesh. Instead, as in *Victor Frankenstein*, it is the faithful assistant—here Hans rather than Igor—who has romantic aspirations toward a mute peasant girl. A scene, approximately thirty minutes into the film, attests to Frankenstein's utter disinterest in women. As he sits

---

[30] Didier C. Deutsch, *MusicHound Soundtracks: The Essential Album Guide to Film, Television and Stage Music* (Detroit: Visible Ink Press, 1999), 4.
[31] Ferreira and Salgueiro, *I Am the Other*, 110.

in a pub with Hans, he notices his enemy the Burgomaster wearing an expensive ring he stole from the scientist during his lengthy exile. While the shots of the Burgomaster and his entourage clearly showcase his young wife's ample cleavage, Victor only has interest in the purloined ring visible on the Burgomaster's hand as it rests on the young woman's heaving bosom. While this conspicuous symbol of maternal largess occupies most of the screen, Victor is oblivious to everything except the ring. Shortly after, Frankenstein bursts into the Burgomaster's chamber confronting the man about the stolen ring and all the other prized possessions he has taken from him during his absence from the village, including Victor's bed upon which lies the voluptuous young wife in her negligée. Of course, Frankenstein again fails entirely to notice her.

In other stage and screen versions of the story, while Victor might have some vague interest in romantic love, he still rejects the notion of natural reproduction involving a man *and a woman*, and promotes instead the notion of a scientific or alchemical approach to creating life. In some instances, the rejection of romance as a means of creating life is implicit, in other versions the rejection of natural procreation is explicit. In Branagh's version, Elizabeth tries to intervene early in Victor's obsessive scientific pursuit, invoking their childhood promise to love each other. But Victor tearfully casts off her plea to leave his laboratory and resume their domestic life in a melodramatic scene that signals his misguided choice of "science" over nature.

> Victor: I must stay.
> Elizabeth: Even if it means you'll die?
> Victor: Yes.
> Elizabeth: Well, let me help you.
> Victor: No, that's impossible.
> Elizabeth: We made a promise. Victor, I beg you.
> Victor: I cannot abandon this work now. It's too important. Not just for me, but, believe me, for everyone. And it must come first.
> Elizabeth: Before us?
> Victor: I love you so much, but . . .
> Elizabeth: Goodbye.

While there is no explicit reference to the natural alternative to creating life in Branagh's version, the scene clearly evokes Victor's choice of patriarchal alchemy over romantic love. We find a more explicit rejection of nature in Jack Smight's 1973 television version, *Frankenstein: The True Story*. Early in the show, Victor storms out of a church where a priest recites platitudes about the accidental death of his brother William, angrily discarding the pious acceptance of God's will to give and take away life. As Victor asks why it is that humans cannot create life from the ashes of bereavement, his loving fiancée Elizabeth responds, "but we can. One day, if God blesses us, when we are man and wife." Victor interrupts her abruptly with a declaration that is crucial to his self-procreating impulse: "so can a pair of animals. Life out of life, that's no miracle. Why can't I raise life out of death?" These words, which do not appear in Shelley's original, clearly indicate that for Victor, procreating with Elizabeth is meaningless, for any rat or pig or dog can do exactly the same.

A similar moment occurs in Boyle's stage version, but later in the narrative, after Victor has given life to the Creature and tries to explain the situation to Elizabeth. Approximately ninety minutes into the production, Dr. Frankenstein exclaims: "I have beaten death! I have done it! I have made a living thing!"

> Elizabeth: But if you wanted to create life –
> Victor: That's it, that's exactly what I wanted!
> Elizabeth: Why not just give me a child? We could have married years ago!
> Victor: No, no, that's not the –
> Elizabeth: Because that is how we create life, Victor—that is the usual way!
> Victor: I am talking about science![32]

As in Smight's version, Boyle's Victor has no interest in the "usual way" animals, such as human beings, create life. The science that Victor refers to, which is in fact nothing more than patriarchal alchemy, is the only acceptable process of procreation for him. As is typical of patriarchal alchemy, Victor's ambition is to do away with the messiness of natural procreation and replace it with the clean artifice of what he calls science. This was the objective of alchemists as well. Fourteenth-century alchemist John of Rupescissa used "science" to cleanse procreation from all the unpleasantness of natural processes. Rupescissa "believed humans could use alchemy to raise corrupted nature to a higher level of perfection, thereby performing through artifice medical cures that were beyond the ordinary course of nature."[33] A masculine desire for self-procreation is rooted in the notion of artifice as a cure for the messiness of nature.

The artifice of male self-procreation seeks to distance alchemical reproduction as much as possible from the darkly intimate, domestic space of natural childbirth, the site of "ultimate abjection," in Julia Kristeva's conception.[34] But the tragic irony of Victor's desire to create life without having to engage in the bestial process of copulation is that his ideal of purity transforms into a disgusting spectacle of abject theatricality, with a miserable monster performing a horrifying pantomime of ghastly gestures and sickening sounds that attest to the impossibility of ever realizing the scientist's obsessive goal of procreating outside the bounds of organic materiality. In one of the more grotesque screen versions of Shelley's novel, Ricardo Islas's *Day of the Beast*, the Creature becomes obsessed with Victor's neglected wife, and spends most of the film pursuing Elizabeth with the express purpose of breeding with her. He eventually catches up with her and, in a repulsively unsettling sequence, assaults and rapes her. Horrified at the prospect of bearing the Monster's child, she rejects life

---

[32] Dear, *Frankenstein, Based on the Novel by Mary Shelley*, 70.
[33] Leah DeVun, *Prophecy, Alchemy, and the End of Time: John of Rupescissa in the Late Middle Ages* (New York: Columbia University Press, 2013), 129.
[34] Julia Kristeva, *Powers of Horror: An Essay on Abjection* (New York: Columbia University Press, 1982), 155.

altogether and shoots herself in the head. Using his alchemical concoctions, Victor resuscitates her in a scene filled with grisly images of gruesome reanimation and a cacophony of melodic wretchedness. In a final moment of caustic dread, the zombified Elizabeth tears Victor to bleeding pieces, leaving him to die as she joins the Creature in what, as the final credits roll, the audience can only imagine will be a spectacular orgy of blood, gore and monstrous coitus.

The audiovisual theatricality of male self-procreation in the stage and screen adaptations of *Frankenstein* discussed earlier serves to separate the moment of the Creature's birth from the rest of the narrative, generally depicted following a relatively realist idiom. In the process, theatricality denaturalizes the birth of the "miserable monster" and positions it outside the parameters of normal reproduction which, in theory, should operate within the contours of realism. As such, theatricality would seem to be an ideal means to celebrate Frankenstein's scientific desire to erase natural procreation, and by extension women, from the reproductive equation. However, as anyone who has ever seen a play or film based on Shelley's novel will know, Frankenstein's aspirations on stage and screen always result in a spectacle of devastating failure and humiliation that delights and enchants the audience. This is not surprising as theatricality, by definition, cannot serve the austere and stringent purposes of science. Theatricality is rooted in overindulgence in sensorial physicality and material stimulation and, as such, it shatters cerebral austerity and exposes patriarchy's ludicrous hubris and misguided cockiness as nothing more than an alchemical farce.

Theatricality *by definition* draws attention to its own artifice and superficiality and, almost by necessity, undermines any claim to a profound and serious scientific discourse. The earnest scientist who indefatigably toils away, alone in an anonymous lab trying to find practical solutions to real problems has little to do with the Victor Frankenstein of stage and screen adaptations, who wallows in the spectacle of vacuous pyrotechnics and indulges in melodramatic proclamations: "it's alive, it's alive," a phrase which, of course, does not appear in Shelley's original. If, as Almut Amberg puts it, "theatricality is the opposite of authenticity," then the ostentatious spectacle of the Creature's birth contradicts the very purpose of science, which is to search for true and authentic answers to humanity's most pressing questions.[35] But again none of this should come as a surprise, since theater and film adaptations of Shelley's novel have always been far less interested in the deep philosophical questions she was pondering than in exploiting the pleasurable paradox of a spectacle of alchemy gone horribly wrong. *Frankenstein* on stage and on screen delights far more than it educates. Shelley may have approved, though, for by most accounts she seems to have enjoyed the frighteningly charming grotesqueries that early-nineteenth-century melodramatic versions of her work presented to their mesmerized audiences.[36]

---

[35] Almut Amberg, *Theatre, Theatricality and Metatheatre in "Behind a Mask" (1866)* (Munich: Grin Verlag, 2020), 4.

[36] Helen M. Buss, D. L. Macdonald, and Anne McWhir, *Mary Wollstonecraft and Mary Shelley: Writing Lives* (Waterloo: Wilfrid Laurier University Press, 2001), 293.

6

Excising the Repulsive

Metaphysics and Psychology in Edison's *Frankenstein* (1910)

Ethan Towns

Edison Studios' *Frankenstein*, written and directed by J. Searle Dawley, is a staple of American silent horror film. Running around fourteen minutes in duration, it was released on March 18, 1910, during a period when narrative films were first being developed. As the first film adaptation of Mary Shelley's seminal novel, it is instructive to look at the practical and moral decisions that influenced this initial cinematic reimagining of the story, its message, and its archetypes. What was included? What was omitted? What rationale motivated these choices, and how were these adaptation priorities depicted onscreen?

The Edison production of *Frankenstein* is a significant milestone in the history of silent horror cinema. This first cinematic adaptation of *Frankenstein*, I argue, highlights an interstitial space between antiquated and modern theories of science. The film deals with a type of metaphysics involving a curious blend of divine inspiration and esoteric science to transform matter—or the self—into a new state of being. This is accomplished through the film's idiosyncratic treatment of alchemic metaphysics and moral psychology. Here, alchemic metaphysics means using supernatural methods to catalyze changes in matter. Moral psychology not only involves ethical considerations, but it can also help us understand the extent to which Victor Frankenstein's fractured identity plays a role in the Monster's creation.[1]

I posit that in Dawley's *Frankenstein* there is a curious tension between alchemic metaphysics and consciousness, with the former being used as a vehicle to investigate the recesses of the latter. As examined herein, the film's representation of monstrosity is

---

[1] In the early twentieth century, moral psychology was largely associated with social values. For instance, in the United States and continental Europe, there was an interest in "providing and devising tests of an individual's moral values and development" (Craig A. Wendorf, "History of American Morality Research, 1894–1932," *History of Psychology* 4, no. 3 (2001): 272), for the benefit of society at large. The assessment of their subjects' ethical agency, in accordance with a predetermined set of principles, is akin to the relationship film producers and censor boards had with contemporaneous audiences.

linked to the early history of silent horror film, to the history of adaptation (from novel to screen), to the producer's desire to create a palatable film for American audiences, and to an interest in aesthetically and intellectually intertwining moral psychology and metaphysics. Through the figure of Frankenstein's Monster, Shelley crystallizes this complex interplay by depicting his gradual antipathy toward the flawed humanity that created him.

It's Alive! Restoring *Frankenstein*

Like many of the earliest silent films, Edison's *Frankenstein* was long thought to have been lost. The film was rediscovered in the 1970s when Alois F. Dettlaff Sr., a film collector from Milwaukee, announced his ownership of a copy after the American Film Institute included it on a list of lost films.[2] In the 1970s, Dettlaff permitted the use of excerpts from the film in a BBC documentary.[3] Having received no compensation or acknowledgment, however, he began to mistrust the intentions of the interested parties and donated a "protected" version of the film to the Academy of Motion Picture Arts and Sciences in 1986.[4] Eventually, Dettlaff held a public screening of *Frankenstein* on October 30, 1993, at the Avalon Theatre in Milwaukee, Wisconsin, and again on April 26–27 in Jersey City, as part of a retrospective on *Frankenstein* films.[5]

The public attention that was generated by these two screenings ultimately led to subsequent restoration efforts, including those by the Library of Congress and the University of Geneva, reflecting a growing international, cultural, and scholarly investment in saving and preserving silent films. After a nitrate print was acquired by the Library of Congress, a 2K scan was performed before photochemical preservation efforts—and digital restoration—could be done. In 2017, one version was published by the National Audio-Visual Conservation Center as a digital MPEG-4 video file, tinted for effect from the original black and white. In 2016, the film was restored by *le comité du Ciné-club universitaire* at the University of Geneva, the very city outside which Lord Byron, John Polidori, and Percy and Mary Shelley resided at the time of the novel's creation, in the Villa Diodati. Graphic designer Julien Dumoulin handled the restoration and retouching, while Swiss musician Nicolas Hafner composed an

---

[2] "In Remembrance: Alois F. Dettlaff, Sr.," *FilmBuffOnline*, available online: http://www.filmbuffonline.com/InRemembrance/AloisDettlaff.htm (accessed February 15, 2021). The film had initially been screened in conjunction with a stage show. This not only illustrates a typical film programming context for the era but also the close relationship between theater and the moving image and, more specifically, with horror. On film's early relationship with the realm of theater, see Rick Altman, *Silent Film Sound* (New York: Columbia University Press, 2004), 124–5. On the Grand Guignol theatrical tradition, see also Winston Wheeler Dixon, *A History of Horror* (New Brunswick and London: Rutgers University Press, 2010), 24.

[3] Evan Lieberman, "*Frankenstein* at the Boundaries of Life, Death, and Film," in *Frankenstein: How a Monster Became an Icon – The Enduring Allure of Mary Shelley's Creation*, ed. Sidney Perkowitz and Eddy Von Mueller (New York: Pegasus Books, 2018), 70.

[4] *FilmBuffOnline*, "Remembrance."

[5] The subtitle for the event was "A Salute to Film Preservation."

original soundtrack on the Wurlitzer organ.[6] Now freely available on numerous video-sharing websites due to its public domain status, Edison's *Frankenstein* circulates widely—in varying conditions—through the efforts of a variety of fan clubs and cultural institutions.

Adapting *Frankenstein* for Silent Cinema

Despite efforts to censor some of its controversial and sensitive content, gothic literature provided a good deal of sordid and salacious material for silent film, from extramarital relationships to criminal acts. In the case of *Frankenstein*, the novel and its contemporaneous stage adaptations were mined for crucial scenes and characters, and reinterpreted to reflect the moralistic concerns of early-twentieth-century America, using what adaptation-theorist Linda Hutcheon describes as "the comfort of ritual combined with the piquancy of surprise."[7] To this end, *Frankenstein* was adapted to emphasize "mystical and psychological elements" rather than "overtly horrific content," so as to appease any potential public morality concerns that may have arisen in America in 1910.[8] This is reinforced in the March 12, 1910 issue of the trade magazine *Moving Picture World*, which reads: "the dissolution [of the monster] through the force of true love is most vividly presented with the repulsive situations eliminated."[9] This is reiterated in Edison's publicity material, published in the same issue, which states that "[t]he actually repulsive situations in the original version have been carefully eliminated in *its visualized form*, so that there is no possibility of its shocking any portion of an audience."[10] While these "repulsive situations" may point to violent content in Shelley's novel, they may also refer to the blasphemy of identifying Victor Frankenstein with God, or to the act of grave robbing, for example. This censorship therefore aligns with American social mores of the early twentieth century, where morality and Christian values were inexorably linked. Literary historian Karen E. Laird argues that "[t]he morality of cinema debate . . . sparked Edison's embrace of adaptation, but also put pressure on the studio to bowdlerize literary source texts in order to appease the moralists."[11]

While Shelley's original novel exhibits a degree of violent content, the Monster's initial appreciation of nature, sensory wonder, and genteel manners challenge the idea of innate evil, as the former is presented by Shelley as the creature's primary instincts, prior to his murderous rage. Shelley's Monster is spurned by the world due to his threatening

---

[6] "Frankenstein 1910." *Jdumoulin.com*, available online: http://www.jdumoulin.com/julien-dumoulin---graphic-and-video-design---frankenstein-1910.html.
[7] Linda Hutcheon, *A Theory of Adaptation* (London and New York: Routledge, 2013), 4.
[8] *Edison Kinetogram*, "Frankenstein (Dramatic)," March 15, 1910, 3.
[9] Chalmers Publishing Company, "Moving Picture World (January–June 1910)," last modified June 14, 2012, available online: https://archive.org/details/movinwor06chal, 392.
[10] Chalmers Publishing Company, "Moving Picture World," 428 (italics are the author's).
[11] Karen E. Laird, *The Art of Adapting Victorian Literature, 1848–1920* (Farnham and Burlington: Ashgate Publishing, 2015), 116.

appearance, not because he is inherently wicked. In the novel, after approaching a home in the countryside whose inhabitants he had been observing, the Monster is driven out by the blind patriarch's son, after having spoken with the boy's father without incident. He retaliates by burning the home to the ground. "Inflamed by pain," the Monster vows, "I vowed eternal hatred and vengeance on all mankind."[12] In the novel, this represents the turning point when the Monster's malicious instincts are triggered. Wanting Victor to share in his misery and wretchedness, the Monster ultimately murders his creator's best friend, younger brother, and wife. For these abominable deeds he feels "triumph" rather than guilt.[13] This raises issues of moral psychology that were very much in circulation in late-Georgian England. It is interesting to note that five years prior to the publication of *Frankenstein*, Mary Shelley's celebrated husband, Percy Bysshe Shelley, had advocated for a more nuanced understanding of moral psychology. In his *Queen Mab: A Philosophical Poem* (1813), Shelley suggests that the new moral psychology would "introduce a great change into established notions of morality . . . there is neither good nor evil in the universe, otherwise than as the events to which we apply these epithets have relation to our own mode of being."[14]

Adapting Shelley's *Frankenstein* to the single-reel silent film format was a daunting challenge for the Edison team, as narrative cinema, still in its infancy, lacked a consolidated sign system to express character psychology. Without sound or dialog, precise, but brief, concrete ideas could be expressed only through intertitles.[15] In *A Theory of Adaptation*, Linda Hutcheon cites comments made by a fictional author, John North, in Louis Begley's novel *Shipwreck*: "Writing a screenplay based on a great novel is foremost a labor of simplification."[16] North further suggests that this is not a matter of just pruning the plot, but also of curating the "intellectual content."[17] This assertion (albeit by a fictional character) is a provocative one, and one that contradicts, to some extent, the notion that the images of cinema have demonstrated broad expressive and conceptual power throughout film history. North's viewpoint is nonetheless noteworthy, as it forces us to consider how complex narrative ideas and character development are translated—and abridged—from page to screen, perhaps especially in the instance of Edison's *Frankenstein*, which runs only fourteen minutes in duration. As noted by Hutcheon, however, runtime need not be viewed as a hindrance, as "adapters actualize or concretize ideas; they make simplifying selections, but also

---

[12] Mary Shelley, *Frankenstein: A Longman Cultural Edition*, ed. Susan J. Wolfson (New York: Pearson Longman, 2007), 108.
[13] Ibid., 109.
[14] Percy Bysshe Shelley, *Queen Mab: A Philosophical Poem [1813]* (London: Create Space Independent Publishing, 2015), 106.
[15] Adapting respected and well-known stories was done to quell concerns about the emerging medium of film, and to borrow a level of prestige from the literary arts, at a time when some observers disregarded film as a frivolous spectacle. In this period, adaptation worked as a form of shorthand; most viewers would have known the story before seeing the film. The first intertitle describes the film as "a liberal adaptation of Mary Shelley's famous story," acknowledging both the wide circulation of the novel and the artistic liberty the filmmakers exercised in their reinterpretation of the literary source.
[16] Hutcheon, *A Theory of Adaptation*, 1.
[17] Ibid.

amplify and extrapolate; they make analogies; they critique or show their respect, and so on."[18]

Dawley, the film's director, clearly had to make "simplifying selections," but he was also able to "concretize ideas," namely the multiple moral dilemmas confronting Victor Frankenstein. To this end, it is interesting to note which aspects of Shelley's novel are maintained in Dawley's film. For example, the Monster is still explicitly jealous of Frankenstein for having found a mate. In the novel, this jealousy results in the Monster's ultimate quest to have a mate fashioned for him, an idea that is developed more fully in James Whale's *Bride of Frankenstein* (1935). Some of the novel's metaphysical and psychological themes are also amplified and extrapolated upon. This is done by changing the context of the Monster's creation (emerging from a boiling cauldron, Dawley's Monster is an alchemic concoction, as explored in detail herein) and by using various compositional and mise-en-scène techniques to express the characters' interior states. For example, the use of mirrors and dream-like compositions in the silent film frame the Monster as an extension—or double—of Frankenstein. While there are no mirrors in the novel, when Shelley's Monster sees his reflection in a pond, he remarks, "I became fully convinced that I was in reality the monster that I am . . . filled with the bitterest sensations of despondence and mortification."[19] This passage, and stage adaptations that incorporated mirrors in a variety of ways, undoubtedly inspired the analogous scene in the film.

Alchemy, Hubris, Good, and Evil

In both Shelley's novel and Edison's film adaptation, Frankenstein's interests are more aligned with alchemy than with modern science. In the novel, Victor Frankenstein is fascinated by the intersection of chemistry and natural philosophy, and with the notion of combining disparate elements to probe "the secrets of life" to create "the perfect human being." Shelley tells the reader that the city of Ingolstadt, where Frankenstein pursues his studies under fictional professors Krempe and Waldman, "housed a medical school and was a well-known center of progressive learning . . . advocacy of free thinking and radical politics," in consequence of which it was "outlawed in 1785."[20] This association of innovative research and transgressive ideology with Frankenstein's own interests sets the stage for his experiments. After finding Professor Krempe "repulsive" for dismissing natural philosophy as antiquated,[21] Frankenstein attends a chemistry lecture by Professor Waldman, and becomes enraptured by the possibilities inherent in its subject matter. According to Waldman, ancient philosophers of chemistry "[penetrated] into the recesses of nature,"[22] by comparison with which "the present

---

[18] Ibid., 3.
[19] Shelley, *Frankenstein*, 190.
[20] Susan Wolfson (ed.) in Shelley, *Frankenstein*, 25n6.
[21] Shelley, *Frankenstein*, 28.
[22] Ibid., 29.

state of the science" is dismally misdirected.[23] His reference to "recesses" suggests that the enlightened alchemist should seek access to forbidden or secluded spaces that are accessible only to those who have the courage to search for it.

In Edison's film, we see Victor Frankenstein leaving for college in the first sequence. In a static long shot—customary for the time—he bids farewell to his parents, dons his top hat, and exits the parlor. Humorously—though perhaps necessarily so, given the extreme time constraints of the film—the next intertitle informs us that "Two years later, Frankenstein has discovered the secret of life," following which he is shown gesticulating theatrically in celebration of his documented discoveries. His study chamber is packed with a curious blend of the macabre, the alchemical, and the scholarly, including skulls, shelved and scattered books, and what appears to be a human head.

In a letter to his fiancée, Elizabeth—shown in close-up for the viewer—Frankenstein states that his mission is to "create into life the most perfect human being that the world has yet known." This epistle quite explicitly calls into question traditional theological conceptions of the divine source of life, as Frankenstein implicitly challenges the notion of God's infallible supremacy in matters of creation. In the novel, Frankenstein's hubris is stated even more explicitly when he boasts that "new species would bless me as its creator and source,"[24] thereby transcending mere scientific curiosity to deify himself through religious language.[25]

Like the novel, the film markedly underscores Frankenstein's hubris. In his quest for perfection and God-like power, Frankenstein's unmitigated pride corrupts his intentions, and he fashions a hideous monster rather than the ideal creature he ostensibly sought to create. Clearly, his unorthodox experiments point to themes of moral depravity. The intertitles note that "the evil in Frankenstein's mind creates a monster." While this abstract "evil" is not explicitly associated with the sins of pride and hubris, it is clear that Frankenstein's aims are compromised, at best. Frankenstein's worst impulses have clearly corrupted his scientific curiosity in the possibility of creating life. This narrative appears to have been designed to set up the climactic conflict that is highlighted at the film's end, where Frankenstein's love for his fiancée is shown to be sufficiently powerful to banish the manifestation of his sinful desires from the world. This classic triumph of good over evil is nowhere to be seen at the end of Shelley's novel. While "a high destiny seemed to bear [Victor Frankenstein] on"[26] toward killing the Monster after it murders Elizabeth, Shelley's hapless protagonist ultimately fails in his efforts. The Monster prepares to kill himself at "the extremity of the globe,"[27] after having a somewhat satanic moral epiphany: "[e]vil thenceforth

---

[23] Ibid.
[24] Ibid., 34.
[25] Later in the novel, the Monster draws further attention to this hubristic perspective when he laments, "I am thy creature: I ought to be thy Adam, but I am rather the fallen angel" (Shelley, *Frankenstein*, 73).
[26] Shelley, *Frankenstein*, 167.
[27] Ibid., 178.

became my good."[28] Shelley's account of events is ultimately a highly nihilistic one in which both characters succumb to their sins, and find neither escape, absolution, nor redemption.

Cauldrons, Creation, and Trick Film

Early films—and early horror films in particular—borrowed elements from contemporary sources, including stage magic, spirit photography, hypnotism, and optical toys. As film scholar Murray Leeder has shown, "where its links with the supernatural are concerned, early cinema's place on a lineage of haunted and haunting media is at least as important as its newness."[29] Often inspired by sources as diverse as X-ray exhibitions and Grand Guignol theater, these visuals were assisted by pioneering special-effects techniques derived from a variety of origins, ranging from the scientific and medical to the artistic.

The Monster's creation scene in Edison's *Frankenstein* features impressive special effects that serve to produce a macabre spectacle. After mixing ingredients and dashing them into an enormous cauldron that is shuttered behind closed doors as the process unfolds, Victor Frankenstein excitedly observes the birth of his creature through a small aperture. Iconographic visual elements—features that are commonplace in other early silent horror films—play an important role in this scene. For example, to the left of the frame sits a skeleton. A common feature in laboratories and science classrooms, the ubiquity of skeletons in early "trick" films is nonetheless striking. As Leeder notes: "Even a cursory survey of early cinema finds that filmmakers were positively fascinated by skeletons: they appear frequently in trick films by Walter R. Booth, Edwin S. Porter, Émile Cohl, Segundo de Chomón and others, as well as [Georges] Méliès and [George Albert] Smith."[30]

The Monster takes shape gradually in the cauldron, starting out as a misshapen globule, then forming a skeletal shell, then gradually gaining flesh to take on human form. Here Dawley is clearly highlighting the macabre attraction of such imagery and foregrounding the Edison Studio's pioneering special effects. In the restored version of the film, produced by the Library of Congress, modern coloring techniques complement this atmosphere. For instance, a dark-red tint completes the Hadean aesthetic of the cauldron scene, reinforcing the transgressive nature of the experiment. Even today, one marvels at how these remarkable effects were achieved in 1910. In a clever maneuver, a dummy was set on fire in the Edison Studio and manipulated through puppetry to descend into the cauldron. The footage was then played in reverse to suggest the formation of the Monster, rather than its destruction. Astonished early-twentieth-century film viewers had never seen anything like it (Figure 6.1).

---

[28] Ibid., 176, citing Milton's *Paradise Lost*.
[29] Leeder, *Supernatural*, 3.
[30] Ibid., 137.

Figure 6.1 Frankenstein's Monster emerges from the cauldron.

Méliès's work is perhaps the most relevant referent in this regard. His *Le manoir du diable* (1896) is frequently cited as the first horror film—a debatable claim, given its emphasis on fantastic effects rather than frightening elements. Just as films of this kind provide a showcase for Méliès's special effects, similar tricks involving skeletons, macabre imagery, and black magic are manifest in Edison's version of Frankenstein's cautionary tale. It bears noting that a cauldron also features prominently in *Le manoir du diable*; after the devil produces the vessel out of thin air, he uses it to create a woman (played by Jehanne D'Alcy, Méliès's wife and frequent collaborator). As in *Frankenstein*, the cauldron is miraculously used to produce a human being. In the Edison film, however, the process is corrupted through the personification of malevolence, reflecting the unconscious evil ostensibly lurking in Victor Frankenstein's soul.

Psychological Horror

Psychologists have long explored questions concerning how our behaviors are conditioned by impinging internal and external forces. Although our psychological and emotional states cannot be visualized, they are often reflected in our behaviors, and psychiatric disorders, and are therefore frequently categorized as "invisible" illnesses. Edison's early film can be situated within the broader subgenre of psychological horror—a prominent subgenre that is almost as old as cinema itself—in which interior states are externalized and visualized in a narrative context in order to disturb viewers.[31]

---

[31] German Expressionism heavily incorporated psychological horror. Through its highly distorted set design, it conveyed the terrifying inner lives of characters—focusing on an unsettling, rather than realistic, depiction of space. Prominent examples include *The Golem: How He Came into the*

As with subsequent films in this vein, Frankenstein's split personality—the "good doctor" and the malicious Monster—externalizes his interior conflict. Although what we later understand as quasi-Freudian filmic developments in representing psychological states were not yet in practice, these basic themes were present in this early film. The audience is meant to be frightened by the disheveled and repulsive Monster, and by extension, they are supposed to be unsettled by Victor Frankenstein's "evil thoughts," thoughts that are portrayed *through* the figure of the Monster. Rather than depicting the Monster as an intelligent being capable of autonomous thought, in Dawley's film it is characterized as an extension of Frankenstein's own malevolent soul. In particular, we are presented with a binary, absolutist interpretation of moral psychology in which matrimonial love is pure and wholesome, whereas the desire to create life outside wedded union is immoral and impure.

In the film, where cinematic technique is in an early stage of development, intertitles tell us that "Instead of a perfect human being, the evil in Frankenstein's mind creates a monster," and elsewhere they point to "Frankenstein's better nature asserting itself." But there are no intertitles illustrating Victor Frankenstein's thoughts directly, or his acts of violence that provoke revenge. To cite Fernando Espi Forcen's recent study of psychiatric elements in horror film, where "a person [may be] unable to integrate some immoral or unacceptable behaviours within the self," Victor Frankenstein is able to overcome his transgressions, if not eradicate the evil that lies within.[32]

While Dawley's *Frankenstein* deals with quite simplistic notions of what constitutes good and evil, the central conflict revolves around the idea that Frankenstein's conscious mind is in conflict with his unconscious desires. While Mary Shelley hints at this deeper connection through Frankenstein's guilt,[33] Dawley's *Frankenstein* operates within the context of the technical limitations imposed by the standard "one-reeler" format of early silent film.[34] After all, filmmakers were still experimenting with the cinematic expression of characters' interior states. Later, more sophisticated examples of these strategies include superimpositions to represent dream states, point-of-view shots to connote attention, and zoom effects or camera dollies to suggest disorientation.[35]

World (Paul Wagener and Carl Boese, 1920), *The Cabinet of Dr. Caligari* (Robert Wiene, 1920), and *Nosferatu* (F. W. Murnau, 1922).

[32] Fernando Espi Forcen, *Monsters, Demons, and Psychopaths: Psychiatry in Horror Film* (Boca Raton: CRC Press, 2016), 16–17.

[33] "I felt as if I had committed some great crime, the consciousness of which haunted me" (Shelley, *Frankenstein*, 126).

[34] Until the narrative and aesthetic codes of psychological horror were consolidated, this linking of psychological elements to the invisible—that is, "the covert"—might have motivated this approach by Edison Studios.

[35] Examples of films that use these techniques include *A Trip to the Moon* (Georges Méliès, 1902), *The Lady in the Lake* (Robert Montgomery, 1947), and *Vertigo* (Alfred Hitchcock, 1958) respectively. They can be used sparingly or for the entire duration of a film, and transcend genre frameworks to focus squarely on character subjectivity.

Keyholes and Reflections: The Psychology of *Frankenstein*

In Edison's *Frankenstein*, there is a noteworthy self-reflexive element in the film's depiction of Frankenstein's observation of the Monster's creation. Literary scholar Elizabeth Young argues that the viewing aperture he uses "simultaneously symbolizes the lens of a camera and the hole through which such images, after the development of projection technology in the 1910s, were projected onto a screen,"[36] thereby connecting Frankenstein's voyeurism with contemporary cinematic apparatuses of production and exhibition. From a psychological perspective, Young observes that the viewing hole is also "a two-way aperture into Frankenstein—a window into his psyche as well as an orifice through which he himself peers."[37] This is supported not only by the conflict between Frankenstein's conscious and unconscious desires but also by the moral conflict between the forces of good and evil *in his mind*, around which the film revolves. The intertitles make this explicit, but through these shots, it is as if we see the evil in Frankenstein's psyche—formally represented by the hellish inferno in the cauldron—cooking the Monster into being. And Frankenstein is positioned as the ideal spectator, awestruck by the spectacle of the creation of his Monster.[38]

Frankenstein's observation of the Monster's creation also contains elements of voyeuristic scopophilia, as described contemporaneously by Sigmund Freud in *Three Essays on the Theory of Sexuality* (1905).[39] While he does not appear to receive sexual gratification from witnessing the drama that unfolds in the cauldron, Victor's melodramatic reactions to the scene—coupled with the Monster's incapacity to comprehend that he is being watched—suggest a sordid pleasure derived from observing the scene in secrecy, while the observed subject is unaware of the observer. Art theorists Thomas Patin and Jennifer McLerran note that Freud's description of scopophilia involves "regarding others as objects and making them the SUBJECT of a controlling GAZE,"[40] and Frankenstein's position of power as creator, over that of the Monster, as creation, is characteristic in this regard. Prior to his formation, the Monster is literally a collection of inanimate elements; it is only when he is animated, and assumes physical and cognitive agency, that Frankenstein's scopophilic power over his creation is lost.

In her seminal essay of 1988, Laura Mulvey explores how power relations—through the scopophilic vehicle of cinema—are structured such that a dominant "male gaze" controls the visual pleasure of film. The closing scene where Frankenstein sees the

---

[36] Elizabeth Young, *Black Frankenstein: The Making of an American Metaphor* (New York and London: New York University Press, 2008), 165.
[37] Ibid., 166.
[38] This sequence was extensively advertised as a "photographic marvel" (as in Chalmers Publishing Company, "Moving Picture World" (January–June 1910)," 436).
[39] Although Frankenstein's pleasure in looking is not associated with genitals, or an exhibitionist subject, it is "connected with the overriding of disgust (as in the case of voyeurs. . .)" (Freud, 157). Transgressive pride in his work supersedes any trepidation he would have about watching the creation unfold.
[40] Jennifer McLerran and Thomas Patin, *Artwords: A Glossary of Contemporary Art Theory* (Westport: Greenwood Press, 1997), 119.

Monster in the mirror, rather than his own reflection, is also of significance here. Mulvey suggests that "male movie star's glamorous characteristics are thus not those of the erotic object of the gaze, but those of the more perfect, more complete, more powerful ideal ego conceived in the original moment of recognition in front of the mirror."[41] This sequence is an inversion of the phenomenon Mulvey describes, as Frankenstein sees a reflection of his darkest characteristics, or his most imperfect self—a persona that is ostensibly overcome and healed by the purity of true love. Rather than recognizing his "more powerful ideal ego" in a beautiful reflection of self, Frankenstein is finally confronted by the flawed manifestation of his Id, which is deemed tamed (at least in the film version), and ultimately less powerful than the bond he shares with Elizabeth.

Through its use of mirrors, Edison's *Frankenstein* deals with the psychologically fractured self by framing Victor Frankenstein and the Monster as one and the same. As I have suggested, the Monster is an extension of Frankenstein's worst impulses; his "evil thoughts" represent his Freudian Id—the locus of immediate gratification and instinct. In Shelley's novel, Victor Frankenstein informs the reader that his "father had taken the greatest precautions that my mind should be impressed with no supernatural horrors"[42] (i.e., unnatural curiosities about life and death). He further notes that "human being in perfection ought always to preserve a calm and peaceful mind, and never . . . allow passion or a transitory desire to disturb his tranquillity."[43] While this could be seen as an overestimation of the extent to which individual agency can exert control over one's mental health, it also points to Frankenstein's "transitory desires" surrounding the supernatural, which haunt his thoughts throughout the rest of the novel.

Following the creation scene, the Monster emerges from the laboratory and stalks Frankenstein through his apartment. When Frankenstein falls exhausted onto his bed the Monster emerges from behind black drapes. The haunted Frankenstein then departs for the comfort of his bourgeois home, and that of his fiancée, Elizabeth. However, Frankenstein's blissful domesticity does not last long, as the intertitles tell us that "[h]aunting his creator and jealous of his sweetheart, for the first time the [M]onster sees himself." Inextricably tied to Frankenstein, the Monster conceives of himself as his creator's shadow—he covets everything his creator has and does, desiring the comfortable life for which he has been abandoned. As Frankenstein is reading in a parlor, situated left-of-frame in a medium-long shot, the Monster enters through a floor-standing mirror right-of-frame. As he harasses his creator, their interaction is reflected in the mirror, and we are constantly made aware of the mirror's Freudian doubling effect (Figure 6.2).

Elizabeth enters but is quickly ushered away by Frankenstein before she is able to see the hideous Monster, who has by now concealed himself. Frankenstein and the Monster then struggle briefly in front of the mirror, until the latter is suddenly confronted by his own reflection. He recoils in disgust, as if conditioned to abhor

---

[41] Laura Mulvey, "Visual Pleasure and Narrative Cinema," in *Feminism and Film Theory*, edited by Constance Penley (London and New York: Routledge, 1988), 63.
[42] Shelley, *Frankenstein*, 32.
[43] Ibid., 36.

Figure 6.2 Frankenstein's Monster terrifies its creator in the parlor.

his own hideousness; monstrous malevolence recognizes itself as such, rather than rejoicing in its wickedness. This aspect of the morality tale is reinforced by the intertitles' description of "Frankenstein's better nature asserting itself" on the wedding night. This sets the stage for a final confrontation following a brief chase scene in the parlor of Victor Frankenstein's home, when the Monster again confronts his own image in the mirror, and disappears *into it*—now appearing only as a reflection. For a few striking seconds, Victor Frankenstein sees only the Monster as he stares at the mirror. Eventually the Monster gradually fades and disappears into the mirror, leaving only Frankenstein's own reflection; he touches the glass in astonishment, as if to confirm that the Monster is truly gone. As he celebrates with Elizabeth, the film's closing scene appears to be a joyful one. But those terrifying seconds when Frankenstein confronts the mirror suggest that the Monster will always live within his psyche.

Musical Cue Sheets

All things considered, whether or not Edison's *Frankenstein* should be characterized as a silent film is contestable. It is "silent" only in the sense that there is no dialog or diegetic sound, but its accompanying musical cue sheets reference well-known opera excerpts and songs of the period, and the film's restorations have featured original scores.[44] James Wierzbicki discusses the film's original musical cue sheets,[45] which included several pieces from Carl Maria von Weber's 1821 opera *Der Freischütz* (The Marksman), possibly including the famous "Wolf's Glen" sequence, described by nineteenth-century American music critic Gustav Kobbé as "the most expressive rendering of the gruesome that is to be found in a musical score."[46] The cue sheets also mix "classical fragments with morsels in varied lighter styles . . . [including] a sentimental salon piece and an old-fashioned parlour song,"[47] balancing music that elicits the horrific with tender melodies, and cues that suggest the gentrified society to which Victor Frankenstein belongs. This intertextual borrowing of music evinces an awareness of how specific selections could impact the emotional response of the viewer, while simultaneously complementing elements of the narrative and mise-en-scène. Moreover, using arrangements from operas such as von Weber's *Der Freischütz* and Wagner's *Lohengrin* might have lent an air of cultural legitimacy to the cinema, which was still broadly recognized as a popular amusement rather than respectable art.

The musical cue sheets help us understand the intended dramatic function of each scene by suggesting the ideal mood the chosen music was intended to elicit. They also demonstrate the early role that the Edison Manufacturing Company played in film exhibition, including anticipating audience reaction to the content of their films, as well as the control that sponsoring organizations exerted over some of the creative aspects of the production, including musical accompaniment.

Conclusions

Overshadowed by James Whale's 1931 classic and subsequent film renderings of Shelley's tale, Edison's *Frankenstein* remains a hidden gem of American silent horror. It exemplifies the era's one-reeler standard, as well as the then-current fashion of adapting classic literature for highly abbreviated filmic presentation. Although its stylistic qualities are customary for the era—including the use of distant framing, frontal staging, studio sets, and theatrical acting—its special effects were highly innovative. Indeed, the Monster's creation scene is advertised in *Moving Picture World* as "possibly the most remarkable ever committed to a film,"[48] and a "photographic marvel."[49]

---

[44] Rick Altman argues that "scholars have for years pursued their arguments in favor of cinema's visual nature," yet it is crucial to interrogate the ways in which contemporary audiences would have *listened* to a film such as this. Altman, *Silent Film Sound*, 6.
[45] James Wierzbicki, *Film Music: A History* (New York: Routledge, 2009), 38.
[46] Gustav Kobbé, *The New Kobbé's Opera Book*, ed. The Earl of Harewood and Antony Peattie (New York: G.P. Putnam's Sons, 1997), 958.
[47] Martin Marks, "Music and the Silent Film," in *The Oxford History of World Cinema*, ed. Geoffrey Nowell-Smith (Oxford: Oxford University Press, 1996), 186.
[48] Chalmers Publishing Company, "Moving Picture World," 428.
[49] Ibid., 436.

But what makes *Frankenstein* counterintuitive in the context of horror cinema is its lack of "overtly" horrific elements or "repulsive situations," a general orientation of the film that is emphasized in industry publications and company ads. Edison Studios issued some important publicity materials in conjunction with the film, revealing that they opted to focus on "mystical and psychological problems,"[50] rather than "repulsive" scenes and situations. This wording may also have been influenced by Edison's effort to frame European films as decadent, in contrast with the ostensibly more wholesome American fare his studio was offering, as US "moving pictures increasingly became inscribed within the rhetoric of moral reform or uplift," in Richard Abel's analysis.[51]

Filmgoers may have nonetheless recoiled in disgust at the appearance and actions of the Monster. For Dawley and Edison, however, it is clear that a conscious elimination of gruesome and bleak content in favor of the "vivid presentation" of "the force of true love" were guiding principles.[52] Rather than depicting the more violent aspects of Shelley's story on the screen—including Elizabeth's murder, the implied suicide of the Monster, and the death of Victor Frankenstein in the desolate Arctic—the film concludes with a cheerful ending and stylish trick-film vanishing effects: Frankenstein and Elizabeth are blissfully married, and the Monster magically disappears into the mirror.

Psychology and theology are other domains that the film seeks to emphasize, given the extent to which it focuses on the mental state of its characters, and on Victor Frankenstein's blasphemous hubris. As the intertitles underline at the outset, "the evil in Frankenstein's mind" is responsible for creating the Monster, and in the final scenes, "the creation of an evil mind is overcome by true love and disappears." While this is a facile moralistic play on Victor Frankenstein's psychiatric state, it ostensibly argues that good and evil have simultaneously impacted the behavior of the protagonist. Frankenstein wants to cure the world of disease, but his transgressive desire to generate life corrupts the process, resulting in the creation of a misshapen monster rather than his imagined "perfect human being." Put differently, Frankenstein's conscious efforts are undermined by his unconscious wickedness, all of which can be interpreted through the Freudian psychical schema of the Id, Ego, and Super-ego, as we have seen. While this may not fit neatly into traditional moral or ethical philosophy, if one's drives and instincts can be associated with unconscious desires, then the malevolence in Frankenstein's mind that creates the Monster can be thought to spring from the instincts of his Id. Essentially, Frankenstein's hubris and immoral desire to create life override his conscience—or Super-ego—resulting in the failure of his Ego to balance his purer intentions and darker impulses.

Whether or not Edison's Frankenstein should even be characterized as a horror film is debatable. *Frankenstein* has had such an indelible impact on popular culture—especially through the Monster—that its association with horror tropes and iconography

---

[50] *Edison Kinetogram*, "Frankenstein (Dramatic)."
[51] Richard Abel, *The Red Rooster Scare: Making Cinema American, 1900-1910* (Berkeley and Los Angeles: University of California Press, 1999), 101.
[52] Chalmers Publishing Company, "Moving Picture World," 392.

is impossible to deny. At the time, however, effort was made to avoid the horror label, so much so that *Moving Picture World* explicitly stated that the filmmakers proactively avoided any scenes or dramatic situations that could be construed as "repulsive" or horrifying. But horror involves a deeper affective character that such advertising blurbs gloss over. While gruesome content or morally suspect subject matter may have been avoided, if the spectator is in any way disposed to react to the creation of the monster as the protagonist does, Frankenstein's abject horror at the sight of his creation may have been experienced by the audience as well.

Notably, the genres the Library of Congress lists on the film's online profile include mad scientist, monster, horror, silent, short, and fiction. The list of subjects the Library provides include experiments, good and evil, and science.[53] While these lists may provide convenient labels for organizing their collection, they foreground the methods we use to categorize films according to narrative and stylistic elements. The keywords "Mad scientist," "Monster," and "Horror" suggest the building blocks of a horror narrative that Noël Carroll would call the "over-reacher plot," one that "criticizes science's will to knowledge" and is concerned with forbidden knowledge of "either the scientific or magical sort," and with the punishment of hapless characters whose hubris compels transgressive actions.[54] In Edison's version, "the evil in Frankenstein's mind" is separate from his conscious efforts but nonetheless qualifies him as archetypical in this sense. Frankenstein is clearly conducting scientific experiments as befits the "Mad scientist" category, but as we have seen, this is intertwined with an interest in alchemy and natural philosophy. The degree to which a "good and evil" plot is emphasized is especially telling in this version of Frankenstein. Victor Frankenstein's prideful overreaching results in the creation of the Monster, yet it is eventually through love, manifest in Frankenstein's feelings for his fiancée, that the Monster is banished from the world. Curiously, these simple keywords indicate a complex interplay between the generic and moralistic conventions that make silent horror cinema—and *Frankenstein* specifically—so singular.

To claim that Mary Shelley's novel contained content that challenged contemporaneous moral standards is to understate the case. In this sense, Shelley is powerfully inspired by the work of her anarchist father William Goodwin, her proto-feminist mother Mary Wollstonecraft, and her celebrated husband Percy Bysshe Shelley (his 1816–18 essay "Speculations on Morals," for example). The novel's disturbing narrative involves violent actions, including murder, and it articulates a deeper concern with the power of creation in a way that would be viewed as blasphemous to many, both in Shelley's time and in Edison's. *Frankenstein*'s story raised new questions about the need to omit or adapt material for mass public consumption. This is not the first such instance, but it is certainly a high-profile case, given the amount of extant corroborating materials that exist. The film is inextricably linked with the early-twentieth-century fascination with mystical metaphysics, which it overtly substitutes

---

[53] "*Frankenstein*," Library of Congress, available online: https://www.loc.gov/item/2017600664/.
[54] Noël Carroll, *The Philosophy of Horror; or, Paradoxes of the Heart* (New York and London: Routledge, 2004), 118.

for horrific material. Furthermore, its depiction of monstrosity conflates physical and moral grotesqueries, given the Monster's creation through Frankenstein's wicked unconscious, and argues that it is subordinate to the affective power of matrimonial love. This curious blend of the modern and the medieval may also relate to the tension in Frankenstein's mind from the start of the film, between his better nature and the evil that compels him to create life.

7

Frankenstein's Organ Transplant

Adaptation in Afro-Futurist and Electronic Dance Musics

Mark A. McCutcheon

Exploring how Mary Shelley's *Frankenstein* is adapted in Afro-Futurist music and electronic dance music (EDM) opens new possibilities for adaptation studies, and forms a case in my larger study of how *Frankenstein*, technology, McLuhan, and Canadian popular culture relate to one another in history and culture. As I argue in that study, *The Medium Is the Monster: Canadian Adaptations of Frankenstein and the Discourse of Technology* (from which this chapter is adapted), *Frankenstein* shaped the modern meaning of the word *technology* as manufactured monstrosity, and Canadian adaptations of *Frankenstein*—many of which also adapt Marshall McLuhan's work—have popularized and disseminated this monstrous sense of technology. Adaptations of *Frankenstein* and McLuhan—together—are numerous enough to form a distinctive tradition in Canadian pop culture. If *Frankenstein* shaped technology's modern meaning, then McLuhan's *Frankenpheme of technology*, as I term it, and Canadian adaptations of *Frankenstein* and McLuhan together have popularized this meaning of technology as manufactured monstrosity. I want to outline two premises of that larger argument about Frankenstein and technology, in order to explain how my approach to adaptation studies challenges some key premises of the field, toward building its capacity. These premises suggest an approach to adaptation studies that is sufficiently expansive, and materially oriented, to address the vast cultural diffusion of a text like *Frankenstein*.

Premise One: Refocusing Adaptation Studies

Adaptation studies is a field where literary, media, and cultural studies intersect, and first emerged to investigate the negotiations and appropriations of literature by film. Conditioned by that originating focus, adaptation studies have tended to privilege extensive, acknowledged, and narrative adaptations, at the expense of shorter, allusive, ephemeral, and lyrical adaptations—although the field also shows greater diversification.

Some of the most productive recent work in adaptation studies has focused on specific authors. *Adaptations of Shakespeare*, a critical anthology of dramatic adaptations of Shakespeare's plays, offers one of the most expansive working theories of adaptation, as "almost any act of alteration performed upon specific cultural works."[1] Taking stock of the overall character of adaptation practice in the context of *Frankenstein*'s proliferating multimedia progeny, Pedro Javier Pardo García suggests the term "cultural intertextuality" to better capture the breadth of citational, generic, discursive, and dialogic practices of interpretation, selection, and recombination that go into adaptation, especially postmodern adaptations like Kenneth Branagh's *Mary Shelley's Frankenstein* (1994): "it is not just that the film perfectly exemplifies the concept," García writes, "but also that its representation of the creature turns it into a walking metaphor of cultural intertextuality."[2] García further acknowledges that the figurative suitability of the text and its main character for commenting on textual production and adaptation—their "perfect correspondence of matter and form"[3]—is something of a commonplace in *Frankenstein* criticism. García's thoughts on adaptation differ from Linda Hutcheon, who argues for "a more restricted . . . definition of adaptation"[4] than that of Fischlin and Fortier, which she cites as indicative of the field's overall current approach. Concerned that such a theory is too vast for critical practice, Hutcheon defines adaptation as both a *product*—an acknowledged, extensive, and specific transcoding of a narrative text—and as a *process*, an engagement—whether knowing or unknowing—with different modes of textual and intertextual telling (e.g., print), showing (e.g., film), or interaction (e.g., video games). Of the adaptor, this process requires creative interpretation; for the audience, it entails "palimpsestic intertextual" engagement.[5] By covering a wide range of forms and media, Hutcheon's theory breaks with the field's tradition; but her theory also reinforces tradition in its orientation to story as the field's "common denominator."[6]

To theorize adaptation studies more expansively, then, is to expand the application of the field's interpretive tools for critiquing varied, divergent, and intersecting orders of discourse and media forms. Adaptation theory's emphasis on story explicitly excludes a wealth of other cultural modes and forms—like music—that warrant consideration as adaptations. Hutcheon specifically excludes "musical sampling" from her theory, on the basis that it "would not qualify as extended engagement."[7] Hutcheon does discuss several music examples throughout the book and details one specific case

---

[1] Daniel Fischlin and Mark Fortier, eds., *Adaptations of Shakespeare: A Critical Anthology of Plays from the Seventeenth Century to the Present* (New York: Routledge, 2000), 4.
[2] Pedro Javier Pardo García, "Beyond Adaptation: Frankenstein's Postmodern Progeny," in *Books in Motion: Adaptation, Intertextuality, Authorship*, ed. Mireia Aragay (Amsterdam: Rodopi, 2005), 240.
[3] Ibid.
[4] Linda Hutcheon, *A Theory of Adaptation* (New York: Routledge, 2006), 9.
[5] Ibid., 22.
[6] Ibid., 10.
[7] Ibid., 9.

of musical scoring, but most of these examples are taken from musical theater and opera.[8] Songs and other musical productions that adapt various texts and media forms remain unaddressed and omitted. But allusive references and condensed adaptations also warrant and reward critical attention (see Baldick, 1987), whether they are pop songs that sample audio from *Frankenstein* films, or even just develop instrumentation traditions that evoke *Frankenstein*.

The present study builds, in particular, on Timothy Morton's idea of "Frankenphemes" (i.e., *Frankenstein* memes) and Christopher Baldick's theory of *Frankenstein*'s modern myth, as well as García's argument for expanding the scope and vocabulary of *Frankenstein* adaptation studies.[9] In his 1987 book *In Frankenstein's Shadow: Myth, Monstrosity, and Nineteenth-Century Writing*, Baldick theorizes *Frankenstein* as a modern myth and thus as a paradox: a text that is at once modern, a critique of modernity, and a "household name" imbued with mythic symbolism.[10] He argues that Frankenstein has achieved this modern mythic status via reductive reproductions of its basic "skeleton story," comprising two pivotal plot points. First, the good doctor makes a living creature out of bits of corpses, and second, this creature turns on him and runs amok.[11] Baldick then shows how this skeleton story gets fleshed out through two main lines of popular interpretation, one of which is the "technological reduction" of the story as "an uncanny prophecy of dangerous scientific inventions."[12] Moreover, while these reductive popularizations constitute practices of creative adaptation, they also represent strategies of interpretive closure, as illustrated by the fixing of the Creature's image in Boris Karloff's iconic 1931 film portrayal.[13]

Baldick argues that the Frankenstein myth manifests itself materially in all the "adaptations, allusions, accretions, analogues, parodies, and plain misreadings which follow upon Mary Shelley's novel."[14] The inclusion of allusions is significant here. Baldick's analysis of *Frankenstein*'s legible impact on nineteenth-century writing and rhetoric is preoccupied with what Hutcheon calls "palimpsestic intertextuality"; that is, the layering and modulation of textual referents and their sometimes recognized, sometimes latent links with one another that produce, in audiences, "intertextual expectations about medium and genre, as well as about specific work."[15] But while Hutcheon reserves these "multilaminated" receptions for extensive, acknowledged adaptations,[16] Baldick excavates some of this specific work's more ephemeral and esoteric reworkings. As Baldick argues, the "kind of connection" found in tracking such a widely popular text as *Frankenstein* is not always "one between a given writer

---

[8] Ibid., 90–3.
[9] García, "Beyond Adaptation."
[10] Chris Baldick, *In Frankenstein's Shadow: Myth, Monstrosity, and Nineteenth-Century Writing* (Oxford: Clarendon Press, 1987), 1.
[11] Ibid., 3.
[12] Ibid., 7.
[13] Ibid., 5.
[14] Ibid., 4.
[15] Hutcheon, *A Theory of Adaptation*, 22.
[16] Ibid., 21.

and a literary 'source,'" but more often a Foucauldian genealogy of "subterranean and invisible diffusion in the cultures which adopt them."[17]

The "subterranean" circulation of *Frankenstein*'s central characters and "skeleton story" in adaptations thus finds an apt encapsulation in Morton's concept of "Frankenphemes": "those elements of culture that are derived from *Frankenstein*, but that are less than a work of art in completion or scale ... an idea derived from Shelley's novel ... repeated in another medium."[18] Morton's examples of "Frankenphemes" include TV commercials, movie scenes, and allusive portmanteaus like "Frankenfoods," which emerged to frame debates over genetically modified organisms (GMOs) in agribusiness.[19] The coinage encapsulates the intertextual practices of condensation and encoding that so widely disperse *Frankenstein*'s modern myth in allusions, quotations, and other miscellaneous ephemera throughout popular culture.

Popular music resounds with adaptation practices, in ways that warrant refocusing a theory of adaptation to account for nonnarrative, nonvisual, and nonextensive adaptations, and to rethink what can count and be studied as adaptation. I explore music adaptations partly because the vocabulary of sound processes and music recording supplies a peculiarly useful terminology for analyzing adaptations, especially less extensive, more citational, and differently interactive adaptations. *Modulation* and *variation* (as in a variation on a theme) are terms that capture the sense of repetition with difference that Hutcheon sees as crucial to adaptations; as with several of the terms suggested here, Hutcheon uses the term *variation* in her own arguments.[20] *Sampling* and *remixing*, borrowed from the parlance of DJ-based music-making, can describe brief, ephemeral, and more meme-like adaptations, and formal rearrangements and recontextualizations, respectively. And *amplification* is a useful way to describe how a meme like a Frankenpheme can "catch on" and reproduce both its forms and its cultural functions (Hutcheon[21] also uses this term in this way).

Neither expanding the vocabulary for adaptation studies nor tracking the "subterranean" diffusions of adaptation means diluting the principle of adaptation. The notion of orders or degrees of adaptation represents a way to uphold and extend Hutcheon's stipulation that adaptations be defined in relation to specific texts, in order for analysis to stay grounded in concrete contexts.[22] Another means to keep the analysis grounded in concrete textual details and historical, material contexts is to itemize some of the common, even cliché, images, tropes, and plot points that mark specific texts as Frankensteinian, or specific textual elements or fragments as "Frankenphemes." Common figures or characters among these adaptations include "mad scientists" of all kinds; grotesquely assembled, "patchwork," or corporate subjects; and mechanical or otherwise manufactured monsters—artificial intelligences, genetically engineered

---

[17] Baldick, *In Frankenstein's Shadow*, 9.
[18] Timothy Morton, *Mary Shelley's* Frankenstein: *A Sourcebook* (London: Routledge, 2002), 47–8.
[19] Ibid., 48.
[20] Hutcheon, *A Theory of Adaptation*, 35, 86.
[21] Ibid., 3.
[22] Ibid., 21.

organisms, rebellious robots, cyborgs, clones, and other such technological doppelgängers. Common plot elements are those that reproduce or vary the reduced "skeleton story" of the novel: stories of technological backfire; robots in revolt; resurrections gone awry; uncontrollable experiments; human-made catastrophes of science and technology; and the awakening to self-awareness of machines. Common images and tropes include unethical R&D, human-induced apocalypse, motifs of Faustian bargains for forbidden knowledge, and recursive reflections on the text's own composition or facticity—especially acknowledgments of composition as collage, "mongrel," or otherwise synthesizing or appropriative; and images or evocations of the technological sublime;[23] that is, representations of technological prowess that test or defy the limits of representation. Genre conventions may also be worth considering: epistolary, gothic, or science fiction modes; unreliable narration; or regressive framing devices, stories embedded within stories. References or allusions to *Frankenstein* or other adaptations are also significant textual elements of adaptation, even when they are used sparingly or in passing.

To be read together with these formal, textual criteria are a number of contextual criteria, aspects of the cultural and economic conditions of production that inform or augment a given text's adaptation strategies. Criteria like these include production modes marked by ambivalence over technology; globally oriented scenes or conditions of production; forms that privilege special effects above other production values; and postmodernist approaches that use and thematize pastiche, or otherwise comment on their own production processes, especially with self-reflexive reference to technology.

Premise Two: *Frankenstein* in Afro-Futurism

While *Frankenstein* adaptations occur in many kinds of popular music, Afro-Futurist music, like funk and rap, and dance music forms based in Afro-Futurism, like house and techno, represent especially resonant reworkings of *Frankenstein*'s gothic theme and its intertextual form.

As theorized by Kodwo Eshun[24] and John Corbett,[25] among others, Afro-Futurism is a Black diasporic music tradition of appropriating science fiction forms, and principles of technological experiment, in Black diasporic cultural production. For example, we find science fiction tropes and experimental appropriations of technology in Black Atlantic music from Sun Ra's jazz to George Clinton's P-Funk, from Lee Perry's Black Ark studio to turntablism and techno. But Afro-Futurism is also a theory—a critique of racist ontology, especially in the music industry,[26] and a challenge to essentialist

---

[23] David Nye, *American Technological Sublime* (Cambridge, MA: MIT Press, 1994).
[24] Kodwo Eshun, *More Brilliant than the Sun: Adventures in Sonic Fiction* (London: Quartet Books, 1998).
[25] John Corbett, *Extended Play: Sounding Off from John Cage to Dr. Funkenstein* (Durham: Duke University Press, 1994).
[26] Ibid.

ideas of Black identity, an avant-garde cultural practice of liberation, counter-memory, and transfiguration.[27] For Corbett, the jazz band leader Sun Ra, the dub-reggae pioneer Lee "Scratch" Perry, and George Clinton of Parliament and Funkadelic fame are three exemplary Afro-Futurist artists who establish and embody the Afro-Futurist tradition in productions and performative personae that articulate a distinctively Frankensteinian "space madness." These artists' music articulates a science fiction aesthetic while their personae represent a marginal and self-consciously monstrous relationship to the mainstream music industry. This "space madness" tradition has been revamped recently by Janelle Monáe, in albums from *The ArchAndroid* (2010) to *Dirty Computer* (2018), which reimagine the African American experience in the imagery of androids and artificial intelligence—together with imagery of auction blocks and segregation. Science fiction turned sonic fiction.

These kinds of music resonate with *Frankenstein*'s constitutive intertextuality in their technical basis in sampling and sequencing. They also resonate with *Frankenstein*'s uncanny gothic thematics in what Simon Reynolds calls their "techno-romantic" scenes of performance. In such scenes, DJs, producers, and dancers alike all take part in practices of high technology and hedonistic excess, experimenting on crowds—and on themselves—like mad scientists.[28] Additionally, DJs and performers exploit playback and production technologies to blur the lines between recording and "liveness,"[29] thus conjuring the technological sublime, the apprehension of ghosts in the machines.[30]

Frankenstein's Organ Transplant

To put these terms to work, and to suggest the interpretive possibilities of nonextensive "Frankenpheme" adaptation, let's consider a specific pattern of this kind of adaptation at work in postmodern Afro-Futurist music. This pattern, in brief, consists of combining Frankensteinian imagery with organ instrumentation in Afro-Futurist music-making, and we hear it in songs like Byron Lee and the Dragonaires' 1964 ska tune "Frankenstein Ska"; in Parliament's album *The Clones of Dr. Funkenstein* (1976); in Michael Jackson's 1984 single "Thriller"; and in the extended "Power" mix of Canadian rap artist Maestro Fresh Wes's single "Let Your Backbone Slide" (1989). In such Afro-Futurist music texts spanning genres and decades, we hear specific combinations of Frankensteinian imagery and organ instrumentation. This diasporic pattern of musical combinations prompts two questions that warrant preliminary consideration as a means

---

[27] Paul Gilroy, *The Black Atlantic: Modernity and Double Consciousness* (Cambridge, MA: Harvard University Press, 1993).
[28] Simon Reynolds, "Ecstasy is a Science: Techno-Romanticism," in *Stars Don't Stand Still in the Sky: Music and Myth*, ed. Karen Kelly and Evelyn McDonell (New York: New York University Press, 1999), 204.
[29] Philip Auslander, *Liveness: Performance in a Mediatized Culture* (London: Routledge, 1999).
[30] Dale Chapman, "Hermeneutics of Suspicion: Paranoia and the Technological Sublime in Drum and Bass Music," *Echo* 5, no. 2 (Fall 2002): 1–18.

to contextualize the subsequent, more detailed discussion of the aforementioned Afro-Futurist music texts that follows: First, how has the organ become such a formulaic and familiar trope of musical metonymy for *Frankenstein*? Second, what might be the cultural functions of this metonymy for Afro-Futurist music?

To address the first question: Steven E. Forry's *Hideous Progenies*[31] looks at performance adaptations of *Frankenstein* since Richard Brinsley Peake's 1823 play *Presumption*. In the process, he identifies a number of popular adaptation strategies established by that play, and later made ubiquitous by its successors; for example, the recasting of Shelley's articulate and well-read creature as a mute, raging monster. Relevant for our purposes are two adaptation strategies in particular: the identification of Frankenstein's Monster with its creator and the trope of the monster's reaction to music.

The identification of the monster with its maker results from the long-standing application of the latter's name to the former, and so references to the monster itself as "Frankenstein" persist in popular culture to this day. For instance, take this rap from Kool Keith, in his "Dr. Octagon" alter ego: "I'm strictly monster, with turtlenecks like Frankenstein."[32] Developing the story's doppelgänger theme in a different, but related, direction, stage and screen adaptations of *Frankenstein* have also consistently identified the unnatural monster with its supernatural counterpart, the vampire; this identification also derives from the famous primal scene of the novel's inception at the Villa Diodati in 1816, when Shelley started her story while John Polidori composed "The Vampyre."[33] In early adaptations, the identification of man-made monster and vampire took place in paired presentations of *Frankenstein* and vampire plays, and in literary works that referred to multiple monsters, in a way that Hollywood has made formulaic in "monster mash" films from *Frankenstein Meets the Wolf Man* (1943) to *Van Helsing* (2004). In early film adaptations, this identification assumed a more industrial than intertextual character: in Universal's *Frankenstein* and *Dracula* franchises of the 1930s and 1940s, actors Boris Karloff and Bela Lugosi became virtually interchangeable by performing similar monster and mad doctor characters among different films. For the 1931 *Frankenstein* film, Lugosi had been considered first for the monster's role that Boris Karloff would make famous. Lugosi, who played the eponymous vampire in *Dracula* (1931), appeared in *Frankenstein* sequels as Dr. Frankenstein's assistant, Ygor, and in *Frankenstein Meets the Wolf Man* (1943) he played the Frankenstein Monster. Similarly, Christopher Lee played the roles of Frankenstein's Monster *and* Dracula for the Hammer horror films of the 1950s and 1960s. To refer to this process of "iconic identification" and "conflation" between Frankenstein and Dracula, especially as dramatized in the careers of Karloff and Lugosi, I'd like to suggest the portmanteau *iconflation*. The processes of icon production, identification, and conflation that this coinage links have significance not just for understanding the popular cultural history of *Frankenstein* but for understanding the function of organ music in this history.

---

[31] Steven E. Forry, *Hideous Progenies: Dramatizations of Frankenstein from Mary Shelley to the Present* (Philadelphia: University of Pennsylvania Press, 1990).
[32] Kool Keith (aka Dr. Octagon), *Dr. Octagonecologyst*. DRMD-50021. Dreamworks, 1997.
[33] Forry, *Hideous Progenies*, 90.

Iconflation becomes a significant component of the musical metonymy in question here.

The iconflation of Karloff's creature and Lugosi's vampire is reproduced in Universal's franchise of Edgar Allan Poe adaptations, where it becomes connected with the trope of the monster's reaction to music. The Universal *Frankenstein* and *Dracula* film soundtracks do not feature any organ music to develop its metonymic association with horror generally and *Frankenstein* specifically. *Bride of Frankenstein* (1935) includes a gospel-style organ arrangement in the scene where the monster meets the blind hermit, but it augments the hermit's ability to soothe the monster's proverbially savage breast with his own violin playing. While this scene of the sublimation of the creature's rage by music was established by the earliest adaptations,[34] it is the opposite of what I'm investigating: the use of organ music to amplify horror in general, and Frankensteinian monstrosity more specifically. As it happens, it's in other period films that the metonymic association of organ music and gothic horror emerges. In Universal's screen versions of Edgar Allan Poe's *The Black Cat* (1934) and *The Raven* (1935), Karloff and Lugosi, respectively, play mad doctors who also play Bach's *Toccata and Fugue in D Minor* on the organ. Paramount's 1931 film *Dr. Jekyll and Mr. Hyde* also sits its mad doctor at the organ to play this music. The diegetic use of Bach's *Toccata and Fugue* in films like these has contributed greatly to the popular cultural association of organ music with gothic and horror narratives. There's an earlier source for this association: Universal's 1925 silent film *The Phantom of the Opera*. The scene in *Phantom* where the heroine unmasks Erik as he plays the organ was a sensation with audiences, and the film's popularity suggested to Universal and other studios the potential market for gothic and horror films, like *The Black Cat* (1934), *The Walking Dead* (1936), and *Return of the Vampire* (1943). It is decidedly ironic, of course, that this *silent* film should contribute so significantly to the metonymic link between organ music and gothic horror.

Between these interwar film uses of organ music, especially Bach's *Toccata and Fugue*, and the postwar Afro-Futurist uses of organ music in records that refer to *Frankenstein*, horrific and humorous Frankenstein figures proliferate throughout American popular culture. For one popular postwar film example: *The Rocky Horror Picture Show* (1975) includes a scene where Riff-Raff teases the creature Rocky; quoting a similar scene from the 1931 *Frankenstein* film, this scene in *Rocky Horror* accompanies its action with organ music. For an Afro-Futurist film example: the opening and closing credits of the 1973 film *Blackenstein* prominently feature organ arrangements.

This brings me to the second question, about the cultural function of this music metonymy for Afro-Futurism, and the aforementioned Afro-Futurist music productions that iconflate *Frankenstein* references together with organ instrumentation. First, the pianist Thelonious Monk created a series of remarkable jazz compositions built around his singularly angular phrasing, highlighted by unusual intervals, dissonance, and displaced notes. Among fellow jazz artists, Monk's musical language was sometimes

---

[34] Ibid., 22.

known as "zombie-music." Pianist Mary Lou Williams explains: "Why 'zombie music'? Because the screwy chords reminded us of music from *Frankenstein* or any horror film."[35] As David McNally observes in his study of zombie and vampire images as responses to global capital, Monk's "'screwy chords' express the rhythms of a world out of joint, a space of reification in which people are reduced to things.... We hear not only the jarring sounds of things coming to life; more than this, we hear the rhythms of zombie-movement, the ferocious sounds of the dance of the living dead."[36] As McNally and music critics like Eshun have discussed, the avant-gardism, alienation effects, and oppositional character of Monk's music—like that of Ra, Perry, and Clinton—have refracted and extended throughout contemporary Black diasporic music, "in genres as diverse as hip-hop and Afrobeat."[37] For example, Kool Keith's "Wild and Crazy" (1997) uses a "zombie-music" piano chord as the downbeat, in a song that names Frankenstein ("Frankenstein's still standing here"), a song whose chorus overlays the dissonant downbeat with *Psycho*-soundtrack high-pitched strings, as the singer croons, "The moon is out / Tonight it's time for experiments." Like Sun Ra before him and rap artists after, Monk adapted and repurposed a selection of popular cultural materials, especially Hollywood film materials, to construct a musical language that would speak to a diasporic African American experience framed and haunted by the legacy of racialized, institutionalized slavery.

Byron Lee and the Dragonaires' "Frankenstein Ska," released in 1964, uses the organ to establish the "crooked beat" that is the signature of ska. The song's organ arrangement evokes Monk's "zombie music" and the clumsy, clunking step of Boris Karloff's hulking, heavy-booted creature.

Parliament's *The Clones of Dr. Funkenstein* opens with a spoken-word "Prelude," in which a campy-spooky organ arrangement strikes up to lead in and accompany a monologue by George Clinton's "Dr. Funkenstein" persona. Parliament's *Clones* album in turn has furnished samples for subsequent dance music, from Armand Van Helden's tribal house anthem "The Witch Doctor" (1994) to Deadmau5's 2006 house track "Dr. Funkenstein."

Another production that has generated further amplifications—from samples in other songs to costumed and choreographed public dance performances—is Michael Jackson's "Thriller" (1984), whose dramatic organ stabs give the song its unmistakable hook. And a *Toccata and Fugue*-like organ arrangement arises late in the song, to accompany its climactic monologue, a campy litany of monster movie references, delivered by Vincent Price. In Price's "Thriller" monologue, "creatures" that "crawl in search of blood" and "grisly ghouls from every tomb" mix with similar figures to make a mash-up of living-dead monster images; together with the organ arrangement, they clearly conjure the specters of *Frankenstein* and *Dracula*, the Hollywood versions of which have made them (alongside George Romero's *Living Dead* franchise) the very

---

[35] Quoted in David McNally, *Monsters of the Market: Zombies, Vampires, and Global Capitalism* (Chicago: Haymarket Books, 2011), 262.
[36] Ibid., 263.
[37] Ibid., 263–4.

stuff of "Thriller's" homage.[38] "Thriller" exploits organ music to amplify its gothic mode; the Afro-Futurist element here lies more in musical arrangement than in lyrical content, as each track juxtaposes the modishly futuristic synthesizers and drum machines of early-1980s pop against the classical- and gospel-derived sounds of organ instrumentation.

The gospel context may suggest why the organ recurs in Afro-Futurist music adaptations of *Frankenstein* more than in other music adaptations. In *Frankenstein*-themed songs by rock artists, and more specifically white rock artists—for example, the Edgar Winter Group, Black Sabbath, the New York Dolls, White Zombie—electric guitar and synthesizer sounds, rather than organs, amplify the *Frankenstein* theme. In this intercultural context, the use of organs by Afro-Futurist artists appears ambivalent. On the one hand, the use of organs instead of guitars to signify *Frankenstein* themes in Black diasporic music might be read to assert cultural difference as musical difference. On the other hand, if the use of organ instrumentation and sampling by Afro-Futurist artists signifies on the organ's place in sacred music by connecting it to the profane theme of Frankensteinian presumption, then it may be read as a critique of essentialist ideas of Black diasporic identity, or as a variant representation of African American double consciousness. The Black diasporic cultural practice of what Julian Jonker calls "black secret technology"—that is, "taking white technology apart and not putting it back together properly"[39]—involves, as the work of Monk and Perry especially dramatizes, transgressing modes of conventional music-making—and, in Perry's case, music recording—as expressions of emancipation from not just slavery proper but also its haunting, revenant legacy.

This brings us to the combination of *Frankenstein* reference and organ instrumentation—or in this case sampling—in rap music. "Let Your Backbone Slide" is a 1989 single by Maestro Fresh Wes, one of the most successful Canadian rap songs. Two specific details of this track, in lyric and instrumentation, are noteworthy here, in order to appreciate the adaptive practice of Maestro's sampling and synecdoche in full effect. The instrumental arrangement of "Backbone" is organized around an organ riff sampled from the 1968 funk track "The Champ" by the Mohawks, a track widely sampled in rap music. In this distinctive pairing of *Frankenstein* reference and organ arrangement, "Let Your Backbone Slide" reproduces the pattern tracked earlier from the Dragonaires to Michael Jackson.

The lyrical references to *Frankenstein* in "Let Your Backbone Slide" are extensive and elliptical. In the last verse of the extended mix of the song, Maestro raps: "It's gettin' out of hand / I've created a monster." This Frankenpheme figures Maestro's self-proclaimed success—a common conceit in rap, and a pointedly bold claim for a debut single—as a Frankensteinian effect of unintended consequences. The lyric sampled here is legible as a commonplace Frankenpheme in everyday speech, but it also resonates with other lyrical details: the recurring imagery of the "spine"; the chorus' reference

---

[38] Michael Jackson, "Thriller," *Thriller*, Sony, 1984.
[39] Julian Jonker, "Black Secret Technology (the Whitey on the Moon Dub)," 2002 Ctheory, article a117, paragraph 32, available online: http://www.ctheory.net/text_file.asp?pick=358.

to "backbone"; the first verse's mention of "vertebrae"; and the song's inspired rhyme about the "sacro-iliac," or tailbone. But lines in the first verse further flaunt this "rap scholar's" learned repertoire, most notably his likening of rap to "a slab of clay that's shapeless" until "I mould it in my hands."[40] Taken together with the lyrical details noted earlier, this verse's self-reflexive rhyme about rap as creative practice alludes with artful economy to the same ancient myths adapted and referenced in Shelley's own novel: the medieval Jewish legend of the golem; the biblical accounts of creation in Genesis and John's gospel; the classical myths of Prometheus and Pygmalion.

"Backbone" thus assembles and reanimates a set of "subterranean"—but identifiable—cultural elements and discourses; the track constitutes a second-order adaptation, in its rehearsal of a clichéd, vernacular Frankenpheme and its sampling of the Mohawks' organ hook. It is significant that the Frankenpheme lyric only occurs on the vinyl "power mix" and video, not on the shorter "radio edit" version—the lyric thus self-reflexively remarks on its own excess: "It's gettin' out of hand." And the track's sampling practice is itself integral to understanding this specific text's representative articulation of the ready-made, bricolage aesthetic of "early hip hop," for which, as Simon Reynolds has put it, "sampling was like Frankenstein's monster, funk-limbs crudely bolted together."[41]

As with "Thriller," so "Backbone" may not at first seem as audibly Afro-Futurist as the more self-consciously avant-garde work of Clinton, Perry, or Monk. The Afro-Futurist aesthetic emerges here as much in the song's musical arrangements as in its lyrics, with their play on Pygmalion and Frankenstein figures. Maestro's track articulates something of the technology discourse that we find in other Canadian adaptations of *Frankenstein*, in its relatively fast tempo and its corresponding lyrical agility. For mainstream rap of the late 1980s, Maestro's lyrics are unusually rapid-fire, more comparable to the style of Public Enemy or Run the Jewels than to that of the Beastie Boys or Dr. Dre, and its tempo is fast for rap—114 beats per minute—accented by an intensive collage of sampling and turntablist effects. The lyrical density of "Backbone" invites headphone concentration, while its detonative breakbeat, a sample of James Brown's "Funky Drummer," invites dance-floor abandon. In the context of pop music in 1989, the beats of "Backbone" resonate as much with UK acid house as its rhymes resonate with US East Coast rap. In this divided transnational perspective, "Let Your Backbone Slide" may be as quintessentially Canadian as pop music gets—it is a technological and transnational acoustic space oddity: Canadian hip house.

The track gains additional interest in its Canadian production context. Maestro signifies on citizenship in his persona's self-description as "un-American" (evoking national difference as well as the American allergy to communism that perennially positions Canada as some purportedly socialist threat). Maestro's self-promotional boasting about success as a jet-setting rap star contrasts ironically with his other self-descriptions as hubristic artist and mad scientist; moreover, all these self-descriptions

---

[40] Maestro Fresh Wes, "Let Your Backbone Slide (Power mix)," *Attic*, 1989.
[41] Simon Reynolds, *Generation Ecstasy: Into the World of Techno and Rave Culture* (London: Routledge, 2013), 45.

join a shape-shifting host of alter egos presented in the track—tactician, Colossus, Tarzan, conductor, builder, playwright—as well as Wesley Williams's rapper pseudonym as "the Maestro." The MC's boastful proliferation of personae signals the track's skillful adoption of this staple convention of the rap genre. What's more, as a Black Canadian cultural production, Maestro's multiple roles signify ironically on official Canadian multiculturalism: the track's voice is a virtual mosaic all to himself. It is not just "the beat," in the words of the track's introductory vocal sample, that "will be played in many parts," but the performing persona itself, a satirical figure of the Canadian multicultural "mosaic" that is rendered ironic by the volume of Frankenphemes in the Maestro's mix.

As demonstrated by Afro-Futurist music generally and the aforementioned tracks specifically, especially Maestro's "Backbone," Black diasporic music has amplified the metonymic associations—the "iconflations"—of zombie and vampire, organ instrumentation and horror intertextuality, such that the sound of organ instrumentation is itself almost sufficient to evoke the modern myth of *Frankenstein* in popular culture. We should also note here the multiple meanings of the word "organ"; although this may go without saying in any discussion of *Frankenstein*, in popular music, and especially in Afro-Futurist music, the sound of the organ has thus become the sound of the body built of—which is to say, *reduced to*—organs, an intermedial "iconflation" of sacred musicality and profane monstrosity, the monstrosity of bodily self-alienation, synecdoche as commodification and exploitation. The organ is the most uncannily named wind instrument, the windpipe that sings in an inhuman voice, but only when compelled to by human machinations.

My second example emerges from the techno-romantic scenes of EDM. Today's dance culture is both diversified and robust, building on a half century of dance scenes that have pivoted on DJ culture and the playback of recorded music: from postwar US record hops and Jamaican sound system clashes to the rapid rise and exaggerated death of disco, which actually lived on in Chicago house, Detroit techno, and New York garage—sounds that fueled the rise of raves in the late 1980s and 1990s, and that continue to drive today's globalized dance music festival culture.

Whether applied to genres (like disco) or media (like vinyl), a Frankensteinian language of death and resurrection articulates three of dance culture's constitutive contexts: the oscillating popularity of dance sounds in the global music market; the culture's techno-romantic representations of excess as experiment; and its uses and fetishizations of technology in reconfigurations of "liveness" in music media and performance practices.

In disco and its electronic successors, the racializing anxieties once visited on rock and roll became compounded by heteronormative anxieties: early house music was reviled by the music press not just as a fad but as an unexpected return of disco, and moreover a kind of disco that amplified a stark, alien minimalism of drum loops, bass lines, and other machine sounds and thus exaggerated the foundational *queerness* of disco. As rave culture codified and popularized (even while sometimes strenuously disavowing) the interface between electronic dance music and MDMA or "Ecstasy," the moral panics that caricatured rave culture as drug culture traded on myths and misconceptions about MDMA that positioned MDMA as a "synthetic" or "designer" drug. Philip Jenkins notes that "the Frankenstein image is so frequently cited in discussions of synthetic drugs because, as in the original tale, a quest for human improvement results instead in the creation of what are identified as terrifying figures."[42] This "quest" activity has long structured raving, clubbing, and other social dance leisure activities and is organized not according to chemical technologies alone but in concert with cultural technologies, chiefly music. This activity is what Reynolds calls "techno-Romanticism": the pursuit of the palace of wisdom on a path of excess "expressed in the discourse of science and technology"; the way in which subcultural scene makers use "the discourse of science and technology" to represent practices of music-making—and drug taking: "In rave," Reynolds writes, "kids play the roles of both Frankenstein and the monster, experimenting on their own nervous systems."[43]

Techno-romanticism also describes the aesthetics of EDM's musical foundation in Afro-Futurism, the tradition of Black Atlantic music- and scene-making in which producers and performers like George Clinton and Kool Keith adopt "mad scientist" personas and in which marginalized and racialized dancers breakdance or jerk their bodies with stylized robotic moves, in empowering practices of "technological identification" whereby "the fearful paradox of the technological age, that machines created as artificial slaves will somehow enslave and even mechanize human beings, is ritually enacted at the discotheque."[44] About rave more specifically, Reynolds adopts a more negative view in describing raving as a zombie-like "living death"; he argues that the dance–drug interface is "an engine for programming sensations ... connotative of enthrallment, of loss of control."[45]

These Frankensteinian figures of dance music's techno-romanticism reverberate with representations of EDM music-making, performance, and consumption in terms of "liveness" and death: representations of EDM as a monstrous synthesis of sampled fragments;[46] as autonomous technology, where "the sequencer and sampler take over";[47] as "soulless" artifice versus authentic presence—recording versus "liveness." The conventional performance of EDM by DJs revolves around a paradox of *live playback*: the improvised, responsive, site-specific selection and sequencing of tracks. EDM culture illustrates Philip Auslander's argument that "the 'live' has always been defined as that which can be recorded"[48]—and, moreover, that "liveness" marks "a site of anxiety, an anxiety that infects all who have an interest in maintaining the distinction between the live and the mediatized."[49] Scholars of media and culture have observed

---

[42] Philip Jenkins, *Synthetic Panics: The Symbolic Politics of Designer Drugs* (New York: New York University Press, 1999), 8.
[43] Reynolds, "Ecstasy is a Science," 204.
[44] Walter Hughes, "In the Empire of the Beat," in *Microphone Fiends: Youth Music and Youth Culture*, ed. Andrew Ross and Tricia Rose (New York: Routledge, 1994), 151.
[45] Simon Reynolds, "Rave Culture: Living Dream or Living Death?" in *The Clubcultures Reader*, ed. Steve Redhead (London: Routledge, 1997), 109.
[46] Reynolds, *Generation Ecstasy*, 45.
[47] Chapman, "Hermeneutics of Suspicion," 17.
[48] Auslander, *Liveness*, 86.
[49] Ibid., 87.

the reconfigurations of aura and authenticity not only between unmediated presence and mediation but also between different kinds of media. Sarah Thornton documents these reconfigurations in dance culture, from early-twentieth-century musicians organizing against jukeboxes and DJs to DJs themselves, by century's end, dreading the "death of vinyl"[50] amid the rise of CDs and digital sound. "Since the mid-eighties," Thornton writes, "'live' qualities have been increasingly attributed to recorded events," while "music performances have become more reliant on recording."[51]

EDM's estranging reconfiguration of liveness converges commodity fetishism and the technological sublime: media live and die and achieve uncanny, monstrous effects, confusing the biological and the technological. From techno-romantic representations of EDM consumption in terms of experiment and automatons to techno-fetishizing representations of EDM production in terms of automatic yet autonomous technology, dance culture is fraught with the discourse of technology as Frankensteinian monstrosity.

Consider Deadmau5, aka Joel Zimmerman, the Canadian producer whose work plays on EDM's structuring tensions between liveness and death. In the first place, he says he came up with his "Deadmau5" pseudonym when he once found a dead rodent in his computer. Deadmau5 produces house music of the "electro" and "progressive" subgenres—popular, accessible dance music styles that are staples at major clubs. And yet his tracks feature gothic motifs, sounds, and references. "Complications" (2008) includes the metronome pulse of an electrocardiogram, which flatlines during sequences when the kick drum cuts out, and then stops when the kick drum resumes, as though the drum beat replaces the heartbeat; the arrangement signals an oscillation from life to death, and back to life—or its digital simulation. The 2009 track "Ghosts 'n' Stuff" propelled Deadmau5 to chart-topping fame; its lyrics open with a disorienting image of shared disembodiment: "It's been so long I've been out of my body with you."[52] The song's hook is a heavy organ riff (which in itself evokes *Frankenstein*, according to the tradition of organ instrumentation discussed above). The companion track "Moar Ghosts 'n' Stuff" (2009) opens with the funeral march of Chopin and modulates this into the organ hook of "Ghosts."

The 2012 track "The Veldt" extends these thematics of death and technics in its adaptation of the eponymous Ray Bradbury story, and its unsettling juxtaposition of major-chord melody, bucolic samples of bird and insect song, and subtly gruesome, dystopian lyrics: "Happy life with the machines . . . Happy technology / Outside the lions run / Feeding on remains."[53] In an interview with CBC, Zimmerman described

---

[50] Sarah Thornton, *Club Cultures: Music, Media, and Subcultural Capital* (Middletown: Wesleyan University Press, 1996), 64.
[51] Ibid., 85.
[52] Deadmau5 [Joel Zimmerman], "Ghosts 'n' Stuff (feat. Rob Swire)," Track 3 on *For Lack of a Better Name*. Virgin/Mau5trap Recordings, 2009.
[53] Deadmau5 [Joel Zimmerman], "The Veldt (Original Mix)," Track 1 on *The Veldt EP*, MAU5053B. Mau5trap Recordings, 2012.

"The Veldt" as a homage to Bradbury's story "in which an unhealthy obsession with technology ends up having murderous consequences."[54]

Deadmau5's performance aesthetic and his productions alike thus dramatize and thematize the Frankensteinian problematic of life, death, and undeath. And in June 2012, Zimmerman reanimated the debate in popular music over "liveness" versus playback: in a *Rolling Stone* interview, he claimed that EDM performers—including himself—"just hit play"—that is, preprogram whole sets—instead of improvising a mix of tracks.[55] In follow-up music press coverage and social media, Zimmerman tried to clarify that he was referring specifically to EDM producers who are expected to perform at concerts and are held—absurdly, he holds—to expectations to perform music "live" the way singer-songwriters would: that is, to play music, not to play it back: "we all hit play," he said, prompting a public controversy over liveness in DJ culture.[56]

In this way, Deadmau5 is extending not just recent traditions in Canadian EDM, but a broader legacy of McLuhan-informed Canadian music-making, like that demonstrated by Glenn Gould. But whereas Gould famously forsook the live concert for the recording studio, Zimmerman, conversely, brings the recording studio to the concert. In the perennial crisis of "liveness" in music, Zimmerman's "just hit play" comments transposed the terms of this crisis more deeply into the already mediatized context of EDM and inflamed deep-seated and long-standing anxieties over technology as labor's monstrous supplement, which perennially recur in music as new instruments, production processes, and performance practices alternately assist or supplant human labor.[57]

Deadmau5's performance practice includes a further detail that furnishes an apt coda to this discussion: when he performs while wearing the mouse-head helmet that lights up with LEDs, he cannot actually see out of the helmet with his own eyes. Instead, he wears video goggles, which means he has to compensate for a millisecond lag between what's happening at the controls and what he sees; suffice to say, for a DJ, Deadmau5 has set himself a risky logistical challenge in the production of his performance spectacle.

Identifying hypermediatization with intoxication, and technology with addiction, and making and playing music in ways that amplify the Frankensteinian figuration of technology, Deadmau5 thus represents a recent, globally popular contribution to the tradition of McLuhanesque *Frankenstein* adaptations in Canada's EDM scene. As a Canadian ambassador of a globalized EDM culture characterized by techno-romanticism and immersive mediatization, Deadmau5 plays on anxieties over liveness and labor in productions and performance practices that dramatize the uncanny

---

[54] Deadmau5 [Joel Zimmerman]. Interview. Q. July 23, 2012.
[55] Josh Eells, "The Rise of the Mau5," *Rolling Stone*, May 7, 2012.
[56] Deadmau5 [Joel Zimmerman], "We All Hit Play," United We Fail [blog], available online: https://web.archive.org/web/20120627035653/http://deadmau5.tumblr.com/post/25690507284/we-all-hit-play (accessed June 23, 2012).
[57] Thomas Porcello, "The Ethics of Digital Audio-Sampling: Engineers' Discourse," *Popular Music* 10, no. 1 (1991): 69–84.

effects of media technologies, and thus amplify the Canadian (and specifically McLuhanesque) discourse of technology of manufactured monstrosity.

As the examples of Maestro Fresh Wes and Deadmau5 show, popular music harbors a profound wealth of adaptation practices. The case of *Frankenstein*'s versions and variations in Afro-Futurist music demonstrates the vast repertoire of knowledge—cultural, historical, technological, and otherwise—that is concentrated and coded in Black Atlantic music. As Angela McRobbie says, it's extraordinary—and underappreciated—"just how much *thinking* there is in black music ... [it] can hardly contain [all its] investment[s] of artistry, politics, history, and literary voice."[58]

And paying attention to such nonextensive gothic adaptations in nonnarrative genres and media thus suggests one way to model a more expansive approach to adaptation studies adequate to the vast, diversified cultural diffusion of massively popular texts like *Frankenstein*.

---

[58] Angela McRobbie, "Thinking with Music," in *Stars Don't Stand Still in the Sky: Music and Myth*, ed. Karen Kelly and Evelyn McDonell (New York: New York University Press, 1999), 43–4.

Part II

Monstrosity in Music, Film, and Videogames

8

Monstrosity as a Queer Aesthetic

Lloyd Whitesell

Gallery

Monsters dot the landscape of queer and trans studies. A clutch of vampires sprang into view in the 1990s, representing the dangers of AIDS, sexual fluidity, and social abjection.[1] Spectral apparitions came to symbolize the precarious presence of queer people within culture.[2] Tales of mismatched body parts stirred memories of damaged identity.[3] With the recent validation of dark feelings and antisocial urges, sightings are on the rise.[4]

Contrary forces animate this discourse: an urge to expose monsters and their likeness as tools of oppression, and a fascination with them as idols of perversity. In his book on homosexuality in the horror film, Harry M. Benshoff vividly describes the social mechanism which forces queer people into the role of the monster by subjecting them to "monstrous signifiers," intended to arouse panic and safeguard the bounds of normality.[5] What better way to inspire horror and incite violence against a group

---

[1] Sue-Ellen Case, "Tracking the Vampire," *differences* 3, no. 2 (1991): 1–20; Ellis Hanson, "Undead," in *Inside/Out: Lesbian Theories, Gay Theories*, ed. Diana Fuss (New York: Routledge, 1991), 324–40; Nina Auerbach, *Our Vampires, Ourselves* (Chicago: University of Chicago Press, 1995).

[2] Terry Castle, *The Apparitional Lesbian: Female Homosexuality and Modern Culture* (New York: Columbia University Press, 1993); Patricia White, *Uninvited: Classical Hollywood Cinema and Lesbian Representability* (Bloomington: Indiana University Press, 1999), 61–93.

[3] Susan Stryker, "My Words to Victor Frankenstein above the Village of Chamounix: Performing Transgender Rage," *GLQ* 1 (1994): 237–54; Jack Halberstam, *Skin Shows: Gothic Horror and the Technology of Monsters* (Durham: Duke University Press, 1995).

[4] For example, Freya Jarman-Ivens, *Queer Voices: Technologies, Vocalities, and the Musical Flaw* (New York: Palgrave Macmillan, 2011), 127–60; Karen E. Macfarlane, "The Monstrous House of Gaga," in *The Gothic in Contemporary Literature and Popular Culture: Pop Goth*, ed. Justin D. Edwards and Agnieszka Soltysik Monnet (New York: Routledge, 2012), 114–34; Charlie Fox, *This Young Monster* (London: Fitzcarraldo Editions, 2017); Laura Westengard, *Gothic Queer Culture: Marginalized Communities and the Ghosts of Insidious Trauma* (Lincoln: University of Nebraska Press, 2019).

[5] Harry M. Benshoff, *Monsters in the Closet: Homosexuality and the Horror Film* (Manchester: Manchester University Press, 1997), 1–30; see 8. On the social uses of monster rhetoric more generally, see Edward J. Ingebretsen, *At Stake: Monsters and the Rhetoric of Fear in Public Culture* (Chicago: University of Chicago Press, 2001). In the words of Jeffrey Jerome Cohen, the monster is "an abjecting epistemological device basic to the mechanics of deviance construction and identity

of people than to declare them embodiments of the unnatural, the menacing, and the obscene? The hate speech of monstrosity has targeted sexual and gender misfits for a long time and in many contexts, from religious abomination, to phobias about disease, to entertainment forms in which queer characters are ritually destroyed. But if such imagery is so often used against us, if it inescapably recalls a history of suffering, then why would queer folk willingly slip into the hateful role? And what is going on psychologically when they do?

Exhibit A: Divine, aka Babs Johnson

In his underground home movie, *Pink Flamingos* (1972), queer filmmaker John Waters immortalized a small-time crime family with delusions of grandeur, whose matriarch boastfully violates taboos against murder, incest, cannibalism, and eating shit.[6] Her saliva is imbued with magical venom. In her garish makeup and bizarre hairstyles, she achieves an aggressive outsider glamour, implying not just bad taste but a willful perversion of taste, while also alluding to the deformities of traditional folk monsters. Scenes of banal domesticity erupt into rivalrous rampages that channel horror and obscenity into assertions of outlaw pride ("We are the filthiest people alive!").

Exhibit B: Tabitha the Ghost Girl

In contrast, "Imago," by Tristan Alice Nieto (from a recent collection of science fiction by transgender writers), adopts a melancholic tone.[7] Set in a near future of advanced biotech, it merges the detective story (as told by the victim) with the zombie thriller (as told by the zombie). The narrator, Tabitha, wakes up postmortem, having been resuscitated by the London police to help solve her murder. "If the body is determined to have died within eighteen hours of arrival, Revivranol will be administered and resuscitation commenced. That's me. I am the body."[8] The wonder drug animates corpses for a few days without forestalling deterioration, leaving the revived vulnerable to amnesia and emotional malfunction. Thus we experience the story by way of a fragmentary, undead subjectivity. As we learn piecemeal, Tabitha is also an albino and formerly blind (now fitted with optical prostheses in the form of multiple airborne wireless butterflies). In life, her albinism elicited phobic reactions, exacerbated by association with the symptoms of a raging pandemic. "You got sick, you turned white, you became agitated, then paranoid, then psychotic, and then you

---

formation"; Jeffrey Jerome Cohen, ed., *Monster Theory: Reading Culture* (Minneapolis: University of Minnesota Press, 1996), ix.
[6] *Pink Flamingos*, directed by John Waters (1972; New Line Cinema).
[7] Tristan Alice Nieto, "Imago," in *Meanwhile, Elsewhere: Science Fiction and Fantasy from Transgender Writers*, ed. Cat Fitzpatrick and Casey Plett (New York: Topside Press, 2017), 347–79.
[8] Ibid., 349–50.

died. I remember how the panic was just as virulent as the disease.... So I became the plague monkey. Patient Zero. Don't touch the albino kid, you'll get the White Death."[9] Allusions to crudely stitched gashes, mob justice, and medical hubris bring to mind the Frankenstein myth. The climactic, frenzied attack by the unkillable narrator satisfies the zombie trope. And yet these violent episodes are cradled within lyrical stretches of haunting memory ("in an instant, as if by some orphean curse, everything vanishes into shadow"),[10] where Tabitha searches the underworld for her lover lost to the plague and rejoins her in the embrace of death.

Exhibit C: Barbara Urselin

In 1977, the editors of the feminist art journal *Heresies* used the image of a historical monster, the werewolf-like Barbara Urselin, on a poster advertising their lesbian issue (Figure 8.1). In the pages of that issue, the original woodcut, taken from an early modern treatise on strange prodigies of nature, accompanies an article by novelist Bertha Harris advancing a theory of lesbian monstrosity in popular fiction. In Harris's view, both monster and lesbian

> have the following traits in common: an ability to make a life outside the social norm that seems both enviable and frightening to those inside; ... marks of difference that are physically manifested and both horrify and thrill; a desire to avenge its own ... outcast misery: through destruction or through forcing a change in the world that will admit it and its kind; [and] an ability to seduce and tempt others into its "evil" ways.[11]

Harris ends by denouncing the "old fearsome disguises, the gruesome costumes of terror,"[12] in favor of lesbian-affirmative rhetoric. But as an independent object, the poster art works differently, recirculating old imagery with mischief and delight. By appropriating this vintage portrait of a woman with hypertrichosis, or excess hair growth, the editors work against the original seventeenth-century intention to exhibit her as a freak stranded on a hill, as well as against 1970s assumptions regarding the abject status of women. Far from being wretched or enraged, this monster is self-possessed, civilized, and sartorially immaculate—an emblem of successfully managed stigma.

I've chosen these preliminary exhibits for their range and disparity; each one explores unique emotional and artistic terrain. But my goal is to move beyond local chronicles of isolated monsters. By considering the significance of monstrous archetypes for the

---

[9] Ibid., 353.
[10] Ibid., 347.
[11] Bertha Harris, "What We Mean to Say: Notes toward Defining the Nature of Lesbian Literature," *Heresies: A Feminist Publication on Art and Politics* 3 (Fall 1977): 5–8; see 7.
[12] Ibid., 8.

136   *Monstrosity, Identity and Music*

Figure 8.1 Poster, *Heresies* (Fall 1977).

many queer artists who work with them, we can detect some unifying principles and bring a scattered host of lost souls under a common roof.

Mantles of Evil

Despite their implication in oppression, monster figures have repeatedly been adopted by queer people as icons of identification and a means of challenging, if not terrorizing, the social order. Two passionate meditations on this reverse discourse appeared in the first flourishing of queer and trans theory. In 1991, performance studies scholar Sue-Ellen Case published her essay "Tracking the Vampire," in which she builds a revisionary myth around this magnetic archetype. In the "dominant discourse," the vampire embodies a hidden menace whose sneak attack adulterates the purity of race and heterosexuality.[13] In the queer "counterdiscourse" as Case sees it, the vampire represents the possibility of "puncturing" or subverting the borders between the

---

[13] Case, "Tracking the Vampire," 6.

realms of the natural and other-than-natural, living and other-than-living—in effect, redefining the sorts of people who can claim the "right to life."[14] On its familiar, dreadful face, the archetype is insidious and life-draining; viewed from the underside, it is powerfully disruptive, striking a "blissful wound into ontology itself."[15] Even so, her account is far from triumphalist. Case's queer vampire has an extremely tenuous presence in cultural representation and can only be tracked with difficulty through thickets of proscription, erasure, and double-crossing.

I want to highlight two psychosocial maneuvers figuring in Case's thesis. First, she returns to her own adolescence as the scene of origin for subsequent "discursive strategies."[16] While careful to disclaim universal validity for her personal story, she sketches a few elements common to subjects of stigma: the shock of insult, the pain of exclusion, the coercion into internal exile. "'Queer' was the site in the discourse at which I felt both immediate identification and shame—a contradiction that both established my social identity and required me to render it somehow invisible."[17] Her words describe the formative queer experience of perverse identification (identifying along the wrong axis), which places one in a position no subject is meant to occupy—a "no-subject" position. Such a subjectivity, formed from the very rhetoric of cultural prohibition, must absorb an inherent breakdown in logic as well as a negative affective charge. Case refers to this psychic process as "identifying with the insult."[18] We can also call it disidentification.[19]

Second, such semi-exiles intuitively resist the predicament thrust on them, struggling to attain a contrary perspective from which to re-evaluate the reviled qualities of their own experience. Some cross to the dark side:

> The queer, unlike the rather polite categories of gay and lesbian, revels in the discourse of the loathsome, the outcast. . . . Unlike petitions for civil rights, queer revels constitute a kind of activism that attacks the dominant notion of the natural. The queer is the taboo-breaker, the monstrous, the uncanny. Like the Phantom of the Opera, the queer dwells underground, below the operatic overtones of the dominant.[20]

Vampire discourse involves a transfer of allegiance or a transposal of ethical coordinates, as a way to "reimagine [one's] strengths."[21]

---

[14] Ibid., 4.
[15] Ibid., 2.
[16] Ibid.
[17] Ibid., 1.
[18] Ibid., 2.
[19] The latter term gained currency in the wake of José Esteban Muñoz's book *Disidentifications: Queers of Color and the Performance of Politics* (Minneapolis: University of Minnesota Press, 1999), as a non-binary concept suspended between identification and "counteridentification" (11).
[20] Case, "Tracking the Vampire," 3.
[21] Ibid., 15.

In another treatise from the 1990s, "My Words to Victor Frankenstein above the Village of Chamounix: Performing Transgender Rage," Susan Stryker disidentifies with Frankenstein's Monster.[22] In Mary Shelley's novel, the man-made creature initially has little understanding of its own condition or reason for being. Upon learning how it came to be created, the monster is sickened, then filled with rage. Confronting Victor Frankenstein high in the French Alps, it demands an audience with its maker. This is the creature that Stryker seeks to emulate, "quick-witted, agile, strong, and eloquent,"[23] speaking back to the men who made her body, tallying her own account of coercion and alienation. The verbal surface of the essay displays a patchwork of discursive modes: critical theory, oracular pronouncement, journal entry, interior monologue, poetry, benediction. "I wanted the formal structure of the work to express a transgender aesthetic by replicating our abrupt, often jarring transitions between genders—challenging generic classification with the forms of my words."[24] By adopting an array of writerly voices, she creates collisions between objective argumentation and the "anguish of my own struggles with gender."[25]

Like Case, Stryker identifies along the wrong axis, seeing herself in the wretched position of the outcast: "I'm such a goddamned freak. . . . Maybe there really is no place for me in all creation. . . . I do war with nature. I am alienated from Being. I'm a self-mutilated deformity, a pervert, a mutant, trapped in monstrous flesh."[26] This psychic incoherence (internal "seams and sutures")[27] spurs her to transvalue the conditions of her oppression: "Hearken unto me, fellow creatures. . . . I call upon you to investigate your nature as I have been compelled to confront mine. I challenge you to risk abjection and flourish as well as have I."[28] Converting abjection to rage, she recognizes her misbegotten identity as a source of "dark power,"[29] "the enlivening power of darkness within yourself."[30]

The better to hold their complexities in mind, it might be helpful to condense the affective structures of disidentification and ethical transposal into a single lapidary scene or pronouncement. Such an utterance occurs in the recent opera *Champion* (2013, music by Terence Blanchard, libretto by Michael Cristofer), based on the life of bisexual prizefighter Emile Griffith. In a scene from his boyhood in the US Virgin Islands, Griffith's fundamentalist cousin subjects him to bouts of physical endurance

---

[22] Stryker, "My Words to Victor Frankenstein above the Village of Chamounix."
[23] Ibid., 243.
[24] Ibid., 237.
[25] Ibid., 250.
[26] Ibid., 246–7; originally set in italics to signal a change of voice. In a more theoretical vein, Stryker describes the paradoxical experience of sustaining subjectivity in a no-subject position: "Transgender rage is a queer fury, an emotional response to conditions in which it becomes imperative to take up, for the sake of one's own continued survival as a subject, a set of practices that precipitates one's exclusion from a naturalized order of existence that seeks to maintain itself as the only possible basis for being a subject" (249).
[27] Stryker, "My Words to Victor Frankenstein above the Village of Chamounix," 241.
[28] Ibid., 240–1.
[29] Ibid., 240.
[30] Ibid., 251.

as punishment for his sinful nature. At a certain point, the young boy snaps out of his misery with a strategic turning of the tables, declaring: "If the devil is inside me, then so be it. Give me evil strength."[31]

This attitude is characterized neither by wholesale opposition to hostile moral codes nor by an abject acceptance of them, but by a dissident reframing of those codes—converting a curse into a protective mantle. In their foundational essays, both Case and Stryker paint vivid portraits of such responses to stigma, and both implicitly acknowledge how queer or transgender modes of creative expression have been shaped by those responses. This is the lead I want to follow here: an intuition that the logic skewing queer subjectivity extends its reach into aesthetic practices. Monsters provide one point of entry.

Obviously, monster rhetoric existed before queer artists got their hands on it. How do they pick through the toxic elements and make it their own? Consider the matter of perspective. At the core of the dominant discourse, monsters represent fearful encounters with Othered beings. Many of these monsters bear no resemblance to the Self; they materialize as brute creatures or alien forces (think of the insectoid extraterrestrial in the 1979 film *Alien*). Some dissemble as fellow human beings until their monstrosity is discovered (think of treacherous android science officer Ash in the same film). Whether otherness makes itself known in terms of species, technology, race, class, disability, gender, sex, or some crossbreed, it figures within a scapegoat narrative whereby the monster is cast out, allowing purity and safety to be restored (for the moment). Queer people, historically subjected to those rituals of exclusion, have answered with a kind of counterspell, inhabiting monstrous subjectivities and looking out through Othered eyes.

For a schematic example, consider Oscar Wilde's novel *The Picture of Dorian Gray* (1891), whose monster is one of the lead characters, a golden boy rotting from the inside. For long passages, Wilde places the reader in Dorian's mind as he descends into depravity and murder. The plot hinges not on keeping the monster out but on *becoming* a monster and making a life as such. This point-of-view structure is motivated by disidentification; it allows Wilde to explore the psychological dilemmas that follow from occupying the position of an unimaginable subject, marked for expulsion. Though the monster archetype insults domestic values, Wilde shows us Dorian ensconced at home, entertaining, enjoying the fruits of his lifestyle, wrapped up in elaborate projects of interior design. The dissonant merging of monstrous and domestic elaborates on the underlying paradox of Dorian's symbolic position (as both alien and native);[32] as does the motif of the portrait in the attic, by fissuring the self into two bodies, one of which is incompletely expelled and secretly cherished.

---

[31] Terence Blanchard, *Champion: An Opera in Jazz*, libretto by Michael Cristofer, 2013.
[32] Scholars of sexual diversity have theorized this subverted binary of belonging as the "proximate other" (Jonathan Dollimore, *Sexual Dissidence: Augustine to Wilde, Freud to Foucault* [Oxford: Clarendon Press, 1991], 33), the "uninvited" family member (White, *Uninvited*, xxiv), and the "stranger at home" (Shane Phelan, *Sexual Strangers: Gays, Lesbians, and Dilemmas of Citizenship* [Philadelphia: Temple University Press, 2001], 36).

Beyond these problems of perspective, Wilde's story dramatizes a shift in ethical coordinates, as Lord Henry Wotton, Dorian's honey-tongued mentor, tempts the younger man with an antinomian philosophy of beauty and pleasure for their own sake. The pertinent theme here is the conversion to a new system of judgment, so that the same behavior, unthinkable under one jurisdiction, becomes valued under another. Yet this double vision admits the dangerous possibility that the new way of seeing lacks ethical coordinates altogether. Wilde wants us to share the thrill Dorian feels at the prospect of leaving morality behind. Though John Waters's audience may be miles apart from that of Oscar Wilde, the same scheme of ethical reframing motivates his films. Waters's characters equate crime with beauty, elevate filth to a cultural ideal, and couple incestuously to unleash divine power. Each enthusiastic inversion is exploited for affective release. As Michael Moon and Eve Kosofsky Sedgwick put it in their discussion of Divine, the "combination of abjection and defiance . . . produces a divinity-effect in the subject, a compelling belief that one is a god or a vehicle of divinity."[33] In all such works, the transfer from one paradigm to another is not necessarily complete or triumphant: an unresolved polarity may leave one stranded between stigma and affirmation. Thus Dorian Gray, for all his gestures toward aesthetic idealism, still suffers a hideous punishment.[34] Is the monster a deviate or a dissenter? A renegade or a regenerate? The trope of ethical undecidability lends itself to multiple realizations.

Appalling Inventions

With this set of theorems in mind, we can turn to some specific works by queer artists in different media who adopt a monstrous aesthetic. Although one can arguably piece together a queer-authored gothic tradition encompassing Wilde's *Dorian Gray*, James Whale's *Frankenstein* films (1931, 1935), Patricia Highsmith's "Ripliad" (1955–91), and recent gaysploitation horror, my goal is to identify an underlying expressive impulse with implications beyond any single generic tradition.[35] So my focus will be on monstrosity in works outside the horror genre.

---

[33] Michael Moon and Eve Kosofsky Sedgwick, "Divinity: A Dossier, A Performance Piece, A Little-Understood Emotion," in *Tendencies*, ed. Eve Kosofsky Sedgwick (Durham: Duke University Press, 1993), 215–51; see 218. Their formulation *abjection* + *defiance* = *divinity* chimes well with the operatic motto introduced earlier: "If the devil is inside me, then so be it. Give me evil strength."
[34] Compare the death sentence dealt out to Salome, another of Wilde's monsters (*Salomé*, 1891).
[35] On the queer sensibility in Whale's horror films, see Benshoff, *Monsters in the Closet*, 40–51, and William J. Mann, *Behind the Screen: How Gays and Lesbians Shaped Hollywood, 1910–1969* (New York: Penguin, 2001), 184–7. On queer-marketed slashers and horror soaps, see Darren Elliott-Smith, *Queer Horror Film and Television: Sexuality and Masculinity at the Margins* (London: I. B. Tauris, 2016).

Vampire

I begin with a synth-pop track by British group the Pet Shop Boys. Formed in the early 1980s by Neil Tennant (lyricist, vocalist) and Chris Lowe (keyboardist, programmer), the duo became immensely successful with their brand of danceable electronic pop, clever lyrics, and deadpan delivery. Their melancholic, detached image aligned with the self-conscious posing of art pop or new wave, projecting a wry attitude toward the conventions of masculinity and authenticity prevalent in rock genres.[36] By ironically mixing sensationalism and banality, and draping monotone vocals over Hi-NRG beats, they cultivated a style fissured by contradictions—an artistic product that "masquerades as good time party music."[37] From the first, their songs evoked a gay subtext, even as the Pet Shop Boys themselves dodged the question of their sexuality. Though Tennant began to publicly acknowledge a gay identity in 1994, the songs remained coy and ambiguous.[38] As Fred E. Maus has shown, their ambivalent aesthetic—opulent sounds and withdrawn utterance, embarrassment and shamelessness—can be understood in terms of an underlying tension between "the desire to express and the desire to withhold" indicative of the closet.[39] His point is not merely that the group's songwriting is constrained by social pressures enforcing certain modes of speaking or keeping silent about homosexuality, but that they have adopted an awareness of such constraints as a central element in their creative strategy.[40]

Consider the song "Vampires," from the album *Nightlife* (1999).[41] Tennant's elliptical lyrics evoke an unnatural family who feed on one another, but the details are indeterminate. Is it a same-sex pair (the speaker and his "boy") or a mixed trio (brothers and sister)? Does the speaker take a submissive role with his mate or do they sometimes trade places? Are their biorhythms strictly nocturnal or can they endure daylight without harm? The allusion to queer desire is barely disguised in the unorthodox lifestyle, physical urges, and not least, the act of coming out as a vampire. Yet this speech act is ironized in more than one respect. If "coming out" is meant to take a stand against a culture of secrecy and scandal, the dynamic is all wrong. The speaker is reticent about the surrounding social world but treats his monstrosity factually and without agitation, as if there were no taboo to negotiate. The potential shock value of

---

[36] Stan Hawkins, "The Pet Shop Boys: Musicology, Masculinity and Banality," in *Sexing the Groove: Popular Music and Gender*, ed. Sheila Whiteley (New York: Routledge, 1997), 118–33.

[37] Interview in *Melody Maker*, November 27, 1993; cited in Hawkins, "The Pet Shop Boys," 127.

[38] Paul Burston, "Honestly" (interview with Neil Tennant), *Attitude*, August 1994.

[39] Fred E. Maus, "Glamour and Evasion: The Fabulous Ambivalence of the Pet Shop Boys," *Popular Music* 20 (2001): 379–93; see 385. Hawkins highlights a statement from Tennant's interview with Burston: "For me, being in the Pet Shop Boys has always been a struggle between total embarrassment and total shamelessness" (Hawkins, "The Pet Shop Boys," 118).

[40] This maneuver of incorporating the surrounding discourse of shame into one's art can be compared to those studied in Richard Meyer, *Outlaw Representation: Censorship and Homosexuality in Twentieth-Century American Art* (New York: Oxford University Press, 2002). "To utilize the negative terms of homosexuality is not necessarily to endorse or accept those terms. It may also be to restage one's own outlaw status within a different register of representation and . . . to counter the terms of one's own subjugation" (8, 12).

[41] Lyrics available online: https://www.petshopboys.co.uk/lyrics/vampires.

his avowal is defused from the beginning in his attempts to downplay any emotional reaction. Instead of affirming an identity, he makes a confession without pride or shock, claiming a deviance that makes no difference (I'm one, you're one too). Nor is there any sense of utopian energy urging us to surmount inequity: what might be construed as an egalitarian model of social relations (we are all monsters together) can just as readily be seen in terms of "top" and "bottom," a weak subject or willing victim conforming to the desires of the more assertive. Furthermore, the speaker forgoes the chance to reap evil strength or dignity from the monster archetype. This vampire is an exceptionally passive predator, not rampaging abroad but waiting placidly for orders. Tennant delivers his lines in a blasé manner, as if he sees nothing disruptive or even remarkable about this post-monstrous world.

Yet the pose of emotional blankness is only one element in a richly layered affective texture. Gothic features such as murmured chanting and bell-like sounds cast a haunting spell. The minor-key chord progression, sliding regularly downward to the sour note of a tritone, adds to the decadent glamour. Edgier sounds spike the mix. Before the song gets started, we are ushered into an empty acoustic space, defined only by the electronically generated stridulations hovering and arcing through. These noises sound both machine-like and insect-like. A stylized animal howl complements the soundscape of an unearthly, humid night. An electric bass prowls in the low register, answered by percussive shudders as of indrawn breath. A burst of metallic clatter breaks out in the pause before the vocalist enters. There are so many signifiers of danger, yet they appear as its muffled echoes, palliated by warm sonorities and entranced by hypnotic patterns, transfixing the listener somewhere between trauma and morbid allure. Amid all this, the singer's cool, subdued expression is profoundly ambivalent: Has he pulled on a mantle of sophistication, or is he stupefied, emotionally numb, sucked dry? After a brief contrasting section in major mode comes an instrumental interlude rocked by musical explosions and alarms. As the singer returns to the opening verse, the sound builds in intensity, with a melodramatic ascent in the strings and strong undertow from an agitated bass. The words devolve into a repetition of "don't worry" as the music becomes increasingly apocalyptic. But which affect is negated by the other?

This song draws heavily on the awareness of stigma and how it warps the discourse around sexual desire. It conveys the impact of double pressures on queer subjects to both confess and repress their deviance, while misdirecting the operation of those forces at every opportunity. The songwriters mock and derail the oppressive dynamic shaping the epistemology of the closet *as well as* the affirmative logic inspiring gay pride. This mischief has both abstract and personal significance. On a personal level, the Pet Shop Boys are giving a nod to the persistent debate among their fans on the question of their sexual orientation, their responsibility to come out, and the gay subtexts in their songs.[42] Tennant was out by the time of this song, so according to the prevailing liberation narrative, he no longer needed to depend on subtexts or subterfuge. By continuing to explore equivocation as a creative strategy even after

---

[42] On the "gay debate" among fans, see Maus, "Glamour and Evasion."

supposedly vacating "the closet," he took a swipe at the homonorms aimed his way, made a meta-comment on the aesthetic for which the group is known, and showed how the emotional structures of oppression remain productive for queer art-forms. On a broader cultural level, he implied that the available scripts for resisting shame are impoverished—that elusiveness can be politically strategic as well as attractive.[43]

In "Vampires," the Pet Shop Boys choose a monster as their mouthpiece, and paradox as their rhetorical figure. Theirs is a strangely de-theatricalized vampire: preoccupied with living arrangements, growing accustomed to his perverse nature, tamping down anxiety despite the highly charged, sinister sonic environment. In their take on the age-old vilification of queer people, they move past fierce counterdiscourse (à la Case and Stryker) to an arch counter-counterdiscourse, as if to say, tongue in cheek, "yes, such things are bothersome, but we've learned how to manage, and frankly, who thinks that way anymore?" They feign nonchalance about monstrosity while in their imaginings they still feel its grip. My collected observations can be distilled into the characteristic tropes identified earlier: the perspectival problem of inhabiting monster subjectivity and creating a lifeworld on waste ground; the uneasy marriage of menace and protected domestic space; and the double framing of ethical behavior. Yet as we can see, these common elements do not limit artists to a single rhetorical device or a simple class of emotions.

Sasquatch

For an example from visual culture, we can turn to Canadian artist Allyson Mitchell. According to her website, "Mitchell is a maximalist artist working in sculpture, performance, installation and film. Her practice melds feminism and pop culture to investigate contemporary ideas about sexuality, autobiography and the body, largely through the use of reclaimed textile and abandoned craft."[44] In 1997, she co-founded the fat-positive performance troupe Pretty Porky and Pissed Off. She took the time to get an advanced degree, completing a PhD in women's studies in 2006. As a political artist, her work engages humorously with third-wave feminism, body-image activism, and lesbian identity. Some of her fundamental principles are articulated in a mini-manifesto entitled "Deep Lez I Statement":

> Deep Lez uses cafeteria-style mixings of craft, context, food, direct action, and human connections to maintain radical dyke politics and resistant strategies. Part quilting bee, part public relations campaign, and part Molotov cocktail, Deep Lez seeks to map out the connections between the second position feminisms that

---

[43] For historical examples from the music world of sexual elusiveness as an expressive choice with wide cultural appeal, see Vincent L. Stephens, *Rocking the Closet: How Little Richard, Johnny Ray, Liberace, and Johnny Mathis Queered Pop Music* (Urbana: University of Illinois Press, 2019).

[44] Allyson Mitchell, "Artist Bio," 2014, available online: https://web.archive.org/web/20150116023625/http://www.allysonmitchell.com/html/bio.html.

sustained radical lesbian politics and the current third-wave feminisms that take apart the foundation on which those politics were built.[45]

While Mitchell defines Deep Lez sensibility primarily in terms of political agency—reclaiming the radical ideas of a previous "bell-bottomed" generation for contemporary urban queers—she also touches on favored materials of cultural production, especially macramé, quilting, and other unfashionable vernacular traditions of fabric art. Elizabeth Freeman has interpreted these parallel reclamation projects, the political genealogy and the vintage materials, as illustrating what she calls "temporal drag": the weighty pull of the past on the present, a reconnection with discarded histories, the mutual entanglement of progressive and retrogressive thinking.[46] The "deep" of Deep Lez refers in part to this historical dimension.

In the same statement, Mitchell expresses a strong interest in monstrosity: "Deep Lez began as a cultural project that informed my art practice. I make lesbian feminist monsters using abandoned domestic handicraft. This has meant the creation of giant 3D Lady Sasquatches and room-sized vagina dentatas."[47] The sasquatch piece took several years to assemble in its final form. For its first outing at the Paul Petro gallery in Toronto (*Lady Sasquatch*, 2005), the installation included "two giant sculptures at a campfire, situated in front of a brown living room set; above the couch is a fun-fur wall hanging."[48] Mitchell continued to expand the piece, adding four oversized figures to create a circle, as well as scattering miniature woodland creatures over the available surfaces. I quote from the artist's notes for the final version:

> *Ladies Sasquatch* is a large scale installation consisting of six gigantic and 25 smaller she-beast sculptures presented on a stage/platform measuring 10 feet x 10 feet. The exhibition includes a soundscape consisting of collaged music samples and nature sound effects. The six giantess sculptures represent lesbian feminist sasquatches. The elements of the installation are constructed with appliqué borg, found textiles and taxidermy supplies and influenced by photographs found in *Playboy* magazines from the 1970's and by the bodies of real fat activists. . . . In an attempt to imagine different sexual currencies *Ladies Sasquatch* valorizes cellulite, dirty fingernails, tattoos, big butts, fangs, collectivity and collaboration.[49]

---

[45] Allyson Mitchell, "Deep Lez I Statement," in *Allyson Mitchell: Ladies Sasquatch*, ed. Carla Garnet, Avril McMeekin, Rose Anne Prevec, and Matthew Hyland (Hamilton: McMaster Museum of Art, 2009), 12–13.
[46] Elizabeth Freeman, "Deep Lez: Temporal Drag and the Specters of Feminism," in *Time Binds: Queer Temporalities, Queer Histories* (Durham: Duke University Press, 2010), 59–93.
[47] Mitchell, "Deep Lez I Statement." Images of the installation *Ladies Sasquatch* (2006–2010) can be found at https://web.archive.org/web/20150111041202/http://www.allysonmitchell.com/html/lady_sasquatch.html.
[48] Freeman, "Deep Lez," 86. Freeman reproduces a photograph of the 2005 version, showing the campfire area with several rodent- or goat-like animals—companions or food for the giant bipeds. More detail about this version appears in Helena Reckitt, "My Fuzzy Valentine: Allyson Mitchell," *C Magazine* 89 (Spring 2006): 14–17.
[49] https://web.archive.org/web/20150111041202/http://www.allysonmitchell.com/html/lady_sasquatch.html.

These giants made of yarn, fun fur, and retro wigs double as stuffed objects and irascible subjects. Their poses suggest action, yet smaller, cuter beasts perch on them as though they haven't moved in a while. Their grouping in a simulated habitat recalls an old natural history display or an anthropological exhibit of tribal customs. Yet these are insolent specimens, mooning the observer, exposing vulvas and incisors, shaking their fists, and roaring. Not only do they loom too large for comfort (up to eleven feet), they appear deformed: one has a massive hunchback, fingers dragging on the ground; one crawls on all fours, head twisted past her shoulder; some with furry teats arranged in patterns like hexagons or bandoliers. Their irregular humanoid shapes suggest anarchic genetic activity boiling under the surface, in defiance of species preservation. Each of the six giantesses has unique markings and morphology; each expresses sasquatch nature in her own way.

Spatial symbolism also exhibits contradictions. The figures face inward toward the fire in a disinviting formation, but cutouts in the base platform allow visitors to pierce the circle and access frontal views. The urge to touch these magnificent plush toys must be hard to resist. In the early version, the campfire area incongruously abutted an indoor leisure setting with corner sofa, wildness clashing with suburban comfort and kitsch.[50] In the final version, the 1970s rec room has disappeared. The she-beasts now occupy an uninterrupted outdoor space, but the comfiness and kitsch survive in their bodily material, as if vital forces have stitched themselves into being out of whatever came ready to hand, no matter how manufactured, left over, or marked down.[51]

What type of monster is a sasquatch? Solitary, forest-dwelling, elusive, it serves as a missing link to primate ancestors. Though it may trespass on the fringes of civilization (stealing one's baby or wife), it has the enviable ability to escape surveillance. The Wildman archetype taps into the double streams of primitivist fantasy and settler guilt, suffered by people who have moved in and forced out the original inhabitants. In her notes for the installation, Mitchell acknowledges the Indigenous origins of the sasquatch legend as well as the history of its appropriation:

> Buried in the memory banks of collective popular culture is the mythical and spiritual creature called Sasquatch. Aboriginal ideas about Sasquatch... have been appropriated by the white Canadian mainstream settler culture, arguably as an expression of racist fears around the "otherness" of native culture and nature in general.[52]

The piece itself, however, uses Indigenous lore as a vehicle of fantasy/fear without establishing any such critical perspective. In other words, Mitchell approaches her

---

[50] Reckitt, "My Fuzzy Valentine," 14.
[51] For more about this piece in relation to monstrosity, domesticity, and affect, see Ann Cvetkovich, "Touching the Monster: Deep Lez in Fun Fur," in *Allyson Mitchell: Ladies Sasquatch*, ed. Carla Garnet, Avril McMeekin, Rose Anne Prevec, and Matthew Hyland (Hamilton: McMaster Museum of Art, 2009), 26–31.
[52] https://web.archive.org/web/20150111041202/http://www.allysonmitchell.com/html/lady_sasquatch.html.

source imagery in an admittedly suspect manner: morally, in plundering someone else's cache of myth, and aesthetically, in recycling degraded cultural forms (*Playboy* spreads, tabloid images of Bigfoot, cheap synthetic fur). In camp fashion, this is a way of signaling that there are no pure, uncompromised symbolic materials; all of us are obliged to work with the idioms we are given.[53]

Where *Ladies Sasquatch* does exert critical pressure is in the realm of gender. Mitchell reworks the notion of the Wildman, translating it from a solitary male into a like-minded but motley group of females. We can supply a contemporary intertext in the lesbian separatist Eden of the Michigan Womyn's Music Festival (1976–2015), whose subculture Mitchell knew firsthand.[54] The Festival was intended to be a place where women could temporarily retreat to the land, cast aside patriarchal baggage, and express their true nature. *Ladies Sasquatch* channels this sense of abandon but in a way that is neither benevolent nor safe. Mitchell's Wild Women revel in their bestiality and dangerous mutation, as if assenting to the phobias of the outside world and reflecting them back as badges of honor. In a fantastic reversal of beauty norms, signs of misshapenness are recoded into expressions of vitality, dignity, and abundance— with an affect that flickers between sexy and scary, cuddly and grotesque, pastoral and explosive. In Mitchell's dream world, queer women may escape surveillance, but they have assimilated stigma into the fabric of their bodies.

Two-face

For my final example, I turn to American rapper Mykki Blanco, who released their debut mixtape, *Cosmic Angel: The Illuminati Prince/ss,* in 2012. Blanco entered the music industry via spoken-word and performance-art milieus, thus gaining credentials as an indie or underground artist rather than a mainstream rapper.[55] Their most important stylistic influences include riot grrrl and queercore, in particular the work of zinester and indie filmmaker Bruce LaBruce and genderqueer performance dynamo Vaginal Davis.[56] True to this post-punk lineage, their music often filters punk or industrial sounds through the lens of hip hop. The name Mykki Blanco originated as a stage persona, alluding to Kimmy Blanco, an alter ego of female rapper Lil' Kim.

---

[53] For a helpful history of sasquatch iconography, see Joshua Blu Buhs, "Camping with Bigfoot: Sasquatch and the Varieties of Middle-Class Resistance to Consumer Culture in Late Twentieth-Century North America," *Journal of Popular Culture* 46 (2013): 38–58. He highlights the camp sensibility in Mitchell's sasquatch piece.
[54] Reckitt, "My Fuzzy Valentine."
[55] Alex Chapman, "The Multiplicities of Mykki Blanco," *Interview Magazine*, April 4, 2012, available online: https://www.interviewmagazine.com/culture/mykki-blanco.
[56] Jenna Sauers, "The Making of Mykki Blanco," *Village Voice*, April 10, 2013, available online: https://www.villagevoice.com/2013/04/10/the-making-of-mykki-blanco/. LaBruce has made overtly queer zombie films; see Darren Elliott-Smith, "Gay Zombies: Consuming Masculinity and Community in Bruce LaBruce's *Otto; or, Up with Dead People* (2008) and *L.A. Zombie* (2010)," in *Zombies and Sexuality: Essays on Desire and the Living Dead*, ed. Shaka McGlotten and Steve Jones (Jefferson: McFarland, 2014), 140–58. For more on Vaginal Davis, see Muñoz, *Disidentifications*, 93–115.

Blanco is transfeminine; a multiplicity of gender expression has always been a feature of their appearances, both live and on video.[57] They came out as HIV-positive in 2015.

Commenting on the song "The Initiation" from their EP *Betty Rubble: The Initiation* (2013),[58] Blanco has stated: "I wanted to create my version of what a 'black American gothic song' sounds like."[59] The video is set in a dangerous all-male underworld, a place of racialized abjection. It begins in epigrammatic fashion with a view of a dark corridor sparsely lit by overhead bulbs, and a stern voice invoking Hell. The eye is drawn to the far end of the corridor and the dim outlines of people expecting someone's approach. The song proper begins, announced by a relentless electronic pulse, sharply metallic in timbre as if slicing the air. We see a hand writhing in distress and the back of a twisting neck, then settle upon a man's face in profile as he begins an incantation. Gradually the visual frame expands to reveal a second face atop the man's head, looking upward, scored by bulging veins. Both faces chant in unison. Blanco embodies a dual-nature monster, like Jekyll and Hyde or a man-beast hybrid. The two faces have independent powers of expression. Depending on which face is dominant, the creature has different bodily orientations and different modes of locomotion, one more bestial. Yet the cranial face, though obscene by body standards, is not very different from the anterior face—no less human. In contrast to other videos in which Blanco appears in both masculine and feminine personas, here they present a singular masculine character, in a torn T-shirt with arm tats. The only trace of gender nonconformity is a glimpse of lacquered fingernails, acknowledging the character's latent feminine nature while forcing it down into a minimal, deniable sign. But any such repressed dualities erupt visibly in the malformed head.

The man crawls over cobblestones and brick walls in deserted back streets, through an ugly, uninhabitable space. He spies a pair of policemen rounding up a group of local youths and checking under their knitted caps. One young white man is exposed as a two-face. As this man is forcibly arrested, Blanco's character casually walks by on two legs wearing a baseball cap, then scurries off out of sight. We experience a hounded, furtive existence from the creature's point of view, hiding one's extra face to avoid capture, dropping to all fours with a sense of relief. Arriving at his destination, the man-creature knocks at a speakeasy panel, using his cranial face to give the password.

At this point the lyrics switch into English (sprinkled with Spanish); the spoken phrases parrot clichés of eroticized dancing as the narrative reaches its dark and violent heart. We enter an underground room (the corridor of the opening), repurposed for blood sport. A gang of single-faced men of color welcome the main character, who for the first time exhibits confident alpha behavior, entering the battle cage to confront a

---

[57] Their gender identity and preferred pronouns have evolved during their career, as evident in published interviews.

[58] Mykki Blanco, "The Initiation," produced by Sinden, video directed by Ninian Doff for MOCAtv. Available online: https://mykkiblancoworld.com/video. Lyrics available online: https://genius.com/Mykki-blanco-the-initiation-lyrics.

[59] Gregory Adams, "Mykki Blanco: 'The Initiation,'" *Exclaim!* May 13, 2013, available online: https://exclaim.ca/music/article/mykki_blanco-initiation. Another queer artist-musician who explores a "Negrogothic" aesthetic is M. Lamar; see Westengard, *Gothic Queer Culture*, 148–60.

masked rival, another two-face. The Latin chant returns as the main character subdues his rival with a series of blood-spattering punches, provoking revulsion among the crowd. At the moment of victory, the winner's cranial face displays an ambiguous, contorted expression. He collects his cash and walks away. The fight club scene stages a painful ritual of belonging through violence against one's own kind, which seems to horrify its onlookers as much as it stokes their bloodlust. This is one of those cases where an incomplete ethical shift leaves us stranded between stigma and affirmation.

As for the vocals, the more you peel away at them, the more they tease as to their meaning. The initial invocation cloaks a real curse under its swagger: a vision of a paradoxical, frozen hell pronounced by a Blakean voice of experience. After this opening line in English, Blanco launches into apparent gibberish, delivered in a growling register beset by the implacable industrial sounds mentioned earlier. Once we catch the phrase "Carpe diem," the unknown tongue resolves into Latin, unexpectedly opening a historical chasm beneath our feet. The evocation of Catholic prayer has long been a gothic mainstay, and here the refrain centers on a simple expression of faith in God. The rest of the text is a mosaic of dead watchwords and sayings, some of which resonate with the macabre scenario. "Hodie mihi, cras tibi" (i.e., Today it's my turn, tomorrow it will be yours) was a warning inscription on medieval tombstones; "Homo homini lupus" an old proverb lamenting man's cruelty to man (in this context carrying lycanthropic overtones). Starting with "seize the night" rather than the day feels like an ominous inversion. And a truly nasty surprise lurks in one of the appeals to God: "Deo vindice" (with God as our defender) was the motto chosen by the pro-slavery Confederacy during the US Civil War. So it seems as if the chant is dense with meaning, until one realizes that its fragments are laid out in alphabetical order. Many serial strings are flawless, as if lifted straight from a dictionary.[60] Such a mechanical operation erodes our sense of a judicious author. Are these rote lists after all, lined up merely for their rhythmic quality and vague aura of antiquity? Are we fools to try to decode them, if their opaqueness is the whole point? Blanco's monologue gives the impression of an intensely alienated subject groping for a cultural prehistory and producing a linguistic monster—a pasted, shambling creation seized with pulses of electricity.

Repertoire

The Monster is not the only archetype with special resonance for queer subjects. Other archetypes often work in tandem with this one. Wilde's *Dorian Gray*, for instance, merges the monster with the ultra-aesthete. The Pet Shop Boys overlay their pallid

---

[60] Blanco: "If I'm going to call myself the 'Illuminati Prince/ss,' what better way to explain that than a rap in what would be the tongue of the Illuminati? I got on Wikipedia and Googled Latin phrases from A to Z, and I just started to cull what I liked and what made sense." Christina Lee, "Mykki Blanco Wanted to Rap in 'the Tongue of the Illuminati' on New EP," *mtv.com*, May 28, 2013, available online: http://www.mtv.com/news/2698931/mykki-blanco-betty-rubble-ep/.

vampire with an impudent, mischievous authorial persona. Allyson Mitchell uses mutant she-beasts to dream of life in the bush. And Mykki Blanco makes their Creature a man of sorrows, defined by his suffering. Monstrosity is a versatile aesthetic stance inviting continued exploration by queer artists, as inflected by variables of gender, race, and ability, and intersecting with other personas such as the Dandy, the Trickster, the Dreamer, and the Victim. By looking for such aesthetic stances, we can trace lines of affinity across differences of stylistic context, social privilege, and individual temper. Each archetype offers a repertoire of creative responses to subjugation, involving accounts of deep injury, strategies of survival, and hard-won caches of heretical knowledge.

9

Twelve-tone Terror

Representing Horror and Monstrosity in Dodecaphonic Film Music

James K. Wright

Throughout the twentieth century, the task of scoring horror films presented composers with both unique challenges and new opportunities to experiment with alternative approaches to tonal organization. As Joe Tompkins points out, this was "due in no small part to horror's characteristic emphasis on monstrosity, otherness, abnormality, and dystopia."[1] Philip Brophy concurs, noting that atonality came to signify "the Other: the monstrous, the grotesque, the aberrant."[2] For many early horror film composers the formula was simple enough: "pastel smears of classical music for the correctly socialized human; dark sludges of avant-garde music for the deviant being."[3] "Deviant music," Tompkins notes, "unleashed to arouse fear and anxiety," provided the perfect accompaniment for "its monstrous visualization."[4]

In this chapter I explore the use of Arnold Schoenberg's systematized atonality—the twelve-tone method (and variants thereof)—in twentieth-century horror film scores, and in monster films in particular. My goals are to consolidate the literature in this area, discuss the nature and effectiveness of dodecaphonic music in horror film scoring, observe the chronological arc of popularity of twelve-tone technique among the most prominent composers who scored for horror films in the twentieth century (an arc that peaks in the 1960s), and examine the astonishingly close lineage between the musical modernists working in the film industries of Europe and North America.

---

[1] Joe Tompkins, "Mellifluous Terror: The Discourse of Music and Horror Films," in *A Companion to the Horror Film*, ed. Harry M. Benshoff (Chichester: Wiley Blackwell, 2014), 197.

[2] Phillip Brophy, "The Secret History of Film Music: Picturing Atonality, Part 1," *The Wire* 168 (February 1998): 30–2, available online: http://www.philipbrophy.com/projects/secrethistoryoffilmmusic/09.html

[3] Ibid.

[4] Tompkins, "Mellifluous Terror," 198.

Atonality as *Sonus Horribilus*

Charles Ives put the case succinctly:

> Why tonality as such should be thrown out for good, I can't see. Why it should always be present, I can't see. It depends, it seems to me, a good deal—as clothes depend on the temperature—on what one is trying to do, and on the state of mind.[5]

If we accept the testimony of countless film composers and film music scholars, the atonal "state of mind" appears to be one of terror, angst, madness, foreboding, monstrosity, and/or the invocation of otherworldliness. When "what one is trying to do" as a film composer is to reflect these states of mind, the historical record is clear: atonality was the early-twentieth-century musical language of choice. When a *sonus horribilus* was called for by the film's plot, character development, or mise-en-scène, it was to atonal compositional languages and techniques that composers tended to turn. Rightly or wrongly, it is noteworthy that in journalistic contexts the word "horror" is often mentioned in connection with Schoenberg's conception of atonality.[6] Indeed Schoenberg once remarked that "when people speak of me, they at once connect me with horror, with atonality, and with composition with twelve notes."[7]

Schoenberg insisted that this need not have been the case. Early on, he dismissed any discussion of the relative beauty of consonance and dissonance, a music-structural dichotomy that has held sway since antiquity. In the *Harmonielehre* (1910), Schoenberg insists that consonances and dissonances are "no more opposites than two and ten are opposites." "The expressions 'consonance' and 'dissonance', which signify an antithesis, are false," he wrote. "It all simply depends on the growing ability of the analyzing ear to familiarize itself with the remote overtones, thereby expanding the conception of what is euphonious, suitable for art, so that it embraces the whole natural phenomenon."[8] After Schoenberg's death in 1951, his student Joseph Rufer summarized this view succinctly: "There are only consonances now; dissonances are merely more remote consonances. The whole matter is relative."[9]

Schoenberg maintained that in time, and with the degree of perceptual effort that should be expected of those who care about the musical art, listeners need not hear

---

[5] Charles Ives, *Essays Before a Sonata, The Majority, and Other Writings*, ed. Howard Boatwright (New York: Norton, 1970), 117.
[6] See, for example: Mark Berry, "Arnold Schoenberg: Beauty and Horror," *TLS: The Times Literary Supplement*, January 25, 2020; Mihir Balantrapu, "Schoenberg's House of Horrors," *The Hindu*, July 30, 2015.
[7] Arnold Schoenberg, "A Self Analysis," in *Style and Idea: Selected Writings of Arnold Schoenberg*, ed. Leonard Stein (Berkeley: University of California Press, 1985), 76.
[8] Arnold Schoenberg, *Theory of Harmony* (Berkeley: University of California Press, 1978), 20–1. For corroborative passages concerning dissonances as "the more remote overtones" of the harmonic series, cf. Schoenberg, *Theory of Harmony*, 316–18 and Schoenberg, "A Self Analysis," 87, 260–1, 271–2, 328–9, 312.
[9] Josef Rufer, *Composition with Twelve Notes Related Only to One Another* [orig. German edition, 1952], trans. Humphrey Searle (New York: MacMillan, 1954), 51.

"dissonant" intervals as anything other than harmonic and melodic entities that are qualitatively distinct from—but not somehow less attractive than, or subordinate to—"consonant" intervals (as red is to blue, for example). By this view, the notion that the "dissonances" were relatively tension-laden intervals, in contrast with smoother and calmer sounding consonances, was nothing more than unnecessary ballast inherited from outmoded nineteenth-century harmonic and psychoacoustic theory, and it needed to be jettisoned. In a nutshell, this was Schoenberg's conception of the "emancipation of dissonance."[10] American composer-conductor Russell Steinberg articulates what is now the most widely held view: "While Schoenberg felt it was just a matter of time till the public became accustomed to 'emancipated dissonance,' even now, over a century later, that is not the case."[11] In short, as compelling as they were for Schoenberg and the Second Viennese School, these propositions and prognostications have not been borne out by subsequent music history, compositional practice, and critical reception, generally, though they continue to inspire debate to the present day.

An important factor that undoubtedly encouraged Schoenberg's vision of a broad-ranging future for atonal music was the rise of German expressionism during the most pivotal years of his career and evolution as an artist. As Theodor Adorno tells us, expressionist music is concerned with interior subconscious experience, where "the depiction of fear lies at the centre."[12] Some have argued that expressionism, atonality, twelve-tone technique, and indeed monster films themselves were consequences, in part, of the cataclysmic and "murderous folly of the Great War [that] chilled western Europe to the bone."[13] In this haunted realm, pungent dissonance must dominate, according to Adorno, and "the harmonious, affirmative element of art is banished."[14] Leonard Meyer concurred: "Schoenberg's music is, to a considerable extent [...] almost hysterically emotional because its intensely directive motion can find no points of real repose," he wrote in *Music, the Arts, and Ideas*. "It is driven frantically toward the unattainable."[15] Thomas Harrison similarly notes that atonality's relative flattening of the expressive range in the pitch domain may not have been of great practical concern for Schoenberg, since extended and unresolved harmonic tension was fully consistent with the goals of his angst-ridden expressionist aesthetic.[16] Writing about Schoenberg's

---

[10] See, for example, Juliane Brand and Christopher Hailey, eds., *Constructive Dissonance: Arnold Schoenberg and the Transformations of Twentieth-Century Culture* (Berkeley: University of California Press, 1997); Stephen Hinton, "The Emancipation of Dissonance: Schoenberg's Two Practices of Composition," *Music and Letters* 91, no. 4 (2010): 568–79.

[11] See Russell Steinberg, "Arnold Schoenberg and Breaking Tonality," February 6, 2013, available online: http://www.russellsteinberg.com/blog/2013/9/26/arnold-schoenberg-and-breaking-tonality.

[12] Theodor Adorno, *Night Music: Essays on Music 1928–1962*, ed. Rolf Tiedemann, trans. Wieland Hoban (London, New York, and Calcutta: Seagull Books, 2009), 275–6.

[13] W. Scott Poole, "After World War I, Horror Movies Were Invaded by an Army of Reanimated Corpses," October 2018, available online: https://longreads.com/2018/10/31/after-world-war-i-horror-movies-were-invaded-by-an-army-of-reanimated-corpses/

[14] Adorno, *Night Music*, 275–6.

[15] Leonard Meyer, *Music, the Arts, and Ideas: Patterns and Predictions in Twentieth-Century Culture* (Chicago: University of Chicago Press, 1967), 243.

[16] Thomas Harrison, *1910: The Emancipation of Dissonance* (Berkeley: University of California Press, 1996), 49.

one-act expressionistic monodrama *Erwartung* (1909), Richard Taruskin states the case rhetorically: "Why, after all, should the inner experiences of a woman discovering her lover's bloody corpse be anything but blood-curdling? Why shouldn't a musical representation of such experiences be horrendously dissonant and ugly?"[17] And about Bernard Hermann's score for John Brahm's classic wartime noir film *Hangover Square* (1945), in which the psychopathic lead character George Harvey Bone suffers from a dissociative identity disorder, filmmaker Steve Collins writes: "Atonality is the trigger for Bone's murderous other half, killing at the sound of [this] music."[18] The critical press was equally merciless about this aspect of Schoenberg's atonal expressionism. After a 1912 performance of Schoenberg's *Five Pieces for Orchestra* in London, conducted by Sir Henry Wood, a critic with the *Daily News* wrote: "We must be content with the composer's own assertion that he has depicted his own experiences, for which he has our heartfelt sympathy."[19]

For evidence that Schoenberg was aware, at some level, of the relative expressive limitations of atonal music—despite his periodic protestations to the contrary—we need to look no further than his *Begleitmusik zu einer Lichtspielszene* ("Accompaniment to a Cinematographic Scene"), Op. 34 (1930), a twelve-tone score that had been commissioned not for a specific film but rather as "stock music" for the silent film music library of Heinrichshofen Verlag.[20] The score features three formal sections that bear titles capturing the filmic emotions Schoenberg had set out to convey: (1) "Imminent Danger," (2) "Fear," and (3) "Catastrophe." Hanns Eisler points to this score—written as it was at precisely the moment when audiences were first being introduced to sound films—as a prime exemplar of musical modernism's powerful potential for accompanying film horror:[21]

> The traditional music written for such scenes has never been remotely adequate to them, whereas the shocks of modern music ... could meet their requirements. Schönberg's music for an imaginary film ... is a landmark pointing the way for the full and accurate use of the new musical resources.[22]

---

[17] Richard Taruskin, "The Poietic Fallacy," *The Musical Times* 145, no. 1886 (Spring 2004): 13–14.
[18] Steve Collins, "The Music of Murder: John Brahm's *Hangover Square* (1945)," available online: https://www.splittoothmedia.com/hangover-square/ (accessed October 16, 2020).
[19] Cited in Donald Brook, *Composers' Gallery: Biographical Sketches of Contemporary Composers* (London: Salisbury Square, 1946), 186.
[20] See the discussion of Schoenberg's dialogue with German film composers around this time in Walter Bailey, *Programmatic Elements in the Works of Schoenberg* (Ann Arbor: UMI Research Press, 1984), 21–2. See also Arnold Schoenberg Centre, "Accompaniment to a Cinematographic Scene, Op 34," Available online: http://www.schoenberg.at/index.php/en/joomla-license-sp-1943310036/begleitungsmusik-zu-einer-lichtspielscene-op-34-1929-1930 (accessed July 2, 2018). It is worth noting that Alfredo Casella and Charles Koechlin, Schoenberg's contemporaries, also composed music for nonexistent films.
[21] Stan Link, "Sympathy with the Devil: Music of the Psycho Post-*Psycho*," *Screen* 45, no. 1 (2004): 5.
[22] Theodor Adorno and Hanns Eisler, *Composing for the Films* (New York: Oxford University Press, [1947] 1994), 36–7.

As if to underline the point, film music scholar David Neumeyer has used the first section of Schoenberg's Op. 34, "Drohende Gefahr" ("Imminent Danger"), to underscore scenes from James Whale's *Frankenstein* (1931), including its well-known "Monster's birth" sequence.[23] Schoenberg's score and the film are contemporaneous (1930–1), and during preproduction for *Frankenstein* Whale was very much under the spell of three German Expressionist films—*The Cabinet of Dr. Caligari* (1919), *Golem* (1922) and *Metropolis* (1927) in particular—each of which would ultimately have an important impact on the visual aesthetics underlying his *Frankenstein*.[24]

The 1930s: "Music, Whoa!"

Carl Laemmle Jr. became a key figure in establishing and promoting the monster horror genre in the films he produced with Universal Pictures in the early- and mid-1930s. Over the objection of his father—the German-born Carl Laemmle Sr., founder of Universal—Laemmle Jr. produced a series of early monster films, including *Dracula* (1931),[25] *Frankenstein* (1931),[26] *The Mummy* (1932),[27] *The Invisible Man* (1933), *The Werewolf of London* (1935),[28] *The Bride of Frankenstein* (1935), *The Invisible Ray* (1936),[29] and *Dracula's Daughter* (1936).[30] Laemmle Jr. was generally *not* a fan of film music, though it must be remembered that the very notion of non-diegetic film music had only begun to acquire normative status with the advent of the "talkies" in the early 1930s, and that there was widespread concern among filmmakers about the ways in which music might interfere with the conveyance of spoken dialog. According to William Rosar:

> In the fall of 1930, when Universal finished its production of Bram Stoker's *Dracula*, the place of music in sound films was the subject of ongoing controversy ... One of Laemmle Jr.'s least concerns was having music in his films, and he was directly responsible for the complete absence of music in at least one of the horror

---

[23] David P. Neumeyer, "Schoenberg at the Movies: Dodecaphony and Film," *Music Theory Online*, no. 1 (February 1993), available online: https://mtosmt.org/issues/mto.93.0.1/mto.93.0.1.neumeyer.php.
[24] See, for example, Sarah Milner, "The Composite Frankenstein: the Man, the Monster, the Myth" (MA thesis, Trent University, 2018), 96.
[25] See Ben Model, "Dracula (1931) – A Horror Movie without Horror Movie Music," Available online: https://www.silentfilmmusic.com/dracula-musical-score/ (accessed October 26, 2019). Note that Philip Glass wrote a score for the film in 1999. See Chris Hicks, "Musical Score Adds Bite to 1931 'Dracula,'" *Deseret News*, October 29, 1999, available online: https://www.deseret.com/1999/10/29/19472847/musical-score-adds-bite-to-1931-dracula.
[26] *Frankenstein* (1931) was sparsely scored by Bernard Kaun. Bernard Kaun was German composer Hugo Kaun's eldest son.
[27] *The Mummy* (1932) was scored by James Dietrich.
[28] *The Werewolf of London* (1935) was scored by Karl Hajos.
[29] Both *The Bride of Frankenstein* (1935) and *The Invisible Ray* (1935) were scored by Franz Waxman.
[30] Both *The Invisible Man* (1933) and *Dracula's Daughter* (1936) were scored by Heinz Roemheld.

films he produced [*Dracula*, 1931]. Later, when he sanctioned the use of music, he ordered that it be dubbed so low that it is almost inaudible in some cases.[31]

It nonetheless soon became clear that in the hands of a capable composer, skillful underscoring would make an indispensable contribution to the *frisson* of horror film. In general, however, Universal's Monster-movie scores of the 1930s adopted the vaguely late-nineteenth-century Romantic style that came to predominate throughout Hollywood's "Golden Age" (roughly 1915–55).[32] As film music scholar Sally Bick points out, composers such as Max Steiner (*King Kong*, 1935), Franz Waxman (*The Bride of Frankenstein*, 1935), George Antheil (*The Plainsman*, 1937), and Hans Salter (*The House of Frankenstein*, 1944) often exploited dissonant passages in their horror film scores, but always within a diatonic context. The incorporation of fully emancipated dissonance was not yet possible in the film industry, as the burgeoning film studios of the 1930s were generally averse to the risks inherent in musical experimentation.[33]

The 1940s: Eisler, Bradley, Salter, and Applebaum

In the 1940s, Schoenberg's American student David Raksin incorporated serial passages in his scores for John Brahm's *The Undying Monster* (1942), Otto Preminger's noir thriller *Laura* (1944), and Abraham Polonsky's noir gangster film *Force of Evil* (1948).[34] Generally, however, as Raksin wrote in a letter to the head of the Music Division of the Library of Congress, "the apprenticeship aspect [on-the-job training for Hollywood film composers] was manifest in a limited encouragement to experiment."[35]

Enter Hanns Eisler. Schoenberg had placed the young Eisler at the very top of his list of "best students" during the early postwar period of 1919–23.[36] During the 1930s, Eisler wrote incidental music for several plays by Berthold Brecht, his friend and frequent collaborator. In 1938, just prior to the Austrian Anschluss, he managed to emigrate to the United States. Eisler settled first in New York, where he taught composition at the New School for Social Research and wrote chamber music and scores for documentary film and radio. In 1940, Eisler repurposed his twelve-tone Chamber Symphony Op. 29 (1932) as a film score for *White Flood* (1940), an educational documentary about the

---

[31] William H. Rosar, "Music for the Monsters: Universal Pictures' Horror Film scores of the Thirties," *The Quarterly Journal of the Library of Congress* 40, no. 4 (1983): 391.
[32] Claudia Gorbman, *Unheard Melodies: Narrative Film Music* (Bloomington: Indiana University Press, 1987).
[33] Sally Bick, "A Double Life in Hollywood: Hanns Eisler's Score for the Film Hangmen Also Die and the Covert Expressions of a Marxist Composer," *The Musical Quarterly* 93, no. 1 (2010): 138, fn 38.
[34] See Sabine Feisst, "Arnold Schoenberg and the Cinematic Art," *The Musical Quarterly* 83, no. 1 (1999): 106.
[35] Letter from David Raksin to Harold Spivacke, Washington, DC, Library of Congress. Reprinted in Roy M. Prendergast, *Film Music: A Neglected Art* (New York and London: W.W. Norton & Co., 1977), 41–2 (date and year of correspondence is not given in the citation).
[36] Letter from Arnold Schoenberg to Robert Emmett Stuart, January 27, 1940, cited in Joseph Auner (ed.), *A Schoenberg Reader* (New Haven: Yale University Press, 2003), 285.

Ice Age and the formation of glaciers,[37] and in 1941 he superimposed a twelve-tone score on Dutch director Joris Ivens's silent documentary film *Regen/Rain* (1929). Both of these scoring experiments were completed under the auspices of the Rockefeller Foundation's "Film Music Project."[38] In 1942, Eisler moved to Los Angeles, where he joined Schoenberg, his old friend Brecht, and a large community of other recently exiled German and Austrian *emigré* artists. Five years later, in collaboration with Adorno, Eisler published an important monograph on film scoring, *Composing for the Films*, in which he advocated for the introduction of modernist techniques and other innovations in the field of film scoring.[39]

In Hollywood, Eisler composed scores for eight films, two of which were nominated for Oscars, including Fritz Lang's *Hangmen Also Die!* (1944), which significantly engages dodecaphonic technique throughout. In 1941, newly arrived in America, Eisler asked:

> Is it really necessary to continue the current Hollywood practice of rehashing "original" scores with crumbs picked up from the table of Tchaikovsky, Debussy, Richard Strauss and Stravinsky? Is a new music material possible? May it not even be more useful and effective?[40]

Indeed, in multiple articles, interviews, and other publications culminating in *Composing for the Films*—and in his own compositional practice—Eisler would unfold a protracted argument that "film music should embrace a contemporary music language."[41] Along the way, he enlisted support for this view from several prominent American composers, including Aaron Copland, George Antheil, and Virgil Thomson, among others.[42] In particular, he noted that "Arnold Schoenberg's twelve-tone method is appropriate for film."[43]

Given the aesthetic underpinnings of Viennese atonal expressionism, it's fair to say that the composers of the Second Vienna School were anything but a lighthearted

---

[37] Tobias Fasshauer, "Hanns Eisler's 'Chamber Symphony op. 69' as Film Music for 'White Flood' (1940)," *Historical Journal of Film, Radio and Television* 18, no. 4 (1998): 509-21.

[38] In 1944, a chamber suite based on this score was premièred at the LA home of Arnold Schoenberg—to whom it was dedicated—in celebration of his seventieth birthday. For a detailed description, describes how Eisler employs twelve-tone technique in *Regen*, see Eisler, 1947, 148-52; see also Sally Bick, "Eisler's Notes on Hollywood and the Film Music Project, 1935-42," *Current Musicology*, no. 86 (Fall 2008): 23-4.

[39] Adorno and Eisler, *Composing for the Films*.

[40] Hanns Eisler, "Film Music – Work in Progress," *Modern Music* 18 (January 1941): 251.

[41] Ibid.

[42] Sally Bick, "Composers on the Cultural Front: Aaron Copland and Hanns Eisler in Hollywood," (PhD Dissertation, Yale University, 2001); Sally Bick, "Copland on Hollywood," in *Copland Connotations: Studies and Interviews*, ed. Peter Dickinson (Rochester: Boydell & Brewer Press, 2002), 39-54.

[43] Eisler, "Film Music," 251; see also Hanns Eisler, "Report Concerning the Project: The Relationship Between Music and the Movies," in *Musik und Politik: Schriften Addenda*, ed. Gunter Mayer. Hanns Eisler Gesammelte Werke, ser. 3, no. 3 (Leipzig: VEB Deutscher Verlag fur Musik, 1982), 185; see also Jennifer Heidebrecht, "12 Degrees of Alienation: A Socio-Political Exploration of Hanns Eisler's Use of the Twelve-Tone Method during Exile (1938-1948)" (MA thesis, University of Calgary, 2020).

club, musically speaking. As Alban Berg lamented to Paul Collaer after the Paris première performance of Darius Milhaud's Fifth Chamber Symphony at the Théâtre des Champs-Elysées: "How I would like to be able to create music as happy as this!"[44] Schoenberg may have had similar reflections when he set the ninth of Albert Giraud's twenty-one poetic melodramas in *Pierrot Lunaire* Op. 21 (1912): "Pierrot! My laughter; I can't remember how to laugh!" ("Pierrot! mein Lachen; hab ich verlernt!"). However, in his twelve-tone comic opera *Von heute auf morgen* (1930) Schoenberg nonetheless insisted that he had proven "that every expression and characterization can be produced with the style of free dissonance."[45] Writing about music and humor, musicologist Fred Fisher clearly disagrees, noting that the "Schoenbergian and post-Schoenbergian school of atonalists" are conspicuously absent from any compilation of music written with humorous intent. "It is perhaps possible to achieve humour in a twelve-tone idiom," he writes, "but it is evidently not easy."[46]

Examples exist, however, of film composers engaging twelve-tone technique with humorous intent. Perhaps the earliest example is found in a score for a somewhat surreal situation in an episode titled "Puttin' on the Dog" (1944), from MGM's *Tom and Jerry* cartoon series. The score was written by early animated film composer Scott Bradley (1891–1977), who had studied briefly with Schoenberg at UCLA in the 1930s. Bradley believed that scoring for animation offered infinitely more compositional flexibility and options than live-action films, and he often enlisted modernist techniques when the storyboard called for them. In the *Tom and Jerry* scene in question, in order to intimidate his bulldog nemesis, Tom had been masquerading as a dog by wearing a head stolen from a canine statue he had discovered. Jerry, his miniscule mouse sidekick, dons the head at one point, and an apparently decapitated Tom chases the diminutive Jerry, who scampers around wearing the head (see Figure 9.1). According to Daniel Goldmark's description of the scene, "the disembodied head making its way across the yard is, by itself, an unsettling image."[47] Bradley describes his engagement of twelve-tone technique in order to convey the sense of "confusion and bewilderment" that the scene demanded:[48]

> You saw this little fellow's feet carrying this big head, and it looked very grotesque.... I was stuck for a new way of describing the action musically.... Everything I tried seemed weak and common. Finally, I tried the twelve-tone scale, and *there it was!* ... I hope Dr. Schoenberg will forgive me for using his system to produce funny music.[49]

---

[44] Paul Collaer, *History of Modern Music*, trans. Sally Abeles (New York: World Publishing, 1961), 92.
[45] Arnold Schoenberg, *Style and Idea*, ed. Leonard Stein and trans. Leo Black (Berkeley: University of California Press, 1984), 244–5.
[46] Fred Fisher, "Musical Humor: A Future as Well as a Past?" *The Journal of Aesthetics and Art Criticism* 32, no. 3 (1974): 376.
[47] Daniel Goldmark, *Tunes for 'Toons* (Berkeley: University of California Press, 2005), 70–1.
[48] Ibid., 70.
[49] Scott Bradley, "Music in Cartoons," in *The Cartoon Music Book*, ed. Daniel Goldmark and Yuval Taylor (Chicago: Chicago Review Press, 2002), 118.

Figure 9.1 Image from Hanna Barbera's *Tom and Jerry* series, episode 16 (1'20"): "Puttin' on the Dog Part 2" (1944).

Even here, however, Bradley's use of the twelve-tone method to connote the surreal and the monstrous is abundantly clear. Bradley also incorporated dodecaphonic technique in his score for *The Cat That Hated People* (MGM, 1948), an animated cartoon about a miserable alley cat who hates humans so much that he launches himself to the moon in a rocket. There he encounters a series of monstrously uncanny creatures, including a disembodied singing mouth, a living claw-hammer that chases a nail and pounds the cat into the ground, a self-playing accordion, and a maniacal pencil sharpener that grinds his tail into a pencil point. These aliens are so unnerving that he launches himself back to earth, where he gratefully announces his relief to be back in "the good ol' USA," for which he ostensibly has a new appreciation. In Bradley's frenetically virtuosic Mickey-mousing score,[50] twelve-tone technique is used quite sparingly, appearing only in fleeting passages in the dystopic and misanthropic opening sequences of the cartoon, as well as during the pencil sharpener sequence on the moon.

Canadian composer Louis Applebaum (1918–2000) is best known for his work as a staff composer with the National Film Board of Canada (NFB), for which he wrote some forty-two documentary film scores during the 1940s and 1950s. Following studies with Roy Harris in New York, Applebaum tried his luck in Hollywood, where he scored the Second World War classic *Tomorrow the World!* (1944) and received an Oscar nomination for his score for *The Story of GI Joe* (1947). Of particular interest

---

[50] For film composers, to "Mickey mouse" is to sync the rhythmic features of a film music soundtrack to the details of the onscreen action. The technique was first used in the animated short film *Steamboat Willie* (Disney Studios, 1928), starring Mickey Mouse (hence "Mickey Mousing").

for our purpose is Applebaum's enlistment of twelve-tone technique in his score for Richard Jarvis's *New Faces Come Back* (1946), an NFB postwar documentary about the monstrous disfigurement experienced by countless air force personnel during the war, and the excruciating reconstructive facial surgery they underwent, as well as the concomitant challenge of reintegrating into society when they returned home. About his score, Applebaum wrote:

> Near the beginning of the film we see the lad's plane crash, his body removed from the burning wreck and taken to an English hospital. For a hospital motif, to signify his long and torturously painful treatments, a theme built on the twelve-tone system was used. The theme appears often in many guises. . . . It acts as a unifying thread for the score.[51]

Applebaum describes how he employed a variety of modernist film scoring "tricks" for the film's climactic operating room scene, techniques that he described in 1974 as "not music in the accepted sense":[52]

> [The young man] sees the Frankenstein monster-like figure of a doctor preparing a hideously savage hypodermic, sees the figure lean over totteringly to apply the anaesthetic—and all goes out of focus as the patient loses consciousness. It is a very effective shot . . . [that] needed a treatment in sound beyond the scope of usual orchestral music. . . . Many separate sounds were recorded on several occasions. . . . Several sharply attacked chords were recorded together with a heavy rippling strum of piano strings in the low register. Various harp glissandi were recorded. A man's breathing close to a microphone was recorded. Little snatches of the twelve-tone hospital theme and a few hymn-like figures were played by various orchestral groups. In all about forty separate sounds were recorded. These were prepared in the cutting room for recording into a continuous sound. Some passages . . . were cut in backwards, some at normal speed, others at increased or lowered speeds, thus altering their pitch and instrumental color. . . . [This] is music whose creation was possible only through film.[53]

We will return briefly to the work of Applebaum and other mid-century Canadian film composers further herein.

A study of this kind would be incomplete without giving at least passing mention to the legendary Hans Salter (1896–1994), who studied at the *Hochschule für Musik und darstellende Kunst Wien* with both Alban Berg and Franz Schreker. Salter was musical director of the Vienna *Volksoper* and later of the Berlin Staatsoper, before

---

[51] Louis Applebaum, "Documentary Music," in *Film Music: From Violins to Video*, ed. James L. Limbacher (Metuchen: Scarecrow Press, 1974), 70–1. Richard Jarvis's *New Faces Come Back* (NFB, 1946), available online: https://www.nfb.ca/film/new-faces-come-back/.
[52] Ibid.
[53] Ibid., 70–1.

being hired in 1928 as a film composer by the Universum-Film Aktiengesellschaft (UFA) in Berlin, the studio that had produced such dystopian silent film horror classics as *Der Golem* and *Metropolis*. In 1937, just prior to the Austrian Anschluss, Salter emigrated to America. Given his rare talent for film work, he was quickly scooped up by Universal Studios, where he worked for nearly thirty years, eventually serving as the studio's music director. Salter is arguably best known for his horror and science-fi film scores, many of them starring Boris Karloff, Bela Legosi, and Lon Chaney Jr. His monster-movie scores include *The Son of Frankenstein* (1939), *The Mummy's Hand* (1940), *Black Friday* (1940), *Man-made Monster* (1941), *The Wolf Man* (1941), *The Ghost of Frankenstein* (1942), *Son of Dracula* (1943), *House of Frankenstein* (1944), *The Invisible Man's Revenge* (1944), *Scarlet Street* (1945), *The 5000 Fingers of Dr. T.* (1953), *The Creature from the Black Lagoon* (1954), and *The Incredible Shrinking Man* (1957).

Lifting up the importance of music in horror film, Salter describes how his approach to the problems it posed was largely technical in nature:

> Horror films were a big challenge for me, because it was obvious when we watched the films that they would not work without the help of the music. . . . You had to create the horror with the music, create a tension that would have been missing on the screen without it. . . . I was able to develop an adequate musical technique for this genre. It was simply a question of applying the right technique.[54]

Yet, as much as Salter's horror film scores show him to be a forward-looking modernist in many respects, he never fully adopted twelve-tone technique.[55] His score for Jack Arnold's *The Creature from the Black Lagoon* (co-composed in collaboration with Henry Mancini and Herman Stein)[56] is nonetheless "remarkably brooding, shifting through a kind of soft serialism, clearly connoting that all is not as it appears," in Philip Brophy's apt description. "As with many other 50s films which explore oceans/jungles/caves/deserts to uncover monsters," Brophy adds, "nature is rendered beautiful but beastly [in this score]; its dissonance is not emancipated, but set loose, ready to terrorize."[57]

---

[54] Interview with Hans Salter (c. 1980), quoted in Helmut G. Asper, *Etwas Besseres als den Tod: Filmexil in Hollywood* (Marburg: Schüren, 2002), 499.
[55] Hans J. Salter, "Als ich 1937 nach Hollywood kam, lag das Land noch immer in tiefster Depression," in *Aufbruch ins Ungewisse: Österreichische Filmschaffende in der Emigration vor 1945*, ed. Christian Cargnelli and Michael Omasta (Vienna: Wespennest, 1993).
[56] The division of score-segment responsibilities between Salter, Mancini and Stein is described in considerable detail in Julia Heimerdinger, "Von 'schreienden Dissonanzen' und 'gedankenlesender Zwölftonmusik': Musikalische Modernen im Hollywoodkino am Beispiel von *Creature from the Black Lagoon* (1954) und *The Cobweb* (1955)," in *Kieler Beiträge zur Filmmusikforschung 8: Symphonische Musik im Film, Filmmusikpädagogik, Anime-Soundtracks* (Kiel, 2012), 80–132.
[57] Brophy, "The Secret History of Film Music," 30–2.

The 1950s: Groundbreaking Scores by Rosenman, Searle, Gold, and Bernard

As with so many aspects of postwar taste and culture, film music norms began to shift in the 1950s, with some film composers opting to employ modernistic techniques more substantively, dodecaphony in particular. In a 1974 interview, British film composer Richard Rodney Bennett recalls:

> I started writing movies in the mid-1950s, and it was a time when I think the old traditions of film music—the symphonic 1930s/40s style—were starting to fade, and ... styles of music were changing. I remember that when I was about sixteen or eighteen I heard some very important film scores ... particularly *East of Eden* by Leonard Rosenman.... Not bang-up-to-the-minute avant-garde music, but it sounded as though the composers had heard Bartók and Berg and Stravinsky, as opposed to just Rachmaninov and Tchaikovsky and Debussy.

Leonard Rosenman (1924–2008)—a student of Schoenberg, Dallapiccola, and Sessions (see Figure 9.2)—is generally credited as the first composer to use a twelve-tone row in a commercial Hollywood film.[58] In *East of Eden* (1955), Rosenman's first film score, he

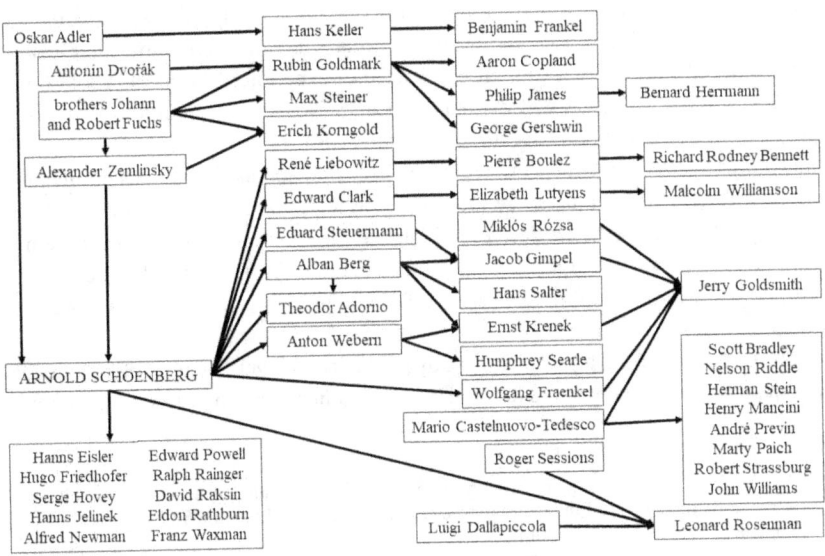

Figure 9.2 Threads of lineage, influence and pedagogy connecting some of the leading composers (many of them film composers) of the twentieth century, most of whom are mentioned in this chapter. In the graphic above, chronology is only very loosely represented by the horizontal positioning of composers' names.

---

[58] Tony Thomas, *Film Score: The Art & Craft of Movie Music* (Burbank: Riverwood Press, 1991), 310.

wrote tonal music for scenes involving teenagers, and atonal music for scenes involving the adults with whom they were in conflict.[59] About the score, David Neumeyer writes that Rosenman's music "transplants the [atonal] manner of Schoenberg's Opus 16 to turn-of-the-century Monterey and the inner turmoil of the James Dean character."[60] Shortly after scoring *East of Eden*, Rosenman wrote another partially atonal score for Nicholas Ray's classic *Rebel without a Cause* (1955), starring James Dean playing the anguished lead character. Tragically, Dean died in an automobile accident on September 30 of that year, a month before the film's October 27 release by Warner Brothers. "Rosenman was rightly credited for having created a specific 'James Dean sound,'" Sabine Feisst notes, "music of revolt and dissonance."[61]

Remarkably, between working on these two landmark James Dean films, Rosenman also wrote the score for Vincent Minnelli's *The Cobweb* (1955), a film that is perhaps of greater interest for our purpose, given the composer's extensive employment of twelve-tone technique.[62] The film is set in a psychiatric clinic where the psychiatrists and staff are as neurotically unstable as the psychiatric patients under their care. In an interview with Roy Prendergast, Rosenman describes how he employed serial technique in the score because at the time he was enthralled with Schoenberg's *Piano Concerto* Op. 42 (the influence of which is abundantly evident in *The Cobweb*), and because he wanted the music to convey the neurotic interior lives of the film's characters: "I wanted more neurosis; much more of the inner workings of the people which, I think, were a bit lacking in the overt action of the film."[63] He felt that his dodecaphonic score would "set off the film as not simply a pot-boiler melodrama which happened to center around an asylum, but rather a film in which this kind of expressionistic music could be, so to speak, mind reading or, as I say, super real."[64] Rosenman's intention was "not to 'ape' or mimic the physical aspect of the screen *mise en scène*," but rather "to show what was going on inside the characters' heads."[65] As Thomas Karban has pointed out, Rosenman's groundbreaking score for *The Cobweb* was considered a "booster for the future use of modern stylistic devices in Hollywood."[66] Following Rosenman's example in this respect, even the normally traditionalist Franz Waxman used dodecaphonic technique in his score for *The Nun's Story* (1959), to underscore a scene in a psychiatric ward.

It bears noting that in an empirical study published in 1989, David Smith and Jordan Witt demonstrated that relative to tonal music, listeners tend to perceive atonal music

---

[59] David Bordwell, Janet Staiger, and Kristin Thompson, *The Classical Hollywood Cinema: Film Style and Mode of Production to 1960* (New York: Columbia University Press, 1985), 74.
[60] Neumeyer, "Dodecaphony and Film."
[61] Sabine Feisst, "Serving Two Masters: Leonard Rosenman's Music for Films and for the Concert Hall," *21st Century Music* 7, no. 5 (2000): 20.
[62] Ibid.
[63] Prendergast, *Film Music*, 119.
[64] Ibid.
[65] Ibid.
[66] Thomas Karban, "Kaum Chancen für Modernes. Filmmusik in Hollywood [Little Chance for the Moderns: Film music in Hollywood]," *Neue Zeitschrift für Musik* 156, no. 4 (1995): 38. Translation from Sabine Feisst, "Serving Two Masters," 20, fn 3.

to be much more strongly associated with feelings of agitation, manic activity, chaotic motion and structure, confusion, and insanity.[67] Indeed, using atonality to connote psychiatric instability has a long history, dating at least from Strauss's *Elektra* (1909) and Schoenberg's *Pierrot Lunaire* and *Erwartung* (1909 and 1912, respectively), and with even earlier precedents in the nineteenth century.[68] As Stan Link has observed: "With aesthetic foundations tied to Freudian psychoanalytic ideas, and development roughly concurrent with that of early cinema, musical expressionism was perhaps destined to constitute the traditional sound of the filmic psychopath."[69]

In the late 1950s and early 1960s, British composer Humphrey Searle wrote two stirring twelve-tone scores for horror films. The first was for the monster film *The Abominable Snowman* (1957), for Hammer Film Productions, and the second for the MGM horror *The Haunting* (1963), a film Martin Scorsese has ranked at the top on his list of the most chilling horror films of all time.[70] After Searle's studies with John Ireland at London's Royal College of Music (RCM) during the mid-1930s, he spent most of the 1937–8 academic year studying music theory and composition with Anton Webern in Vienna.[71] A polyglot, Searle translated two major German-language books on the Second Vienna School into English: *Die Komposition mit zwölf Tönen* (1952) by Schoenberg's student Josef Rufer,[72] and Walter Kolneder's *Eine Einführung in die Musik von Anton Webern* (1961),[73] the first attempt at a comprehensive monograph on Webern's works. Searle was one of the leading pioneers of serialism in Britain, and he used his role as a producer at the BBC (1946–8) to promote the cause of serial composers.

At age seventeen, Viennese-born composer Ernest Gold (1921–99) enrolled in Vienna's *Akademie für Musik und darstellende Kunst*, where in 1937 he briefly studied with Schoenberg's student Erwin Ratz. Like the Jewish families of so many of his Austrian contemporaries, Gold's family soon emigrated to America following the Anschluss in March of 1938. Gold first employed twelve-tone technique in passages

---

[67] David J. Smith and Jordan N. Witt. "Spun Steel and Stardust: The Rejection of Contemporary Compositions," *Music Perception* 7, no. 2 (1989): 169–85.

[68] See for example Diane Penney, "The Method Behind the Madness: Schoenberg's *Erwartung*," in *Freie Referate 13: Mahler/Schönberg*, ed. Hermann Danuser and Tobias Plebuch (Kassel: Bärenreiter Verlag, 1998), 396–402; Julia Heimerdinger, "Music and Sound in the Horror Film and Why Some Modern and Avant-garde Music Lends Itself to it So Well," *Seiltanz. Beiträge zur Musik der Gegenwart* 4 (2012): 4–16; Robert Quist, "Atonality in Music and the Upheavals of High Modernity," in *Catastrophe and Philosophy*, eds. JeiDong Ryu, Sarah K. Corrigan, Kwon Jong Yoo, John Ross, Steven Cresap, and Diana Prokofyeva (Washington, DC: Lexington Books, 2018), 205–17; Fernando E. Forcen, *Monsters, Demons, and Psychopaths: Psychiatry in Horror Film* (Boca Raton: CRC Press, 2016)

[69] Link, "Sympathy," 1.

[70] "From Alfred Hitchcock to Stanley Kubrick: Martin Scorsese Named the 11 Greatest Horror Films of All Time," *Far Out Magazine*, 2020, available online: https://faroutmagazine.co.uk/martin-scorsese-11-favourite-horror-films-list-hitchcock-kubrick/.

[71] See Humphrey Searle and Anton von Webern, "Conversations with Webern," *The Musical Times* 81, no. 1172 (1940): 405–6.

[72] Rufer, *Composition*.

[73] Walter Kolneder, *Anton Webern: An Introduction to His Works*, trans. Humphrey Searle (Berkeley, CA: University of California Press, 1968).

of his score for Stanley Kramer's *On the Beach* (1959), a film adaptation of Nevil Shute's eponymous novel of 1957 about a post-nuclear apocalypse in Australia. Given the bleak nature of Shute's novel, Gold decided that he could employ dodecaphonic technique to powerful effect if he used it to signal the presence of radioactive fallout.[74] "I used the twelve-tone set approach in this sequence to bring out the chain reaction of radiation, the billiard balls analogy used in freshman physics," Gold told film music scholar Gregory Burt. "This is precisely where I like the twelve-tone system—it is like physics to me."[75]

Another important British film composer who explored modernist techniques extensively in his horror film scores of the 1950s and 1960s is James Bernard (1925–2001), a composer who had served with the Royal Air Force during the war and subsequently studied with Herbert Howells at the Royal College of Music, London (1947–9).[76] A characteristic example of Bernard's engagement with modernist technique is seen in the music he used to accompany the appearance of a "giant Thing, half-man, half-cactus" in *The Quartermass Xperiment* (1955, released in America with the title *The Creeping Unknown*), a Hammer horror about a space fungus that transforms an astronaut into a deadly monster.[77] About this score, Bernard's biographer David Huckvale writes: "Most astonishing of all, for an English film score of the mid-1950s, is Bernard's use of tone clusters."[78] In contrast to the aversion to musical modernism that dominated at Universal Studios and elsewhere, Bernard was impressed with Hammer's adventuresome approach to music in permitting modernist idioms:

> I give full marks to Hammer and to Anthony Hinds [screenwriter, producer and son of Hammer Films founder William Hinds], because he encouraged this. They never raised their eyebrows at the comparative weirdness of the sounds . . . I've always found atonal and twelve-tone music to be unappealing. . . . But then I found myself doing the same kind of thing—it was the sort of sound I needed for the film [*The Quartermass Xperiment*].[79]

In a syndicated review for *London Calling* (March 8, 1956), Paul Dehn applauds Bernard's music in *The Quartermass Xperiment*: "A subordinate contribution to my 'shivers' was the music by James Bernard . . . [who] has taken his main theme, which consists of two notes a semitone apart, from the peculiar rhythm of the monster's heartbeat."[80] For its obstinate semitonal monster motif we might think of Bernard's title

---

[74] Feisst, "Arnold Schoenberg and the Cinematic Art," 106.
[75] Gregory Burt, *The Art of Film Music* (Boston: Northeastern University Press, 1994), 48.
[76] James Abbott, "An Interview with Composer James Bernard, Part II," *The Jade Sphinx*, September 14, 2011. Available online: http://thejadesphinx.blogspot.com/2011/09/interview-with-composer-james-bernard_14.html
[77] David Huckvale, *James Bernard, Composer to Count Dracula: A Critical Biography* (Jefferson: McFarland, 2006), 53.
[78] Ibid., 52.
[79] Ibid.
[80] Ibid., 54. It should be noted that Dehn may have been somewhat biased about Bernard's score, given that he and Bernard were lifelong partners.

music for *The Quartermass Xperiment* as an important precursor to John Williams's nerve-fraying main theme for *Jaws* (1975), an Oscar-winning horror film score that created such a sensation some twenty years later. Bernard's monster horror film work with Hammer Film Productions includes his scores for *The Curse of Frankenstein* (1957), *Dracula* (1958), *The Kiss of the Vampire* (1962), *The Gorgon* (1964), *Dracula: Prince of Darkness* (1966), *The Plague of the Zombies* (1966), *Frankenstein Created Woman* (1967), *The Devil Rides Out* (1968), *Dracula Has Risen from the Grave* (1968), *Frankenstein Must Be Destroyed* (1969), *Taste the Blood of Dracula* (1970), *Scars of Dracula* (1970), *Frankenstein and the Monster from Hell* (1974), and *The Legend of the Seven Golden Vampires* (1974).[81]

The 1960s: Lutyens, Frankel, and Goldsmith's "Monkeying Around"

If ever there were a heyday—all things being relative—for the use of twelve-tone technique in film scoring, it was the 1960s. In Britain, two composers, in particular, Elisabeth Lutyens (1906–83) and Benjamin Frankel (1906–73), followed in the footsteps of Searle in their adoption of the twelve-tone method for horror film work. Lutyens came to be known as "the Horror Queen" for the series of scores she wrote for both Hammer Films and Amicus Productions. The monstrously green nail polish Lutyens wore in public only consolidated this image, a reputation in which she apparently reveled.[82] Together with Searle and her husband Edward Clark (the British conductor who had studied with Schoenberg in Berlin from 1910 through 1912), Lutyens was among Britain's leading champions of the continental avant-garde. Though her serial technique was often employed flexibly, Lutyens was known in some circles as "twelve-tone Lizzie," for her committed engagement of a very personal variant of twelve-tone technique in virtually all of her mature film scores and concert music.[83] Dodecaphonic film scores by Lutyens during the 1960s include her music for a creepy Hammer thriller on the topic of child molestation (*Never Take Sweets from a Stranger*, 1960), an Amicus horror involving a werewolf, a vampire and a disembodied hand (*Dr. Terror's House of Horrors*, 1965), a Lippert Pictures sci-fi film about zombies and alien robots (*The Earth Dies Screaming*, 1965), an Amicus horror about a series of mysterious deaths resulting from the evil presence of the Marquis de Sade's unearthed skull (*The Skull*, 1965), as well as *The Psychopath* (1966) and *The Terrornauts* (1967). Lutyens also frequently wrote scores for radio and television, including a densely dissonant twelve-tone score for a wordless BBC documentary by David Thompson titled *Francis Bacon: Paintings, 1944-1962* (1963), featuring Bacon's grotesquely monstrous, surreal, and

---

[81] Huckvale, *James Bernard*, 76.
[82] Kimberly Lindbergs, "Elisabeth Lutyens: The Horror Queen of Film Composers," *Cinebeats*, March 11, 2020. Available online: https://cinebeats.wordpress.com/2020/03/11/elisabeth-lutyens-the-horror-queen-of-film-composers.
[83] Anthony Payne, "Lutyens's Solution to Serial Problems," *The Listener*, December 5, 1963.

expressionistic paintings.[84] It was undoubtedly through Lutyens's horror film music that many British and Americans filmgoers first received exposure to dodecaphonic music.[85]

British composer Benjamin Frankel may have scored more important films such as *The Importance of Being Ernest* (1952), *The Night of the Iguana* (1964), and *The Battle of the Bulge* (1965), but as a film composer he is perhaps best remembered for his twelve-tone score for *The Curse of the Werewolf* (1961), a Hammer monster film featuring the young Oliver Reed in the starring role as the half-man-half-werewolf, and the first English-language film to feature dodecaphonic music extensively.[86] A few years earlier, Frankel had experimented in a limited way with twelve-tone passages in his scoring of solitary-confinement sequences in Peter Glenville's *The Prisoner* (1955).[87] As Gregory Newbold has shown in his fine analytical study of Frankel's music for *The Curse of the Werewolf*, this score exemplifies Frankel's unique and personal form of twelve-tone technique, in which he sought to reconcile it with tonality.[88] Frankel adopted serialism during the last fifteen years of his compositional career, due in part to the encouragement of his friend Hans Keller,[89] whose own friend and teacher had been Oskar Adler, who had also been Arnold Schoenberg's early childhood companion and musical mentor (these common threads of lineage, influence, and pedagogy are traced in Figure 9.2).[90]

Perhaps on the strength of Louis Applebaum's reputation for engaging with innovative film scoring techniques (as demonstrated in *New Faces Come Back*, 1946, discussed earlier), the Canadian composer was invited to collaborate with Toronto electronic music guru Myron Schaeffer on the soundtrack of Canada's first feature-length horror film: Julian Roffman's 3D surrealist extravaganza, *The Mask* (1961). The story involves a psychiatrist who comes into possession of a mysterious primeval mask that causes him to experience increasingly disturbing and sadistic visions, dreams that begin to alter his character and eventually drive him to madness. Throughout the score, Applebaum extensively engages twelve-tone technique and other modernist compositional devices.[91] Roffman even corresponded with Timothy Leary in the hope that his dream sequences would recreate a filmic experience akin to an LSD trip.[92]

---

[84] David Thompson (dir.), *Francis Bacon: Paintings 1944–62* (London: Samaritan Films, 1962).
[85] Cat Kenwell, "Scores for Horrors: The Underappreciated Queen of Hammer and Amicus Horror," *Horror Tree*, available online: https://horrortree.com/wihm-scores-for-horrors-the-underappreciated-queen-of-hammer-and-amicus-horror/.
[86] Huckvale, *James Bernard*, 585–6.
[87] Mervyn Cooke, *The History of Film Music* (Cambridge: Cambridge University Press, 2008), 247.
[88] Gregory S. Newbold, "Benjamin Frankel's Serial Film Score for *The Curse of the Werewolf*: An Historical Context and Analysis" (MA thesis, University of Iowa, 2017).
[89] Newbold, "Serial Film Score," 5–7.
[90] Christopher Wintle, "Hans Keller (1919–1985): An Introduction to His Life and Works," *Music Analysis* 5, no. 2/3 (1986): 344.
[91] Myron Schaeffer, "The Electronic Music Studio of the University of Toronto," *Journal of Music Theory* 7, no. 1 (Spring 1963): 73–81.
[92] R. J. Nadon, "The Mask (1961)—Canada's Horror History," *Killer Canuck*, October 1, 2020, available online: https://www.youtube.com/watch?v=NNGES5QbHeg.; see also Kevin Lyons, "The Mask

Reviewer Kevin Lyon heaped praise on Applebaum's scoring of these sequences in particular:

> Louis Applebaum's score during these visions suddenly becomes strikingly wild.... With its squelching synths, water drips, rapid arpeggios, ominous rumbles and assorted inexplicable noises . . . [this is] some of the most effective experimental music heard in any 1960s film.[93]

About this "chilling 3D psychedelic nightmare from the north," one monster film blogger describes the score as a triumph of the genre:

> This film would have scared the frozen snot out of you back in 1961, and it's still eerie as hell to this day! I get the heebie-jeebies just writing about it! The combined musical composition skills of Louis Applebaum and the wacky electronic genius of Myron Schaeffer makes for a pretty heady stew. Be very careful listening to this stuff; we will not be responsible![94]

Another Canadian horror film from this period, *The Bloody Brood* (1959), tells the story of a hapless drug dealer, Nico (Peter Falk), who investigates the death of his brother after ingesting hamburger laced with shards of glass. Under the film's musical director Louis Applebaum, Canadian composer Harry Freedman (1922–2005) provided the largely dodecaphonic score. From 1945 to 1951, Freedman had studied at the University of Toronto with John Weinzweig, the prominent Canadian pedagogue and dodecaphonist, and he had also received sporadic instruction from both Messiaen and Copland during summer sessions at Tanglewood. Freedman later scored the supernatural satanic horror film *The Pyx* (1973), starring Christopher Plummer and Karen Black.

From 1979 to 1981, Harry Freedman served as president of the Guild of Canadian Film Composers. An active member of the Guild at the time was Canadian film composer Eldon Rathburn (1916–2008), who had been briefly mentored by Schoenberg in the mid-1940s, and who later incorporated serial technique in two scores he wrote for documentary films produced by the National Film Board of Canada: *Universe* (1960) and *Sky* (1963). Curiously—given that it was essentially a planetary science documentary—*Universe* was a crucially important source of inspiration for Stanley Kubrick's landmark sci-fi film *2001: A Space Odyssey* (1968).[95]

In 1961, even the relatively traditional Hungarian-American film composer Miklós Rózsa (1907–95) tried his hand with twelve-tone technique to personify Satan in the

---

(1961)," *The EOFFTV (Encyclopedia of Fantastic Film and Television) Review*, February 1, 2020, available online: https://eofftvreview.wordpress.com/2020/02/01/the-mask-1961/.

[93] Lyons, "The Mask."
[94] Eegah and Tabonga, "The Mask (1961): Louis Applebaum and Myron Schaeffer—'Put The Mask On Now'," *Monster Movie Music*, April 19, 2008, available online: https://monstermoviemusic.blogspot.com/2008/04/mask-applebaumschaeffer-put-mask-on.html.
[95] James K. Wright, *They Shot, He Scored: The Life and Music of Eldon Rathburn* (Montreal: McGill-Queen's University Press, 2019), 75–82.

"Temptation of Christ" theme from his score for Nicholas Ray's *King of Kings*. One wonders whether Rózsa might have had additional exposure to serialism through the work of Jerry Goldsmith (1929–2004) around that time, as Goldsmith attended his weekly film music course at the University of Southern California during the 1950s.[96]

Jerry Goldsmith is undoubtedly best known for his chilling twelve-tone score for director Franklin Schaffner's classic 1968 sci-fi film, *Planet of the Apes*, based on Pierre Boulle's novel *La Planète des Singes* (1963). Vincent Gassi writes about the relative rarity of twelve-tone scoring techniques in Hollywood before and after Goldsmith's landmark score:

> The paucity of scores drawing on twelve-tone technique before and after [*Planet of the Apes*] brings into stark view the lack of "modernism" in Hollywood.... Though film composers did occasionally push beyond tonal barriers, serialism, unlike music written for the concert stage, never became a standard approach to film scoring.[97]

Never before or since has a film composer employed dodecaphonic technique as thoroughly and effectively as Goldsmith in this austere score. "It stands alone in its extensive use of tone rows and their permutations throughout the entire score," writes Gassi.[98] The score is also a fine example of the employment of twelve-tone technique to create an anempathetic perspective on the film's dystopic diegesis. Twenty years before *Planet of the Apes*, Eisler and Adorno had pointed out that rather than looking to the techniques of musical modernism to provide new means for conveying the depths of emotional angst and terror, in some cases these techniques might be engaged to convey a sense of removed coolness or even indifference; that is, to suggest alienation and a sense of horrified recoil from the impinging forces of modernity. "The new music is capable of expressing absence of expression, quietude, indifference and apathy with an intensity beyond the power of traditional music," they wrote in *Composing for the Films*.[99] In short, Eisler and Adorno propose that modernistic techniques may be best suited to what Michel Chion calls an "anempathetic" mood, a kind of musical coldness toward what is happening onscreen, an indifference which in itself can have a chilling effect.[100] In *Unheard Melodies*, Claudia Gorbman draws attention to the unique power of anempathetic music, a sonic backdrop that seems to be "indifferent to violence or human tragedy."[101] In this respect and others, Goldsmith's landmark score for *Planet of*

---

[96] See Chapter 1 from Carrie Goldsmith's aborted biography of her father, posted on February 2, 2004, http://www.jerrygoldsmithonline.com/spotlight_biography_preview.htm; see also Goldsmith's obituary, "Jerry Goldsmith: Prolific Film and Television Composer," *The Independent*, October 10, 2011, available online: https://www.independent.co.uk/news/obituaries/jerry-goldsmith-550152.html.
[97] *The Independent*, "Prolific," 4.
[98] Ibid., 3–4.
[99] Adorno and Eisler, *Composing for the Films*, 40.
[100] Michel Chion, *Audio-Vision: Sound on Screen* (New York: Columbia University Press, 1994), 8.
[101] Gorbman, *Unheard Melodies*, 159–61.

the Apes opens up new and exciting insights into the expressive potential of music and the moving image in horror film.

In view of the renown and impact of *Planet of the Apes*, it is easy to overlook the fact that it was in John Huston's biopic, *Freud* (1962), that Goldsmith first experimented with serial technique in a film score. The score garnered Goldsmith the first of his many Academy Award nominations (eighteen in all during his long Hollywood career). About Goldsmith's score for *Freud*, reviewer James Southall opines:

> It's very hard to imagine any film made in Hollywood today having music as unfailingly modern as this. Huston chose to make his film in black-and-white, and one could certainly say there's more than a noirish hint to Goldsmith's music—it's unsettling, sometimes creepy, a turbulent study of the human mind. Don't come here expecting melody—this is one of the most uncompromisingly atonal scores of the composer's career. . . . It's scarcely believable that Goldsmith was so confident, so early in his career, to write a score like this.[102]

Seventeen years later, Ridley Scott imported large segments from Goldsmith's score for *Freud* and combined them with the composer's original music for *Alien* (1979), arguably the granddaddy of all American monster films of the 1970s and 1980s.[103] Scott decided to use large score segments from *Freud* after Terry Rawlings, the sound editor for *Alien*, somewhat arbitrarily decided to use *Freud* excerpts in the "temp score" that was employed while Goldsmith was completing his music. Goldsmith was thoroughly incensed by Scott's decision, and he implored the director to allow him to write additional material that he felt would work better with the rest of his score. But Scott was resolute in his decision to redeploy large chunks of the score from *Freud* in *Alien*. Notwithstanding the overwhelming success of *Alien*, both at the box office and on the awards circuit, Goldsmith remained furious about Scott's decision for the rest of his life. It is unsurprising that Goldsmith scored only one of the *Planet of the Apes* sequels—*Escape from the Planet of the Apes* (1971)—as subsequent directors turned to Leonard Rosenman to score *Beneath the Planet of the Apes* (1970), and *Battle for the Planet of the Apes* (1973).

Three Degrees of Separation

At age sixteen, Goldsmith first studied composition with Mario Castelnuovo-Tedesco, who had worked as a film composer on over one hundred with MGM. Castelnuovo-Tedesco's impact on Hollywood film music is significant: the list of prominent film

---

[102] James Southall, "Freud: An Uncompromisingly Dark Journey into the Human Mind—Music by Jerry Goldsmith," *Movie Wave—Film Music Reviews*, available online: http://www.movie-wave.net/titles/freud.html.

[103] Charlie Brigden, "The Great Unknown: The Story behind Jerry Goldsmith's Score for *Alien*," *RogerEbert.com*, May 17, 2017, available online: https://www.rogerebert.com/features/the-great-unknown-the-story-behind-jerry-goldsmiths-score-for-alien.

composers who studied with him includes Henry Mancini, Nelson Riddle, Herman Stein, André Previn, Marty Paich, Scott Bradley, and John Williams (see Figure 9.2). During his formative years, Goldsmith also studied with Jacob Gimpel, Wolfgang Fraenkel, and Ernst Krenek. Gimpel had studied with Edward Steuermann who was a student of Schoenberg, and Krenek had studied with both Alban Berg and Anton Webern, as had Fraenkel (see Figure 9.2). It is little wonder that Goldsmith was well acquainted with serial technique. As shown in Figure 9.2, Schoenberg also taught numerous other Hollywood film composers, including David Raksin, Ralph Rainger, Edward Powell, Alfred Newman, Hugo Friedhofer, Serge Hovey, Leonard Rosenman, and Franz Waxman.[104] Friedhofer is noteworthy for his two scores written for films about the monstrous Jack the Ripper: *The Lodger* (1944) and *Man in the Attic* (1953). In this chapter we have also briefly discussed the film work of Bernard, Bradley, Eisler, Frankel, Gold, Hermann, Krenek, Lutyens, Rathburn, Rosenman, Salter, and Serle, all of whom are shown in Figure 9.2, which reflects the astonishingly close threads of lineage, influence, and pedagogy that connect these composers.

Conclusion

Apart from whatever benefits might accrue from taking a synoptic look at the employment of twelve-tone technique in twentieth-century horror film scores, what else can be gleaned from the preceding pages? We have seen that at mid-century, the British horror film studios—Hammer and Amicus in particular—were generally much more musically adventuresome than their American counterparts. We have also seen that the "era" of twelve-tone technique in film music—which rises slowly in the 1940s, gains momentum in the 1950s, reaches a zenith in the 1960s, subsides in the 1970s, and disappears almost entirely from the scoring palette of film composers during the past forty years—appears to have been an ephemeral one. The end of this trend coincides roughly with the end of the period during which serial orthodoxy enjoyed its greatest prominence among avant-garde composers of Western art music: "The last musical style of significance to enjoy some duration, some temporary stability, was Serialism," wrote George Rochberg in 1971, "and that lasted less than two full generations, from 1923 to about 1965."[105]

Some have suggested that tonal music has been dominant in Western culture because, as Irving Kolodin's has pointed out, it possesses "an extraordinary affinity for aural recognition, mental recollection, and emotional response."[106] As we have

---

[104] See Sabine Feisst, *Schoenberg's New World: The American Years* (Oxford: Oxford University Press, 2011).

[105] George Rochberg, "The Avant-Garde and the Aesthetics of Survival," *New Literary History* 3, no. 1 (1971): 73. About Rochberg's "apostasy," see also Alan Gillmor, "The Apostasy of George Rochberg," *Intersections: Canadian Journal of Music* 29, no. 1 (2009): 32–48.

[106] Irving Kolodin, *The Continuity of Music: A History of Influence* (New York: Knopf, 1969), 357. I am grateful to Vincent Gassi for highlighting Kolodin's insights in "The Forbidden Zone, Escaping

seen, numerous twentieth-century film composers would have mounted a vociferous challenge to this assertion. It is nonetheless clear that the expressive emotional range of atonal music has proven to be relatively limited. While it is well suited to the dramatic contexts of expressionistic art and theater, and to the underscoring of angst-ridden noir and horror films, the test of time has proven that the atonal state of mind appears not to be one that adapts well to other expressive contexts.

Perhaps we should let Rochberg have the last word. In the mid-1960s, in a move that shocked his contemporaries—especially after his nearly twenty years as a devoted serialist—Rochberg dismissed many of the techniques and tenets of musical modernism when he could no longer reconcile himself with their limited expressive range. After his teenaged son died of a brain tumor in 1964, Rochberg began to look for new modes of musical expression, languages that were equal to the emotional depths of his all-too-human experience. In this respect, he found twelve-tone technique and other avant-garde modes of musical ideation inadequate. In a 2005 interview with National Public Radio, pianist Marc-Antonio Barone described how—whether writing in a neo-tonal language or with twelve-tone technique—Rochberg's technical and formal approach was always governed by "what, in the human condition, he was trying to express."[107]

Through the middle years of the twentieth century, I have argued, the twelve-tone method proved to be a highly effective technique for expressing the "inhuman" conditions of monstrosity and madness in film. As with countless artistic technical innovations and movements of the past, however, serialism was a sustained but ultimately ephemeral fashion, and it seems to be almost entirely absent from the technical palette of twenty-first-century film composers.

Earth and Tonality: An Examination of Jerry Goldsmith's Twelve-tone Score of Planet of the Apes" (PhD dissertation, York University, 2019), 1.

[107] Joel Rose, "Music Interviews: The Evolution of George Rochberg," *National Public Radio*, June 4, 2005, available online: https://www.npr.org/templates/story/story.php?storyId=4680395

10

The Horror, the Horror!

White Women are the True Monsters in Jordan Peele's *Get Out*

Frederick W. Gooding Jr.

Jordan Peele's 2017 directorial debut in the movie *Get Out* was surprising on several levels. First, it publicly showcased a successful transition from the comedic sketches for which he was prominently known (i.e., "Key & Peele" show on Comedy Central) into a completely different genre in horror (i.e., laugh or cry, right?). Second, the movie—despite its unique content—was a crossover box office hit, which meant that such financial success was only possible with patronage from more than just "black audiences." Meaning, many white audience members patronized the film and it was covered extensively through mainstream media, allowing for this low-budgeted sleeper to rise in prominence and become part of popular parlance. Third, the movie cleverly fused and used historically racialized themes to provoke anxiety and dread in its viewers.

Yet, upon further analysis, Peele was rightfully rewarded for reminding us about a horrific reality routinely taking place off-screen and outside of the theater—Black bodies have always been under threat of systemic exploitation and destruction by their economically and politically more powerful white counterparts. Although *Get Out* brought to life the living (dead?) horror of being trapped in a Black body in modern society, the question remains whether this nightmare was purely entertaining, puzzlingly educational, or possibly exceptional for American audiences—all of which are quite scary propositions.

Good Horror Is Where You Least Expect It

Alfred Hitchcock once famously explained the difference between surprise and suspense.[1] Surprise is when the audience is caught off guard by whatever new piece of

---

[1] Varun Chaubey, "How Hitchcock Generated Suspense in His Films," *Medium*, April 28, 2019, available online: https://medium.com/the-film-odyssey/how-hitchcock-generates-suspense-in-his-films-1ef60a4ad153.

information that the director chooses to instantly reveal. Surprise is certainly effective, but its effect is quite fleeting. Conversely, suspense best develops when the audience actually has a piece of information beforehand (i.e., knowledge of some attendant, lurking danger) and then must wait for time to pass to see how the building conflict will be resolved. It is the difference between watching a couple eat at a dinner table inside a restaurant and a bomb suddenly exploding from underneath the table versus the camera showing the maître d' place a bomb underneath the dinner table without the audience knowing at what point the bomb may go off while the couple is dining, unwittingly aware of the ticking bomb underneath.

Peele effectively builds suspense in the movie *Get Out* by placing a relatively isolated Black male character in the middle of a white family dynamic. Many viewers may suspect that this simple juxtaposition will cause racial tension and, for the most part, they are right! Despite the pleasantries, the tension builds between the two sides (Black and white), and the suspense continues to build. Viewers know this is a "social tension bomb," but do not know when that bomb will go off.

Yet, it is the positionality of white women characters in *Get Out* that is most horrifying. While the movie certainly contains several elements designed to induce feelings of discomfort within the viewer, this analysis posits that white women are the primary sources of horror in the movie. More specifically, there are two white women of note we shall analyze here: Rose Armitage, the girlfriend of the protagonist, and Missy Armitage, Rose's mother. Together, both white women serve as the two principal levers of horror against the protagonist, Chris Washington (played by Daniel Kaluuya).

SPOILER ALERT: please be advised and forewarned that reading further will result in the referencing of specific plot points which will either assume that the reader has viewed the film Get Out, *or will not mind reading scene descriptions that will reveal key plot points.*

A Thorny Rose Indeed

First, we will focus on the daughter, Rose. When we first meet her, our suspicions are naturally aroused, as it is the beginning of a thriller movie. Questions entertained by the viewer possibly include: "Is this for real? How sincere is the romantic connection between Rose and Chris?" Peele starts by centering one of the primordial fears that many of the white audience members may share: namely, a fear (this is a horror movie, after all) of interracial mixing within a romantic context. Otherwise known as "Hollywood's Third Rail,"[2] onscreen depictions of Black males expressly intimate with white females are still relatively far and few between. This concept unfortunately connects to the rabid negrophobia that infected the Southern United States in the aftermath of enslavement.

---

[2] Frederick Gooding Jr., *Black Oscars: From Mammy to Minny, What the Academy Awards Tell Us about African Americans* (Lanham: Rowman & Littlefield, 2020).

Negrophobia was perhaps the ultimate example of projecting one's racial fears upon another as a form of social control and protection. Many whites held this irrational belief that all Black men shared one singular mission and purpose which was to commit lewd and lascivious acts with white women.[3] If the white man was part of the "master race," then any connection or contact between Black men and white women would necessarily challenge and fly in the face of this so-called power of purity. Thus, any hint of contact—God forbid, romantic contact—had to be discouraged and punished where need be. To this extent, the Alabama-based Equal Justice Initiative headed by MacArthur grant winner Bryan Stevenson has conducted a thorough study documenting close to 4,000 extrajudicial lynchings,[4] many of which included so-called offenses for crossing imagined social boundaries with real, often fatal, consequences that not so much imperiled white women as such, but rather white women as property of white men—the true target of such insult.

In the years that followed the high-peak lynching years, Hollywood, insofar that it reflects and reinforces mainstream society, followed suit by not producing movies that approached Hollywood's Third Rail. Here, Hollywood could say with a straight face that in order to be responsive to the paying public, its hands were tied with respect to what images it could produce and introduce. The fact that you, the reader, will likely struggle to think of at least three recent movies featuring an interracial A-list couple—featuring a Black male and an A-list white female movie star—underscores how so many movie studios still observe this principle. More specifically, given the gendered power dynamic that is named white male supremacy, interracial relationships are not necessarily the problem, for movies that prominently feature interracial A-list talent when there is a white male and a nonwhite female are much more abundant (e.g., "The Bodyguard," "Grown Ups," "Monster's Ball"). The pairing of a Black male and a white female is the image that is still at issue.

For whatever it is worth, Hollywood's Third Rail remains untouched in this movie as well—although there are roughly three principal windows within the movie whereby the couple is depicted expressing their intimacy through kissing: (1) at the movie's beginning when the couple first connects onscreen, (2) early evening after the weird "auction" party, and (3) the evening after Chris first meets Rose's parents. First, Rose freely kisses Chris upon arriving at his apartment to pick him up for the trip to her parents' home. At the conclusion of the opening scene in Chris's apartment, while he is seen kissing Rose once again while "on top," the scene cuts immediately to Chris as a passenger in Rose's car. If the kiss continued and evolved into a full-blown lovemaking session, well, perhaps we are to utilize our collective imaginations here. Further, notice how Peele cleverly suggests that Chris's appeal through the white female gaze was highest toward the beginning of the movie, when he appears to have been "rewarded"

---

[3] See generally, Mia Bay, "Remembering Racism: Rereading the Black Image in the White Mind," *Reviews in American History* 27, no. 4 (1999): 646–56.

[4] See, generally, Equal Justice Initiative, "Lynching in America: Confronting the Legacy of Racial Terror," (Montgomery: Equal Justice Initiative, 2017), available online: https://eji.org/reports/lynching-in-america/.

with unforced intimacy after applying white shaving cream to his face in efforts to "tidy up" and look more respectable right before Rose arrives. Also of note is the dialog wherein Chris somewhat anxiously asks Rose about meeting her parents for the first time (i.e., "Do they know I'm Black?") and Rose answers: "No. Should they?" While subtle, it is significant to note that very early in the movie, Rose first establishes herself as a liar—now whether it is for good or evil, the audience must decide—but this is the beginning of a "little white lie" that is told seemingly without consequence.

Speaking of discerning lies from truth, another scene of kissing intimacy was seen when the couple took a break from the party and social pressures accompanying publicly performing for a mostly older, white audience (one that may be more historically steeped in racially problematic thinking). They are outside with daylight with other guests in the vicinity (reducing the chances of sexual intercourse) by a body of water; against this background Rose validates herself once again as one who "gets it" by suggesting to Chris, "This sucks. Let's go home." Chris emotionally responds over the prospects of him being "free" from the rather awkward social ordeal he has endured thus far and states, "I love you," to which Rose responds, "I love you too, baby." As this scene is before the violent and chaotic climax, the audience is about to soon discover the limitations of Rose's so-called love for Chris's Black body, perhaps the travesty being that it was only the body she loved and not the person embodied inside.

For the third and most romantically intense scene roughly one-third into the movie, Rose is later depicted casually brushing her teeth in her undergarments within Chris's presence. Chris just arrived earlier that day at her parent's home and had a relatively awkward exchange with Rose's brother at dinner. The couple appears to be settling in for the night and briefly processing Chris's emotional resiliency in not being too perturbed over such slightly unpleasant interactions, with the unspoken understanding that this was not the first time Chris has been subject to such treatment. They both reciprocate intimate contact, freely kissing and embracing as they even lay down side by side on the bed with an overhead camera shot. The scene ends shortly after Chris recites the cryptic lines: "You know, with my genetic makeup, shit gonna go down. I'm a beast. I'm a beast!" The couple is next seen in bed sleeping together in the dark before Chris exits to encounter Rose's mother over an infamous cup of tea. In returning to Chris's lines about being a beast, perhaps Peele was showing the emotional intimacy of an interracial couple making light of the racial tensions in their relationship.

While it would be inappropriate for Rose's father or brother to call Chris a beast directly, Chris self-titling himself as such could be viewed as an inside joke, even one with potential sexual meaning if "beast" possibly refers to his imputed performance later that evening. Here, Rose still flies under the radar as moments before, she appears to distance herself from her relatives and the party attendees from the next day by exasperatedly declaring that "they are so white," perhaps as a generic insult to mean that these individuals are devoid of larger cultural understanding. Peele cleverly plays upon assumed notions of white female purity and Rose has now given the audience enough reason to distance herself from all the other, truly problematic white people that Chris may have to encounter. It is unclear with so many other commentaries challenged in this movie why Peele elected not to explicitly challenge in a visual manner Hollywood's Third Rail. However, the point holds that the couple is never depicted having sexual intercourse while onscreen. Perhaps this would have been too scary for audience members.

To delve further into the issue, let us be honest—the actress who plays Rose Armitage, Allison Williams, is not and was not an A-list actor at the time of casting for the movie *Get Out*. Before Williams was cast as Rose Armitage, her biggest claims to fame were: (1) a five-year run on the HBO series *Girls* from 2012 to 2017, and (2) in 2014 she starred in the title role on NBC's live television presentation of the musical *Peter Pan Live!*. Thus, Williams's Rose character still comports with the Third Rail analysis insofar that Williams had only two notable television roles (one of which was a paid cable channel) and was not a highly prized white female A-list movie actress who had to consider complicating "her brand" by associating intimately with a Black male. It is an open question as to what factored into Peele's casting decision, but this author wonders aloud how Peele's strategic use of whiteness helped make the character and the interracial couple more believable. Is it not possible that the audience may have had an even more difficult time accepting the interracial union as "real" if Williams herself were indeed a high-profile A-list actress, replete with buxom features and blonde hair? While these features are not necessarily standard requisites for contemporary offerings such as "Wonder Woman 1984" or "Black Widow," they do remain front and center in recent creations such as "Atomic Blonde" or "Bombshell." In other words, Williams, cast as the petit brunette in Rose, perhaps was unassuming enough in appearance to make the couple's union all the more believable.

What is fascinating is that, even for a movie that directly engages the topic of white privilege, Allison Williams possibly represents white privilege off-screen as well as on it. As the daughter of two well-known names in show business (her father is former NBC *Nightly News* anchor Brian Williams and her mother, Jane Gillian Stoddard, is a well-regarded television producer), her "opportunity" to become an actress was likely made easier than the average person looking to truly "catch a break."

While some viewers may initially scrutinize the sincerity of the relationship between Chris and Rose (do they truly have affection for one another, or is the attraction based upon fascination?), Peele pulls out a clever diversion trick to counter skepticism by transforming Rose into an advocate. As Rose drives to her parents' home for a weekend getaway, the couple has an interaction with a police officer after hitting a deer that jumped in the road. Yet, it is Rose who speaks up on her Black boyfriend's behalf when the officer asks Chris, who was not the driver, but was sitting in the passenger seat, for his identification, perhaps as an example of fake white virtue signaling. If anything, Chris remains a bit reserved during the interaction but Rose boldly intervenes on Chris's behalf, successfully thwarting the possible microaggression by the officer. She then becomes the audience's white balance test—meaning she is the normal metric by which all other white characters are judged. However, despite Rose appearing to be the most liberal of her family, confirmation of her involvement with the horrific body transplant scheme comes with Chris's discovery of a shoebox in her room, presumably with pictures of past victims inside.

A Spot O' Tea

Missy Armitage, as Rose's mother, is an effective character because at first glance, she too is immediately shrouded and protected by the common veneers of white respectability. She presents with a genteel demeanor akin to a middle-school teacher who is resigned to no longer become stressed over incomplete assignments. This character trope is familiar to many in the viewing audience, as many, if not virtually all, have had a white female authority figure providing instruction and/or education at some point in their life. It is natural and normal for white women to be placed in key positions of trust and power, even if not made to be the "leader" of an organization.[5] Missy's reassuring presence subtly pulls upon the audience's puppet strings of socialization, whereby we all have been educated to believe that white women are worthy of our unquestioned trust. This unquestioned trope is all the more horrifying when we recall that such "socialization is a powerful means of political control."[6]

If anything, Missy appears to take a back seat to her husband's (i.e., Dean's) possible off-color comments. The viewing audience does not immediately suspect Missy of any malicious motives because she appears reasonable and rational. The same evening after Chris declared, "I'm a beast," he awakes in the middle of the night unable to sleep. He goes outside to see inexplicably one of the property's caretakers running past him robotically at full speed. Not knowing that this is the spirit of Dean's father inhabiting a new Black body at this point, Chris tries to shrug off the strange encounter before meeting Missy who invites Chris to simply "sit with" her in the study. Using smoking as the pretext, Missy offers to "help" Chris. Lo and behold, the audience discovers later that this offer of help was the lever for planned harm. This is what makes the offer so insincere and insidious.

Thus, with Missy serving as the resident hypnotherapist in the home, it becomes readily apparent that this is no ordinary chat in the dead of night. Rather, it is Missy's spoon that slowly (and audibly) encircles her tea cup that sets in motion Chris's hypnosis into the "sunken place." Even still, audience suspicion is kept at bay when Chris comments on how his desire for smoking instantly vanished—for those of us who have watched enough material from the Ad Council over the years, the audience of course understands Chris's abandonment of a physically destructive vice as a positive development, and therefore Missy's tea cup routine—while weird—is not necessarily morbidly evil.

---

[5] This dynamic is only underscored and affirmed by older etiquette manuals that instruct women to "take charge" insofar that they can relieve the "helpless husband" of domestic worry—thereby creating a confusing power dynamic whereby women were vested with uncontested authority, but within a limited context. Naturally, by being closer to white males within a white male–dominated patriarchy, some white women have endeavored to extend both this mindset and the boundaries of their domain at least to professional areas within their control (e.g., elementary education, nursing). See Maida, "What Etiquette Books Teach Us about Women," *Athena Talks*, January 1, 2018, available online: https://medium.com/athena-talks/what-etiquette-books-teach-us-about-women-90edbd67fcbc.

[6] Joel Spring, *American Education* (New York: Routledge, 2016), 14.

However in actuality, Missy plays an important role within a larger, heavily orchestrated operation whereby her daughter Rose lures Black subjects to her home, possibly with the implied promise of sexual gratification. Once inside the home, the subject is then exposed to the mother, Missy, who uses their mind and thoughts as a weapon against them before the father and neurosurgeon, Dean, actually performs the consciousness transfer operation, transplanting a white person's mind into a Black body. After building considerable suspense, the audience eventually learns that Rose and Missy are part of some macabre, experimental operation that allows whites to manipulate and cheat death—only by fusing their consciousness into a Black body—a Black body that previously was in possession of a resident consciousness, and therefore must be suppressed or displaced to make way for the invasive white consciousness to take control and direct the body's actions. If the prior sentence evokes distant memories of colonialism, particularly as expressed through the monopolized trade of tea by the British, then the use of a tea cup to start Chris's descent into the sunken place is perhaps not accidental.

Missy therefore performs the hypnosis technique to prepare the victim for soul transfer, the implication being that the mind must be pliable and nonresistant in order to make room for the new (white) consciousness to take residence inside the new Black body. Missy purports to be an ally offering to help Chris live longer by no longer damaging his body through recreational smoking, while secretly and patiently precipitating the conditions for his untimely demise via an unauthorized and diabolical lobotomy. This dynamic presents a delicious new twist—whereas many horror movies focus upon death as a means by which an individual's consciousness would be wrongfully taken from one's body, the twist here is that a Black individual's consciousness is trapped inside their own body, sitting in the passenger seat as some other form of white consciousness drives the body—akin to Chris being a passenger in Rose's car en route to her family's home.

Here, Peele indeed constructs a scenario that sounds absolutely horrifying—where, through constant conditioning and destructive propaganda, colonized victims of color spend a lifetime imprisoned in their own minds, unable to truly exercise their naturally endowed rights according to their own free will as recognized by a governing society that vests value in their common humanity.

Adding to the horror of this operational scheme is that it takes place under the unassuming roof of an upper-middle-class, white-owned home on a private, secluded, amply sized lot. This means that the literal destruction of Black bodies is potentially allowable and permissible in broad daylight without fear of castigation under the guise of protected personal property—perhaps serving as a connection to a time when plantation owners were likewise allowed extreme leniency in the dastardly, savage, and horrific treatment of their enslaved workers under the guise of personal property. Thus, adding to the horror scene is perhaps the suggestion by Peele that such murder and abuse of Black bodies may be more common than what we expect; that it occurs in plain daylight without the cover of darkness. If anything, no neighbor was the wiser as to what was truly happening inside the Armitage home, just as no citizen was in a position to question a local plantation owner during enslavement about detailed movements in the early morning hours. Under the socially constructed rules of whiteness and politeness, such specifics were rarely discussed during plantation owners' official Christian visits to church on Sundays in town.

Further, Missy's hypnosis sets Chris in motion toward the "sunken place," a concept that was given a name by Peele in the movie, but yet is a condition with which many nonwhites in society are familiar. For those who "live in the hyphenated space" (i.e., Asian American, Latinx American, Native American, African American, etc.) psychologically speaking, the "sunken place" is likely the most horrifying idea of all. For this concept speaks to the representative fear of a nonwhite American confident in their identity, ultimately selling out their culture in favor of assimilating wholesale and without resistance to the identity of whiteness (although we must note for the record, that Chris Washington is played by British American actor Daniel Kaluuya[7]). These more explicit and express form of whiteness can be seen as taking on property qualities based on an ability to elicit consistently similar systematic responses along the lines of a "dog whistle." Conversely, Peele cleverly creates a "dog whistle," or a "metaphor that pushes us to recognize that modern racial pandering always operates on two levels: inaudible and easily denied in one range, yet stimulating strong reactions in the other"[8] when he crafts the mental construct of the "sunken place" for nonwhite members of the audience. While anecdotal, there is strong evidence through the creation of several "Get Out!" memes that the "sunken place" as a collective concept has indeed stimulated strong reactions in its audience.

Before the movie *Get Out* was even contemplated, it is no secret that visits to the "sunken place" were forced upon enslaved Black Americans for generations when, after being ripped away from their homeland, roots, and culture, they were forced to adopt and adapt to white cultural norms for survival. Thus, traditional names, original languages, cultural traditions, religious rites, and sacred foods were all sacrificed on account of having the opportunity to survive the truly horrific, unimaginable dystopia called enslavement to some and "a land of Cavaliers and cotton fields" to others.[9]

It is unknown how many scores of enslaved Black bodies actually endured what we saw essentialized as a spoon encircling a tea cup—a visit to the sunken place that might otherwise be a massive case of undiagnosed "Stockholm Syndrome," where a captive victim begins to adopt confusing, positive feelings for their captors, likely confusing their sole source of food, water, and survival as an act of grace or goodwill. Thus, to be brainwashed or psychologically disoriented into participating in one's own oppression is likely the most horrible, horrific, and scariest proposition that could occur to a Black person within a white-dominated society. For it can be argued that for those

---

[7] See generally, Christopher D. Shea, "Samuel L. Jackson and Others on Black British Actors in American Roles," *New York Times*, March 9, 2017, available online: https://www.nytimes.com/2017/03/09/movies/samuel-jackson-black-british-african-american-actors.html.

[8] Ian Haney López, *Dog Whistle Politics: How Coded Racial Appeals Have Reinvented Racism and Wrecked the Middle Class* (Oxford: Oxford University Press, 2014), 3.

[9] Joseph M. Flora and Lucinda Hardwick, eds., *The Companion to Southern Literature: Themes, Genres, Places, People, Movements, and Motifs* (Baton Rouge: Louisiana State University Press, 2002), 309.

who survived the Holocaust of Enslavement,[10] their perseverance, tenacity, and grit demonstrated that even if they were not free in the body, they at least were free in spirit and mind.

We often overlook white women's roles as active supporters of institutionalized, discriminatory practices given their "special relationship" with white men.[11] White males traditionally have been highlighted as having constructed a society premised upon white male-dominant patriarchy. Yet, it is white women who, as the daughters, wives, sisters, mothers (and perhaps mistresses) of white men, both indirectly and directly tangibly benefit from such white male patriarchy. You simply cannot have it both ways. Indeed, many white women see themselves as subjugated victims of white male patriarchy, yet this is only partially true. While many white women are devalued (i.e., receive less pay for similar work and education), subjugated, and objectified by white men, the special relationship they hold as the beneficiaries of white men still privileges them over any other grouping of nonwhite individuals.[12]

Peele adds to the pervading sense of horror building in the movie when Missy, initially posing as wanting to "help" Chris with his smoking problem, in actuality is merely prepping his mind for potential brainwashing. Hence, the true horror is revealed when it comes from an unsuspecting source, or the trusted individual who was scheming and plotting against our protagonist the entire time. What makes Missy's character one of the most horrifying in the entire movie is that her actions—when viewed in retrospect—cause one to become suspicious about the character's overall sincerity. When in our current age, our society still grapples with racially divisive issues, bonds of trust are tentatively formed across such racial divides in hopes of forging bridges of communication for better race relations. Insincere actions only erode any existing bonds of trust, thereby heightening the fear or apprehension of being double-crossed. For example, in retrospect, the audience must call into question Rose's so-called defense of Chris against the intervening police officer. We now know that her intervention was fueled by her own self-interest. Rose is not a Black Lives Matter advocate. She is concerned about covering her tracks and ensuring that Chris does not officially register as missing after having made contact with police, provided the planned consciousness transplant goes through without a hitch.

---

[10] John Henrik Clarke, *Christopher Columbus & the Afrikan Holocaust: Slavery & the Rise of European Capitalism* (New York: A & B Books, 1992), 5: "The struggle over the legacy of Columbus and the correct history of African Holocaust of Enslavement is at the heart of the contemporary conflict over the curriculum reform in our schools."

[11] "Yes, white women write exhaustively about being suppressed . . . yet, many ironically benefit from their interactions with white males that they critique. White women are also the mothers, grandmothers, sisters, daughters, aunts, nieces, wives and mistresses of white males which despite their subordinate state relative to white males, nonetheless positions them differently and accords them significant status and privilege above other groups." Frederick Gooding Jr., *You Mean, There's Race in My Sports?: The Complete Guide for Understanding Race & Sports in Mainstream Media* (Silver Spring: On the Reelz Press, 2016), 116.

[12] For example white women are uniquely positioned to both berate and yet benefit from established policies of affirmative action. See generally, Victoria M. Massie, "White Women Benefit Most from Affirmative Action—and Are among Its Fiercest Critics," *Vox*, June 23, 2016, available online: https://www.vox.com/2016/5/25/11682950/fisher-supreme-court-white-women-affirmative-action.

Soul Controller

With *Get Out* in 2017, Jordan Peele masterfully constructed a story whereby white women "helped" Black people reach the sunken place, thereby privileging themselves as active facilitators in the psychological destruction of Black consciousness. The idea of being dispossessed of one's consciousness, only to serve as an imprisoned spectator unable to resist inside one's own body absolutely sounds like the stuff of a horror movie. But do you want to hear something truly scary? This sunken place scenario was actually the stuff of a family movie made by Disney – Pixar's 2021 release, *Soul*, starring Jamie Foxx and Tina Fey. How *Soul* connects to *Get Out* is critically important because due to the invisibility of Whiteness and Niceness, many whites face difficulty recognizing more nuanced, subtle, suave, and sophisticated manifestations of ideological narratives that are not as racially explicit but are just as problematic.[13]

Soul is the story about middle-aged, middle-school jazz teacher Joe Gardner, who on the eve of his big break to play on stage with an admired jazz great unexpectedly dies, refuses to accept his premature death, and tries to get back to his body on Earth. Gardner therefore connects with Tina Fey's character (i.e., "22") in the "Great Before" to fulfill his goal of living his life to the fullest. Gardner and 22 succeed in getting back to Earth, but the only problem is Gardner ends up occupying the body of a cat sitting on his disembodied body's lap in the hospital bed. It is 22 who actually occupies Gardner's body.

In reflecting upon Peele's genius buildup of suspense throughout the movie *Get Out*, the audience gets a chance to review and reassess the actions of all of the white characters in the movie only after the big twist and reveal toward the movie's climax (i.e., Chris being strapped in a chair with Dean ready to alter his brain). Many audiences reported a similar experience with the quite famous twist in supernatural thriller *Sixth Sense* by M. Night Shyamalan that will not be revealed here. Further, Peele's movie perhaps provides a skeletal key with which to unlock similar patterns of insincere attempts of white performative diversity still at play (under the auspices of aid or assistance) hidden in plain sight with the animated movie *Soul*. Examining the key art poster for *Soul*, Ray Gardner is clearly the focus. His head is surrounded by a halo formed by the "O" in *Soul*, which could also be interpreted as the sun in the background. Yet upon closer inspection, one can also see a cat walking in front of Gardner's character.

The horror! The horror!

If you were a Black person looking to see your image reflected in what was billed as "Pixar's first-ever animated movie featuring a black lead protagonist,"[14] then you may have been sold a bill of goods. For in actuality, the Black male actor Jamie Foxx voices

---

[13] Gooding Jr., *You Mean, There's Race in My Sports?*, 5.
[14] Charles Solomon, "'Soul' Features Pixar's First Black Lead Character," *New York Times*, December 28, 2020.

the cat and white female Tina Fey voices the Black male body when they are together on planet Earth.

Thus the movie *Soul* is actually titled after Tina Fey's character, who is the "soul" of the main Black body upon which the audience is focused while on Earth! The movie experience therefore revolves around a Black male character dependent upon a white female character to get his life—and more importantly, his body—back. 22 is in charge of moving Gardner's body as Gardner fights to regain full control of his body. The movie *Soul* also underscores the point that white women have always had the ability to manipulate; once in possession of Gardner's body, she then has the authority and power of choice to opt whether to stay in Ray Gardner's body or not.

Only this time, despite having made a "deal" to help each other—Gardner helps 22 find her spark and 22 helps Gardner make it back to Earth—it is Fey who reneges, and selfishly abandons Gardner (literally in his cat suit). Gardner fights to get his body back, only to realize how "selfish" he was, with the climactic scene occurring when Gardner agrees to sacrifice his own body in favor of 22's possession of it.

Thus, only four years after Peele's release, his horror prediction came true, whereby Black consciousness is displaced in favor of a white female, under the subculture-specific auspices of jazz, all in the name of good fun and family entertainment by Disney-owned Pixar. The only difference here is that the Black male in *Soul willingly* abandons his consciousness whereas in *Get Out*, Chris attempted to fight this process, as punctuated by the famous scene of the tear running down his right cheek.

Is this not the definition of horror? What was once famously feared in 2017 is now unceremoniously celebrated in 2021? Perhaps Peele predicted as much in the opening scene of *Get Out* when the camera pans over Chris's apartment to provide context for his career as a photographer, and we see an ominous photograph that at first pass appeared innocuous—a photograph of a young, white child with a black mask covering their face.[15] In so many ways (pardon the expression) *Soul* brings to life the idea of dispossessed Black consciousness just a few years later.

White Women Cannot Have It Both Ways

White women occupy a liminal space whereby they are simultaneously active observers and passive preservers of white male privilege, which by extension becomes white privilege for all involved. Moreover, with the white women working in concert with the more violent, blunt, and direct white males (e.g., Rose's father and brother), the white women in this movie help maintain the façade that all is "normal" at the Armitage house until it becomes painfully obvious that it is far from normal. In other words, the white female presence is sinister insofar that it purports to anesthetize,

---

[15] Adding to the layered meaning of the movie, it is only through "flash photography" that Chris unwittingly interrupts (albeit temporarily) the psychological conditioning of the "sunken place" when he takes a picture of Andre Logan King (as played by LaKeith Stanfield).

sanitize, and rationalize the horror of dastardly destructive racist behavior and beliefs. Peele's masterful setup in the movie *Get Out* leans on the assumption that whiteness is "invisible" and therefore is regarded as "normal."[16] It is safe to say that white (or European) "American norms, ideas, and theories about education are deeply embedded" in the majority of our existing institutions, which may stunt or slow the critical thinking process necessary to challenge and change damaging narratives perpetuated by such institutions.[17]

Therefore, white characters simply behaving as "nice" within existing institutional frameworks support this structure—even if not actively engaging oppressive tactics towards nonwhites. Even within an unequal system, "'nice' people can accept and even distribute . . . unfair rewards and punishments."[18] The two white women characters profiled (i.e., Rose and Missy) fit into this category of appearing to be nice, but directly benefit from the ugly and evil vestiges of racial discrimination.

Are white women really that innocent or innocuous? Or, do they simply benefit from a system that still sees them as property? Any assault or affront against them is indirectly an insult against the larger system to which they are beholden—and from which they derive their imputed importance and power. After all, what is the source of value for white women as *white women*? As individual human beings, of course, they have value insofar that they exist on the planet and share in the gift of life. As women they have supreme value as a gender that is essential and vital for human survival. Yet, white women have been held up consistently as the trophies, or markers of white male conquest that exemplify that which is beautiful, attractive, and pure within the white power structure. Further, as awkward as this conversation may seem, being "respectful," "polite," or "nice" in not acknowledging the darker chapters of our historical past can only serve to silence the voices most desperate to be heard.[19]

White women live and function within a "White racial frame." Sociologist Joe Feagin reminds us that such framing emerges when whites are in control, and it includes "deep emotions, visual images, and the accented sounds of spoken language. Powerful emotions, deep negative feelings about Americans of color frequently shape how Whites behave and interact," often without any conscious or deliberate action required.[20]

Advancing this idea further, whiteness can actually be viewed as a proprietary right, stemming from the country's origins in taking lands already inhabited by Native Americans as property, and then by "employing" or deploying enslaved Africans as

---

[16] Richard Dyer, *White: Essays on Race and Culture* (New York: Routledge, 1997), 45.
[17] Jennifer S. Simpson, *I Have Been Waiting: Race and U.S. Higher Education* (Toronto: University of Toronto Press, 2003), 127.
[18] Mica Pollock, *Everyday Antiracism: Getting Real about Race in School* (New York: New Press, 2008), 52–3.
[19] Enrique Aleman, "Through the Prism of Critical Race Theory: 'Niceness' and Latina/o Leadership in the Politics of Education," *Journal of Latinos and Education* 8, no. 4 (2009): 290–311.
[20] Joe R. Feagin, *The White Racial Frame: Centuries of Racial Framing and Counter-framing* (New York: Routledge, 2013), 14.

chattel to work and develop these same confiscated lands.[21] This property right is not absconded just because white women are subjugated relative to white men.

Even when white women are specifically held out as attractive, their beauty has been leveraged as a measuring stick of acceptance on two levels: for nonwhite women, many have felt pressure to approach the white beauty standard, whereas for nonwhite men, many have sought to gain in power. This occurs either psychologically in harnessing a piece of white power as expressed through white beauty, or in physically "taking a piece" of ownership—a key reason why imputed sexual contact is so contested (i.e., Hollywood's Third Rail), because it represents a "taking" or tapping into the dominant class's sexual energy.

When Chris discovers the box containing photographs of possible past victims, it could be that Peele is suggesting that Rose's sexual energy was being used as a lure for unassuming nonwhite (male) victims. The presumption behind this is that white beauty is "strong enough" to make men literally go base, uncivilized, and tribal, and lose momentary consciousness and immediately think solely about intercourse above their original self-interested programming for survival which may suggest guarded contact due to the attendant social consequences that might result. At least, this was the myth perpetuated upon Black men, especially after the era of enslavement and during the failed Reconstruction.

In either event, the unsuspecting evil roles of Rose and Missy play upon the audience's assumptions that white women are typically nice, neutral, and not involved with direct, violent, and racist action. I therefore posit that the actions of Rose and Missy were the most harmful—Dean merely executed the procedure at the tail end, which pales in comparison to all the other steps undertaken by Rose and Missy to even make such a procedure possible. Audiences in American society have been conditioned to accept white women as innocent, based upon a cumulative familiarity built up by mainstream Hollywood over the years, "because no one has to be nice to someone to whom they have no connection or obligation."[22] White women onscreen still benefit from such momentous goodwill building through decades of cinema and image creation, despite the limitations of white male gaze as theorized by insightfully incisive scholars such as Judith Butler or Laura Mulvey. Thus, for the greatest twist of all, with the audience "being nice" (inside their minds) to the white women depicted onscreen, viewers suspend their judgment (and potential castigation) of white female imagery which remains cloaked and protected by the "benefit of the doubt," and the movie's suspense continues to build. Meanwhile, the audience members willingly take a temporal visit to a "sunken place" of their own, whereby they step aside and allow for mainstream Hollywood programming to take control when it comes to implicating white women properly within the savagely violent matrix of racism.

As horrifying as this sounds, there may be hope if we can only use our flash cameras to take more accurate pictures of society, warts and all. Williams was definitely

---

[21] Cheryl I. Harris, "Whiteness as Property," *Harvard Law Review* 106, no. 8 (1993): 1713–24.
[22] Angelyne Mitchell and Danille. K. Taylor, eds., *The Cambridge Companion to African American Women's Literature* (Cambridge: Cambridge University Press, 2009), 71.

complicit in Peele's plan to make palpable the horrifying message of never taking for granted the possible sources of destructive, racist thoughts and actions. Says Allison Williams, "I was looking for a role that would weaponize everything that people take for granted about me. So I instantly signed on to it."[23]

The horror! The horror!

---

[23] Jada Yuan and Hunter Harris, "The First Great Movie of the Trump Era," *Vulture*, February 22, 2018, available online: https://www.vulture.com/article/get-out-oral-history-jordan-peele.html.

11

Indigeneity as Monstrosity in *The Four Skulls of Jonathan Drake*[1]

Murray Leeder

In 1997, Isabel Cristina Pinedo noted the relative absence of treatments of race in horror scholarship.[2] This situation has changed substantially in the almost twenty-five years since then, and studies of race in classical American horror film are increasingly common.[3] However, the role played by Indigeneity has been less explored.[4] Almost beyond count is the number of horror films that take place in some distant part of the world or that vaguely evoke "native magic" for their horrific goings-on. Many take place in or otherwise connect to wildly fictionalized versions of the Caribbean (e.g., *White Zombie* [1932], *I Walked with a Zombie* [1943], and a host of other zombie films), though others feature similarly imaginary versions of Africa (e.g., *Captive Wild Woman* [1943], *Voodoo Woman* [1958], *The Leech Woman* [1960]), Southeast Asia (*Revolt of the Zombies* [1936]) or Oceania (*King Kong* [1933]). South America is a rarer setting, with the prominent exception of *Creature from the Black Lagoon* (1954); it is a location somewhat more available to the realm of fantastical high adventure stories like *The Lost World* (1925/1960). The silent era had a short cycle of Indigenous-

---

[1] Thanks to Drs. Gary D. Rhodes, Lorne Holyoak and Michael R. Paradiso-Michau for their comments on drafts of this chapter.
[2] Isabel Cristina Pinedo, *Recreational Terror: Women and the Pleasures of Horror Film Viewing* (Albany: SUNY Press, 1997), 111.
[3] E.g., Robin R. Means Coleman's *Horror Noire: Blacks in American Horror Films from the 1890s to Present* (New York: Routledge, 2011) and Elizabeth Young's *Black Frankenstein: The Making of an American Metaphor* (New York: NYU Press, 2008). "Classical horror" is something of a vague and homogenizing term, but I am treating it here as representing the genre's mode before the key shakeups represented by *Psycho* (1960), *Rosemary's Baby* (1968) and *Night of the Living Dead* (1968).
[4] There are, of course, some exceptions, among them Aalya Ahmad's "Blood in the Bush Garden: Indigenization, Gender, and Unsettling Horror," in *The Canadian Horror Film: Terror of the Source*, ed. Gina Freitag and André Loiselle (Toronto: University of Toronto Press, 1995), 47–66, Ariel Smith's "This Essay Was Not Built on an Ancient Burial Ground," *Offscreen* 18, no. 8 (August 2014), available online: https://offscreen.com/view/ancient-burial-ground, and Gail de Vos and Kayla Lar-son, "Cowboy Smithx's *The Candy Meister*—First Nations Horror," in *Horror: A Companion*, ed. Simon Bacon (Oxford: Peter Lang, 2019), 175–80. The recent emergence of Indigenous horror directors like Mark J. Marin (Navajo/Laguna Pueblo/Washoe), Roger Boyer (Saulteaux/Ojibway), Cowboy Smithx (Piikani/Kainai), Nyla Innuksuk (Inuit) and Jeff Barnaby (Mi'gmaq) should motivate considerably more discourse.

themed werewolf films that "not only drew upon the folkloric traditions but also upon the popularity of 'Indian' films,"⁵ but Hollywood horror films mostly do not deal with the Indigenous peoples native to their own hemisphere at all, except in the Caribbean context.

This chapter will discuss one of the exceptions, *The Four Skulls of Jonathan Drake* (1959). In this obscure, but fascinating film, supernatural forces at work are given an Indigenous South American provenance and are explicitly lodged within colonial violence and guilt, albeit in a rather partial and inchoate manner. The film ultimately reinscribes narratives of white innocence. To borrow from Robin R. Means Coleman's distinction between Black horror films and Blacks in horror films,⁶ this is decidedly an "Indigenous peoples in horror" film (in contrast with *The Dead Can't Dance* [2013], *The Smudging* [2016] or *Blood Quantum* [2019]); it is a film wholly reflective of settler anxieties, embodied in its peculiar racially mixed villain, Dr. Emil Zurich (Henry Daniell).

Horror and Indigeneity

"I heard of the discovery of the American hemisphere and wept with Safie over the hapless fate of its original inhabitants." So states none other than Frankenstein's Monster in Mary Shelley's 1818 novel.⁷ The Creature has been eavesdropping on the education of Safie and the moment provides an interesting anti-colonial gesture, where the monster and the young Turkish exile are joined in pathos over the violence and exploitation intrinsically linked with the narrative of "discovery." It also provides a useful example of the shadowy role, both allusive and elusive, that Indigeneity has played in the foundational works of horror literature and in horror theory.

Indigenous peoples are referred to no fewer than five separate times in what is probably the most read, cited, and taught essay in the field of horror studies, "An Introduction to the American Horror Film" by Robin Wood. Often reprinted, this piece, often informally called the "Return of the Repressed," was originally published in *The American Nightmare: Essays on the Horror Film* (1979), a chapbook that accompanied a horror screening series in Toronto. Engaging with the confluence of Karl Marx and Sigmund Freud around the question of repression, Wood argues that horror film compulsively stages the release of repression in the form of that many-faced being called "the monster." Wood offers us the "basic formula" for the horror film: "normality is threatened by the monster."⁸ Wood argues that, while not inevitably

---

⁵ Gary D. Rhodes, *The Birth of the American Horror Film* (Edinburgh: Edinburgh University Press, 2018), 201.
⁶ Means Coleman, *Horror Noire*, 7–8.
⁷ Mary W. Shelley, *Frankenstein; or, the Modern Prometheus* (Boston: Sever, Francis & Co., 1869), 94.
⁸ Robin Wood, "An Introduction to the American Horror Film," in *American Nightmare: Essays on the Horror Film*, ed. Andrew Britton, Richard Lippe, Tony Williams, and Robin Wood (Toronto: Festival of Festivals, 1979), 14.

progressive, horror has powerful transgressive potential in its ability to dramatize the fragility of society's repressive apparatuses. The monster itself is pointedly not especially defined, except as that which results when repression fails, or perhaps by implication as anything which has the power to threaten normality.

Wood develops this point in greater detail earlier in the essay, describing the processes of Othering, whereby what is repressed in the self is projected onto the Other instead. Wood writes:

> A particularly vivid example—and one that throws light on a great many classical Westerns—is the relationship of the Puritan settlers to the Indians in the early days of America. The Puritans rejected any perception that the Indians had a culture, a civilization, of their own; they perceived them not merely as savage but, literally, as devils or the spawn of the Devil; and, since the Devil and sexuality were inextricably linked in the Puritan consciousness, they perceived them as sexually promiscuous, creatures of unbridled libido. The connection between this view of the Indian and Puritan repression is obvious: a classic and extreme case of the projection on to the Other of what is repressed within the Self in order that it can be discredited, disowned, and if possible annihilated.[9]

Here Wood suggests that the "inconvenient Indian" was in a way also very convenient,[10] providing a dumping ground for the Euro-American psyche. The construction of the "Indian" in what would become the settler imagination owes little to anything factual but much to the need to create that savage, warlike, and libidinous Other against whom to project their own self-construction of New World purity and innocence. When listing those things that are repressed by Euro-American culture, Wood returns to this point with a reference to John Ford's *Drums along the Mohawk* (1939), in which a preacher refers to the Indians as "sons of Belial," but which also includes a Christianized comic relief "Indian," Blue Back.[11] Another, briefer citation of Indigenous peoples by Wood is a quick reference to John Carpenter's film *Assault on Precinct 13* (1976), where he notes parenthetically that one of the leaders of the racially diverse revolutionary army is "clad as an Indian."[12]

Wood invokes Indigenous peoples again when he itemizes those things that are repressed within society and how they play into horror films. Noting that, as was common in the formative period of the 1930s, horror films with exotic, foreign settings tend to evoke a "'savage,' unsuccessfully colonized culture," he goes on to mention two then-recent horror films that openly present Indigenous characters and mythologies, *The Manitou* (1978) and *Prophecy* (1979).[13] Since Wood is also a scholar of the Western, he invokes it frequently as a neighboring genre to horror. He even suggests that the

---

[9] Ibid., 9.
[10] I play here on the title of Thomas King's *The Inconvenient Indian: A Curious Account of Native People in North America* (Minneapolis: University of Minnesota Press, 2018).
[11] Wood, "An Introduction to the American Horror Film," 10.
[12] Ibid., 11.
[13] Ibid.

generalness of his basic formula for the horror film—again, "Normality is threatened by the monster"—is not a weakness but a strength: "It suggests the possibility of extension to other genres: substitute for 'Monster' the term 'Indians' . . . and one has a formula for a large number of classical Westerns."[14] Wood moves on from the point quickly, but the slippage between "Monster" and "Indian" is a telling one, suggesting that the colonizer's conceptions of Indigeneity and monstrosity are tightly linked. Another monster theorist, Jeffrey Jerome Cohen, similarly notes that "In the United States, Native Americans were presented as unredeemable savages *so* that the powerful political machine of Manifest Destiny could push westward with disregard."[15]

The horror genre, for Wood, is uniquely equipped to challenge the repressive apparatus of Western civilization, those that make us, in his words, "into monogamous heterosexual bourgeois patriarchal capitalists."[16] And while the repression or overt suppression of Indigeneity and of Indigenous peoples is just one example that he evokes among many, it is worth noting the almost subliminal role they play in Wood's essay. They are the repressed even within a discussion of repression.

Other scholars have investigated the significance of Indigenous peoples to North American horror and supernatural media, often focusing on the figure of the ghost.[17] With reference to Freud's conception of the Uncanny, which is another important formulation for many horror theorists, Renée L. Bergland observes that:

> The sense of unsettledness in the word *unheimlich* [uncanny] is important, because it evokes the colonialist paradigm that opposes civilization to the dark and mysterious world of the irrational and savage. Quite literally, the uncanny is the unsettled, the not-yet-colonized, the unsuccessfully colonized, or the decolonized.[18]

In race-themed horror films, there is often a sort of reverse colonialism at play, where "savage" subjects, artifacts, and forces, sometimes supernatural, leave their "exotic" confines and make themselves known in the core of "civilization." *The Four Skulls of Jonathan Drake* is such a narrative and anticipates the "race horror" films that Pinedo describes as "explicitly cod[ing] the monster as a racial Other,"[19] albeit via a narrative

---

[14] Ibid., 14.
[15] Jeffrey Jerome Cohen, "Monster Culture (Seven Theses)," in *Monster Theory: Reading Culture*, ed. Jeffrey Jerome Cohen (Minneapolis: University of Minnesota Press, 1996), 8. Original emphasis.
[16] Wood, "An Introduction to the American Horror Film," 8.
[17] Examples not otherwise cited here include Kathleen Brogan's *Cultural Haunting: Ghosts and Ethnicity in Recent American Literature* (Charlottesville: University of Virginia Press, 1998), Kathryn Troy's *The Specter of the Indian: Race, Gender, and Ghosts in American Séances, 1848–1890* (Albany: SUNY Press, 2017) and Colleen E. Boyd and Coll Thrush's edited collection *Phantom Past, Indigenous Presence: Native Ghosts in North American Culture & History* (Lincoln: University of Nebraska Press, 2011). While I do not want to erect hard boundaries between ghosts and monsters, my focus on monstrosity here hopes to avoid rehashing the familiar "Indian burial ground" territory.
[18] Renée L. Bergland, *The National Uncanny: Indian Ghosts and American Subjects* (Hanover: The University Press of New England, 2000), 11.
[19] Pinedo, *Recreational Terror*, 112.

surprise. Before examining the film more closely, however, I want to draw on another important theorist of the monster, Eve Tuck (Unangax̂). With C. Ree, Tuck writes:

> What is a monster? (A monster is one who has been wronged and seeks justice). Why do monsters interrupt? (Monsters interrupt when the injustice is nearly forgotten. Monsters show up when they are denied; yet there is no understanding the monster). How does one get rid of a monster? (There is no permanent vanquishing of a monster; monsters can only be deferred, disseminated; the door to their threshold can only be shut on them for so long).[20]

This version of the monster resembles Wood's conception insofar as it is disruptive to colonial civilization, but more pointedly so—it is aimed specifically at seeking justice rather than simply undermining structures. Tuck and Ree's description seems very relevant to *The Four Skulls of Jonathan Drake*, which is fundamentally about achieving revenge for past atrocities waged in the name of American capitalism, but that theme is conspicuously downplayed and unacknowledged within the film itself.

The Return of the Native: *The Four Skulls of Jonathan Drake*

The Four Skulls of Jonathan Drake is a US film but plainly not a Western, and its Indigenous peoples are not "inconveniently close," as Wood puts it,[21] but distant from both the film's setting and the location of its production. Nothing but the film's backstory unfolds in South America, though it is fixated on headhunting and the practice of collecting *tsantsas*, shrunken heads. The film's action unfolds in a nameless American university town, though it has no classroom scenes and features no students; owing to its low budget, the film's scope is extremely small, mostly moving between two houses.

The story involves a wealthy American family, the Drakes, who are under a bizarre intergenerational curse. For close to two centuries, every male member has died mysteriously at age sixty, only for his head to be severed and vanish before burial. Later, their skulls appear in a hidden cabinet in the family crypt, but no one knows who places them there or how. In the film's opening moments, this complicated fate befalls Kenneth Drake (Paul Cavanaugh) and is supposed to happen in turn to his brother, Professor Jonathan Drake (Eduard Franz).[22] *The Four Skulls of Jonathan Drake* supplies a pair of bland young, vaguely romantic white leads in the policeman Lt. Jeff Rowan

---

[20] Eve Tuck and C. Ree, "A Glossary of Haunting," in *Handbook of Autoethnography*, ed. Stacey Holman Jones, Tony E. Adams and Carolyn Ellis (New York: Routledge, 2013), 649. For a different perspective on monstrosity that mixes scholarship and art, see Eric Gansworth's (Onondaga) *Breathing the Monster Alive* (Treadwell: Bright Hill Press, 2006).
[21] Wood, "An Introduction to the American Horror Film," 10.
[22] The fact that Kenneth and Jonathan are brothers and both sixty yet are never described as twins is one of the screenplay's numerous points of incoherence.

(Grant Richards) and Alison Drake (Valerie French). Together, they provide the horror film's stock skeptical characters who initially resist and scoff at the supernatural (Rowan especially) but ultimately must embrace its reality in order to help defeat the monster.

As we learn, a curse was laid on the Drake brothers' great-grandfather, Captain Wilfred Drake (1813–73), and has carried through the generations. As Jonathan explains to his daughter Alison, Captain Drake had a trading station on the Upper Amazon River. "Jivaro Indians," as the film terms them,[23] kidnapped his Swiss agent, and Captain Drake led an expedition to rescue him. But when they reached the Jivaro village, they found him beheaded. Then Drake and his men exacted a terrible vengeance. Says Jonathan Drake, "The captain and his men killed every Jivaro man and male child, except one, the Chingui [or] witch doctor. He escaped and hid in the jungle. And he's the one who's put the curse on every Drake male descendent."

Jonathan Drake regularly hallucinates floating skulls. Lieutenant Rowan investigates the crimes against the Drake family and begins to suspect that the culprit is a family friend, archaeologist Dr. Emil Zurich. Though Rowan is slow to acknowledge it, Zurich *is* the murdered Swiss agent, still using the same name more than a century later. He enacts the curse through the proxy of Zutai (Paul Wexler), the original witch doctor, who immobilizes his victims using curare poison, beheads them after death, and then hides their skulls in a secret panel in the Drake crypt. In the end, Zutai self-immolates in a puff of smoke, and Zurich is defeated by Rowan and his allies, with Jonathan Drake taking on himself the task of severing Zurich's head from the "jungle Indian" body on which it sits; it rapidly turns into a bare skull, signaling the end of the Drake family curse.

The film opens by evoking the core of the Western literary canon, with a quote from William Shakespeare. Despite the film's skull imagery, the quote is not from *Hamlet* but from *Julius Caesar*: "The evil that men do lives after them." These words recur throughout the film and come to represent the curse on the Drake family, their ancestor's actions and the forces arrayed against them. In certain ways, *The Four Skulls of Jonathan Drake* anticipates narratives like *The Shining* (1980) and *Poltergeist* (1982), in which "the site of spectral terror, the terrible place, is often a cemetery buried underneath a contemporary mansion; the injustice is literally in the foundation and produces a haunting based on revenge."[24] But the film tellingly acknowledges the horrific foundations of the colonial nation of the United States at a series of slight removes. Bergland notes how "land ownership may be the source of the [American] nation's deepest guilt," and the film shows some awareness of how "American nationalism must

---

[23] Anthropologist Steven Lee Rubenstein notes that the exonym "Jivaro" is regarded by the Shuar people, probably the rough model for Zutai's people, as an insult and is used pejoratively by Euro-Ecuadorians ("Circulation, Accumulation, and the Power of Shuar Shrunken Heads," *Cultural Anthropology* 22, no. 3 [2007]: 384). Nonetheless, I here use the film's word "Jivaro" in place of "Shuar," since it seems even more inappropriate to apply the real name to this insulting fictionalized representation.

[24] Tuck and Ree, "A Glossary of Haunting," 652. *The Four Skulls of Jonathan Drake* has obvious affinities with the hoary "old Indian burial ground" narrative through its focus on human remains, even if it presents a less spectral, more embodied monster.

be predicated on haunted grounds: the land is haunted because it is stolen."[25] Likewise, the Drake family crypt contains secrets tracing back to the foundation of the family fortune on colonial exploitation, theft, and bloodshed.

Both Zurich and Zutai are kept alive—or something like it—by curare flowing through their veins. They also use a curare-covered stiletto to immobilize their victims. A real-life paralyzing agent used by many Indigenous South American cultures for hunting and documented by Europeans as early as Columbus,[26] curare joins the tsantsas in the film's mélange of Indigenous Amazonian signifiers and becomes a magical substance that does whatever the screenplay requires of it. Zurich says his plan is to make the Drake family "pay for the evil of [its] ancestors," and his modus operandi includes collecting four souls via the transformation of their heads into tsantsas, but he also seems to operate under a curse himself. He insists that when Jonathan Drake is killed and the male line of the Drake line finally extinguished, "then the ancient pledge will be fulfilled and I shall rest." The muddled nature of Zurich's motivations speaks to an unwillingness of the film to commit to its own subject matter: the history of violence and exploitation on which American society rests.

The final revelation about Zurich is that he is himself a monstrous patchwork: not only "a living dead thing" but "the head of a decapitated white man on the body of a jungle Indian." Throughout the film he wears gloves and, when introduced, he refrains from shaking hands with Rowan. These clues that there is something "wrong" with his body are eventually clarified once his shirt is ripped open, revealing not only a line of scars but exposed brown flesh beneath his neck. He exemplifies Jeffrey Jerome Cohen's thesis that "The Monster is the Harbinger of Category Crisis,"[27] not precisely mixing or blending races so much as co-occupying them in a Frankensteinian amalgam.

Within the film's overall incoherence, the nature of Zurich's relationship with Zutai is also profoundly unclear: How is it that Zurich is putting the curse into practice when it was Zutai who initially saved Zurich? Regardless, there is an interesting dichotomy between Zutai, who is obviously racialized and monstrous in appearance, and Zurich, who is ostensibly a respectable academic—and a Caucasian. Zurich is also a perverse variation on the classic James Fenimore Cooper protagonist, the "white man who knows Indians,"[28] reconfigured for horror: not a daring frontier hero who harmonizes civilization and "savagery," but a treacherous infiltrator who cloaks his savage nature behind expertise and (white) respectability.

The Four Skulls of Jonathan Drake also provides a peculiar variation on alarmist tropes about miscegenation or even passing, here based less around the question of lineage and shading (as in *The Imitation of Life* [1959]) than on the creation of a miniature racial hierarchy within a single body: Zurich's white head stitched to an

---

[25] Bergland, *The National Uncanny*, 9–10.
[26] Jill Carl, Mario Schwarzer, Doris Klingelhoefer, Daniel Ohlendorf and Daniel A. Groenberg, "Curare—A Curative Poison: A Scientometric Analysis," *PLOS One* 9, no. 11 (November 2014): 1.
[27] Cohen, "Monster Culture (Seven Theses)," 6.
[28] Richard Slotkin, *Gunfighter Nation: The Myth of the Frontier in Twentieth-Century America* (Norman: University of Oklahoma Press, 1998), 16.

Indigenous body. This hierarchy is further reproduced in Zurich's relationship with the silent Jivaro Zutai, to whom he issues instruction, despite the fact that Zutai (and not Zurich) is the creator.[29] Zurich is also an unusually literal example of what's been called "the white man's Indian,"[30] a creation of the colonial imagination with scant reference to any actual Indigenous people. So is Zutai, of course, and unsurprisingly for 1959, he is played by a white actor in makeup—but Zurich is more pointedly so, since his "Indianness" is preserved as a climactic narrative surprise.

Why does the film focus on the Jivaro people? A 1921 issue of *National Geographic Magazine* reported that:

> The third element of the Ecuadorian population comprises the wild and savage Indian tribes of the Oriente, typified by the Jivaro or headhunters. These latter Indians, while nominally under the government of Quito, are so far removed by the inaccessibility of their home territory that Ecuadorian laws rest lightly upon them, and they are in many aspects as primitive today as when America was discovered.... The Indians of the Oriente are much more savage and uncivilized than their brethren of the western Andes. They come into contact with the whites occasionally, since the country they inhabit is very inhospitable in its climate, its dense, trackless jungles, and to a certain extent, in its human population as well.[31]

The Jivaros are thus depicted in *National Geographic* as being particularly "savage" people even among "savages." *The Four Skulls of Jonathan Drake* also came five years after *Jivaro* (1954), a lavish 3-D adventure film about gold hunters in Brazil. One assumes, as well, that the filmmaker saw tsantsas as a promising concept around/ upon which to build a horror film, as tsantsas themselves had widely circulated in the spaces of both academia and exploitation. For example, in 1940 it was reported that five tsantsas were acquired by the Beckmann & Gerety Carnival and that "they plan to build a sideshow exhibit around the five human heads, and interest biological professors and students in college towns on the carnival route."[32] In 1949, the children's novel *Amazon Adventure* by Willard Price also dealt with the Jivaros and shrunken heads, further attesting to the mainstream visibility of this theme in postwar American culture.[33]

One wonders if the screenwriters looked to tsantsas as an alternative to the "voodoo dolls" that had appeared in earlier films like *White Zombie* (1932) and *I Walked with*

---

[29] One is reminded of stories like *A Man Called Horse* (1970), where the reward for "going native" is not simply tribal membership but chiefdom.
[30] Angela Aleiss, *Making the White Man's Indian: Native Americans and Hollywood Movies* (London: Praeger, 2005).
[31] H. E. Anthony, "Indian Headhunters of the Interior an Interesting Study in the South American Republic," *National Geographic Magazine* 40, no. 4 (October 1921): 328.
[32] "If You Had 5 'Tsantsas,' Just What Would You Do?" *The Decatur Daily Review*, May 12, 1940, 20.
[33] *Tsantsas* have appeared in numerous subsequent popular horror or supernatural narratives (*Beetlejuice* [1988], *The Mummy Returns* [2001], *Pirates of the Caribbean: At World's End* [2007], *The Princess and the Frog* [2009], etc.), mostly making minor appearances and seldom with Shuar or even Amazonian specificity.

a Zombie (1943), possibly due to overexposure. *The Four Skulls of Jonathan Drake* has been listed as a zombie film, though words like "zombie" and "voodoo" are never spoken;[34] TV listings in the 1990s misrepresented it as a film about "an ancient, deadly voodoo curse."[35] One quality that *The Four Skulls of Jonathan Drake* shares with a great many pre-*Night of the Living Dead* (1968) zombie films is a fascination with ritual. We watch Zutai steal Kenneth's head and place it in a wicker basket. We see him later produce that head, whereupon Zurich boils it, extracts its skull (with implausible ease), boils it, and produces a tsantsa. Zutai transports both tsantsas and skulls and doses his victims with curare. We also see Zurich don a ceremonial mask. The white characters learn something of these practices in a book called "Ancient Witchcraft and, (*sic*) the Black Arts."

In terms of performance, Zutai and Zurich's actions gain ritualistic implications because they are smooth and practiced (they have, after all, done them before). I here use the words "ritual" and "ritualistic" advisedly, as contested terms, "used by missionaries in reference to Indigenous religious ceremonies . . . [which] imply that Indigenous religions are not legitimate religions, but more cult-like, thus implying an element of evil."[36] And that is precisely the case in *The Four Skulls of Jonathan Drake*. While Zurich and Zutai are putatively punishing the primal offenses of the Drake family, a sense of justice does not come across strongly since their actions are presented as superstitious, savage, eerie, and evil, though their supernatural powers are diegetically treated as real.

Horror theorist Andrew Tudor draws a distinction between modes of "secure horror" and "paranoid horror."[37] In the former, "human beings possess significant volition, while authorities and institutions generally remain credible protectors of the social order."[38] Threats and monsters arise, of course, but only to be sent away. The paranoid mode, on the other hand, has little faith in authority and does not do as much to ultimately preserve the status quo: "Lacking control of our inner selves, we have no means of resisting, and there is a certain inevitability to humanity's final defeat."[39] Tudor argues that around 1960, the secure mode starts to recede in favor of the paranoid one. It is perhaps no surprise to find that *The Four Skulls of Jonathan Drake* operates mostly in the secure mode, which Tudor intriguingly describes as "horror's first world," while offering subtle hints of the paranoid. To be sure, it casually glorifies traditional authority through the figure of the policeman Lieutenant Rowan, but his worldview of hard-headed rationalism ("curses don't have anything to do with facts") limits his

---

[34] E.g., David Stanley, Karen Stanley and Deborah Magee, "Celluloid Zombies: A Research Study of Nurses in Zombie-Focused Feature Films," *Journal of Advanced Nursing* 75, no. 8 (August 2019): 1751–63.
[35] "The Four Skulls of Jonathan Drake," *The Akron Beacon Journal*, June 23, 1995, 217.
[36] Gregory Younging, *Elements of Indigenous Style: A Guide for Writing by and about Indigenous Peoples* (Edmonton: Brush Education, 2018), 59.
[37] Andrew Tudor, *Monsters and Mad Scientists: A Cultural History of the Horror Movie* (Oxford: Basil Blackwell, 1989), 103.
[38] Ibid.
[39] Ibid.

ability to solve the case and protect those at risk. Jonathan Drake is a figure of white academic authority, but admits that his studies in the occult have done little to protect him and his family from their curse: "For all these years of study at the university, how little I've actually learned." And Dr. Zurich is a murderer and a monster beneath his respectable professorial front, who has apparently spent years (decades?) posing as a friend to the Drake family while secretly plotting its ritual extinction. But these hints of paranoia are swept aside as Rowan and Drake adjust their worldviews to counter Zurich's plans, and the basic underpinnings of their patriarchal colonial institutions, the police and the university, remain unchallenged.

Zurich's profession as an archaeologist bears particular examination. He belongs to one of the fields that helped secure the narrative of Indigenous peoples as primitive, savage Others, as "specimens" for white science, while also secretly practicing Indigenous magic. It is not uncommon in films built on real or purported Indigenous legends, like *The Last Wave* (1977), *The Manitou* (1978), or *Q: The Winged Serpent* (1982), to have a scene where its white protagonist seeks out the advice of a white professional who delivers exposition about Indigenous mysticism. But Zurich is both that interpreter figure and the villain or monster himself. In an inversion of the "going native" narrative,[40] he passes for a respectable academic while secretly practicing Indigenous magic. Zurich is introduced as someone who "deals with the dead, not the living"—appropriate, considering that he is dead—yet he speaks in the present tense about the practices of the Jivaros, helping construct them as atavistic holdovers of an ancient time and as occupying the spectral state of being simultaneously immortal and dead (undead, you might say).

Though Zurich is presumably a South American specialist, he is described more generally as an expert on "primitive cultures" and his house is decorated indiscriminately with artifacts from different parts of the Global South, including Africa, Oceania, and South America. Rowan snatches one of them up while questioning Zurich, irking the professor with his casual disdain for these artifacts. The main floor of Zurich's house projects a veneer of upper-middle-class respectability, all the more so for its curated Indigenous content, while the basement is a more chaotic mélange of white science (test tubes) and pseudo-Indigenous magic (bubbling cauldrons, masks and fetishes).[41] The structure of Zurich's house thus mirrors that of his body.

When Rowan asks him about shrunken heads near the end of the film, Zurich cannot resist the opportunity to deliver a lecture. He monologues:

> Throughout history, some of our strongest cultures were based on the taking of heads. When the practice was abandoned or suppressed, the local civilization degenerated and soon disappeared. Even today the practice flourishes in several parts of the world: the Philippines, India, New Guinea, the upper regions of the Amazon. Until a few years ago, it was prevalent in civilized Europe.

---

[40] Karen O'Reilly, *Key Concepts in Ethnography* (Los Angeles: SAGE, 2009), 88–92.
[41] For a discussion of the interplay between white science and Black magic in horror films, see Carol J. Clover, *Men, Women and Chain Saws: Gender in the Modern Horror Film* (Princeton: Princeton University Press, 1992), 97–9.

Zurich is notably the only character identified as European (Swiss, but also marked by Daniell's priggish English accent). He goes on to explain that "When the head of a strong, valiant enemy is properly taken, the possessor acquires the spirit of the soul, the vital spark that kept his enemy alive, a degree of immortality." Zurich's explanations of headhunting appear reasonably accurate, and in other contexts his opposing neat demarcations between savagery and civilization and refusing to denounce the supernatural as mere ignorant superstition may seem enlightened. But Daniell delivers Zurich's lines in the tone of half-unhinged villainy.

Though Rowan is the man of action and the film's locus of traditional authority, in the climax he must ultimately cede the final destruction of the monster to Jonathan Drake, who beheads Zurich with his enemy's weapon. As Drake indicates, it—the curse and the film alike—will not be over "till the head of the white man is severed from the brown body." He asserts that nothing will be destroyed "but evil, nothing human. These men, white and Indian, died 180 years ago." He does the grim duty of severance, in-scene but out of frame, and in the film's final moments, the body disappears altogether, leaving only Zurich's skull, over which appear the words "THE END."

Conclusion: Vanishing Americans

"When European Americans speak of Native Americans, they always use the language of ghostliness. They call Indians demons, apparitions, shapes, spectres, phantoms, or ghosts. They insist that Indians are able to appear and disappear suddenly and mysteriously, and also that they are ultimately doomed to vanish."[42]

Like most films made in the classical Hollywood style, *The Four Skulls of Jonathan Drake* ends with the impression of absolute closure—and like most classical horror films, that means the destruction of the monster. Here, that also explicitly means the end of the curse, and thus presumably the primal guilt over the massacre perpetrated in the early nineteenth century by Captain Wilfred Drake. Colonial relations are neutralized and made traceless. Notably, ending the curse does not mean making any sort of restitution to the Indigenous peoples massacred by Captain Drake; the fact that they are still living is something that the film barely acknowledges. It invokes colonial atrocities only to consign them to the past. The myth of settler innocence is embodied by the annoyingly naïve Alison, who has been carefully insulated from the knowledge of the crimes of her ancestors ("I've always wanted to keep you from this," her father says); the ending even implies love between her and Lieutenant Rowan, foregrounding heterosexual romance themes as the endings of classical horror films so often do. Tudor's "secure mode" prevails, and neither Jonathan nor Alison Drake is ever forced to confront their status as long-term beneficiaries of colonial violence.

---

[42] Bergland, *The National Uncanny*, 1.

In their previously quoted essay, Eve Tuck and C. Ree note that:

> Settler colonialism is the management of those who have been made killable, once and future ghosts—those who have been destroyed, but also those that are generated in every generation.... Settler horror, then, comes about as part of this management, of the anxiety, the looming but never arriving guilt, the impossibility of forgiveness, the inescapability of retribution.[43]

This is a particularly useful insight to bring to bear on *The Four Skulls of Jonathan Drake*. It demonizes the prospect of justice by reframing it as an evil curse, and even that curse is forestalled by the defeat of Zurich at the film's close. It ultimately shows itself as a narrative about managing settler anxiety, with an underlying subject—how the wealth and privileges of white civilization derive from genocide—that can only stand to be hinted at.

Zurich and Zutai not only die but *vanish*, with Indigenous bodies and haunting colonial specters conveniently self-erasing. All that remains is a skull that, like the tsantsas the film has so frequently dangled about, seems certain to become a mere specimen or souvenir.

---

[43] Tuck and Ree, "A Glossary of Haunting," 642.

12

A "Distaste for... Allegory" or
In the Bowels of Horror[1]

Daniel Humphrey

Reading Horrorgorically

In the decades since Mary Shelley's *Frankenstein* was first consumed by a hungry readership, horror literature has engendered a broad array of well-considered interpretations. Read over the decades as everything from a nightmarish representation of the creation and inevitable revolt of the proletariat,[2] to an account of post-Enlightenment tendencies to reconceptualize humanity's origins,[3] *Frankenstein*, horror's incontestable urtext, inaugurated a long-held tradition of reading supernatural gothics and horrific science fiction according to exegetical practices. Establishing a working definition of allegory, Daisy Delogu remarks that

> In general, one can identify two broad allegorical practices. One writes allegorically by hiding or disguising one's true meaning, whether to confine knowledge to select publics, or to protect writers from the consequences of subversive or dangerous discourses. One can also read allegorically, by seeking meanings other than those which are readily apparent in an effort to supplement—or supplant—a base text.[4]

The subtitle to Shelley's novel, "The Modern Prometheus," clearly invites a critical engagement in the pursuit of the first of these two practices, and yet scholars' and critics' habitual analyses in search of metaphorical or parabolic meanings can also be seen as reflecting the deeply unsettling ways in which this particular novel, and much of

---

[1] I thank Mindy Bergman, Kimberly Nichele Brown, Bill Nichols, and Pedro Rojas for their help and insight in the research and writing of this essay.
[2] Franco Moretti, "The Dialectic of Fear," in *Signs Taken for Wonders: On the Sociology of Literary Forms* (London: Verso, 1983), 83–108.
[3] Ian Balfour, "Allegories of Origins: Frankenstein after the Enlightenment," *SEL: Studies in English Literature 1500–1900* 56, no. 4 (Autumn 2016): 777–98.
[4] Daisy Delogu, *Allegorical Bodies: Power and Gender in Late Medieval France* (Toronto: University of Toronto Press, 2015), 20.

what it inspired, resonates with the reader. In her now-canonical attack on the modern hermeneutic impulse, Susan Sontag laments how content interpretation effectively "tames the work of art" and indicates, indeed, "a wish to replace it by something else."[5] To cite the fictional version of Shelley seen in *Bride of Frankenstein* (1935), one is surely more comfortable with a "moral lesson—the punishment that befell a mortal man who dared to emulate God,"[6] than a raw, literalist nightmare about reanimated dead tissue in humanoid form furiously pursuing its assembler to the ends of the earth.

We hardly need to survey the literature of horror allegory here: vampires as queer seducers, rampaging apes as the racial other, alien pod people as communist menace. By the late 1970s, the genre brought with it the stripped-down specter of the "mad slasher," infusing the genre with a ruthless efficiency that eschewed a long history of strongly allegorical horror. Replacing metaphorically rich work like *Rosemary's Baby* (1968) and *Don't Look Now* (1973) with an almost mechanistically engendered sense of dread, the new tradition was damned by critics for purported shallowness, and potentially pernicious effects, while raking in profits for any producer willing to stake a claim on an unoccupied holiday (Halloween, Friday the 13th, Valentine's Day, "prom night," etc.). Even here, though, the killers' impossible strength and uncanny knowledge (how *does* Michael Meyers know how to drive a car, having spent his entire adult life in a mental hospital?) tend to forestall a realist ethos and the desire to claim meaning via allegorical subtext persisted in reviews and, later, scholarly analysis of these films. "[W]e're faced," Paul Malcolm tells us in *LA Weekly*, "with the nature and mutability of evil," in *Jason Goes to Hell: The Final Friday* (1993), "as Jason becomes the simultaneous source and cessation of sin."[7] In a retrospective analysis, Klaus Rieser extends and amends Carol Clover's argument about horror's "final girl" to argue that *Halloween* (1978) rehearses the adolescent female's trajectory of "outgrow[ing] her intrauterine world" in order "to get out of [the] 'motherly' body as much as to get away from the monster"—all this as a journey "between girlhood and full-fledged motherhood."[8]

Of course, realist shockers like *Henry: Portrait of a Serial Killer* (1986) or unnerving home invasion nightmares such as *The Strangers* (2008) can be justified as simple terror machines. What one sees on screen is possible, even plausible, in the real world—we have all been horrified by the accounts of mass killings we see on the evening news. Art, as the mimetic practice Plato describes, is giving us a plausible reality that functions according to Aristotle's prescription; as summarized by Susan Sontag: "it arouses and purges dangerous emotions."[9] Then again, when we call these seemingly simplest of horror films "roller coasters" or "amusement park rides," we are still effectively

---

[5] Susan Sontag, "Against Interpretation," in *Against Interpretation and Other Essays* (New York: Farrar Straus Giroux, 1966), 8, 10.
[6] William Hurlbut and John L. Balderston, *Bride of Frankenstein: The Original Shooting Script*, ed. Philip J. Riley (Absecon: MagicImage Filmbooks, 1989), 64.
[7] Paul Malcolm, "*Jason Goes to Hell: The Final Friday*" (Review). *LA Weekly*, August 20–26, 1993, 56.
[8] Klaus Rieser, "Masculinity and Monstrosity: Characterization and Identification in the Slasher Film," *Men and Masculinities* 3, no. 4 (April 2001): 379. Rieser develops ideas from Carol Clover, "Her Body, Himself: Gender in the Slasher Film," in *The Dread of Difference: Gender and the Horror Film*, ed. Barry Keith Grant (Austin: University of Texas Press, 2015), 68–115.
[9] Sontag, "Against Interpretation," 4.

metaphorizing them, just at a different level: the awe-inspiring, seemingly supernatural technology of the cinema is tamed into little more than a county fair attraction. In short, allegory continues as a constituent part of the horror genre, and yet, despite allegory's comforting effects, it has its own particularly discomforting consequences. I am not the first, indeed not the hundredth person to suggest this.

The Fear of Allegory

Horror films, unlike suspense thrillers, rarely show us things that could plausibly happen or might possibly exist, if ever they seemed to do so. For decades, forms of realism may or may not have factored into the equation of a specific example of the genre, but either way, a novelist, screenwriter, or director was not expected to demonstrate plausibility. If the modern horror creator could capture the readers'/spectators' imagination, engage their emotions, and/or successfully trigger their hermeneutical impulse to decipher impossible creatures and previously unthinkable situations, questions of plausibility were not raised. Indeed, the very unbelievability of vampires, werewolves, and eighty-foot gorillas can be considered a crucial part of the equation. The interpretations such texts prompt, however, hardly have the function of assuaging us, contra Sontag. If anything, they can make these works more troubling. Terrence Rafferty considers a moment in David Cronenberg's *The Fly* (1986) when the protagonist, at the height of the AIDS epidemic, suddenly notices disturbing changes in his body: "There are few scenes in movies more unbearable than the one in which he staggers away from the mirror, sits on the edge of the tub, and says to himself, 'Am I dying?'" Rafferty calls this, "subtext with a vengeance."[10] It almost comes as a relief when the film shifts gears from a realistic look at corporeal degradation and finally becomes the creature feature audiences expected.

One often thinks that the allegorical subtexts of horror films somehow validate them in the eyes of critics as something more than thrill rides or, for earlier generations, carnival sideshow attractions: Near the beginning of his celebration of the genre in American popular culture, Stephen King assures his reader that "the tale of horror, no matter how primitive, is allegorical by its very nature."[11] In his excellent study, *Shocking Representation: Historical Trauma, National Cinema, and the Modern Horror Film*, Adam Lowenstein argues that, due to its allegorical function, horror films should be taken as seriously as *Shoah* (1985) and *Hiroshima, mon Amour* (1959) in their ability to exhibit and process the psychic wounds of social catastrophe.[12] More recently, Lowenstein has argued that even the most widely condemned, so-called "torture porn"

---

[10] Terrence Rafferty, "*Dead Ringers*" (Review). *The New Yorker*, October 3, 1988, 92–4.
[11] Stephen King, *Danse Macabre* (New York: Everest House, 1981), 42.
[12] Adam Lowenstein, "Introduction: The Allegorical Moment," in *Shocking Representation: Historical Trauma, National Cinema, and the Modern Horror Film* (New York: Columbia University Press, 2005), 1–16.

horror films of the last twenty-five years continue to provide such a salutary function.[13] Nevertheless, the fact remains that allegory, even more than the horror genre, is generally held in suspicion in academic criticism. For the most part, the aversion to it takes the form of a dismissiveness, with allegory seen as a decidedly old fashioned, even premodern mode of discourse. In one of the more thoughtful studies on the subject, Edwin Honig's *Dark Conceit*, we read that "a distaste for the *idea* of allegory" actually "goes back a long way in the history of Western thought," and that, in fact, allegory has always been regarded with acute suspicion.[14] Honig gives examples of this suspicion dating as far back as ancient Greece.[15]

The reason for this suspicion can be summarized with a statement found in Angus Fletcher's *Allegory: The Theory of a Symbolic Mode*. He writes, "In the simplest terms, allegory says one thing and means another. It destroys the normal expectation we have about language, that our words 'mean what they say.' [. . .] Pushed to an extreme, this ironic usage would subvert language itself."[16] Published in 1964, two years before Jacques Derrida introduced the practice of deconstruction and revolutionized literary theory, Fletcher's diagnosis of allegory's subversive powers might now seem simplistic, or at least unremarkable.[17] Nevertheless, the sense that allegory can be seen as both a naively old-fashioned practice and a potentially revolutionary threat is an insight worth noting, especially when confronted with work that fits into well-worn genre formations while also triggering surprisingly strong responses to its metaphorical implications.

One text that certainly triggered a strong reaction upon its debut is Pier Paolo Pasolini's art-house adaptation *Salò, or the 120 Days of Sodom* (1975), based on a 1785 novel by the Marquis de Sade, featuring torture, rape, coprophagia, and murder. The film is generally defined as a Marxist allegory that means to reflect upon Italian consumerism-as-fascism in the 1970s while also pointing toward an imminent late-capitalist apocalypse.[18] Just prior to *Salò*'s release (and Pasolini's own grisly murder), the filmmaker said: "In this film, sex is nothing but allegory, the metaphor for the commodification of bodies subjected to power."[19] Subsequently, in an essay originally published in *Le Monde*, Roland Barthes asked the rhetorical question: *Salò* "obviously

---

[13] Adam Lowenstein, "Spectacle Horror and *Hostel*: Why 'Torture Porn' Does Not Exist," *Critical Quarterly* 53, no. 1 (2011): 42, 43, 55–6.
[14] Edwin Honig, *Dark Conceit: The Making of Allegory* (Evanston: Northwestern University Press, 1959), 6. [Emphasis in the original].
[15] Ibid.
[16] Angus Fletcher, *Allegory: The Theory of a Symbolic Mode* (Ithaca: Cornell University Press, 1964), 2.
[17] In delivering the lecture "Structure, Sign, and Play in the Discourse of the Human Sciences" at Johns Hopkins University in 1966, Derrida effectively introduced the practice of deconstruction to academia, forever shattering the notion of a straightforward and unambiguous denotative function in language. It was later published as Chapter 10 of: Jacques Derrida, *Writing and Difference* (Chicago: University of Chicago Press, 1978), 278–93.
[18] See Naomi Greene, "*Salò*: The Refusal to Consume," in *Pier Paolo Pasolini: Contemporary Perspectives*, ed. Patrick Rumble and Bart Testa (Toronto: University of Toronto Press, 1994), 232–42.
[19] Quoted in Richard Brody, "Pasolini's Theorem," *The New Yorker*, December 29, 2011, available online: https://www.newyorker.com/culture/richard-brody/pasolinis-theorem.

touches a nerve—but which one?"[20] which he then went on to answer by devoting several paragraphs to decrying the film's *failure* to function straightforwardly as the allegory Pasolini claimed it to be. Barthes ended his review by claiming that *Salò*, "as the outcome of a long string of errors," paradoxically enough, succeeds. It succeeds, in Barthes's ultimate analysis, precisely in its irreclaimability.[21] In other words, it promises a horrific allegory but ends conveying the horror of a dysfunctional allegorical text. Allegory, here, has itself become monstrous.

Allegories and Insects

More recently, and in terms of a reliably efficient horror subgenre (the mad scientist melodrama and torture-porn new extremism), *Village Voice* critic Karina Longworth referred to the low-budget feature *The Human Centipede (First Sequence)* (Tom Six, Netherlands, 2009), in one of a surprisingly high number of positive reviews, as a "torture-porn game-changer."[22] She did this, however, without really explaining what the "game" is, or indeed, how it has been changed. A cultural phenomenon in the United States from almost the moment its trailer appeared on YouTube in the spring of 2010, *The Human Centipede* boasts a central idea that captured the collective imagination of almost all who heard about it. In what surely invites an allegorical reading attending to race, nationality, gender, and the still resonant specter of the Second World War, the film presents a paradigmatically evil German scientist who captures and imprisons a Japanese man and two American women for nefarious reasons. In due time, he surgically grafts them together, male-to-female-to-female, anus-to-mouth-to-anus-to-mouth, to create a single organic unit: the titular human centipede—with three brains, six arms, six legs, and, key to the whole appalling but mesmerizing spectacle, one digestive tract. Longworth's modest analysis of the film is not at the level of Barthes's reading of Pasolini's project, and *The Human Centipede* is no *Salò*. Although her feminist concerns surface in the review, Longworth does not mention the centipede's sexist lineup, in which the man, even as a man of color who doesn't speak English, is accorded the position at the beginning of the sequence, so that the two women are both forced into silence and forced to consume his noxious waste. Nevertheless, like Barthes's *Le Monde* essay, the *Voice* review intelligently skirts many of the concerns raised by the film under its scrutiny, only to ultimately explain the aesthetically modest film's arresting power. "The film itself is not as scat-pornographic as you might think," Longworth writes.

---

[20] Roland Barthes, "Pasolini's *Salò*: Sade to the Letter," in *Pier Paolo Pasolini*, ed. Paul Willemen (London: British Film Institute, 1977), 64.
[21] Ibid., 66.
[22] Karina Longworth, "Tom Six's Torture-Porn Game Changer *The Human Centipede (First Sequence)*," *The Village Voice*, April 27, 2010, available online: https://www.villagevoice.com/2010/04/27/tom-sixs-torture-porn-game-changer-the-human-centipede-first-sequence/.

[T]here's no excrement onscreen. [. . .] Never as explicit as a *Saw* or *Hostel* film, *Centipede* disarms the viewer with comedy early on, then swiftly shifts into the shit (literally and figuratively), managing to maintain a steady aura of stomach-churning dread through the end purely from performance and suggestion.[23]

Satirized by Comedy Central's popular *South Park* series and recreated even more directly by that network's *Tosh.O*—in which series host Daniel Tosh devotes an entire episode to nothing more than an epic description of the plot of the film to a delighted/revolted studio audience—the narrative's basic conceit has so transfixed observers that the film itself is almost superfluous. Evidencing the appeal, if that is really the right word, of its bizarre conceit, one can point to *Human Centipede* T-shirts, coffee mugs, and Christmas decorations that appeared by the end of 2010. To explain the appeal of the film's not-so-buried subtext, however, one must turn to a meme on the internet that was part of a series titled "Bad Luck Brian." Each features the same photograph of a particularly awkward-looking male teenager with red hair, a loud plaid sweater, and silver braces on a set of teeth revealed by a goofy smile. The photo is sandwiched between before-and-after captions demonstrating how utterly cursed this young man's life is. "Confesses to murder on his death bed/makes a miraculous recovery" and "has a pet rock/it runs away" are two typical examples. More cryptically, however, are these: "gets invited to play a game/Saw" and "gets rimjob/Human Centipede." Here, allusions to two violent horror films are encountered. There is also an allusion to gameplaying in the first example and mouth-to-anus sexual contact in the second. With these jokes, we begin to understand the "game" that has "changed" for Karina Longworth. It is one of violence, of course, one often played in torture-porn horror, and one that is always already metaphorized in the sex we perform in the bedroom, sex club, private party, or wherever games of sex are played.[24] More precisely, one could say it is a game in which sex and violence inspire and are inspired by each other. These games of sex-as-violence and violence-as-sex present newly disquieting implications that emerge with particular force while watching *The Human Centipede*—hence the change identified by Longworth. As we shall see, this disquiet resonates in the film as a result of the functioning of allegory in a way that signifies while paradoxically casting doubt on the epistemological status of what it is allegory claims to represent. Watching this film, as horrifyingly simple as its central situation seems to be, the palpable oscillation between what is seen (three bodies grafted together) and implied (a single digestive tract as a metaphor for a kind of occulted sexual practice) creates an uncanny effect: one in which the practice of representation seems to lose its grounding. (See Figure 12.1.)

Now, if the term "torture porn" connects the violence of films like *Saw* (2004), *Hostel* (2005), and *Martyrs* (2008) to sado-masochistic sexual desire filtered through

---

[23] Ibid.
[24] For an understanding of the ways in which sex has been theorized as violence, see: Andrea Dworkin, *Intercourse* (New York: Basic Books, 2008) and Leo Bersani, "Is the Rectum a Grave?" in *AIDS: Cultural Analysis/Cultural Activism*, ed. Douglas Crimp (Cambridge, MA: MIT Press, 1988), 197–222.

Figure 12.1 Linked together: *The Human Centipede*.

a pornographic gaze, then the sexual allegory undergirding *The Human Centipede* involves practices that move across the seemingly discrete boundaries of the BDSM universe: anilingus, group sex, and coprophagia.[25] As presented in the film, these practices remain forced upon unwilling victims, but torture is hardly what one first thinks of when faced with the film's high-concept scenario. In other words, watching the film, one can understand how an even moderately sexually adventurous spectator might see *The Human Centipede* as presenting a nightmare image of (consensual) three-way oral/anal stimulation and, ultimately, fecal ingestion.[26] If the visible connection point between one person's gastrointestinal tract and the next is doubly acculted from *The Human Centipede* thanks to the welcome presence of gauze bandaging where the bodies are joined, the film's even more disturbing evocation of feces consumption is, as a result, also obscured. It is, however, never far from the spectator's thoughts.

A key scene in the film strongly evokes both a general BDSM allegory at the heart of the film as well as the specific act of coprophagia. Having successfully joined the bodies of his three captives together, the doctor has taken them to his back lawn. Like an owner training a new dog fresh from the breeder, he makes simple, if demeaning, demands of his new "creature." When the man at the front of the chain rejects the humiliation and starts to crawl away, taking the two attached women along with him, the doctor's performative rage explodes. Before the doctor can whip the exposed back of his sloughing prisoner(s), however, the captive male begins to moan and falls onto his forearms while speaking in untranslated Japanese. It quickly becomes clear he is

---

[25] Torture porn as a term is contested by Adam Lowenstein in "Spectacle Horror and *Hostel*: Why 'Torture Porn' Does Not Exist," but from the perspective I adopt in this chapter it seems apt.

[26] As one will recall, in *Salò*, coprophagia was practiced as happily by the torturers as it was unhappily by the torturer's victims. The question of consent was never suggested.

defecating involuntarily into the mouth of the woman behind him. This evocation of scatological practice is so strong, and presumably so upsetting to sensitive filmgoers, that the scene has been removed from the R-rated iteration of the film, rented via Redbox and other seemingly more conservative distributors.[27]

Via the doctor's ominous riding crop, leather boots, and dialog, the film unmistakably evokes extreme sex play of the kind one finds in specialized pornographic videos and, presumably, the edgier sex clubs of liberal urban metropolises. In this way the allegory evokes the seemingly ambiguous line between consent and non-consent in SM sex play. Additionally, the demands of the mad doctor, "feed her, feed her, hard! Swallow it, bitch!" remind one of a similar scene in *Salò*, in which a fascist libertine demands that a young captive eat feces off the floor, screaming simply "*mangi!*" or "eat." For its part, *Salò* also seems to be suggesting that the consent manufactured in repressively desublimated states is so overdetermined as to be inauthentic at its core. Beyond using allegory to blur the discrete boundaries between consent and non-consent, to suggest the ambivalence at the heart of so-called consensual torture, if not quite a sense of ambivalence at the heart of non-consensual torture, *The Human Centipede* also attacks the comforting, but only apparent, distinction between suggestion and signification through visual and sonic evidence.

As Barthes wrote of Pasolini's film: "Eat excrement? Gouge an eye, add a few needles to tonight's dinner? You see it all: the plate, the turds, the mess, the packet of needles. [. . .] As they say, *you're spared nothing.*"[28] For Barthes, this is Sade "to the letter." It is also a fair working description of the pornographic gaze, one for which no equivocation is allowed; in pornography, we see the central action of the scene, images which seem to mean what is shown. If such ultimate sexual images function, as Bill Nichols and others argue, as signifiers of authenticity, they do so surely because they are authentically exactly what they are, no less and—*symbolically*—no more: a cum shot is a cum shot is a cum shot. They don't exist to *depict* anything. They exist to *prove* sex happened.[29] Pornography signifies the literal itself. And yet, as horrifying as *The Human Centipede* is, its most revolting acts are hidden from view, with only the occasional muffled gagging sound presenting a clue to what, exactly, is going on. The fact that the buttocks and the faces of the victims are clothed in bandages suggests not merely "good taste" on the part of the filmmakers in terms of the presentational aspects of the film but their confidence in an erotic rather than a pornographic strategy. This speaks suggestively to the anxieties attending the practice of hermeneutics: there's something important, perhaps horrible or at least distasteful going on that we cannot actually see on the surface. It also highlights coprophagia's suitability as a metaphor in the service of a deconstructive reappraisal of metaphor and allegory as such.

---

[27] It can still be found in the "unrated director's cut" shown theatrically and available on DVD, Blu-ray, and streaming platforms.
[28] Barthes, "Pasolini's *Salò*," 65. Emphasis in the original.
[29] See Bill Nichols, *Representing Reality: Issues and Concepts in Documentary* (Bloomington: Indiana University Press, 1991), particularly Chapter VII, "Pornography, Ethnography, and the Discourses of Power" (201–28) co-authored by Christian Hansen and Catherine Needham.

The Excremental "Vision"—Out of Sight/Not Out of Mind

Evoking the filmmaker's taste, specifically *good* taste, in this context might well register as a pun, something which points toward the ways in which allegory, like figures of speech including puns, offers acceptable alternatives to all too unappetizing ideas. Reading Edwin Honig's claim about a *distaste* for allegory only furthers one's sense that there is something both "anal-retentive" and excremental about allegory, or, more precisely, there is something about allegory that wants to both hide and convey an excremental vision. The concept of an "excremental vision" was popularized in psychoanalytic and New Left criticism by Norman O. Brown, who first used it to assess the work of Jonathan Swift, whose scholars have long felt obliged to account for that author's scatological passages.[30] According to Brown, Swift, in early works such as *Gulliver's Travels* (1726) and even more scandalously in his final poetry, uses "the anal function" as a "decisive weapon in his assault on the pretensions, the pride, even the self-respect of mankind."[31]

This suggests a far more direct assault on the sensibilities of the reader than the genteel user of polite allegories might wage, but like Swift and *Salò*, *The Human Centipede* hardly offers polite allegories. In its blunt severity, Six's seemingly modest horror film does violence to the idea one might have of allegory as a polite discourse of evasion or even, a la Swift, as an acerbically requisitioned tool in the service of savage social satire. It suggests instead the often-conflicted relationship to both dignity and self-presentation inherent is allegory itself, its attempt to both acknowledge and contain the violent surfeit of emotions human existence presents. *The Human Centipede* accords with the role of feces in the work of Swift as Brown understands it, but it also manages to say something about the allegorical function itself as the processing of the unacceptable. And like allegory, *The Human Centipede*'s horrific digestive referent cannot be directly shown. It is only implied.

The film's fecund scenario obviously invites innumerable potential allegorical readings: From its dramatization of the passage from food to shit, to even more fully digested (and, as Pasolini would say innutritious) shit, might the film not be argued to be a liberal allegory attacking the logic of so-called trickle-down economics? As three separate bodies are forced together into one monstrous whole, might it not conversely be seen as a mordant parody of the kind of forced collectivization that right-wing critics

---

[30] For instance, both J. Churton Collins and R. H. Fry contest long-standing claims that the worst of Swift's fecal obscenities were the result of late-in-life mental illness, reminding their readers that Catholic theology has had a long, if oft forgotten, tradition of evoking human waste in its discourses. J. Churton Collins, *Jonathan Swift: A Biographical and Critical Study* (London: Chatto & Windus, 1893), 259–60; Roland Mushat Fry, "Swift's Yahoos and the Christian Symbols of Sin," *Journal of the History of Ideas* 15, no. 2 (April 1954): 201–17. More commonsensically, Carole Fabricant points out that "Swift actually lived in a landscape in which excrement was a prominent—not to mention highly visible and necessarily obtrusive—feature," and that the author's thematic interest in it must be historicized with that in mind. Carole Fabricant, *Swift's Landscape* (Baltimore: Johns Hopkins University Press, 1982), 24.

[31] Norman O. Brown, *Life against Death: The Psychoanalytical Meaning of History* (Middletown: Wesleyan University Press, 1959), 179.

claim obligatory single-payer health care to be? Whatever the case, the central conceit of a seemingly infinite and entropic slippage of content from body to body suggests the infinite slippage of discursive meaning through language, oral or otherwise, that the deconstructionists have charted. Furthermore, the film's central situation insists on the identicality of shit and symbol.

According to Brown,

> [the] infantile state of anal eroticism takes the essential form of attaching symbolic meaning to the anal product. [. . .] When infantile sexuality comes to its [. . .] end, non-bodily cultural objects inherit the symbolism originally attached to the anal product, but only as second-best substitutes for the original (sublimations). Sublimations are thus symbols of symbols.[32]

Conceived in this way, *The Human Centipede* is both an allegory about allegory, one suggesting deeper, often supremely disquieting meanings behind the skin, sutures, and discrete diapers of narrative, and a warning about the instability, and perhaps ultimate emptiness, of the "meanings" we think we find entering and exiting as discourse through the (human) body politic. The fact that the director's two less popular sequels, *The Human Centipede II (Full Sequence)* (2011) and *The Human Centipede III (Final Sequence)* (2015), proved both far too much and not enough of an extension of this project seems like an utterly predictable, and thematically suitable, direction for this trilogy of entropy, one that began with such a perfectly calibrated statement.

The Bowels of the Earth

Instead of continuing this discussion by progressing on to the increasingly dissatisfying and uninteresting second and third entries in Tom Six's Centipede trilogy, I would like to conclude with a brief examination of a film that undertakes something similar to what Six ultimately does, but on a much bigger canvas and for a much larger group of spectators, if to somewhat different effect. If the audience for the second and third films in the Centipede trilogy became progressively smaller as the onscreen "centipede" grew longer and longer, Jordan Peele's notedly allegorical hit, *Get Out* (2017), was followed by an even more ambitious film, *Us* (2019), that attracted as much initial attention and an equally impressive box office.[33] If, in Barthes's verbiage, Pasolini and Six touched a nerve or two with their allegories, the issues of race and racism in America, especially since the beginning of the Trump era, touch an entire body of long-frayed nerves. Therefore, one might well have expected Peele's first foray into Black horror to have come across as a particularly discomforting film, certainly for what turned out to be

---

[32] Ibid., 191.
[33] According to the website Boxofficemojo.com, as of February 13, 2021, *Get Out* grossed $255,583,642, while *Us* made about four hundred thousand dollars less: $255,184,580.

a significant crossover audience that included a substantial number of liberal white attendees.

Nevertheless, *Get Out*—an allegory of liberal America's white appropriation of Black bodies filmed at the end of Barack Obama's presidency—was widely celebrated. It received rhapsodic reviews and a surprising number of prestigious nominations and awards for a horror film, including an Oscar nomination for Best Picture and the Academy Award itself for Best Original Screenplay. *Us*, on the other hand, if every bit as widely seen, was not as widely loved. Conscripting Pasolini once again, who created a number of allegories he presented in a series of what he called "unconsumable films," we can say—paraphrasing his thoughts—that although audiences may have eaten and happily digested *Get Out*, *Us*, while similarly chewed and swallowed, instead gave many of its spectators indigestion.[34] The audience approval rating for Peele's sophomore effort on the consumer review site Rotten Tomatoes stands at only 59 percent positive, compared with 86 percent for *Get Out*.[35]

Critics, on the other hand, were, initially, at least, enthusiastic about both films, if a bit less so about *Us* (*Get Out*: received 98 percent positive reviews, *Us*: earned 93 percent positive notices). Peele's sophomore effort received no Oscar nominations and many reviewers who may have been unwilling to condemn a film they probably realized they didn't quite understand with a negative rating, nevertheless, complained in the body of their reviews about what they saw as its unfocused thematic concerns.[36] Offering a nightmarish account of a race of human clones beneath the continental United States that emerges three decades after a single Black girl from the surface is captured and enslaved there, *Us* takes the uncanny persecuting double allegory introduced to the cinema in Paul Wegener and Stellan Rye's *The Student of Prague* (1913) and spins it into a frenzy of complications.

Critical Indigestion

Time's Stephanie Zacharek claimed that with *Us*, "Peele goes even deeper into the conflicted territory of class and race and privilege. [. . .] But this time, he's got so

---

[34] Explaining the unexpected success of two of his own widely viewed, but ultimately rejected, "unconsumable films" (*Teorema* (1968) and *Porcile* (1969)), Pasolini said, "the consumers put them in their mouths, but then they spit them out or pass the night with a tummy ache." Pier Paolo Pasolini, *Pier Paolo Pasolini: A Future Life* (Rome: Associazione Fondo Pier Paolo Pasolini, 1989), 109. See also my brief discussion of Pasolini's conception of unconsumable films. Daniel Humphrey, *Archaic Modernism: Queer Poetics in the Cinema of Pier Paolo Pasolini* (Detroit: Wayne State University Press, 2020), 54–6.

[35] "Jordan Peele," *Rotten Tomatoes*, February 11, 2021, available online: https://www.rottentomatoes.com/celebrity/jordan_peele.

[36] Rotten Tomatoes, "Jordan Peele." A very rough attempt to identify African American film critics' reviews of *Us* and compare their positive and negative ones against the larger sampling of critics on the Rotten Tomatoes website suggests no discrepancy based on race. Two of the twenty-eight critics who gave the film it a negative review are identifiable as Black through their thumbnail photographs, corresponding to the 7 percent overall number of negative reviews.

many ideas he can barely corral them, let alone connect them."[37] Richard Lawson, in *Vanity Fair*, concedes the film offers a "worthy allegory" about "inequality" and "class struggle" (one that expands far beyond *Get Out*'s allegory focused primarily on the fetishization of the Black body) but deems *Us* to be "a jumble of fascinating threads that Peele fails to weave together."[38] Like *The Human Centipede* and *Us*, both of which create an uncanny frisson out of the specter of human beings linked in a chain, Lawson, in his review, stumbles into suggesting that the metaphorical use of "thread," and the idea of a weaving together of separate entities, is more than simply a structural issue leading to either the success or failure of a thematic pattern.[39] Indeed these exposed and tangled threads, themselves allegorizing the trauma of the African American experience and the impossibility of social cohesion in the United States, seem to be exactly what Peele means us to grapple with. That we fail to do so adequately may be, precisely, the point.

If Tom Six offers daisy-chain anilingus as a metaphor for obscene symbolization itself, Peele, offsetting his doppelgänger theme, folds into his narrative a similarly disturbing concatenation of the Reagan-era body politic in the form of a nightmare-nostalgic vivification of the (in)famous "Hands Across America" celebration of 1986. Promoted as "the biggest community event in the history of the world,"[40] the continent-wide chain of human beings stretching hand in hand across the continental United States began as an attempt to create a heart-warming metaphor of the power of people coming together to fight a color-blind conception of hunger and homelessness. Participants donated a small sum of money to the charity USA for Africa in order to take part. In the months leading up to its occurrence, Hands Across America was embraced by people across the political, racial, and cultural spectrum. However, when the proverbial dust settled, the event was seen as a somewhat embarrassing attempt to deflect attention away from the unraveling of the nation's social safety net via little more than a feel-good exercise, and it would be thought of, at best, as "a factoid often referenced in comic fashion, if anyone happens to remember it at all."[41] At worst, it

---

[37] Stephanie Zacharek, "Jordan Peele's *Us* is Dazzling to Look At. But What Is It Trying to Say?" *Time*, March 15, 2019, available online: https://time.com/5552617/review-us-jordan-peele/.

[38] Richard Lawson, "Jordan Peele's *Us* Stabs Itself in the Foot." *Vanity Fair*, March 20, 2019, available online: https://www.vanityfair.com/hollywood/2019/03/jordan-peeles-us-stabs-itself-in-the-foot.

[39] A week after Lawson's negative review of *Us* appeared on the *Vanity Fair* website, a second notice, by African American critic K. Austin Collins, appeared offering a positive assessment. However, Collins also found the film's thematic and allegorical levels confused. "*Us* [. . .] trades elegance for abundance, piling on symbol after symbol until the sum can't help but seem to lead nowhere." The difference between the two critics' perspectives is that Collins, while not quite seeing the thematic confusion as a *positive* feature, gives the film a strongly positive review anyway, as, simply, a fun horror movie. Therefore, in a way he does warn us against the presence of the allegories in the film, "[D]on't overthink them," he says. K. Austin Collins, "Jordan Peele's *Us* is Just a Horror Movie, and That's a Good Thing." *Vanity Fair*, March 26, 2019, available online: https://www.vanityfair.com/hollywood/2019/03/jordan-peeles-us-dont-overthink-it

[40] Lily Tomlin, Hands Across America P.S.A. quoted in, Yohana Desta, "*Us*: What Was Hands Across America, the Creepy Event That Inspired Jordan Peele?" *Vanity Fair*, March 22, 2019, available online: https://www.vanityfair.com/hollywood/2019/03/us-movie-hands-across-america.

[41] Tyler Coates, "Why Hands across America Is So Vital to Jordan Peele's *Us*," *Esquire*, March 21, 2019, available online: https://www.esquire.com/entertainment/movies/a26883876/hands-across-america-us-movie-explained/.

can be seen as nothing more than a self-promoting stunt dreamed up by white music producer Ken Kragen which only netted a relatively modest fifteen million dollars to fight hunger and homelessness.[42] More sadly, it was a stunt that, if anything, actually deflected attention away from systemic poverty and its corollary, systemic racism. In Jordan Peele's estimation, Hands Across America functioned in a "cultlike" way: "an insistence that as long as we have each other, we can walk blindly past the ugliness and evil that we may be a part of."[43]

But in the film's first frames, before we can begin to think about how the thematically resonant concept of Hands Across America serves Peele's socially engaged thriller, we are presented with introductory white text on a black background: "There are thousands of miles of tunnels beneath the continental United States. . . . Abandoned subway systems, unused service routs, and deserted mine shafts. . . . Many have no known purpose at all."[44] Here, we might well begin to wonder how this follow-up to *Get Out*, one of the most metaphorically acute films about race in America, could be trying to suggest something allegorical that resonates with the historical Underground Railroad, a project that led escaped slaves northward to freedom,[45] or we might think about how the reference on screen to the "United States" is echoed in the film's actual title. From here we move to the film's first scene, in which we see a mock commercial on a 1980s cathode ray television promoting Hands Across America in a way that uncannily suggests the final, lengthiest (500-person-long) human centipede in the conclusion to Six's trilogy: "What has 12 million eyes 192 million teeth, and stretches from the Golden Gate Bridge all the way to the Twin Towers? It's Hands Across America, a 4,000-mile-long chain of Good Samaritans standing hand in hand through fields of grain, past purple mountains, and across fruited plains, from sea to shining sea!"[46]

On the shelves surrounding the television we see VHS cassettes of iconic 1980s films that suggest, in turn, split or conjoined identities (*The Man with Two Brains* [1983]), the façade of American exceptionalism (*The Right Stuff* [1983]), cavernous terrors beneath the earth (*The Goonies* [1985]), and an unceasingly horrifying (nine films worth!) suburban corridor in the Reagan era's popular imaginary (*A Nightmare on Elm Street* [1984]). We also see a Rubik's Cube that suggests the difficulty we might have in getting all these cinematic references to line up. All this is thrown at the spectator in the film's first two minutes. As it continues, this story of evil doppelgangers, a demonic

---

[42] Adeel Hassan, "Your Wednesday Briefing," *The New York Times*, May 25, 2016, available online: https://archive.nytimes.com/www.nytimes.com/indexes/2016/05/25/nytnow/nytnow-email/index.html.

[43] Jordan Peele quoted in Erik Piepenburg, "*Us* Took Hands across America and Made It a Death Grip." *The New York Times*, March 26, 2019, available online: https://www.nytimes.com/2019/03/26/movies/us-hands-across-america.html.

[44] Chapter 1, *Us*, written and directed by Jordan Peele (Universal City: Universal Pictures Home Entertainment, 2019), Blu-ray.

[45] Such a suggestion would have been particularly strong in 2019, just three years after the publication of Colson Whitehead's best-selling novel, *The Underground Railroad*, which literalizes the metaphorical railroad of American history with one that runs on tracks through a subterranean tunnel. See Colson Whitehead, *The Underground Railroad* (New York: Doubleday, 2016).

[46] Chapter 1, *Us*.

Figure 12.2 Linked together: *Us*.

fun fair, home invasions, and a monstrous apocalypse presents us with a surfeit of clearly metaphorical signifiers appropriate for the horror genre: a Whac-a-Mole game, a rickety roller coaster, and a T-shirt featuring an image from Michael Jackson's *Thriller* (which obviously means something more disturbing today than it would have in the 1980s). When we see a homeless man holding a sign reading Jeremiah 11:11 for a second time, we no longer wonder what the scripture says ("Therefore, thus says the LORD, Behold, I am bringing disaster upon them that they cannot escape. Though they cry to me, I will not listen to them"),[47] but think instead about the doubled numerals and the colon that separates them and what that may be signifying in terms of digital coding, in other words, how the reference seems to allude to coding as such.

As the film's metaphors pile up, its allegorical vectors cross each other horizontally and vertically. In terms of horizontality, the anti-racist Underground Railroad of historical consciousness stretches northward from the south while the Hands Across America event of popular consciousness, along with Peele's clones' nightmarish reenactment, stretches, like the racist Manifest Destiny, from the Atlantic to the Pacific. (See Figure 12.2.) In the vertical register, on the other hand, an underworld of the enslaved clones lies beneath the surface of 1980s America.[48] Surely, as one sits in the theater trying to put it all together as the end credits roll, one can be forgiven for thinking that Peele was simply unable to "connect," let alone "weave together," all the various "fascinating threads" he presents in his ambitious second feature. And yet, if *The Human Centipede* uses a horrifying allegory to suggest dark, dead matter slipping through our systems of discursivity, *Us* cannily reflects the ways in which allegories, visual and narrative, spatial, historical, and temporal, are hopelessly tangled up within

---

[47] New Revised Standard Version.
[48] If one were to develop a more traditional allegorical reading of the film, surely this vertical dimension is the true, beating heart of the film. It shows us a ferocious underclass of impoverished Americans, both Black and white, attempting to emerge from the lower depths to challenge the false narrative of a classless society, a narrative promulgated by the misleading symbolism of the lateral Hands Across America stunt. I thank Kimberly Nichele Brown for sharing her insights on *Us* as an allegory of the underclass as I was completing this chapter.

American society's imperfect and largely fictive understandings of the republic's historical consciousness. As the film's many strands successfully fail to come together, its obvious lack of cohesion stands in stark contrast to the ersatz unity of Reagan's America.

Conclusion

Pier Paolo Pasolini was so disturbed with the trendy success of his national-popular films of the early 1960s that he had to follow them up in the late 1960s with his "unconsumable films." A few years later, after his "Trilogy of Life" was widely embraced for what he believed were all the wrong reasons, he struck another blow against his own audience with *Salò*, his ultimate unconsumable masterpiece. For his second film, Peele left behind the project of crafting the kind of neat allegory epitomized by *Get Out*, a Pasolinian failure in the sense that it was enthusiastically embraced by the very white liberal establishment it intended to excoriate. With *Us*, Peele appropriately demonstrates the ultimate failure of allegory to move or enlighten us beyond discrete, easily containable concerns raised in order to account for and assuage broader, still aching traumas associated with the allegorical and racist constructions of nationhood and community. If *The Human Centipede* leaves us with metaphors that cannot be stomached, *Us* provides knotted allegories that cannot but be untangled, allegories we must nevertheless confront and engage with, if always at our own peril.

13

Tragic Wraiths, Seductive Sirens, and Man-Eating Vampires

Female Monstrosity in *The Witcher 3: Wild Hunt* Video Game

Sarah Stang

Given their centrality in countless mythologies, folktales, legends, as well as works of art, literature, and popular culture, monsters offer insights into how various cultures view and define themselves in relation to the Other. For media scholars interested in questions of representation and identity politics, monsters are rich objects of analysis because, regardless of how fantastical they are, they often represent that which is feared, hated, reviled, and repressed while also being fascinating and irresistible figures. Indeed, scholars have long noted that the monster often functions as a tool of oppression or repression that polices the symbolic borders of what or who is permissible. In other words, to step outside of social norms risks either "attack by some monstrous border patrol or (worse) to become monstrous oneself."[1]

This has always been particularly true for women: not only are women often the victims of monstrous aggression in mythology, folklore, and popular culture, they are also commonly portrayed *as* the monsters. As J. J. Cohen has observed, women are punished for their transgression with a monstrous transformation: "the woman who oversteps the boundaries of her gender role risks becoming a Scylla, Weird Sister, Lilith, ... or Gorgon."[2] Indeed, as feminist scholars such as Barbara Creed[3] and Jane Caputi[4] have demonstrated, the design of female monsters in mythology and popular culture often draws on the fear and hatred of the female body. Whether related to sexuality, reproductive processes, or aging, the female body—especially the transgressive or

---

[1] Jeffrey Jerome Cohen, "Monster Culture (Seven Theses)," in *Monster Theory: Reading Culture*, ed. Jeffrey Jerome Cohen (Minneapolis: University of Minnesota Press, 1996), 12.
[2] Ibid., 9.
[3] Barbara Creed, *The Monstrous-Feminine: Film, Feminism, Psychoanalysis* (New York: Routledge, 1993).
[4] Jane Caputi, *Goddesses and Monsters: Women, Myth, Power, and Popular Culture* (Madison: University of Wisconsin Press, 2004).

non-normative female body—is framed as subhuman, abject, and a monstrous threat to the patriarchal order.

The female monster therefore too often functions as a misogynistic construct, used to warn, control, and punish transgressive women. Monsters—often drawn from mythology and presented as enemies for the player to fight—are ubiquitous in video games. Given that most mainstream games are designed by teams composed entirely or mostly of men,[5] it is no surprise that much of the misogyny inherent in the design of female monsters is manifest conspicuously in games as well. Many scholars have addressed female monstrosity in film, but when it comes to video games the topic is largely understudied—a notable gap, given how much the often stereotypical, problematic, and harmful representation of women in games has been otherwise discussed.[6] To contribute to addressing that gap, this chapter is a close reading of a selection of female monsters in the critically acclaimed and commercially successful dark fantasy roleplaying game *The Witcher 3: Wild Hunt*,[7] based on *The Witcher* series of fantasy novels by Andrzej Sapkowski. Through an analysis of the wraith, the siren, and the vampire, I argue that this game—like most roleplaying games—remediates misogynistic assumptions about women's bodies and behaviors established throughout Western mythology, folklore, and popular culture. As I demonstrate, video games are particularly fruitful objects of study for critical feminist analysis because they position the player as a normative (usually a straight, white, and male) representative of patriarchal society who must confront and slay monsters that are often coded as non-male and non-normative. These games therefore provide a reenactment of patriarchal violence, forcing players to be complicit in the marginalization of women by symbolically portraying them as monstrous Others that must be destroyed in order to "win the game."

Female Monstrosity

Feminist scholars have long argued that transgressive women—those who do not adhere to the heteronormative constraints regarding appearance and behavior assigned to them within a patriarchal worldview—are presented as the sexual Other through monstrous archetypes, such as the witch, vampire, siren, and succubus. Feminist

---

[5] International Game Developers Association (IGDA), "Developer Satisfaction Survey 2019 Summary Report," Available online: https://igda.org/dss/ (accessed November 20, 2019).

[6] For example, see Alicia Summers and Monica K. Miller, "From Damsels in Distress to Sexy Superheroes: How the Portrayal of Sexism in Video Game Magazines has Changed in the Last Twenty Years," *Feminist Media Studies* 14, no. 6 (2014): 1028–40; Edward Downs and Stacy L. Smith, "Keeping Abreast of Hypersexuality: A Video Game Character Content Analysis," *Sex Roles* 62, no. 11 (2010): 721–33; Teresa Lynch, et al., "Sexy, Strong, and Secondary: A Content Analysis of Female Characters in Video Games Across 31 Years," *Journal of Communication* 66, no. 4 (2016): 564–84; among many others.

[7] CD Projekt Red, *The Witcher 3: Wild Hunt*. CD Projekt, Microsoft Windows, 2015.

philosopher Julia Kristeva[8] used the psychoanalytical concept of the abject—that which disturbs and disrupts normative identity, evokes reactions of disgust and horror, and must be cast out or repressed—to explore how patriarchal religious rituals position women as unclean and impure. She demonstrated that within patriarchal society there is an underlying assumption that women, as abject subjects, are always teetering on the brink of evil and must be controlled and oppressed.[9] Along with religious ritual, mythologies, fairy tales, folklore, and popular culture are tools to control human behavior—means for the patriarchy to keep women in check.

Barbara Creed's foundational analysis of female monstrosity—what she termed the "monstrous-feminine"—in horror film demonstrated the ways that cinematic female monsters embody the abject.[10] Creed observed that "all human societies have a conception of the monstrous-feminine, of what it is about woman that is shocking, terrifying, horrific, abject."[11] However, these are more than just female versions of male monsters, as "the reasons why the monstrous-feminine horrifies her audience are quite different from the reasons why the male monster horrifies his audience."[12] Namely, the transgressive female physicality of these cinematic monsters is what makes them so disturbing and abject, particularly monsters that reproduce without male input, possess phallic symbols, and penetrate or castrate their victims. These monsters evoke male anxieties about being emasculated and feminized, meaning that "the feminine is not per se a monstrous sign; rather, it is constructed as such within a patriarchal discourse which reveals a great deal about male desires and fears."[13] As this chapter shows, this same patriarchal discourse that was critiqued by film scholars decades ago continues to plague the game industry.

The act of categorizing women as various kinds of monstrous archetypes is important to my analysis because this chapter draws extensively on the in-game bestiary in *The Witcher 3* as evidence for how the game frames and presents monstrous women. In *The Witcher* series, the player adopts the role of Geralt, a "witcher," or professional monster slayer. Unsurprisingly, players fight monsters almost continuously throughout the game and many of these monsters are based on creatures from European mythology. Once a monster is defeated, it appears in the game's bestiary with a detailed description and a strategy for how best to defeat it. As I have argued elsewhere, as an instrument of classification, the historical and ludic bestiary "works as an apparatus of abjection, which itself normalizes our culture of misogyny by explaining over and over, in matter-of-fact naturalistic descriptions complete with tables, pictures, and statistics, that women are monsters and the female body is horrifying."[14] As Debra Hassig has

---

[8] Julia Kristeva, *Powers of Horror: An Essay on Abjection*, trans. Leon S. Roudiez (New York: Columbia University Press, 1982).
[9] Ibid., 91.
[10] Barbara Creed, "Horror and the Monstrous-Feminine: An Imaginary Abjection," *Screen* 27, no. 1 (1986): 44–71, https://doi.org/10.1093/screen/27.1.44; Creed, *The Monstrous-Feminine*.
[11] Ibid., 44.
[12] Creed, *The Monstrous-Feminine*, 3.
[13] Creed, "Horror and the Monstrous-Feminine," 70.
[14] Sarah Stang and Aaron Trammell, "The Ludic Bestiary: Misogynistic Tropes of Female Monstrosity in Dungeons & Dragons," *Games & Culture* 15, no. 6 (2020): 743, https://doi.org/10.1177

argued, the allegories within bestiaries would compare women to animals through creatures like the succubus or the siren, associate animals with an unkempt and lustful sexuality, and equivocate that sexuality with evil.[15] Female monsters therefore function to literally dehumanize women and present their sexuality as evil. Many digital games have bestiaries accessible through in-game menus or available as paratextual material, and creatures usually do not appear in the in-game bestiaries until they are encountered and defeated by the player character for the first time, meaning that these murdered beast-women are collected like trophies. Like the *Pokémon* series' imperative "gotta catch em' all," a dedicated player will likely want to fill their bestiary with all the possible enemy types. These games thereby encourage players to seek out these monsters and slay them—even invading their communities, lairs, or nests without provocation in order to murder them.

Broken Hearts and Vengeful Brides

There are several kinds of wraiths in the world of *The Witcher*, though the ones referred to simply as "wraiths" are gender-neutral in their bestiary description but portrayed as male-coded. These generic wraiths are not described in much detail; rather, they are simply "spirits who, for one reason or another, remain in our world after their body breathes its last."[16] They endure "endless, indescribable pain" and are filled with envy and anger that causes them to attack the living, but the cause of that anger and pain is unknown. Otherwise, nearly every other specific type of humanoid wraith in *The Witcher 3* is female. More importantly, these female wraiths are all given tragic backstories in which their deaths or suicides were caused by the betrayal, infidelity, or death of their beloved. These tragic experiences force them to exist in a state of perpetual undead torment, consumed by rage and broken heartedness. They also seem to prey primarily or exclusively on men, demonstrating that they are not just angry at all living beings, they are specifically seeking vengeance.

Noonwraiths, who "resemble sun-scorched women dressed in long, white robes," are described in the bestiary as "the spirits of young women and girls who died violent deaths right before their weddings. Driven mad with pain and anger, they wander the fields searching for their unfaithful lovers or backstabbing rivals, though they will kill anyone who does not get out of their way in time." Their nocturnal variant, the nightwraith, described as "a pale, withered woman in a tattered dress," is similarly tragic and enraged. These spirits are tethered to the world of the living by an item of "intense emotional significance," such as "a wedding ring or torn veil," thereby reinforcing the emphasis on marriage, or marriage interrupted, as that which determines their existence.

/1555412019850059.

[15] Deborah Hassig, *The Mark of the Beast: The Medieval Bestiary in Art, Life, and Literature* (New York: Routledge, 2000), 72.
[16] All quotes unless otherwise specified are from the in-game bestiary of *The Witcher 3: Wild Hunt*.

Figure 13.1 A screenshot of the noonwraith from the "Devil by the Well" side quest.

The wraith, with her skeletal, corpse-like appearance (Figure 13.1) is a literal embodiment of the abject, since, as Kristeva underlines, "the corpse . . . is the utmost of abjection. It is death infecting life."[17] The monster signifies the boundary between the human and the nonhuman, and since the corpse is the nearest thing to a human while not being human, it blurs that boundary. Because of this blurring, the living dead are both uncanny and abject figures. By literalizing the breakdown of the distinction between human and nonhuman, subject and object, the living corpse, whether in the form of a zombie, skeleton, or wraith, effectively evokes reactions of fear, horror, and disgust—in other words, it is an abject subject. For this reason, the living dead are particularly popular video game enemies. As Tanya Krzywinska argues, zombies are the perfect video game enemy because "they are strong, relentless, and already dead; they look spectacularly horrific; and they invite the player to blow them away without guilt or a second thought."[18]

However, even if that violence is thoughtless, it is not necessarily innocent or apolitical. Carly Kocurek points out that monstrosity, like "zombification," is used as a veil to mask and justify the violent murder of countless digital characters in games. She argues that constructing video game enemies as monsters and designating them as execution targets for players is a type of dehumanizing cultural violence that justifies their murder.[19] In this sense, Kocurek argues that "the broad deployment of monstrousness as a justification for killing in video games implicitly suggests that

---

[17] Kristeva, *Powers of Horror*, 4.
[18] Tanya Krzywinska, "Zombies in Gamespace: Form, Context, and Meaning in Zombie-Based Video Games," in *Zombie Culture: Autopsies of the Living Dead*, ed. Shawn McIntosh and Marc Leverette (Lanham: Scarecrow Press, 2008), 153.
[19] Carly Kocurek, "Who Hearkens to the Monster's Scream? Death, Violence and the Veil of the Monstrous in Video Games," *Visual Studies* 30, no. 1 (2015): 80.

those who can be killed are inherently monstrous."[20] Indeed, although like many video game protagonists Geralt is effectively a mass murderer, he is still considered a heroic figure. This is, of course, a problem common in many video games, which often task the player with adopting the role of a "hero" who enacts violence against enemies. Because video games are interactive, this makes the player complicit in that violence if they wish to continue playing the game. Although this does not necessarily encourage violent behavior in the real world, violence against monstrous enemies can provide a virtual reenactment of real-world heteropatriarchal violence directed at female, queer, or otherwise non-normative bodies. As I have argued in my previous work:

> Like many horror films, the act of murdering monstrous women is a violent and cathartic reestablishment of normative, dominant, and patriarchal order. Analyzing and deconstructing the cultural objects involved in this mediated symbolic violence are therefore important components of a feminist project.[21]

The way noonwraiths and nightwraiths fight Geralt is significant to their status as gendered monsters. When threatened, the wraiths scream and claw—both common attacks for female monsters in games—but they also create illusory copies of themselves to trick the player.[22] The bestiary describes the way these "mirror images" circle the player as "a kind of morbid parody of a dance." This "ghastly ritual," as the bestiary calls it, also drains the player's health and heals the wraith, therefore positioning her as a kind of vampire. This is noteworthy because, as Creed has discussed,[23] the vampire is a feminized monster and historical vampire myths were commonly related to menstruation, as it was believed women needed to replenish their lost blood. In addition, the imagery of a woman "draining" a male victim through a "dance" which is actually a deceptive illusion evokes the succubus, the siren, the vamp, or even the black widow or *femme fatale*—archetypes of female monstrosity or villainy that literally or symbolically consume and destroy their male victims. As part of this deception, the wraiths can also turn invisible and immaterial, and must be forced into a corporeal form before they can be harmed. Deception and illusion are common tactics of the monstrous-feminine, sending the message that women are too weak to attack a man directly. They must rather use underhanded methods to trick, deceive, and lie. Besides wraiths, several other female monsters in *The Witcher 3* use these tactics, such as the siren and the vampire as I discuss herein, while male monsters almost never do.

The bestiary advises that, once the wraith has been forced into her corporeal form, the player can "mount a fast attack with a silver blade, preferably one coated in specter oil." Although the association may not have been intentional, this plan of attack calls up imagery of sexualized violence, especially the word "mount" together

---

[20] Ibid., 88.
[21] Stang and Trammell, "The Ludic Bestiary," 732.
[22] Sarah Stang, "Shrieking, Biting, and Licking: The Monstrous-Feminine in Video Games," *Press Start* 4, no. 2 (2018): 18–34.
[23] Creed, *The Monstrous-Feminine*.

with the instruction to penetrate the wraith with a blade coated in oil, like a lubricant. This sexualized violence is repeated with the side quest entitled "The White Lady," in which Geralt must defeat a noonwraith "somewhat like a maid in appearance, though her visage is ghastly and sullied." The quest giver explains that four men from the village got drunk and decided to seek out the wraith to "plough" her, in order to get her to "bugger off." This attempt to gang rape the wraith ended in their deaths, but it demonstrates that even undead women in the world of *The Witcher* are not safe from sexualized violence.[24] The White Lady, as it turns out, is the ghost of a woman who committed suicide on her wedding day because she did not want to be married off to the man her parents chose for her. Geralt lures her out using the dagger she used to kill herself, then proceeds to fight and "kill" her to dispatch her spirit.

In the bestiary, the nightwraiths and noonwraiths are described as exuding an "immense sadness" and howling as though they are suffering. One noonwraith, called the "Devil by the Well" even evokes sympathy in the heart of the witcher himself, an unusual experience for a man whose attitude toward monsters is limited to either "despis[ing] the particularly cruel ones or [being] repulsed by the disgusting ones." Geralt is even apparently "haunted by thoughts of the young woman whose horrible death and powerful emotions had transformed her into that terrible monster," though this is only noted in the bestiary and never acknowledged in the game otherwise. This combination of sympathy and horror is a staple of gothic fiction.[25] And the ghostly bride or woman in white—a tragic woman in a white dress whose broken heart has caused her to haunt the world of the living—is a well-known figure in urban legends, ghost stories, and gothic horror, including works for children such as Tim Burton's film *Corpse Bride*. Before their deaths, these wraiths were almost always brides or brides-to-be, and marriage is a woman's entire raison d'être within the patriarchal world of *The Witcher* series, so being robbed of that, either by their betrothed's betrayal or by death, is the ultimate tragedy. In this sense, female wraiths are not only more tragic, vindictive, and vengeful than their male counterparts, but since their relationship to a man—typically a relationship characterized by betrayal or loss—is what defined them in life and in death, they are also made monstrous in relation to their gender.

As Angela Wright observes, in the 1700s, around the time of the earliest gothic novels, "Women's rights to property and legal representation remained suspended upon their marriage, and they were expected to consolidate and incorporate their 'very being

---

[24] Like much medieval-inspired fantasy written by men, *The Witcher* is full of casual references to rape alongside pillaging and murder. Aside from seeing bandits and soldiers dragging screaming women out of their homes, in *The Witcher 3*, the player encounters rooms full of the naked corpses of murdered women, their bodies butchered and displayed by serial killers in horrific and sexualized ways, as well as sex workers being tied up and tortured by their male clients.

[25] For examples of this, see Samantha Holland, Robert Shail, and Steven Gerrard, *Gender and Contemporary Horror in Film* (Bingley: Emerald Group Publishing, 2019); Helen Hanson, *Hollywood Heroines: Women in Film Noir and the Female Gothic Film* (London and New York: I. B. Tauris, 2007); and Diana Wallace, "Uncanny Stories: The Ghost Story As Female Gothic," *Gothic Studies* 6, no. 1 (2018): 57–68.

or legal existence' with their husband's."[26] Emma Clery has argued that this "civil death" required of married women reduced them to "ghosts" or "the living dead" and they manifested as the supernatural in gothic fiction: "[women] are the ghosts in [the law's] machine."[27] Indeed, Avril Horner observes that gothic heroines were defined by their lack of agency, "disadvantaged and disempowered by the workings of primogeniture and property law."[28] Similarly, the wraiths of *The Witcher 3* are women victimized by patriarchal power structures whose living death is directly connected to their marital status. That a man is the one who lures them, fights them, and violently destroys them, thereby preventing them from exacting their vengeance upon other men, demonstrates the wraiths' continued oppression in the face of masculine dominance.

On the other hand, the very act of transforming into a monster in order to seek vengeance upon the world—killing unfaithful lovers and would-be rapists—is an enactment of agency that these women were denied in life. Some more contemporary gothic fiction writers similarly attempt to grant agency to the gothic heroine, who, as Horner argues, has started to "express desires that challenge traditional roles" and, in order to empower herself, has begun to "embody, quite literally, the unruly and even the abject."[29] Horner further claims that twentieth-century "Gothic texts featuring abject and/or vampiric bodies have been used very effectively by women writers to deconstruct cultural assumptions about the female body and female desire."[30] *The Witcher 3*, as a game written and designed entirely by men and featuring a male protagonist, always positions monstrous women as horrific creatures, collected in the game's bestiary alongside all the other monsters Geralt has slain. However, they do indeed use the power of their own monstrosity to get what they want (though what they want is almost always only vengeance against the men who wronged them).

For example, one of the longer side quests in the game has the player encounter the ghost of a woman named Anabelle whose home was invaded by angry peasants intent on murdering her father. Rather than risking the rape and murder that awaited her, she drank a potion that induced a state of death-like paralysis. During this paralysis, her lover Graham came to rescue her, but upon finding her apparently dead, he fled in his grief. Anabelle awoke after the peasants had left but was unable to move or speak. Rats had started feasting on the corpses, and they ate her alive—she felt everything, but could do nothing. This torment, and the belief that her lover had abandoned her to this horrific fate, caused her spirit to haunt the tower. Geralt, seeking to exorcise her, was tasked with helping her make peace with what happened and forgive Graham.

---

[26] Angela Wright, *Gothic Fiction: A Reader's Guide to Essential Criticism* (Basingstoke: Palgrave Macmillan, 2007), 136.
[27] Emma J. Clery, *The Rise of Supernatural Fiction 1762-1800* (Cambridge: Cambridge University Press, 1995), 126, https://doi.org/10.1017/CBO9780511518997.
[28] Avril Horner, "Women, Power and Conflict: The Gothic Heroine and 'Chocolate-Box Gothic,'" *Caliban* 27 (2010): para 4, https://doi.org/10.4000/caliban.2218.
[29] Ibid., para 7. She discusses examples such as Fay Weldon's *The Life and Loves of a She-Devil* (1983), Angela Carter's *Nights at the Circus* (1984), Jeanette Winterson's *Sexing the Cherry* (1988), Jody Scott's *I, Vampire* (1986), and Anna Livia's *Minimax* (1991).
[30] Horner, "Women, Power and Conflict," para 10.

Anabelle requests that Geralt bring her bones to Graham, so he can bury her to make amends. However, whether the player agrees to this or not, Anabelle is revealed to be a plague maiden or "pesta," a type of evil female spirit that spreads disease and "delights in dealing pain and suffering, in hearing the howling and moaning of men." Like the other female wraiths, she is a floating, skeletal woman wearing a tattered dress; however, she is significantly more grotesque, as she is "covered in scabs and boils, with rats scurrying about all around her." Although her story is tragic and her rage justified, the plague maiden is blamed for gleefully spreading disease to others and she apparently controls rats, the very creatures that ate her alive—in this sense, cruelly and ironically, she appears to want to make others suffer as she did. Aside from the ableist description of her "resembling an ill woman whose flesh rots off her bones"—ableist in that it frames illness as monstrous and horrific—the fact that the bestiary claims that she particularly delights in the suffering of *men* reinforces her positioning as the monstrous-feminine. In Anabelle's case, her "making peace" with Graham results in his death: if the player brings Graham her bones, she appears in her true form and kills him before disappearing, presumably to haunt and spread disease to others; if the player brings Graham to her instead, she reveals her true form to him and insists he kiss her to prove his love.

Like the other female wraiths, Anabelle's face is skeletal, with rotting flesh stretched taut over her skull. She has only a few teeth and her nose, lips, and lower jaw are missing, leaving her unnaturally long, prehensile tongue hanging out of her mouth (Figure 13.2). Kissing her, then, is truly a trial for Graham, a test of his commitment and love. He passes the test, kissing her after she slowly licks his face with her long

Figure 13.2 A screenshot of the plague maiden challenging her former lover to prove his love by kissing her.

tongue—a revolting twist on a loving caress. As they kiss, she regains her human appearance and Graham gasps and dies, presumably poisoned. Anabelle kneels over his corpse, exclaiming "at last" with a tone of relief and exultation before disappearing, ready to join her beloved in death. While this is certainly a twisted take on the cliché of true love's kiss breaking an evil curse, it does set Anabelle's spirit free. Whether her release results from Graham proving his love, or from the satisfaction of having killed him, either way she is presented as cruel, vengeful, unforgiving, and murderous.

The other wraiths in the game who remain after death due to broken hearts and are so filled with sorrow and rage that they murder the living are all women, suggesting that the plague maiden's gender is no coincidence. The bestiary even briefly acknowledges how odd it is that these creatures should be all female:

> As the name "plague maiden" suggests, these wraiths take the appearance of females, though exactly why that is remains a mystery. Some speculate they, like other such specters, arise from the powerful emotional charge associated with certain circumstances of death, such as death preceded by a long and particularly painful illness.

There really is no mystery to the plague maiden's gender, since powerful emotions and prolonged, painful illnesses are both feminized in Western society, especially in the gothic tradition. All the female wraiths exist because of broken hearts and prolonged suffering, thereby reinforcing a misogynistic cultural association between women and mental and emotional instability. Presumably, men must also have their hearts broken and suffer for long periods of time in the world of *The Witcher*, but they do not become murderous wraiths as a result.

It is worth recalling that many of the creatures in *The Witcher* games are inspired by European folklore, and the wraiths are no exception. The plague maiden, for example, "has roots in European folklore,"[31] and the noonwraith is similar to the Polish Noon Witch, or Lady Midday, a specter that causes madness and heat stroke. According to *The Witcher 3: Wild Hunt Artbook*, noonwraiths and nightwraiths, both drawn from Slavic mythology, are particularly tragic figures:

> Usually they are born of some horrible tragedy tied to ill-fated love. Women falling victim to such events become—depending on the time of day in which they die—either noonwraiths or nightwraiths, with grief, longing, or a thirst for vengeance having cursed them and driven them insane.[32]

Another female wraith in *The Witcher 3*, called the beann'shie, is derived from the Irish legend of the banshee, a female spirit that wails, shrieks, and howls to herald the death of a family member. They resemble the other wraiths in that they are floating skeletal women with long hair, and the bestiary describes them as "pale, tear-streaked

---

[31] Marcin Batylda et al., *The Witcher 3: Wild Hunt Artbook* (CD Projekt Red, 2015), 168.
[32] Ibid., 169.

women with shriveled faces and wrinkled, corpse-like bodies." It also claims that they "are the spirits of women stuck between life and death due to traumatic experiences," thereby repeating the same trope of victimized, tragic female specters that haunt the living due to their own trauma. In these stories of ghostly women who cause illness and death, femininity is tied to suffering, danger, abjection, and madness. The wraiths in *The Witcher 3* send the message that women cannot control themselves, and that they will be overcome by grief or rage if their hearts are broken or they are denied heterosexual marriage, therefore further drawing on the misogynistic history of pathologizing women's emotions by labeling them hysterical, out of control, and mad. Even The White Lady's story suggests that men believed the wraith just needed sex (i.e., gang rape) to "cure" her, and that although this did not work, she apparently needed to be penetrated by a man's silver sword in order to be dispatched.

"A Monster in a Beautiful Woman's Body": The Bait-and-Switch *Femme Fatale*

The Witcher series seems particularly preoccupied with the idea of female monsters disguising themselves to deceive their male victims, like the plague maiden who first appeared to Geralt as the ghost of a human woman in order to gain his sympathy and manipulate him, before revealing her true, horrific form. This "bait-and-switch reveal" of the monster reinforces her positioning as a *femme fatale*—the archetype of female villainy made famous in the film noir genre that encompasses any kind of attractive, self-serving woman who uses her seduction and charm to manipulate, deceive, and ultimately betray the male protagonist for her own ends.[33] While the *femme fatale* is a relatively recent label for this archetype, this positioning of woman as deceptive, seductive, and predatory is ancient and ubiquitous—seen in the form of the succubus, siren, vamp, man-eater, black widow, enchantress, and so on. This figure embodies misogynistic distrust and fear of female sexuality—especially the threat it poses to heterosexual men—as well as patriarchal attempts to control that sexuality by framing it as monstrous and evil. Unsurprisingly, there are countless manifestations of this archetype in games, of which *The Witcher 3* is a prime exemplar.

Succubi in *The Witcher 3* are conventionally attractive women with horns and goat legs who wear revealing clothing (or nothing at all) and are also covered in spiral markings or tattoos (Figure 13.3). According to *The Witcher 3*'s bestiary, succubi do not mean to harm humans, unlike other monsters. Rather, "they are motivated by one thing and one thing only: an insatiable lust. They try in vain to slake this by engaging in sexual acts with any other humanoid species they encounter." While this is pleasurable for their "victims," their never-ending desire has "pushed more than one man to madness or even death." Although they do not kill their lovers, succubi need

---

[33] See Mary A. Doane, *Femmes Fatales: Feminism, Film Theory, Psychoanalysis* (New York: Routledge, 1991).

Figure 13.3 A screenshot of succubi reveling at the feet of one of the main antagonists of *The Witcher 3: Wild Hunt*.

their "vital energies" to survive—they give men pleasure in exchange for those energies and can hold them spellbound for as long as they wish. In the few side quests in which Geralt interacts with succubi, the player can choose either to fight and murder them or to let them live in peace. In one side quest, if players choose to spare the succubus, Geralt claims that they do so because although she is a monster, she is "a sentient one, and basically harmless." However, the succubus accuses Geralt of only sparing her because she has "ample breasts and a pretty face." Several times in the series, Geralt claims that he does not kill sentient creatures—though, of course, he does not hesitate if they have harmed a human, if a human has paid him to murder them for any reason (even if their presence is simply an inconvenience and they would have posed no threat if left undisturbed), or if he happens to stumble upon their nest or lair while exploring or treasure hunting. True, most creatures will usually attack Geralt on sight, but he has invaded their home and, since he is a witcher—a *professional monster slayer*—they would immediately perceive him as a threat. Occasionally, Geralt can converse with sapient monsters and in the dialog options the player can choose violence or a peaceful resolution, either by leaving them alone, or convincing them to leave the area.

Ample breasts and a pretty face, however, are not enough to save all monsters. Sirens are another sapient species of conventionally attractive women with animal body parts, yet unlike the succubus, the player is allowed no opportunities to show them mercy or even converse with them. While the bestiary insists that the succubus means no harm even if her rapacious sexual appetite can be dangerous, sirens are literal man-eaters:

> Like skilled hunters setting out wooden ducks to lure in drakes, sirens ... lure men near—using their own bodies as decoys. They can transform to resemble beautiful

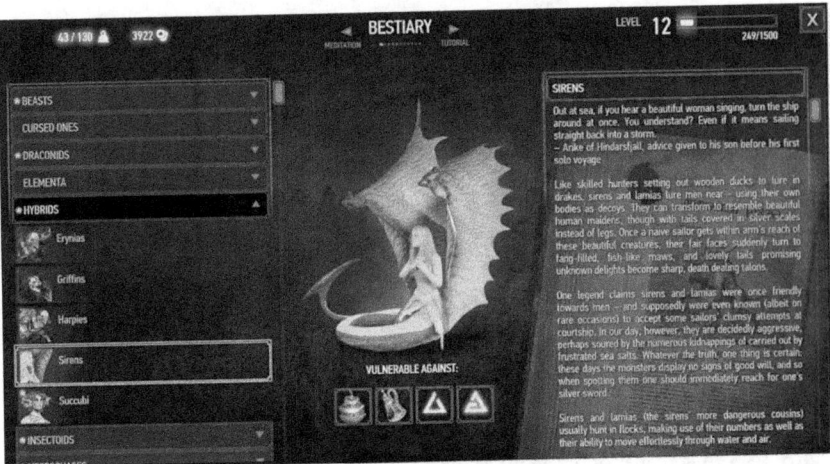

Figure 13.4 Screenshot of the bestiary entry for sirens. Note how they are categorized as "hybrid" monsters alongside succubi, but they are treated with neither mercy nor sympathy.

human maidens, though with tails covered in silver scales instead of legs. Once a naive sailor gets within arm's reach of these beautiful creatures, their fair faces suddenly turn to fang-filled, fish-like maws, and lovely tails promising unknown delights become sharp, death dealing talons.

As described in the bestiary, according to legend sirens were once friendly and even occasionally romantically interested in men. They grew aggressive, however, "perhaps soured by the numerous kidnappings" carried out by frustrated men, presumably in order to rape them (Figure 13.4).

That they use "their own bodies as decoys" is important, because as Mary Ann Doane has argued, femininity is used as a masquerade in order for non-normative women—especially queer women—to survive in a patriarchal world:

> The very fact that we can speak of a woman "using" her sex or "using" her body for particular gains is highly significant—it is not that a man cannot use his body in this way but that he doesn't have to.[34]

This type of masquerade, in which a woman plays up her sexuality to manipulate men, "is aligned with the *femme fatale*" and "regarded by men as evil incarnate" because it represents a power that women can potentially use against them.[35] For the sirens, that

---

[34] Mary Ann Doane, "Film and the Masquerade: Theorising the Female Spectator," in *Feminist Film Theory: A Reader*, ed. Sue Thornham (Edinburgh: Edinburgh University Press, [1982] 1999), 139.
[35] Ibid.

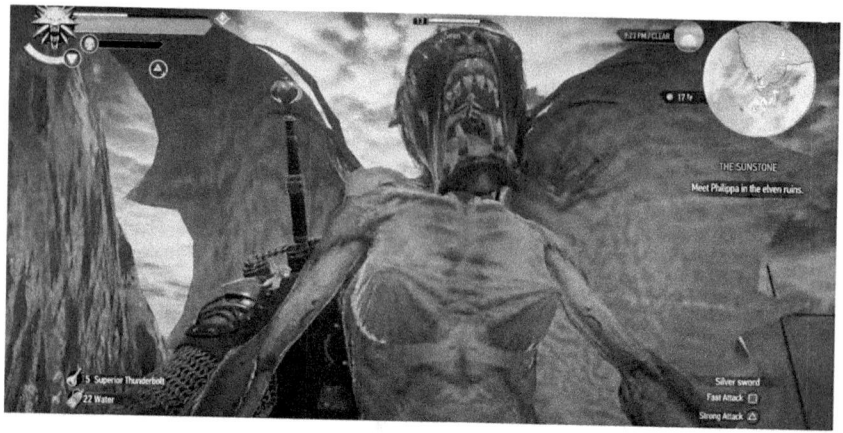

Figure 13.5 A screenshot of the more monstrous form the siren takes when she attacks. Note the gaping mouth, sharp fangs, and the way her body appears aged and withered.

power is also the phallic power they wield once they shed their alluring forms and attack with their sharp teeth, claws, and strength in numbers (Figure 13.5).

Sirens are all-female and they hunt in flocks, adhering to the classic imagery, discussed by Creed, of "the lesbian as a deadly siren who waits for her male prey while savouring an erotic embrace with her amoral sisters."[36] While sirens might be framed as "amoral" monsters deserving of death in the decidedly patriarchal world of *The Witcher*, their anger at men seems justified—they were, after all, being *kidnapped*. Although the game's narrative insists that they prey on men, their hostility is justified given that they are fighting off men who would invade their homes and kidnap, rape, or murder them. The bestiary, however, leaves no room for mercy or sympathy and instead encourages players to immediately reach for their swords once they have spotted a siren. Similarly, *The Witcher 3: Wild Hunt Artbook* describes them, in no uncertain terms, as evil and horrific monstrosities: "Sirens are bloodthirsty, treacherous creatures that lure naïve travelers in close with their illusory female forms and then, when escape is impossible, transform into hideous monsters and tear their unfortunate victims to shreds."[37]

Threatened sirens let out a horrifying, ear-piercing shriek that can stun Geralt—a twisted version of the alluring siren's song, though just as dangerous. Although their appearance is inhuman once they shed their attractive disguises, when they die, their upper bodies revert to their more human form (Figure 13.6), thereby reminding players that they are murdering women who are nearly human. From the corpses of these women, the player can harvest body parts—their vocal cords and hair—for use in potions. When witches in the game use human body parts to brew potions and

---

[36] Barbara Creed, "Lesbian Bodies: Tribades, Tomboys and Tarts," in *Sexy Bodies: The Strange Carnalities of Feminism*, ed. Elizabeth Grosz and Elspeth Probyn (New York: Routledge, 1996), 86–7.
[37] Batylda et al., *The Witcher 3*, 180.

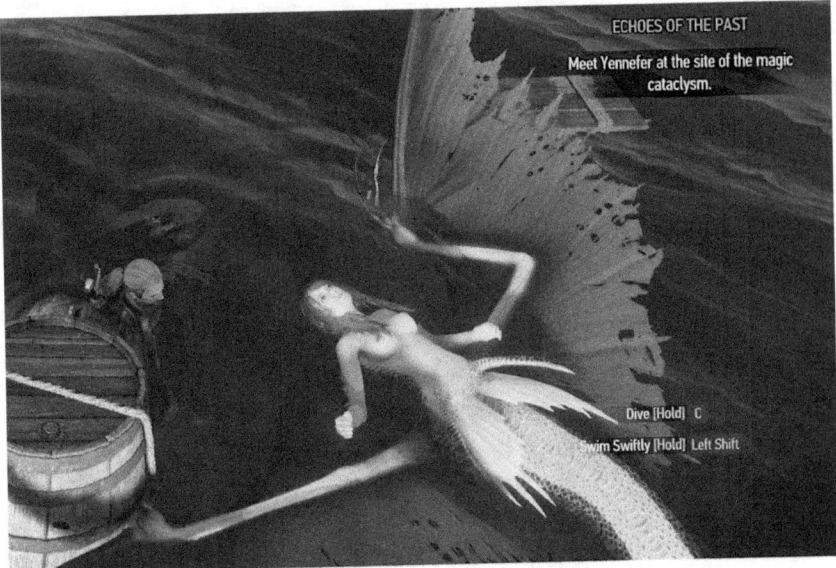

Figure 13.6 Screenshot of a siren's corpse floating on the water. Note how it has reverted to its more humanoid appearance, thereby suggesting that this is the siren's "true" form and they only adopt the more monstrous form pictured in Figure 13.5 when they are threatened.

soups, it is framed as evil and revolting, but when Geralt harvests monster body parts to brew, it is unquestioned and accepted, even when those parts are from the human halves of those monsters. This resemblance to humans is unimportant in the world of *The Witcher*, however, because as with many fantasy games, it is populated by sapient, humanoid beings that are treated with disgust or consternation. The sirens are regularly called "sea whores" and "cunts" by non-player characters—nasty, gendered insults that are somewhat ironic given that sirens do not have sex with men, nor do they appear to have human genitals. These insults serve to highlight the fact that within this world, sirens are indeed seen as women, but they are unacceptable women deserving only punishment and death. Perhaps the succubus is tolerated simply because she, unlike the sirens, is still willing to have sex with men.

Similarly, the female vampires or "bruxae" in *The Witcher 3* downloadable content entitled *Blood and Wine* initially appear as beautiful young women but transform into ghastly, naked, emaciated women with sharp teeth, long claws, and gray skin stretched taught across muscle and bone, thereby once again embodying the trope of the female monster being both seductive and deceptive, with a horrifying "true" or alternative form when she attacks. Described as a "womanoid" and "a monster in a beautiful woman's body" in the game's bestiary, *The Witcher 3*'s playing card game features a bruxa card that reads, "A vile, bloodthirsty, man-eating hag. Kind of like my mother-in-law," thereby revealing the game's casual misogyny as well as its use of terms typically associated with the monstrous-feminine: vile, bloodthirsty, man-eating, hag

Figure 13.7 A screenshot of the bruxa card from Gwent, the card game in *The Witcher 3: Wild Hunt*.

(Figure 13.7). Creed[38] has observed that female vampires are both predatory and sexual and, as previously discussed, given their tendency to "drain" their victims, vampires can be interpreted as the same kind of manifestation of the monstrous-feminine as the succubus and the wraiths.

The bruxa slashes at Geralt with her claws and bites him with her fangs, but her greatest threat is her voice, as she "can screech with such force that the shockwave will knock even a huge man down, making him easy prey for the vampires." This stunning, shocking, paralyzing shriek, screech, or scream is the same tactic used by the beann'shies and sirens and is a common weapon in the monstrous-feminine arsenal. It is also a particularly feminized weapon: Terms like "screech," "shriek," "scream," and "wail" are often used to refer to female voices, whereas, as Michel Chion has noted in *The Voice in Cinema*, a man's cry is often called a shout rather than a scream, suggesting a calculated and purposeful demonstration of aggressive power or a primal marking of territory.[39] When the wraiths, bruxae, or sirens use their voices as weapons to

---

[38] Creed, *The Monstrous-Feminine*.
[39] Michel Chion, *The Voice in Cinema*, trans. Claudia Gorbman (New York: Columbia University Press, [1982] 1999).

disarm the men who threaten them, they are not revealing weakness or fear. They use their voices in that calculated and purposeful (and masculine) way, suggesting that this screech is one way in which they claim phallic power for themselves. This echoes a tactic taught in many women's self-defense courses, as victims are encouraged to scream to startle their attackers and give them an opportunity to escape or fight back.

While female monsters in these games never try to escape, they use the moment in which the protagonist is stunned, to fight back, usually by clawing, stabbing, or biting the player, thereby using their bodies as weapons to claim and wield the penetrative phallic power that women are typically denied in patriarchal society. This threat of penetration is a key attribute of the monstrous-feminine since, as Creed has thoroughly demonstrated,[40] female monsters are not terrifying because of their supposed lack that reminds the male subject of his own fear of castration (as Freud had argued); rather, they are terrifying precisely because they threaten penetration with their phallic parts or castration with their fanged mouths or *vagina dentata*. Either way, they feminize their male victims. Even the female scream, which normally functions to signal distress or vocalize terror is turned against the protagonist and used to harm him. In this sense, the danger the monstrous-feminine poses in the form of deadly teeth, claws, and screams is associated with embodied, natural, primal, and animalistic power, whereas masculine danger is in the form of the sword—an inorganic tool used by the man. Of course, these monsters all lose in the end, slain by the protagonist wielding his apparently more powerful phallic symbol. He serves and restores the symbolic order, while the transgressive female monster is punished with death for attempting to take phallic power for herself, using her hybrid or transformative, animalistic body. Although their voices are used as a weapon while they fight, once these creatures are defeated they do indeed scream in agony, a lengthy sound that subtly shifts from an inhuman and monstrous snarl or shriek to an all-too-human scream of pain and anguish. This human scream upon death is unique to these female monsters, thereby underscoring their resemblance to, or former status as, human women and perhaps emphasizing the tragedy of their existence in this hostile patriarchal world.

Becoming Willfully Monstrous

In her book *Goddesses and Monsters*, Jane Caputi has demonstrated how "popular culture serves as a repository of ancient and contemporary mythic and folkloric images and narratives, personalities, icons, and archetypes."[41] As I have demonstrated in this chapter, games are an important site of analysis and intervention, meriting critique from feminist media scholars given the overt and symbolic ways that popular culture remediates and reinforces the construction of woman as monster. While I have only examined one video game in this chapter, it is important to note that these kinds of

---

[40] Creed, *The Monstrous-Feminine*.
[41] Caputi, *Goddesses*, 4.

horrific female monsters that clearly embody misogynistic assumptions and fears are ubiquitous in fantasy, science fiction, and horror games. And, as I have previously argued, games are particularly problematic tools of meaning-making because they position players as heroic, normative representatives of the patriarchal symbolic order and force them to enact violence against marginalized bodies thinly disguised as monstrous creatures.[42] Like all monstrous creatures, the wraith, siren, or vampire—or any of their various iterations—signifies a threat to patriarchal society and so must be dehumanized and categorized as evil. An effective way of dehumanizing someone is to make them literally half-animal, like the succubus or siren, or transform them into a corpse-like creature, like the vampire or wraith—a violation of natural boundaries that also categorizes them as an abject subject who is "heterogenous, animal, metamorphosed, altered."[43]

The abject is that which "does not respect borders, positions, rules. The in-between, the ambiguous, the composite"[44] and for feminist scholar Deborah Covino, the abject woman is subversive and liberating: she "immerse[s] herself in the significances of the flesh, becoming willfully monstrous as she defies the symbolic order."[45] Patricia Yaeger has similarly proposed that women should seek a grotesque and sublime feminist aesthetic by embracing their own unruly bodies.[46] Regardless of the problematic way they are victimized and vilified, these creatures all draw on the image of a powerful, willfully monstrous woman. In this sense, within the ambiguity of the monster, lies the potential for feminist reclamation and empowerment. However, while the monster, like the abject itself, is an inherently ambiguous, transgressive figure, the female monster in a game like *The Witcher 3* is a misogynistic construct, designed by men to be confronted and slain by a male protagonist.

The siren is framed as a deceptive "sea whore" and the female vampire is called "a vile, bloodthirsty, man-eating hag," and both are deserving only of death. The succubus is allowed to survive only if she is willing to have sex with men but mean them no harm. Even when the female monster is framed in a sympathetic way like the wraith, she is doomed to a tragic, undead existence full of wrath and madness, either because her heart was broken by a man, or because she was never able to fulfill her "purpose" and become a wife and mother. The design and narrative framing of these monsters, especially given that the hero is a straight white man, send the clear message that this game was designed for a presumed male player—that this story was not intended for women to enjoy.[47] This is not to diminish the power of oppositional

---

[42] Stang, "Shrieking, Biting, and Licking"; Stang and Trammell, "The Ludic Bestiary."
[43] Kristeva, *Powers of Horror*, 207.
[44] Ibid., 4.
[45] Deborah C. Covino, *Amending the Abject Body: Aesthetic Makeovers in Medicine and Culture* (Albany: SUNY Press, 2004), 29.
[46] Patricia Yaeger, "The 'Language of Blood': Toward A Maternal Sublime," *Genre* 25, no. 1 (1992): 5–24.
[47] In Dmitri Williams, Nicole Martins, Mia Consalvo, and James Ivory, "The virtual census: Representations of gender, race and age in video games." *New Media and Society* 11, no. 5 (2009): 830–1; it is recognized that the most likely cause for these patterns of representation is "a combination of developer demographics and perceived ideas about game players among marketers. The stereotype

or subversive reading, nor am I arguing that there should be no female monsters in games. However, space must be made for powerful, active, willfully monstrous women who are not victimized and vilified. Games offer the opportunity to virtually embody the monstrous Other and see the world through their eyes, so perhaps instead of playing as the monster slayer, players could enact the role of the vengeful wraith or siren protecting herself from her would-be rapists. Perhaps game developers could start to re-envision monstrosity as an empowering manifestation of non-normativity or transgression that pushes back against oppressive patriarchal narratives.

of game players as only young, white males who want to be powerful white adults may be driving the content-creation process, even as the player base becomes older and more diverse." For this reason, the feminist potential of these characters is undercut by authorial intention and bias.

Bibliography

Abbott, James. "An Interview with Composer James Bernard, Part II." *The Jade Sphinx*, September 14, 2011. http://thejadesphinx.blogspot.com/2011/09/interview-with-composer-james-bernard_14.html.

Abel, Richard. *The Red Rooster Scare: Making Cinema American, 1900–1910*. Berkeley and Los Angeles: University of California Press, 1999.

Adams, Gregory. "Mykki Blanco: 'The Initiation.'" *Exclaim!*, May 13, 2013. https://exclaim.ca/music/article/mykki_blanco-initiation.

Adorno, Theodor. *Night Music: Essays on Music 1928–1962*. Edited by Rolf Tiedemann, Translated by Wieland Hoban. London, New York, and Calcutta: Seagull Books, 2009.

Adorno, Theodor and Hanns Eisler. *Composing for the Films*. New York: Oxford University Press, [1947] 1994.

Ahmad, Aalya. "Blood in the Bush Garden: Indigenization, Gender, and Unsettling Horror." In *The Canadian Horror Film: Terror of the Source*, edited by Gina Freitag and André Loiselle, 47–66. Toronto: University of Toronto Press, 1995.

Aldiss, Brian. *Trillion Year Spree: The History of Science Fiction*. New York: Atheneum, 1986.

Aleiss, Angela. *Making the White Man's Indian: Native Americans and Hollywood Movies*. London: Praeger, 2005.

Aleman, Enrique. "Through the Prism of Critical Race Theory: 'Niceness' and Latina/o Leadership in the Politics of Education." *Journal of Latinos and Education* 8, no. 4 (2009): 290–311.

Altman, Rick. *Silent Film Sound*. New York: Columbia University Press, 2004.

Altman, Rick. *The American Film Musical*. London: British Film Institute, 1987.

Amberg, Almut. *Theatre, Theatricality and Metatheatre in "Behind a Mask" (1866)*. Munich: Grin Verlag, 2020.

Anthony, H.E. "Indian Headhunters of the Interior an Interesting Study in the South American Republic." *National Geographic Magazine* 40, no. 4 (October 1921): 327–73.

Applebaum, Louis. "Documentary Music." In *Film Music: From Violins to Video*, edited by James L. Limbacher, 66–72. Metuchen: Scarecrow Press, 1974.

Arnett, Jeffrey Jensen. "The Psychology of Emerging Adulthood: What is Known, and What Remains to be Known." In *Emerging Adults in America: Coming of Age in the 21st Century*, edited by Jeffrey Jensen Arnett and Jennifer Lynn Tanner, 303–30. Washington: American Psychological Association, 2006.

Arnold Schoenberg Centre. "Accompaniment to a Cinematographic Scene, Op 34." July 2, 2018. http://www.schoenberg.at/index.php/en/joomla-license-sp-1943310036/begleitungsmusik-zu-einer-lichtspielscene-op-34-1929-1930.

Asper, Helmut G. *Etwas Besseres als den Tod: Filmexil in Hollywood*. Marburg: Schüren, 2002.

Auerbach, Nina. *Our Vampires, Ourselves*. Chicago: University of Chicago Press, 1995.

Auslander, Philip. *Liveness: Performance in a Mediatized Culture*. London: Routledge, 1999.

Bailey, Walter. *Programmatic Elements in the Works of Schoenberg*. Ann Arbor: UMI Research Press, 1984.

Balantrapu, Mihir. "Schoenberg's House of Horrors." *The Hindu*, July 30, 2015.

Baldick, Chris. *In Frankenstein's Shadow: Myth, Monstrosity, and Nineteenth-Century Writing*. Oxford: Clarendon Press, 1987.

Balfour, Ian. "Allegories of Origins: Frankenstein after the Enlightenment." *SEL Studies in English Literature* 88, no. 4 (2006): 777–98.

Barthes, Roland. "Pasolini's Salò: Sade to the Letter." In *Pier Paolo Pasolini*, edited by Paul Willemen, 64–6. London: British Film Institute, 1977.

Bateson, Gregory. *Steps to an Ecology of the Mind*. Chicago: University of Chicago Press, 1972.

Batylda, Marcin, et al. *The Witcher 3: Wild Hunt Artbook*. CD Projekt Red, 2015.

Baumann, Rebecca. *Frankenstein 200: The Birth, Life, and Resurrection of Mary Shelley's Monster*. Indianapolis: Indiana University Press, 2018.

Bay, Mia. "Remembering Racism: Rereading the Black Image in the White Mind." *Reviews in American History* 27, no. 4 (1999): 646–56.

Behrendt, Stephen C. "Novel into Drama." *Presumption: or, the Fate of Frankenstein* (electronic edition). Edited by Stephen Behrendt for Romantic Circles. Boulder: University of Colorado, 2001. https://romantic-circles.org/editions/peake/apparatus/drama.html (accessed May 15, 2021).

Bennett, Betty T., ed. *Selected Letters of Mary Wollstonecraft Shelley*. Baltimore: Johns Hopkins University Press, 1995.

Benshoff, Harry M. *Monsters in the Closet: Homosexuality and the Horror Film*. Manchester: Manchester University Press, 1997.

Bergland, Renée L. *The National Uncanny: Indian Ghosts and American Subjects*. Hanover: The University Press of New England, 2000.

Berry, Mark. "Arnold Schoenberg: Beauty and Horror." *TLS: The Times Literary Supplement*, January 25, 2020.

Bersani, Leo. "Is the Rectum a Grave?" In *AIDS: Cultural Analysis/Cultural Activism*, edited by Douglas Crimp, 197–232. Cambridge: MIT Press, 1988.

Bick, Sally. "A Double Life in Hollywood: Hanns Eisler's Score for the Film Hangmen Also Die and the Covert Expressions of a Marxist Composer." *The Musical Quarterly* 93, no. 1 (2010): 90–143.

Bick, Sally. "Copland on Hollywood." In *Copland Connotation: Studies and Interview*, edited by Peter Dickinson, 39–56. Rochester, New York: Boydell Press, 2002.

Bick, Sally. "Eisler's Notes on Hollywood and the Film Music Project, 1935–42." *Current Musicology* 86 (Fall 2008): 7–39.

Blanchard, Terence. *Champion: An Opera in Jazz*, libretto by Michael Cristofer, 2013.

Blanco, Mykki. "The Initiation." Produced by Sinden, video directed by Ninian Doff, June 5, 2013 for MOCAtv. https://mykkiblancoworld.com/video.

Bolter, Jay, Blair MacIntyre, Maribeth Gandy, and Petra Schweitzer. "New Media and the Permanent Crisis of Aura." *Convergence* 12, no. 1 (February 2006): 21–39.

Bolton, H. Philip. *Women Writers Dramatized: A Calendar of Performances from Narrative Works Published in English to 1900*. London and New York: Mansell, 2000.

Bordwell, David, Janet Staiger, and Kristin Thompson. *The Classical Hollywood Cinema: Film Style and Mode of Production to 1960*. New York: Columbia University Press, 1985.

Boyd, Colleen E. and Coll Thrush, eds. *Phantom Past, Indigenous Presence: Native Ghosts in North American Culture & History*. Lincoln: University of Nebraska Press, 2011.

Bradley, Scott. "Music in Cartoons." In *The Cartoon Music Book*, edited by Daniel Goldmark and Yuval Taylor, 115–20. Chicago: Chicago Review Press, 2002.

Brand, Juliane and Christopher Hailey, eds. *Constructive Dissonance: Arnold Schoenberg and the Transformations of Twentieth-Century Culture*. Berkeley: University of California Press, 1997.

Brigden, Charlie. "The Great Unknown: The Story Behind Jerry Goldsmith's Score for Alien." *RogerEbert.com*, May 17, 2017. https://www.rogerebert.com/features/the-great-unknown-the-story-behind-jerry-goldsmiths-score-for-alien.

Brody, Richard. "Pasolini's Theorem." *New Yorker*, December 29, 2011. https://www.newyorker.com/culture/richard-brody/pasolinis-theorem.

Brogan, Kathleen. *Cultural Haunting: Ghosts and Ethnicity in Recent American Literature*. Charlottesville: University of Virginia Press, 1998.

Brook, Donald. *Composers' Gallery: Biographical Sketches of Contemporary Composers*. London: Salisbury Square, 1946.

Brophy, Phillip. "The Secret History of Film Music: Picturing Atonality, Part 1." *The Wire* 168 (February 1998): 30–2. http://www.philipbrophy.com/projects/secrethistoryoffilmmusic/09.html.

Brown, Norman O. *Life Against Death: The Psychoanalytical Meaning of History*. Middletown: Wesleyan University Press, 1959.

Browne, Max. *The Romantic Art of Theodor von Holst 1810–44*. London: Lund Humphries, 1944.

Browne, Max. *Theodor von Holst: His Art and the Pre-Raphaelites 1810-2010*. Cheltenham: The Holst Birthplace Museum, 2010.

Buhs, Joshua Blu. "Camping with Bigfoot: Sasquatch and the Varieties of Middle-Class Resistance to Consumer Culture in Late Twentieth-Century North America." *Journal of Popular Culture* 46, no. 1 (2013): 38–58.

Burston, Paul. "Honestly" (interview with Neil Tennant). *Attitude*, August 1994.

Burt, Gregory. *The Art of Film Music*. Boston: Northeastern University Press, 1994.

Buss, Helen M, D. L. Macdonald, and Anne McWhir. *Mary Wollstonecraft and Mary Shelley: Writing Lives*. Waterloo: Wilfrid Laurier University Press, 2001.

Caputi, Jane. *Goddesses and Monsters: Women, Myth, Power, and Popular Culture*. Madison: University of Wisconsin Press, 2004.

Carl, Jill, Mario Schwarzer, Doris Klingelhoefer, Daniel Ohlendorf and Daniel A. Groenberg, "Curare – A Curative Poison: A Scientometric Analysis." *PLOS One* 9, no. 11 (November 2014): 1.

Carroll, Noël. *The Philosophy of Horror; or, Paradoxes of the Heart*. New York and London: Routledge, 2004.

Case, Sue-Ellen. "Tracking the Vampire." *differences* 3, no. 2 (1991): 1–20.

Castle, Terry. *The Apparitional Lesbian: Female Homosexuality and Modern Culture*. New York: Columbia University Press, 1993.

CD Projekt Red. *The Witcher 3: Wild Hunt*. CD Projekt. Microsoft Windows, 2015.

Chalmers Publishing Company. "Moving Picture World (Jan–Jun 1910)." https://archive.org/details/movinwor06chal (accessed June 14, 2012).

Chapman, Alex. "The Multiplicities of Mykki Blanco." *Interview Magazine*, April 4, 2012, https://www.interviewmagazine.com/culture/mykki-blanco.

Chapman, Dale. "Hermeneutics of Suspicion: Paranoia and the Technological Sublime in Drum and Bass Music." *Echo* 5, no. 2 (Fall 2002): 1–18. http://www.echo.ucla.edu/volume5-issue2/chapman/chapman.pdf.

Chaubey, Varun. "How Hitchcock Generated Suspense in His Films." *Medium*, April 28, 2019. https://medium.com/the-film-odyssey/how-hitchcock-generates-suspense-in-his-films-1ef60a4ad153.

Chion, Michel. *Audio-Vision: Sound on Screen*. New York: Columbia University Press, 1994.

Chion, Michel. *The Voice in Cinema*. Translated by Claudia Gorbman. New York: Columbia University Press, [1982] 1999.

Clarke, Andrew. "Loder and Sons, Bath: A Band of Musicians." In *Musicians of Bath and Beyond: Edward Loder and his Family (1809–1865)*, edited by Nicholas Temperley, 76–105. Woodbridge, Suffolk: The Boydell Press, 2016.

Clery, Emma J. *The Rise of Supernatural Fiction 1762–1800*. Cambridge: Cambridge University Press, 1995.

Clover, Carol. "Her Body, Himself: Gender in the Slasher Film." In *The Dread of Difference: Gender and the Horror Film*, edited by Barry Keith Grant, 68–115. 2nd ed. Austin: University of Texas Press, 2015.

Clover, Carol J. *Women and Chain Saws: Gender in the Modern Horror Film*. Princeton: Princeton University Press, 1992.

Coates, Tyler. "Why Hands Across America Is So Vital to Jordan Peele's Us." *Esquire online*, March 21, 2019. https://www.esquire.com/entertainment/movies/a26883876/hands-across-america-us-movie-explained/.

Cohen, Jeffrey Jerome, ed. *Monster Theory: Reading Culture*. Minneapolis: University of Minnesota Press, 1996.

Cohen, Jeffrey Jerome. "Monster Culture (Seven Theses)." In *Monster Theory: Reading Culture*, edited by Jeffrey Jerome Cohen, 3–25. Minneapolis: University of Minnesota Press, 1996.

Coleman, Deirdre. "Claire Clairmont and Mary Shelley: Identification and Rivalry Within the Tribe of the Otaheite Philosophers." *Women's Writing* 6, no. 3 (1999): 309–28.

Collaer, Paul. *History of Modern Music*. Translated by Sally Abeles. New York: World Publishing, 1961.

Collins, K. Austin. "Jordan Peele's Us is Just a Horror Movie, and That's a Good Thing." *Vanity Fair*, March 26, 2019. https://www.vanityfair.com/hollywood/2019/03/jordan-peeles-us-dont-overthink-it.

Collins, Steve. "The Music of Murder: John Brahm's Hangover Square (1945)." October 16, 2020. https://www.splittoothmedia.com/hangover-square/.

Cooke, Mervyn. *The History of Film Music*. Cambridge: Cambridge University Press, 2008.

Corbett, John. *Extended Play: Sounding Off from John Cage to Dr. Funkenstein*. Durham: Duke University Press, 1994.

Covino, Deborah C. *Amending the Abject Body: Aesthetic Makeovers in Medicine and Culture*. Albany: SUNY Press, 2004.

Cox, Jeffrey N. *Seven Gothic Dramas, 1789–1825*. Athens: Ohio University Press, 1992.

Creed, Barbara. "Horror and the Monstrous-Feminine: An Imaginary Abjection." *Screen* 27, no. 1 (1986): 44–71. https://doi.org/10.1093/screen/27.1.44.

Creed, Barbara. "Lesbian Bodies: Tribades, Tomboys and Tarts." In *Sexy Bodies: The Strange Carnalities of Feminism*, edited by Elizabeth Grosz and Elspeth Probyn, 86–103. New York: Routledge, 1996.

Creed, Barbara. *The Monstrous-Feminine: Film, Feminism, Psychoanalysis*. New York: Routledge, 1993.

Bibliography

Cvetkovich, Ann. "Touching the Monster: Deep Lez in Fun Fur." In *Allyson Mitchell: Ladies Sasquatch*, edited by Carla Garnet, Avril McMeekin, Rose Anne Prevec, Matthew Hyland, 26–31. Hamilton: McMaster Museum of Art, 2009.

Dangerfield, Elma. *Byron and the Romantics in Switzerland 1816*. London: Ascent Books, 1978.

Davis, Erik. *TechGnosis: Myth, Magic, and Mysticism in the Age of Information*. Berkeley: North Atlantic Books, 2015.

de Bruin-Molé, Megen. *Gothic Remixed: Monster Mashups and Frankenfictions in 21st-Century Culture*. New York: Bloomsbury, 2019.

de Vos, Gail and Kayla Lar-Son. "Cowboy Smithx's The Candy Meister." In *Horror: A Companion*, edited by Simon Bacon, 175–80. Oxford: Peter Lang, 2019.

Deadmau5 [Joel Zimmerman]. "Interview." *Q*. Toronto: CBC Radio, 23 July 2012. https://www.youtube.com/watch?v=Zeb3dGbhvTM.

Deadmau5 [Joel Zimmerman]. "We All Hit Play." *United We Fail* [blog], 23 June, 2012. https://web.archive.org/web/20120627035653/http://deadmau5.tumblr.com/post/25690507284/we-all-hit-play.

Dear, Nick. *Frankenstein, Based on the Novel by Mary Shelley*. London: Faber & Faber, 2011.

Delogu, Daisy. *Allegorical Bodies: Power and Gender in Late Medieval France*. Toronto: University of Toronto Press, 2015.

Denson, Shane. "Incorporations: Melodrama and Monstrosity in James Whale's Frankenstein and Bride of Frankenstein." In *Melodrama! The Mode of Excess from Early America to Hollywood*, edited by Frank Kelleter, Barbara Krah, and Ruth Mayer, 209–28. Heidelberg: Universitätsverlag Winter, 2007.

Denson, Shane. "Postnaturalism: Frankenstein, Film, and the Anthropotechnical Interface." Bielefeld: Transcript-Verlag, 2014.

Denson, Shane. "Tarzan und der Tonfilm: Verhandlungen zwischen 'Science' and 'Fiction.'" In *"Ich Tarzan." Affenmenschen und Menschenaffen zwischen Science und Fiction*, edited by Gesine Krüger, Ruth Mayer, and Marianne Sommer, 113–30. Bielefeld: transcript Verlag, 2008.

Denson, Shane and Ruth Mayer. "Grenzgänger: Serielle Figuren im Medienwechsel." In *Populäre Serialität: Narration - Evolution - Distinktion*, edited by Frank Kelleter, 185–203. Bielefeld: transcript Verlag, 2012.

Derrida, Jacques. *Writing and Difference*. Chicago: University of Chicago Press, 1978.

Derrida, Jacques. *The Truth in Painting*. Translated by Geoff Bennington and Ian McLeod. Chicago: University of Chicago Press, 1987.

Desta, Yohana. "Us: What Was Hands Across America, the Creepy Event that Inspired Jordan Peele?" *Vanity Fair*, March 22, 2019. https://www.vanityfair.com/hollywood/2019/03/us-movie-hands-across-america.

Deutsch, Didier C. *MusicHound Soundtracks: The Essential Album Guide to Film, Television and Stage Music*. Detroit: Visible Ink Press, 1999.

DeVun, Leah. *Prophecy, Alchemy, and the End of Time: John of Rupescissa in the Late Middle Ages*. New York: Columbia University Press, 2013.

Dixon, Winston Wheeler. *A History of Horror*. New Brunswick and London: Rutgers University Press, 2010.

Doane, Mary Ann. "Film and the Masquerade: Theorising the Female Spectator." In *Feminist Film Theory: A Reader*, edited by Sue Thornham, 131–45. Edinburgh: Edinburgh University Press, [1982] 1999.

Doane, Mary Ann. *Femmes Fatales: Feminism, Film Theory, Psychoanalysis*. New York: Routledge, 1991.

Dollimore, Jonathan. *Sexual Dissidence: Augustine to Wilde, Freud to Foucault*. Oxford: Clarendon Press, 1991.

Douthwaite, Julia V. and Daniel Richter. "The Frankenstein of the French Revolution: Nogaret's Automaton Tale of 1790." *European Romantic Review* 20, no. 3 (July 2009): 381–411.

Downs, Edward, and Stacy L. Smith. "Keeping Abreast of Hypersexuality: A Video Game Character Content Analysis." *Sex Roles* 62, no. 11 (2010): 721–33.

Du Bois, W.E.B. *The Souls of Black Folk*. Boston: Bedford Books, [1903] 1997.

Dumoulin, Julien. "Frankenstein 1910." http://www.jdumoulin.com/julien-dumoulin---graphic-and-video-design---frankenstein-1910.html (accessed April 10, 2021).

Dworkin, Andrea. *Intercourse*. New York: Basic Books, 2008.

Dyer, Richard. *White: Essays on Race and Culture*. New York: Routledge, 1997.

Eco, Umberto. "Innovation and Repetition: Between Modern and Post-Modern Aesthetics." *Daedalus* 114, no. 4 (1985): 161–84.

Eco, Umberto. "The Myth of Superman." Translated by Natalie Chilton. *Diacritics* 2, no. 1 (1972): 14–22.

Edison Kinetogram. "Frankenstein (Dramatic)." March 15, 1910.

Eegah and Tabonga. "The Mask (1961): Louis Applebaum and Myron Schaeffer – 'Put The Mask On Now.'" *Monster Movie Music*, April 19, 2008. https://monstermoviemusic.blogspot.com/2008/04/mask-applebaumschaeffer-put-mask-on.html.

Eells, Josh. "The Rise of the Mau5." *Rolling Stone*, May 7, 2012.

Eisler, Benita. *Byron: Child of Passion, Fool of Fame*. New York: Vintage Books, 2000.

Eisler, Hanns "Film Music – Work in Progress." *Modern Music* 18 (January 1941): 591–4.

Elliott-Smith, Darren. "Gay Zombies: Consuming Masculinity and Community in Bruce LaBruce's Otto; or, Up with Dead People (2008) and L.A. Zombie (2010)." In *Zombies and Sexuality: Essays on Desire and the Living Dead*, edited by Shaka McGlotten and Steve Jones, 140–58. Jefferson: McFarland, 2014.

Elliott-Smith, Darren. *Queer Horror Film and Television: Sexuality and Masculinity at the Margins*. London: I. B. Tauris, 2016.

Equal Justice Initiative. "Lynching in America: Confronting the Legacy of Racial Terror." Montgomery: Equal Justice Initiative, 2017. https://eji.org/reports/lynching-in-america/.

Eshun, Kodwo. *More Brilliant than the Sun: Adventures in Sonic Fiction*. London: Quartet Books, 1998.

Fabricant, Carole. *Swift's Landscape*. Baltimore: Johns Hopkins University Press, 1982.

Far Out Magazine. "From Alfred Hitchcock to Stanley Kubrick: Martin Scorsese Named the 11 Greatest Horror Films of All Time." 2020. https://faroutmagazine.co.uk/martin-scorsese-11-favourite-horror-films-list-hitchcock-kubrick/.

Fasshauer, Tobias. "Hanns Eisler's 'Chamber Symphony op. 69' as Film Music for 'White Flood' (1940)." *Historical Journal of Film, Radio and Television* 18, no. 4 (1998): 509–21.

Feagin, Joe R. *The White Racial Frame: Centuries of Racial Framing and Counter-Framing*. New York: Routledge, 2013.

Feisst, Sabine. "Arnold Schoenberg and the Cinematic Art." *The Musical Quarterly* 83, no. 1 (1999): 93–113.

Feisst, Sabine. "Serving Two Masters: Leonard Rosenman's Music for Films and for the Concert Hall." *21st Century Music* 7, no. 5 (2000): .

Ferreira, Seabra and Maria Aline Salgueiro. *I Am the Other: Literary Negotiations of Human Cloning*. Westport: Praeger, 2005.

FilmBuffOnline. "In Remembrance: Alois F. Dettlaff, Sr." http://www.filmbuffonline.com/InRemembrance/AloisDettlaff.htm (accessed February 15, 2021).

Fischlin, Daniel, and Mark Fortier, eds. *Adaptations of Shakespeare: A Critical Anthology of Plays from the Seventeenth Century to the Present*. New York: Routledge, 2000.

Fisher, Fred. "Musical Humor: A Future as Well as a Past?" *The Journal of Aesthetics and Art Criticism* 32, no. 3 (1974): 375–83.

Fletcher, Angus. *Allegory: The Theory of a Symbolic Mode*. Ithaca: Cornell University Press, 1964.

Flora, Joseph M. and Lucinda Hardwick, eds. *The Companion to Southern Literature: Themes, Genres, Places, People, Movements, and Motifs*. Baton Rouge: Louisiana State University Press, 2002.

Florescu, Radu. *In Search of Frankenstein: Exploring the Myths Behind Mary Shelley's Monster*. London: Robson Books, 1999.

Forcen, Fernando E. *Monsters, Demons, and Psychopaths: Psychiatry in Horror Film*. Boca Raton: CRC Press, 2016.

Forry, Steven E. *Hideous Progenies: Dramatizations of Frankenstein from Mary Shelley to the Present*. Philadelphia: University of Pennsylvania Press, 1990.

Forry, Steven Earl. *Hideous Progenies: Dramatizations of Frankenstein from the Nineteenth Century to the Present*. Philadelphia: University of Pennsylvania Press, 1990.

"The Four Skulls of Jonathan Drake." *The Akron Beacon Journal*, June 23, 1995.

Fox, Charlie. *This Young Monster*. London: Fitzcarraldo Editions, 2017.

"Frankenstein." Library of Congress. https://www.loc.gov/item/2017600664/.

The Frankenstein Monster #12 (September 1974). Roy Thomas, editor-in-chief. New York: Marvel, 1974.

The Frankenstein Monster #16 (May 1975). Len Wein, editor-in-chief. New York: Marvel, 1974.

Fraying, Christopher. *Frankenstein: The First Two Hundred Years*. London: Real Art Press, 2017.

Freedman, Carl. "Hail Mary: On the Author of Frankenstein and the Origins of Science Fiction." *Science Fiction Studies* 29, no. 2 (2002): 253–64.

Freeman, Elizabeth. "Deep Lez: Temporal Drag and the Specters of Feminism." In *Time Binds: Queer Temporalities, Queer Histories*, edited by Elizabeth Freeman, Judith Halberstam, and Lisa Lowe, 59–93. Durham: Duke University Press, 2010.

Freud, Sigmund. *The Uncanny*. Translated by David McLintock. New York: Penguin, 2003.

Friedman, Lester D. and Allison B. Kavey. *Monstrous Progeny: A History of the Frankenstein Narratives*. New Brunswick: Rutgers University Press, 2016.

Gansworth, Eric. *Breathing the Monster Alive*. Treadwell: Bright Hill Press, 2006.

García, Pedro Javier Pardo. "Beyond Adaptation: Frankenstein's Postmodern Progeny." In *Books in Motion: Adaptation, Intertextuality, Authorship*, edited by Mireia Aragay, 223–42. Amsterdam: Rodopi, 2005.

Gassi, Vincent. "The Forbidden Zone, Escaping Earth and Tonality: An Examination of Jerry Goldsmith's Twelve-tone Score of Planet of the Apes." PhD dissertation, York University, 2019.

Gillmor, Alan. "The Apostasy of George Rochberg." *Intersections: Canadian Journal of Music* 29, no. 1 (2009): 32–48.

Gilroy, Paul. *The Black Atlantic: Modernity and Double Consciousness*. Cambridge, MA: Harvard University Press, 1993.

Glut, Donald. *The Frankenstein Catalog*. Jefferson: McFarland, 1984.

Goffman, Erving. *Frame Analysis: An Essay on the Organization of Experience*. New York: Harper, 1974.

Goldsmith, Carrie. "Preview of the Aborted Jerry Goldsmith Biography." February 2, 2004. http://www.jerrygoldsmithonline.com/spotlight_biography_preview.htm.

Gooding, Jr., Frederick. *Black Oscars: From Mammy to Minny, What the Academy Awards Tell Us about African Americans*. Lanham: Rowman & Littlefield, 2020.

Gooding, Jr., Frederick. *You Mean, There's Race in My Sports?: The Complete Guide for Understanding Race & Sports in Mainstream Media*. Silver Spring: On the Reelz Press, 2016.

Gorbman, Claudia. *Unheard Melodies: Narrative Film Music*. Bloomington: Indiana University Press, 1987.

Gordon, Jane Anna and Lewis R. Gordon. "When Monsters No Longer Speak." In *Political Phenomenology: Essays in Memory of Petee Jung*, edited by Hwa Yol Jung and Lester Embree, 331–52. Dordrecht: Springer, 2016.

Greene, Naomi. "Saló: The Refusal to Consume." In *Pier Paolo Pasolini: Contemporary Perspectives*, edited by Patrick Rumble and Bart Testa, 232–42. Toronto: University of Toronto Press, 1994.

Gunning, Tom. "Cinema of Attractions: Early Film, Its Spectator and the Avant-Garde." In *Early Cinema: Space-Frame-Narrative*, edited by Thomas Elsaesser and Adam Barker, 56–62. London: British Film Institute, 1990.

Halberstam, Jack. *Skin Shows: Gothic Horror and the Technology of Monsters*. Durham: Duke University Press, 1995.

Hand, Richard J. "Paradigms of Metamorphosis and Transmutation: Thomas Edison's Frankenstein and John Barrymore's Dr Jekyll and Mr Hyde." In *Monstrous Adaptations: Generic and Thematic Mutations in Horror Film*, edited by Richard J. Hand and Jay McRoy, 9–19. Manchester: Manchester University Press, 2007.

Hanson, Ellis. "Undead." In *Inside/Out: Lesbian Theories, Gay Theories*, edited by Diana Fuss, 324–40. New York: Routledge, 1991.

Hanson, Helen. *Hollywood Heroines: Women in Film Noir and the Female Gothic Film*. London and New York: I. B. Tauris, 2007.

Harkup, Kathryn. "The Science Behind the Fiction: Frankenstein in Historical Context." *Natural History* 126, no. 4 (April 2018): 34.

Harris, Bertha. "What We Mean to Say: Notes toward Defining the Nature of Lesbian Literature." *Heresies: A Feminist Publication on Art and Politics* 3, no. 2 (1977): 5–8.

Harris, Cheryl I. "Whiteness as Property." *Harvard Law Review* 106, no. 8 (1993): 1713–24.

Harrison, Thomas. *1910: The Emancipation of Dissonance*. Berkeley: University of California Press, 1996.

Hassan, Adeel. "Your Wednesday Briefing." *The New York Times*, May 25, 2016. https://archive.nytimes.com/www.nytimes.com/indexes/2016/05/25/nytnow/nytnow-email/index.html.

Hassig, Deborah. *The Mark of the Beast: The Medieval Bestiary in Art, Life, and Literature*. New York: Routledge, 2000.

Hawkins, Stan. "The Pet Shop Boys: Musicology, Masculinity and Banality." In *Sexing the Groove: Popular Music and Gender*, edited by Sheila Whiteley, 118–33. New York: Routledge, 1997.

Heidebrecht, Jennifer "12 Degrees of Alienation: A Socio-Political Exploration of Hanns Eisler's Use of the Twelve-Tone Method during Exile (1938–1948)." Unpublished MA Thesis, University of Calgary, 2020.

Heider, Fritz. *Ding und Medium*. 1926. Berlin: Kulturverlag Kadmos, 2005.

Heimerdinger, Julia. "Music and Sound in the Horror Film and Why Some Modern and Avant-garde Music Lends Itself to it So Well." *Seiltanz. Beiträge zur Musik der Gegenwart* 4 (2012): 4–16.

Hicks, Chris. "Musical Score Adds Bite to 1931 'Dracula.'" *Deseret News*, October 29, 1999. https://www.deseret.com/1999/10/29/19472847/musical-score-adds-bite-to-1931-dracula.

Hill, Daisy. *Young Romantics: The Shelleys, Byron and Other Tangled Lives*. London: Bloomsbury, 2010.

Hinton, Stephen. "The Emancipation of Dissonance: Schoenberg's Two Practices of Composition." *Music and Letters* 91, no. 4 (2010): 568–79.

Hirschmann, Kris. *Frankenstein*. San Diego: ReferencePoint Press, 2012.

Hitchcock, Susan Tyler. *Frankenstein: A Cultural History*. New York: W. W. Norton, 2007.

Holland, Samantha, Robert Shail, and Steven Gerrard. *Gender and Contemporary Horror in Film*. Bingley: Emerald Group Publishing, 2019.

Honig, Edwin. *Dark Conceit: The Making of Allegory*. Evanston: Northwestern University Press, 1959.

Horner, Avril. "Women, Power and Conflict: The Gothic heroine and 'Chocolate-box Gothic.'" *Caliban* 27 (2010): 319–30.

Horton, Robert. *Frankenstein*. New York: Columbia University Press/Wallflower, 2014.

Huckvale, David. *James Bernard, Composer to Count Dracula: A Critical Biography*. Jefferson: McFarland, 2006.

Hughes, Walter. "In the Empire of the Beat." In *Microphone Fiends: Youth Music and Youth Culture*, edited by Andrew Ross and Tricia Rose, 147–57. New York: Routledge, 1994.

Humphrey, Daniel. *Archaic Modernism: Queer Poetics in the Cinema of Pier Paolo Pasolini*. Detroit: Wayne State University Press, 2020.

Hurlbut, William and John L. Balderston. *Bride of Frankenstein: The Original Shooting Script*. Edited by Philip J. Riley. Absecon: MagicImage Filmbooks, 1989.

Hutcheon, Linda. *A Theory of Adaptation*. London and New York: Routledge, 2013.

Hutcheon, Linda. *A Theory of Adaptation*. New York: Routledge, 2006.

"If You Had 5 'Tsantsas,' Just What Would You Do?" *The Decatur Daily Review*. May 12, 1940.

The Independent. "Jerry Goldsmith: Prolific Film and Television Composer." October 10, 2011. https://www.independent.co.uk/news/obituaries/jerry-goldsmith-550152.html.

Ingebretsen, Edward J. *At Stake: Monsters and the Rhetoric of Fear in Public Culture*. Chicago: University of Chicago Press, 2001.

International Game Developers Association (IGDA). "Developer Satisfaction Survey 2019 Summary Report." Last modified November 20, 2019. https://s3-us-east-2.amazonaws.com/igda-website/wp-content/uploads/2020/01/29093706/IGDA-DSS-2019_Summary-Report_Nov-20-2019.pdf.

Ives, Charles. *Essays Before a Sonata, The Majority, and Other Writings*. Edited by Howard Boatwright. New York: Norton, 1970.

Jancovich, Mark. "Frankenstein and Film." In *The Cambridge Companion to Frankenstein*, edited by Andrew Smith, 190–204. Cambridge: Cambridge University Press, 2016.

Jarman-Ivens, Freya. *Queer Voices: Technologies, Vocalities, and the Musical Flaw*. New York: Palgrave Macmillan, 2011.

Jenkins, Philip. *Synthetic Panics: The Symbolic Politics of Designer Drugs*. New York: New York University Press, 1999.

Johnson, Barbara E. "Allegory and Psychoanalysis." *The Journal of African American History* 88, no. 1 (Winter 2003): 66–70.

Jonker, Julian. "Black Secret Technology (the Whitey on the Moon Dub)." *Ctheory*, article a117, 2002, http://www.ctheory.net/text_file.asp?pick=358.

Kabatchnik, Amnon. *Blood on the Stage, 1800–1900: Milestone Plays of Murder, Mystery, and Mayhem*. Washington: Rowman and Littlefield, 2017.

Karban, Thomas. "Kaum Chancen für Modernes. Filmmusik in Hollywood [Little Chance for the Moderns: Film music in Hollywood]." *Neue Zeitschrift für Musik* 156, no. 4 (1995): .

Kenwell, Cat. "Scores for Horrors: The Underappreciated Queen of Hammer and Amicus Horror." *Horror Tree*. https://horrortree.com/wihm-scores-for-horrors-the-underappreciated-queen-of-hammer-and-amicus-horror/.

King, Stephen. *Danse Macabre*. New York: Everest House, 1981.

King, Thomas. *The Inconvenient Indian: A Curious Account of Native People in North America*. Minneapolis: University of Minnesota Press, 2018.

Klock, Geoff. *How to Read Superhero Comics and Why*. New York: Continuum, 2002.

Kobbé, Gustav. *The New Kobbé's Opera Book*. Edited by The Earl of Harewood and Antony Peattie. New York: G.P. Putnam's Sons, 1997.

Kocurek, Carly. "Who Hearkens to the Monster's Scream? Death, Violence and the Veil of the Monstrous in Video Games." *Visual Studies* 30, no. 1 (2015): 79–89.

Koepnick, Lutz. *The Dark Mirror: German Cinema Between Hitler and Hollywood*. Berkeley: University of California Press, 2002.

Kolneder, Walter. *Anton Webern: An Introduction to His Works*. Translated by Humphrey Searle. Berkeley: University of California Press, 1968.

Kolodin, Irving. *The Continuity of Music: A History of Influence*. New York: Knopf, 1969.

Kristeva, Julia. *Powers of Horror: An Essay on Abjection*. Translated by Leon S. Roudiez. New York: Columbia University Press, 1982.

Krzywinska, Tanya. "Zombies in Gamespace: Form, Context, and Meaning in Zombie-Based Video Games." In *Zombie Culture: Autopsies of the Living Dead*, edited by Shawn McIntosh and Marc Leverette, 153–68. Lanham: Scarecrow Press, 2008.

Laird, Karen E. *The Art of Adapting Victorian Literature, 1848–1920*. Farnham and Burlington: Ashgate Publishing, 2015.

Lavalley, Albert J. "The Stage and Film Children of Frankenstein: A Survey" in *The Endurance of Frankenstein: Essays on Mary Shelley's Novel*, edited by George Levine and U.C. Knoepflmacher, 243–89. Berkeley: University of California Press, 1979.

Lawson, Richard. "Jordan Peele's Us Stabs Itself in the Foot." *Vanity Fair*, March 20, 2019. https://www.vanityfair.com/hollywood/2019/03/jordan-peeles-us-stabs-itself-in-the-foot.

Lee, Christina. 2013. "Mykki Blanco Wanted to Rap in 'the Tongue of the Illuminati' on New EP." *mtv.com*, May 28, 2013. http://www.mtv.com/news/2698931/mykki-blanco-betty-rubble-ep/.

Leeder, Murray. *Horror Film: A Critical Introduction*. New York: Bloomsbury, 2018.

Leeder, Murray. *The Modern Supernatural and the Beginnings of Cinema*. London: Palgrave Macmillan, 2017.

Lieberman, Evan. "Frankenstein at the Boundaries of Life, Death, and Film." In *Frankenstein: How a Monster Became an Icon – The Enduring Allure of Mary Shelley's Creation*, edited by Sidney Perkowitz and Eddy von Mueller, 67–83. New York: Pegasus Books, 2018.

Lindbergs, Kimberly. "Elisabeth Lutyens: The Horror Queen of Film Composers." *Cinebeats*, March 11, 2020. https://cinebeats.wordpress.com/2020/03/11/elisabeth-lutyens-the-horror-queen-of-film-composers.

Link, Stan. "Sympathy with the Devil: Music of the Psycho Post-Psycho." *Screen* 45, no. 1 (2004): 1–20.

Longworth, Karina. "Tom Six's Torture-Porn Game Changer The Human Centipede (First Sequence)." *The Village Voice*, April 27, 2010. https://www.villagevoice.com/2010/04/27/tom-sixs-torture-porn-game-changer-the-human-centipede-first-sequence/.

López, Ian Haney. *Dog Whistle Politics: How Coded Racial Appeals Have Reinvented Racism and Wrecked the Middle Class*. Oxford: Oxford University Press, 2014.

Lowenstein, Adam. *Shocking Representation: Historical Trauma, National Cinema, and the Modern Horror Film*. New York: Columbia University Press, 2005.

Lowenstein, Adam. "Spectacle Horror and Hostel: Why 'Torture Porn' Does Not Exist." *Critical Quarterly* 53, no. 1 (2011): 42–60.

Luhmann, Niklas. *Art as a Social System*. Translated by Eva M. Knodt. Stanford: Stanford University Press, 2000.

Luhmann, Niklas. *Die Gesellschaft der Gesellschaft*. Frankfurt: Suhrkamp, 1997.

Luhmann, Niklas. *Die Kunst der Gesellschaft*. Frankfurt: Suhrkamp, 1995.

Lynch, Teresa, Jessica E. Tompkins, Irene I. van Driel, and Niki Fritz. "Sexy, Strong, and Secondary: A Content Analysis of Female Characters in Video Games across 31 Years." *Journal of Communication* 66, no. 4 (2016): 564–84.

Lyons, Kevin. "The Mask (1961)." *The EOFFTV (Encyclopedia of Fantastic Film and Television) Review*, February 1, 2020. https://eofftvreview.wordpress.com/2020/02/01/the-mask-1961/.

Macfarlane, Karen E. "The Monstrous House of Gaga." In *The Gothic in Contemporary Literature and Popular Culture: Pop Goth*, edited by Justin D. Edwards and Agnieszka Soltysik Monnet, 114–34. New York: Routledge, 2012.

Magner, Lois N. *A History of the Life Sciences, Revised and Expanded*. New York: Marcel Dekker, 2002.

Magoun, Alexander B. "Why Frankenstein Became Electric [Scanning Our Past]." *Proceedings of the IEEE* 107, no. 2 (Febuary 2019): 488–98.

Maida, "What Etiquette Books Teach Us About Women." *Athena Talks*, January 1, 2018, https://medium.com/athena-talks/what-etiquette-books-teach-us-about-women-90edbd67fcbc.

Malcolm, Paul. "Jason Goes to Hell: The Final Friday." *LA Weekly*, August 20–26, 1993. 56.

Mann, William J. *Behind the Screen: How Gays and Lesbians Shaped Hollywood, 1910–1969*. New York: Penguin, 2001.

Marks, Martin. "Music and the Silent Film." In *The Oxford History of World Cinema*, edited by Geoffrey Nowell-Smith, 183–92. Oxford: Oxford University Press, 1996.

Mary Wollstonecraft Shelley. *Frankenstein or The Modern Prometheus the 1818 Text*. Edited by James Rieger. Chicago: The University of Chicago Press, 1974.

Maus, Fred E. "Glamour and Evasion: The Fabulous Ambivalence of the Pet Shop Boys." *Popular Music* 20, no. 3 (2001): 379–93.

McConnell, Jenny. "National Theatre Live: Frankenstein Encore Screening, October 2013." *The Irish Journal of Gothic and Horror Studies* 13 (2014): 152–5.

McCutcheon, Mark A. *The Medium Is the Monster: Canadian Adaptations of Frankenstein and the Discourse of Technology*. Edmonton: Athabasca University Press, 2018.

McLerran, Jennifer, and Thomas Patin, eds. *Artwords: A Glossary of Contemporary Art Theory*. Westport: Greenwood Press, 1997.

McLuhan, Marshall. *The Mechanical Bride: Folklore of Industrial Man*. London: Routledge and Kegan Paul, 1951.

McLuhan, Marshall. *Understanding Me: Lectures and Interviews*, edited by Stephanie McLuhan and David Staines. Cambridge, MA: MIT Press, 2004.

McLuhan, Marshall. *Understanding Media: The Extensions of Man*. Corte Madera: Gingko Press, [1964] 2003.

McNally, David. *Monsters of the Market: Zombies, Vampires, and Global Capitalism*. Chicago: Haymarket Books, 2011.

McRobbie, Angela. "Thinking with Music." In *Stars Don't Stand Still in the Sky: Music and Myth*, edited by Karen Kelly and Evelyn McDonell, 37–49. New York: New York University Press, 1999.

Means Coleman, Robin R. *Horror Noire: Blacks in American Horror Films from the 1890s to Present*. New York: Routledge, 2011.

Mellor, Anne K. "Making a Monster." In *Mary Shelley's Frankenstein*, edited by Harold Bloom, 43–59. New York: Infobase Publishing, 2007.

Meyer, Leonard. *Music, the Arts, and Ideas: Patterns and Predictions in Twentieth-Century Culture*. Chicago: University of Chicago Press, 1967.

Meyer, Richard. *Outlaw Representation: Censorship and Homosexuality in Twentieth-Century American Art*. New York: Oxford University Press, 2002.

Milner, Sarah. "The Composite Frankenstein: The Man, the Monster, the Myth." MA Thesis, Trent University, 2018.

Mitchell, Allyson. "Artist Bio." 2014. https://web.archive.org/web/20150116023625/http://www.allysonmitchell.com/html/bio.html.

Mitchell, Allyson. "Deep Lez I Statement." In *Allyson Mitchell: Ladies Sasquatch*, edited by Carla Garnet, Avril McMeekin, Rose Anne Prevec, and Matthew Hyland, 12–13. Hamilton: McMaster Museum of Art, 2009.

Mitchell, Angelyn, and Danille K. Taylor, eds. *The Cambridge Companion to African American Women's Literature*. Cambridge: Cambridge University Press, 2009.

Model, Ben. "Dracula (1931) - A Horror Movie without Horror Movie Music." October 26, 2019, https://www.silentfilmmusic.com/dracula-musical-score/.

Moers, Ellen. *Literary Women*. London: The Women's Press, 1978.

The Monster of Frankenstein no. 1 (January 1973): "Mary Shelley's Frankenstein." Gary Friedrich, writer. Mike Ploog, pencils and inks. John Costanza, letters. New York: Marvel, 1973.

The Monster of Frankenstein no. 2 (March 1973): "Bride of the Monster." Gary Friedrich, writer. Mike Ploog, pencils and inks. Dave Hunt, colors. John Costanza, letters. New York: Marvel, 1973.

The Monster of Frankenstein no. 3 (May 1973): "The Monster's Revenge!" Gary Friedrich, writer. Mike Ploog, pencils and inks. Dave Hunt, colors. Charlotte Jetter, letters. New York: Marvel, 1973.

The Monster of Frankenstein no. 4 (July 1973): "Death of the Monster!" Gary Friedrich, writer. Mike Ploog, pencils. John Verpoorten, inks. Glynis Wein, colors. Artie Simek, letters. New York: Marvel, 1973.

Moon, Michael, and Eve Kosofsky Sedgwick. "Divinity: A Dossier, A Performance Piece, A Little-Understood Emotion." In *Tendencies*, edited by Eve Kosofsky Sedgwick, 215-51. Durham: Duke University Press, 1993.

Moretti, Franco. *Signs Taken for Wonders: On the Sociology of Literary Forms*. London: Verso, 1983.

Morton, Timothy. *Mary Shelley's Frankenstein: A Sourcebook*. London: Routledge, 2002.

Mulvey, Laura. "Visual Pleasure and Narrative Cinema." In *Feminism and Film Theory*, edited by Constance Penley, 57-68. London and New York: Routledge, 1988.

Muñoz, José Esteban. *Disidentifications: Queers of Color and the Performance of Politics*. Minneapolis: University of Minnesota Press, 1999.

Myrone, Martine, ed. *Gothic Nightmares: Fuseli, Blake and The Romantic Tradition*. London: Tate Publishing, 2006.

Nadon, R.J. "The Mask (1961) – Canada's Horror History." *Killer Canuck*, October 1, 2020. https://www.youtube.com/watch?v=NNGES5QbHeg.

Neumeyer, David P. "Schoenberg at the Movies: Dodecaphony and Film." *Music Theory Online* no. 1 (February 1993): 1-6. https://mtosmt.org/issues/mto.93.0.1/mto.93.0.1.neumeyer.php.

Newbold, Gregory S. "Benjamin Frankel's Serial Film Score for The Curse of the Werewolf: An Historical Context and Analysis." MA thesis, University of Iowa, 2017.

Nichols, Bill. *Representing Reality: Issues and Concepts in Documentary*. Bloomington: Indiana University Press, 1991.

Nieto, Tristan Alice. "Imago." In *Meanwhile, Elsewhere: Science Fiction and Fantasy from Transgender Writers*, edited by Cat Fitzpatrick and Casey Plett, 347-79. New York: Topside Press, 2017.

Nitchie, Elizabeth. "The Stage History of Frankenstein." *The South Atlantic Quarterly* 41 (1942): 384-98.

Nowlan, Alden and Walter Learning. *Frankenstein: A Full-Length Play*. Woodstock: Dramatic Publishing, 1981.

Nüsslein-Volhard, Christiane. *Coming to Life: How Genes Drive Development*. San Diego: Kales Press, 2006.

Nyberg, Amy Kiste. *Seal of Approval: The History of the Comics Code*. Jackson: University Press of Mississippi, 1998.

Nye, David. *American Technological Sublime*. Cambridge, MA: MIT Press, 1994.

O'Reilly, Karen. *Key Concepts in Ethnography*. Los Angeles: SAGE, 2009.

Pasolini, Pier Paolo. *Pier Paolo Pasolini: A Future Life*. Rome: Associazione Fondo Pier Paolo Pasolini, 1989.

Payne, Anthony. "Lutyens's Solution to Serial Problems." *The Listener*, December 5, 1963.

Peake, Richard Brinsley. "Presumption, or the Fate of Frankenstein." In *Seven Gothic Dramas*, edited by Jeffrey N. Cox, 385-425. Athens: Ohio University Press, 1992.

Penney, Diane. "The Method Behind the Madness: Schoenberg's Erwartung." In *Freie Referate 13: Mahler/Schönberg*, edited by Hermann Danuser and Tobias Plebuch, 396-402. Kassel: Bärenreiter Verlag, 1998.

Phelan, Shane. *Sexual Strangers: Gays, Lesbians, and Dilemmas of Citizenship*. Philadelphia: Temple University Press, 2001.

Picart, Carolyn Joan. *Remaking the Frankenstein Myth on Film*. New York: SUNY Press, 2003.

Picart, Caroline Joan. "Visualizing the Monstrous in Frankenstein Films." *Pacific Coast Philology* 35, no.1 (2000): 17–34.

Picart, Carolyn Joan, Frank Smoot and Jayne Blodgett, *The Frankenstein Film Sourcebook*. Westport: Greenwood Press, 2001.

Picart, Caroline Joan ("Kay") S., Frank Smoot, and Jayne Blodgett. *The Frankenstein Film Sourcebook*. Westport: Greenwood, 2001.

Piepenburg, Erik. "Us Took Hands Across America and Made It a Death Grip." *New York Times*, March 26, 2019. https://www.nytimes.com/2019/03/26/movies/us-hands-across-america.html.

Pinedo, Isabel Cristina. *Recreational Terror: Women and the Pleasures of Horror Film Viewing*. Albany: SUNY Press, 1997.

Ping, Tang Soo. "Frankenstein, 'Paradise Lost,' and 'The Majesty of Goodness.'" *College Literature* 16, no. 3 (Fall 1989): 255–60.

Pisani, Michael V. *Music for the Melodramatic Theatre in Nineteenth-Century London and New York*. Iowa City: University of Iowa Press, 2014.

Pollock, Mica. *Everyday Antiracism: Getting Real about Race in School*. New York: New Press, 2008.

Poole, W. Scott. "After World War I, Horror Movies Were Invaded by an Army of Reanimated Corpses." October 2018. https://longreads.com/2018/10/31/after-world-war-i-horror-movies-were-invaded-by-an-army-of-reanimated-corpses/.

Porcello, Thomas. "The Ethics of Digital Audio-Sampling: Engineers' Discourse." *Popular Music* 10, no. 1 (1991): 69–84.

Porter, Lynnette. "It's Alive! But What Kind of Creature is National Theatre Live's 'Frankenstein'?" *Studies in Popular Culture* 35, no. 2 (2013): 1–21.

Prendergast, Roy M. *Film Music. A Neglected Art*. New York and London: W.W. Norton & Co., 1977.

Pruska-Oldenhof, Izabella and Robert K. Logan. "The Spiral Structure of Marshall McLuhan's Thinking." *Philosophies* 2, no. 9 (2017): 1–15.

Quist, Robert. "Atonality in Music and the Upheavals of High Modernity." *Catastrophe and Philosophy* (2018): 205–17.

Rafferty, Terrence. "Dead Ringers." *New Yorker*, October 3, 1988, 92–4.

Raub, Emma. "Frankenstein and the Mute Figure of Melodrama." *Modern Drama* 55, no. 4 (Winter 2012): 454–5.

Reckitt, Helena. "My Fuzzy Valentine: Allyson Mitchell." *C Magazine* 89 (2006): 14–17.

Reed, Edward S. "The Separation of Psychology from Philosophy: Studies in the Sciences of Mind, 1815–1979." In *Routledge History of Philosophy Volume VII: The Nineteenth Century*, edited by C. L. Ten, 248–96. London and New York: Routledge, 2005.

Reynolds, Simon. "Ecstasy is a Science: Techno-Romanticism." In *Stars Don't Stand Still in the Sky: Music and Myth*, edited by Karen Kelly and Evelyn McDonell, 199–205. New York: New York University Press, 1999.

Reynolds, Simon. "How Rave Music Conquered America." *The Guardian*, August 2, 2012. http://www.theguardian.com/music/2012/aug/02/how-rave-music-conquered-america.

Reynolds, Simon. "Rave Culture: Living Dream or Living Death?" In *The Clubcultures Reader*, edited by Steve Redhead, 102–11. London: Routledge, 1997.

Reynolds, Simon. *Generation Ecstasy: Into the World of Techno and Rave Culture*. Boston: Little, Brown & Co., 1998.

Rhodes, Gary D. *The Birth of the American Horror Film*. Edinburgh: Edinburgh University Press, 2018.

Rieser, Klaus. "Masculinity and Monstrosity: Characterization and Identification in the Slasher Film." *Men and Masculinities* 3, no. 4 (April 2001): 370–92.

Rigby, Mair. "'Do You Share My Madness?' Frankenstein's Queer Gothic." In *Queering the Gothic*, edited by William Hughes and Andrew Smith, 36–54. Manchester: Manchester University Press, 2009.

Roberts, Marie [Mulvey-], *Gothic Immortals: The Fiction of the Brotherhood of the Rosy Cross*. London: Routledge, 1990,

Rochberg, George. "The Avant-Garde and the Aesthetics of Survival." *New Literary History* 3, no. 1 (1971): 71–92.

Rosar, William H. "Music for the Monsters: Universal Pictures' Horror Film scores of the Thirties." *The Quarterly Journal of the Library of Congress* 40, no. 4 (Fall 1983): 390–421.

Rose, Joel. "Music Interviews: The Evolution of George Rochberg." *National Public Radio*. June 4, 2005. https://www.npr.org/templates/story/story.php?storyId=4680395.

Rotten Tomatoes. "Jordan Peele." https://www.rottentomatoes.com/celebrity/jordan_peele (accessed February 11, 2021).

Rubenstein, Steven Lee. "Circulation, Accumulation, and the Power of Shuar Shrunken Heads." *Cultural Anthropology* 22, no. 3 (2007): 357–99.

Rufer, Josef. *Composition with Twelve Notes Related Only to One Another [Original German Edition. 1952]*, Translated by Humphrey Searle. New York: MacMillan, 1954.

Sally, Bick, "Composers on the Cultural Front: Aaron Copland and Hanns Eisler in Hollywood." PhD Dissertation, Yale University, 2001;

Salter, Hans J. "Als ich 1937 nach Hollywood kam, lag das Land noch immer in tiefster Depression." In *Aufbruch ins Ungewisse: Österreichische Filmschaffende in der Emigration vor 1945*, edited by Christian Cargnelli and Michael Omasta, 107–15. Vienna: Wespennest, 1993.

Santos, Cristina. *Unbecoming Female Monsters: Witches, Vampires, and Virgins*. Lanham: Lexington Books, 2017.

Sauers, Jenna. "The Making of Mykki Blanco." *Village Voice*, April 10, 2013, https://www.villagevoice.com/2013/04/10/the-making-of-mykki-blanco/.

Schaeffer, Myron. "The Electronic Music Studio of the University of Toronto." *Journal of Music Theory* 7, no. 1 (Spring, 1963): 73–81.

Schiff, Gert. "Theodore Matthias Von Holst." *The Burlington Magazine* 105, no. 718 (1963): 23–32.

Schoenberg, Arnold. "A Self Analysis." In *Style and Idea: Selected Writings of Arnold Schoenberg*, edited by Leonard Stein, 76–8. Berkeley: University of California Press, 1985.

Schoenberg, Arnold. *Style and Idea*. Edited by Leonard Stein. Translated by Leo Black. Berkeley, California: University of California Press, 1984.

Schoenberg, Arnold. *Theory of Harmony*. Berkeley: University of California Press, 1978.

Scott, Grant F. "Victor's Secret: Queer Gothic in Lynd Ward's Illustrations to Frankenstein (1934)." *Word & Image* 28, no. 2 (2012): 206–32.

Searle, Humphrey and Anton von Webern. "Conversations with Webern." *The Musical Times* 81, no. 1172 (1940): 405–6.

Sedgwick, Eve Kosofsky. *The Epistemology of the Closet*. Berkeley: University of California Press, 1990.

Shea, Christopher D. "Samuel L. Jackson and Others on Black British Actors in American Roles." *New York Times*, March 9, 2017. https://www.nytimes.com/2017/03/09/movies/samuel-jackson-black-british-african-american-actors.html.

Shelley, M. Wollstonecraft. *Frankenstein, or, The Modern Prometheus*. 2nd ed. Edited by Dorothy K. Scherf and D. Lorne Macdonald. Peterborough: Broadview Press, 1999.

Shelley, Mary. *Frankenstein*. Mineola: Dover, 1994.

Shelley, Mary. *Frankenstein*. Edited by Johanna M. Smith. Boston: Bedford, [1831] 1992.

Shelley, Mary, *Frankenstein: Complete, Authoritative Text with Biographical, Historical, and Cultural Contexts, Critical History, and Essays from Critical Perspectives*. 2nd ed. Edited by Johanna M. Smith. Boston: Bedford/St. Martin's, 2000.

Shelley, Mary. *Frankenstein, or The Modern Prometheus*. New York: Bedford / St. Martin's Press, [1831] 2000.

Shelley, Mary. *Frankenstein; or, The Modern Prometheus*. Oxford: Oxford University Press, 2008.

Shelley, Mary. *Frankenstein: A Longman Cultural Edition*. Edited by Susan J. Wolfson. New York: Pearson Longman, 2007.

Shelley, Mary and Lynd Ward. *Frankenstein: The Lynd Ward Illustrated Edition*. Mineola: Dover Publications. 2016. First published 1934.

Shelley, Mary Wollstonecraft. *Frankenstein*. Illustrated by Bernie Wrightson. Milwaukie: Dark Horse, 2008.

Shelley, Mary Wollstonecraft. *Frankenstein; or, the Modern Prometheus*. Boston: Sever, Francis & Co., 1869.

Shelley, Mary Wollstonecraft and Elizabeth Nitchie. "Mathilda." *Studies in Philology* 56 no. 3 (1959): i-104.

Shelley, Percy Bysshe. *Queen Mab: A Philosophical Poem* [1813]. London: Create Space Independent Publishing, 2015.

Shohet, Lauren. "Reading Milton in Mary Shelley's Frankenstein." *Milton Studies* 60, no. 1–2 (2018): 157–82.

The Silver Surfer no. 7 (August 1969): "The Heir of Frankenstein." Stan Lee, writer. John Buscema, pencils. Sal Buscema, inks. Sam Rosen, letters. New York: Marvel, 1969.

Simpson, Jennifer S. *I Have Been Waiting: Race and U.S. Higher Education*. Toronto: University of Toronto Press, 2003,

Slotkin, Richard. *Gunfighter Nation: The Myth of the Frontier in Twentieth-Century America*. Norman: University of Oklahoma Press, 1998.

Slusser, George. "The Frankenstein Barrier." In *Fiction 2000: Cyberpunk and the Future of Narrative*, edited by George Slusser and Tom Shippey, 46–71. Athens: University of Georgia Press, 1992.

Smith, Ariel. "This Essay Was Not Built on an Ancient Burial Ground" *Offscreen* 18, no. 8 (August 2014): https://offscreen.com/view/ancient-burial-ground

Smith, David J. and Jordan N. Witt. "Spun Steel and Stardust: The Rejection of Contemporary Compositions." *Music Perception* 7, no. 2 (1989): 169–85.

Solomon, Charles. "'Soul' Features Pixar's First Black Lead Character." *New York Times*, December 28, 2020.

Sontag, Susan. *Against Interpretation and Other Essays*. New York: Farrar Straus Giroux, 1966.

Southall, James. "Freud: An Uncompromisingly Dark Journey into the Human Mind – Music by Jerry Goldsmith." *Movie Wave – Film Music Reviews.* http://www.movie-wave.net/titles/freud.html.

Sowa, Joanna. "When Does a Man Beget a Monster? (Aristotle's De Generatione Animalium)." *Collectanea Philologica* 19, no. 1 (2016): 5–13.

Spadoni, Robert. *Uncanny Bodies: The Coming of Sound and the Origins of the Horror Genre.* Berkeley: University of California Press, 2007.

Spivak, Gayatri Chakravorty. "Can the Subaltern Speak?" In *Can the Subaltern Speak?: Reflections on the History of an Idea,* edited by Rosalind Morris, 21–78. New York: Columbia University Press, 2010.

Spring, Joel. *American Education.* New York: Routledge, 2016.

St Clair, William. *The Godwins and the Shelleys: The Biography of a Family.* London: Faber and Faber, 1990.

St. Clair, William. "The Impact of Frankenstein." In *Mary Shelley in Her Times,* edited by Betty T. Bennett and Stuart Curran, 38–63. Baltimore: Johns Hopkins University Press, 2000.

St. Clair, William. *The Reading Nation in the Romantic Period.* Cambridge: Cambridge University Press, 2004.

Stang, Sarah. "Shrieking, Biting, and Licking: The Monstrous-Feminine in Video Games." *Press Start* 4, no. 2 (2018): 18–34.

Stang, Sarah, and Aaron Trammell. "The Ludic Bestiary: Misogynistic Tropes of Female Monstrosity in Dungeons & Dragons." *Games & Culture* 15, no. 6 (2020): 730–47.

Stanley, David, Karen Stanley and Deborah Magee, "Celluloid Zombies: A Research Study of Nurses in Zombie-Focused Feature Films." *Journal of Advanced Nursing* 75, no 8 (August 2019): 1751–63.

Steinberg, Russell. "Arnold Schoenberg and Breaking Tonality." February 6, 2013. http://www.russellsteinberg.com/blog/2013/9/26/arnold-schoenberg-and-breaking-tonality.

Stephens, Elizabeth. "'Dead Eyes Open:' The Role of Experiments in Galvanic Reanimation in Nineteenth-Century Popular Culture." *Leonardo* 48, no. 3 (2015): 276–7.

Stephens, Vincent L. *Rocking the Closet: How Little Richard, Johnny Ray, Liberace, and Johnny Mathis Queered Pop Music.* Urbana: University of Illinois Press, 2019.

Stilling, Dennis. "Editor's Preface." In *The Theology of Electricity: On the Encounter and Explanation of Theology and Science in the 17th and 18th Centuries,* edited by Ernst Benz, vii–xiii. Eugene: Pickwick Publications, 2009.

Stryker, Susan. "My Words to Victor Frankenstein above the Village of Chamounix: Performing Transgender Rage." *GLQ* 1, no. 3 (1994): 237–54.

Summers, Alicia, and Monica K. Miller. "From Damsels in Distress to Sexy Superheroes: How the Portrayal of Sexism in Video Game Magazines Has Changed in the Last Twenty Years." *Feminist Media Studies* 14, no. 6 (2014): 1028–40.

Taruskin, Richard. "The Poietic Fallacy." *The Musical Times* 145, no. 1886 (Spring, 2004): 7–34.

Thomas, Tony. *Film Score: The Art & Craft of Movie Music.* Burbank: Riverwood Press, 1991.

Thornton, Sarah. *Club Cultures: Music, Media, and Subcultural Capital.* Middletown: Wesleyan University Press, 1996.

Tompkins, Joe. "Mellifluous Terror: The Discourse of Music and Horror Films." In *A Companion to the Horror Film,* edited by Harry M. Benshoff, 186–204. Chichester: Wiley Blackwell, 2014.

Troy, Kathryn. *The Specter of the Indian: Race, Gender, and Ghosts in American Séances, 1848-1890*. Albany: SUNY Press, 2017.

Tuck, Eve and C. Ree. "A Glossary of Haunting." In *Handbook of Autoethnography*, edited by Stacey Holman Jones, Tony E. Adams and Carolyn Ellis, 639-58. New York: Routledge, 2013.

Tudor, Andrew. *Monsters and Mad Scientists: A Cultural History of the Horror Movie*. Oxford: Basil Blackwell, 1989.

Twitchell, James B. *Dreadful Pleasures: An Anatomy of Modern Horror*. Oxford: Oxford University Press, 1985.

Von Mueller, Eddy. "The Face of the Fiend: Media, Industry, and the Evolving Image of Frankenstein's Monster." In *Frankenstein - How A Monster Became an Icon - The Science and Enduring Allure of Mary Shelley's Creation*, edited by Sidney Perkowitz and Eddy Von Mueller, 136-61. New York: Pegasus, 2018.

Wallace, Diana. "Uncanny Stories: The Ghost Story As Female Gothic." *Gothic Studies* 6, no. 1 (2018): 57-68.

Wallerstein, Immanuel Maurice. *The Modern World-System in the Longue Durée*. Boulder: Paradigm Publishers, 2004.

Ward, Lynd. *Storyteller without Words: The Wood Engravings of Lynd Ward*. New York: Harry N. Abrams, 1974.

Wendorf, Craig A. "History of American Morality Research, 1894-1932." *History of Psychology* 4, no. 3 (2001), 272-88.

Westengard, Laura. *Gothic Queer Culture: Marginalized Communities and the Ghosts of Insidious Trauma*. Lincoln: University of Nebraska Press, 2019.

White, Patricia. *Uninvited: Classical Hollywood Cinema and Lesbian Representability*. Bloomington: Indiana University Press, 1999.

Wierzbicki, James. "How Frankenstein's Monster Became a Music Lover." *Journal of the Fantastic in the Arts* 24, no. 2 (2013): 246-63.

Wierzbicki, James. *Film Music: A History*. London and New York: Routledge, 2009.

Williams, Dmitri, Nicole Martins, Mia Consalvo, and James Ivory. "The Virtual Census: Representations of Gender, Race and Age in Video Games." *New Media and Society* 11, no. 5 (2009): 815-34.

Winter, Sarah A. "'A Mass of Unnatural and Repulsive Horrors': Staging Horror in Nineteenth-Century English Theater." In *The Palgrave Handbook of Horror Literature*, edited by Kevin Corstorphine and Laura R. Kremmel, 139-54. New York: Palgrave Macmillan, 2018.

Wintle, Christopher. "Hans Keller (1919-1985): An Introduction to His Life and Works." *Music Analysis* 5, no. 2-3 (1986): 343-65.

Wolf, Werner. "Framing Borders in Frame Stories." In *Framing Borders in Literature and Other Media*, edited by Werner Wolf and Walter Bernhart, 179-206. Amsterdam: Rodopi.

Wolf, Werner. "Introduction: Frames, Framings and Framing Borders in Literature and Other Media." In *Framing Borders in Literature and Other Media*, edited by Werner Wolf and Walter Bernhart, 1-40. Amsterdam: Rodopi, 2006.

Wolf, Werner, and Walter Bernhart, eds. *Framing Borders in Literature and Other Media*. Amsterdam: Rodopi, 2006.

Wood, Robin. "An Introduction to the American Horror Film." In *American Nightmare: Essays on the Horror Film*, edited by Andrew Britton, Robin Wood, and Richard Lippe, 7-28. Toronto: Festival of Festivals, 1979.

Wright, Angela. *Gothic Fiction: A Reader's Guide to Essential Criticism*. Basingstoke: Palgrave Macmillan, 2007.

Wright, James K. *They Shot, He Scored: The Life and Music of Eldon Rathburn*. Montreal: McGill-Queen's University Press, 2019.

The X-Men no. 40 (January 1968): "The Mark of the Monster!" Roy Thomas, writer. Don Heck, pencils. George Tuska, inks. Artie Simek, letters. New York: Marvel, 1968.

Yaeger, Patricia. "The 'Language of Blood': Toward A Maternal Sublime." *Genre* 25, no. 1 (1992): 5–24.

Young, Elizabeth. *Black Frankenstein: The Making of an American Metaphor*. New York and London: New York University Press, 2008.

Younging, Gregory. *Elements of Indigenous Style: A Guide for Writing By and About Indigenous Peoples*. Edmonton: Brush Education, 2018.

Yuan, Jada, and Hunter Harris. "The First Great Movie of the Trump Era." *Vulture*, February 22, 2018. https://www.vulture.com/article/get-out-oral-history-jordan-peele.html.

Zacharek, Stephanie. "Jordan Peele's Us is Dazzling to Look At. But What Is It Trying to Say?" *Time*, March 15, 2019. https://time.com/5552617/review-us-jordan-peele/.

Filmography

Adamson, Al, dir. *Dracula vs. Frankenstein*. 1971; Independent-International Pictures.
Adamson, Al, dir. *Dynamite Brothers*. 1974; Asam Film Company Inc.
Adamson, Al, dir. *Black Heat*. 1976; Independent-International Pictures.
Adamson, Al, dir. *Black Samurai*. 1977; SA Vail Productions.
Alazraki, Benito. *Frankenstein, el vampiro y compañía*. 1962; Frankenstein, the Vampire and Company.
Allen, Irwin, dir. *The Lost World*. 1960; 20th Century Fox.
Anderson, Paul W. S., dir. *Alien vs Predator*. 2004; 20th Century Fox.
Annakin, Ken, dir. *The Battle of the Bulge*. 1965; Warner Brothers.
Arnold, Jack, dir. *The Creature from the Black Lagoon*. 1954; Universal Pictures.
Arnold, Jack, dir. *The Incredible Shrinking Man*. 1957; Universal Pictures.
Asquith, Anthony, dir. *The Importance of Being Ernest*. 1952; Universal-International.
Avery, Tex, dir. *The Cat That Hated People*. 1948; Metro-Goldwyn-Mayer.
Baker, Roy Ward, dir. *Scars of Dracula*. 1970; Hammer Film Productions.
Baker, Roy Ward, and Chang Cheh, dirs. *The Legend of the 7 Golden Vampires*. 1974; Hammer Film Productions.
Barahm, John, dir. *Hangover Square*. 1945; 20th Century Fox.
Barton, Charles, dir. *Abbott and Costello Meet Frankenstein*. 1948; Universal Pictures Company Inc.
Barton, Charles, dir. *Abbott and Costello Meet the Killer, Boris Karloff*. 1949; Universal-International.
Beaudine, William, dir. *Jesse James Meets Frankenstein's Daughter*. 1966; Embassy Pictures.
Beebe, Ford, dir. *The Invisible Man's Revenge*. 1944; Universal Pictures.
Berman, Lionel, and David Wolff, dirs. *White Flood*. 1940; Frontier Films.
Bertino, Bryan, dir. *The Strangers*. 2008; Universal Pictures.
Brahm, John, dir. *The Undying Monster*. 1942; 20th Century Fox.
Brahm, John, dir. *The Lodger*. 1944; 20th Century Fox.
Branagh, Kenneth, dir. *Mary Shelley's Frankenstein*. 1994; TriStar Pictures.
Browning, Tod, dir. *Dracula*. 1931; Universal Pictures.
Cabanne, Christy, dir. *The Mummy's Hand*. 1940; Universal Pictures.
Cahn, Edward L., dir. *Voodoo Woman*. 1958; American International Pictures.
Cahn, Edward L., dir. *The Four Skulls of Jonathan Drake*. 1959; Premium Pictures.
Carpenter, John, dir. *Halloween*. 1978; Compass International Pictures.
Cohen, Larry, dir. *Q - The Winged Serpent*. 1982; United Film Distribution Company.
Cooper, Merian C. and Ernest B. Schoedsack, dirs. *King Kong*. 1935; RKO Radio Pictures.
Craven, Wes, dir. *A Nightmare on Elm Street*. 1984; New Line Cinema.
Cronenberg, David, dir. *The Fly*. 1986; 20th Century Fox.
Cunha, Richard E., dir. *Frankenstein's Daughter*. 1958; Astor Pictures.
Curtiz, Michael, dir. *The Walking Dead*. 1936; Warner Brothers.
Dawley, J. Searle, dir. *Frankenstein*. 1910; Edison.
Dein, Edward, dir. *The Leech Woman*. 1960; Universal Pictures.

Dekker, Fred, dir. *The Monster Squad*. 1987; TriStar Pictures.
DemichelI, Tulio and Hugo Fregonese, dirs. *Dracula vs. Frankenstein*. 1969; Castilla Films.
DeMille, Cecil B., dir. *The Plainsman*. 1937; Paramount Pictures.
Dmytryk, Edward, dir. *Captive Wild Woman*. 1943; Universal Pictures Company Inc.
Docter, Pete, dir. *Soul*. 2020; Walt Disney Pictures, Pixar Animation Studios.
Donner, Richard, dir. *The Goonies*. 1985; Warner Brothers.
Feeney, John, dir. *Sky*. 1963; National Film Board of Canada.
Fenton, Leslie, dir. *Tomorrow the World!*. 1944; United Artists.
Fisher, Terence, dir. *The Curse of Frankenstein*. 1957; Hammer Film Productions.
Fisher, Terence, dir., *The Revenge of Frankenstein*. 1958; Hammer Film Productions.
Fisher, Terence, dir. *Dracula*. 1958; Hammer Film Productions.
Fisher, Terence, dir. *The Curse of the Werewolf*. 1961; Hammer Film Productions.
Fisher, Terence, dir. *The Gorgon*. 1964; Hammer Film Productions.
Fisher, Terence, dir. *The Earth Dies Screaming*. 1965; 20th Century Fox.
Fisher, Terence, dir. *Dracula: Prince of Darkness*. 1966; Hammer Film Productions.
Fisher, Terence, dir. *Frankenstein Created Woman*. 1967; Hammer Film Productions.
Fisher, Terence, dir. *The Devil Rides Out*. 1968; Hammer Film Productions.
Fisher, Terence, dir. *Frankenstein Must Be Destroyed*. 1969; Hammer Film Productions.
Fisher, Terence, dir. *Frankenstein and the Monster from Hell*. 1974; Hammer Film Productions.
Francis, Freddie, dir. *The Evil of Frankenstein*. 1964; Hammer Film Productions.
Francis, Freddie, dir. *Dr. Terror's House of Horrors*. 1965; Amicus Productions.
Francis, Freddie, dir. *The Skull*. 1965; Paramount Pictures.
Francis, Freddie, dir. *The Psychopath*. 1966; Paramount British Pictures.
Francis, Freddie, dir. *Dracula Has Risen from the Grave*. 1968; Hammer Film Productions.
Franco, Jesús, dir. *Marquis de Sade's Justine*. 1968; Corona Filmproduktion.
Franco, Jesús, dir. *Count Dracula*. 1970; Filmar Compagnia Cinematografica.
Franco, Jesús, dir. *Dracula, Prisoner of Frankenstein*. 1972; Fénix Cooperativa Cinematográfica.
Frankel, Cyril, dir. *Never Take Sweets from a Stranger*. 1960; Hammer Film Productions.
Fregonese, Hugo, dir. *Man in the Attic*. 1953; 20th Century Fox.
Freund, Karl, dir. *The Mummy*. 1932; Universal Pictures.
Gilling, John, dir. *The Plague of the Zombies*. 1966; Hammer Film Productions.
Girdler, William, dir. *The Manitou*. 1978; AVCO Embassy Pictures.
Glenville, Peter, dir. *The Prisoner*. 1955; Columbia Pictures.
Guest, Val, dir. *The Quatermass Xperiment*. 1955; Hammer Film Productions.
Guest, Val, dir. *The Abominable Snowman*. 1957; Hammer Film Productions.
Halperin, Victor, dir. *White Zombie*. 1932; Halperin Productions.
Halperin, Victor, dir. *Revolt of the Zombies*. 1936; Victor and Edward Halperin Productions.
Hart, Harvey, dir. *The Pyx*. 1973; Host Productions (Quebec).
Hillyer, Lambert, dir. *Dracula's Daughter*. 1936; Universal Pictures.
Hillyer, Lambert, dir. *The Invisible Ray*. 1936; Universal Pictures.
Hitchcock, Alfred, dir. *Vertigo* 1958; Paramount Pictures.
Honda, Ishirō, dir. *Godzilla*. 1954; Toho Studios.
Honda, Ishirō, dir. *King Kong vs Godzilla*. 1962; Toho Studios.
Honda, Ishirō, dir. *The War of the Gargantuas*. 1966; Toho Studios.
Honda, Ishirō, dir. *Frankenstein Conquers the World*. 1965; Toho Studios.

Honda, Ishirō, dir. *Furankenshutain Tai Baragon* [Frankenstein vs Baragon]. 1965; Toho Studios.
Hoyt, Harry O., dir. *The Lost World*. 1925; First National Pictures.
Huston, John, dir. *Freud*. 1962; Universal-International.
Huston, John, dir. *The Night of the Iguana*. 1964; Metro-Goldwyn-Mayer.
Ivens, Joris, dir. *Regen/Rain*. 1929; Capi-Holland.
Jarvis, Richard, dir. *New Faces Come Back*. 1946; National Film Board of Canada.
Julian, Rupert, dir. *The Phantom of the Opera*. 1925; Universal Pictures.
Kaufman, Philip, dir. *The Right Stuff*. 1983; Warner Brothers.
Kazan, Elia, dir. *East of Eden*. 1955; Warner Brothers.
Kenton, Erle C., dir. *The Ghost of Frankenstein*. 1942; Universal Pictures.
Kenton, Erle C., dir. *House of Frankenstein*. 1944; Universal Pictures.
Kenton, Erle C., dir. *House of Dracula*. 1945; Universal Pictures Company Inc.
Kluska, Jennifer and Derek Drymon, dirs. *Hotel Transylvania: Transformania*. 2021; Sony Pictures.
Koch, Howard W., dir. *Frankenstein 1970*. 1958; Aubrey Schenck Productions.
Kramer, Stanley, dir. *On the Beach*. 1959; United Artists.
Kroitor, Roman and Colin Low, dirs. *Universe*. 1960; National Film Board of Canada
Kubrick, Stanley, dir. *2001: A Space Odyssey*. 1968; Metro-Goldwyn-Mayer.
Lamont, Charles, dir. *Abbott and Costello Meet Dr. Jekyll and Mr. Hyde*. 1953; Universal-International.
Lamont, Charles, dir. *Abbott and Costello Meet the Mummy*. 1955; Universal-International.
Landers, Lew, dir. *The Raven*. 1935; Universal Pictures.
Landers, Lew, dir. *Return of the Vampire*. 1943; Columbia Pictures.
Lang, Fritz, dir. *Metropolis*. 1927; UFA (Universum-Film).
Lang, Fritz, dir. *Hangmen Also Die!*. 1944; United Artists.
Lang, Fritz, dir. *Scarlet Street*. 1945; Universal Pictures.
Lanzmann, Claude, dir. *Shoah*. 1985. New Yorker Films.
Laugier, Pascal, dir. *Martyrs*. 2008; Wild Bunch.
Lee, Rowland V., dir. *The Son of Frankenstein*. 1939; Universal Pictures.
Leone, Damien, dir. *Frankenstein vs The Mummy*. 2015; Image Entertainment.
Levey, William A., dir. *Blackenstein*. 1973; Prestige Pictures.
Lubin, Arthur, dir. *Black Friday*. 1940; Universal Pictures.
Ludwig, Edward, dir. *Jivaro*. 1954; Paramount Pictures.
Mamoulian, Rouben, dir. *Dr. Jekyll and Mr. Hyde*. 1931; Paramount.
Marcus, Adam, dir. *Jason Goes to Hell: The Final Friday*. 1993; New Line Cinema.
Martinez Solares, Gilberto, dir. *Santo y Blue Demon contra Los Monstruos* [Santo and Blue Demon vs. the Monsters]. 1970; Cinematográfica Sotomayor.
McNaughton, John, dir. *Henry: Portrait of a Serial Killer*. 1986; Greycat Films.
Méliès, Georges, dir. *Le manoir du diable*. 1896; Star Film.
Méliès, Georges, dir. *A Trip to the Moon*. 1902; Star Film Company.
Milestone, Lewis, dir. *All Quiet on the Western Front*. 1930; Universal Pictures.
Minnelli, Vincente, dir. *The Cobweb*. 1955; Metro-Goldwyn-Mayer.
Montgomery, Robert, dir. *The Lady in the Lake*. 1947; Metro-Goldwyn-Mayer.
Murnau, F. W., dir. *Nosferatu*. 1922; Prana Film.
Neill, Roy William, dir. *Frankenstein Meets the Wolf Man*. 1943; Universal Pictures.
Pasolini, Pier Paolo, dir. *Salò, or the 120 Days of Sodom*. 1975; United Artists.
Peele, Jordan, dir. *Get Out*. 2017. Universal Pictures.

Peele, Jordan, dir. *Us*. 2019; Universal Pictures.
Polanski, Roman, dir. *Rosemary's Baby*. 1968; Paramount Pictures.
Polonsky, Abraham, dir. *Force of Evil*. 1948; Metro-Goldwyn-Mayer.
Post, Ted, dir. *Beneath the Planet of the Apes*. 1970; 20th Century Fox.
Preminger, Otto, dir. *Laura*. 1944; 20th Century Fox.
Ray, Nicholas, dir. *Rebel Without a Cause*. 1955; Warner Brothers.
Ray, Nicholas, dir. *King of Kings*. 1961; Metro-Goldwyn-Mayer.
Reiner, Carl, dir. *The Man with Two Brains*. 1983; Warner Brothers.
Resnais, Alain, dir. *Hiroshima, mon Amour*. 1959; Cocinor.
Roddam, Franc, dir. *The Bride*. 1985; Columbia Pictures.
Roeg, Nicolas, dir. *Don't Look Now*. 1973; British Lion Films.
Roffman, Julian, dir. *The Bloody Brood*. 1959; Meridian Films Ltd.
Roffman, Julian, dir. *The Mask*. 1961; Warner Brothers.
Roth, Eli, dir. *Hostel*. 2005; Lions Gate Films.
Rowland, Roy, dir. *The 5000 Fingers of Dr. T*. 1953; Columbia Pictures.
Sangster, Jimmy, dir., *The Horror of Frankenstein*. 1970; Hammer Film Productions.
Sasdy, Peter, dir. *Taste the Blood of Dracula*. 1970; Warner Brothers.
Schaffner, Franklin, dir. *Planet of the Apes*. 1968; 20th Century Fox.
Scott, Ridley, dir. *Alien*. 1979; 20th Century Fox.
Sharman, Jim, dir. *The Rocky Horror Picture Show*. 1975; 20th Century Fox.
Sharp, Don, dir. *The Kiss of the Vampire*. 1962; Hammer Film Productions.
Siodmak, Robert, dir. *Son of Dracula*. 1943; Universal Pictures.
Six, Tom, dir. *The Human Centipede (First Sequence)*. 2009; Bounty Films.
Six, Tom, dir. *The Human Centipede II (Full Sequence)*. 2011; Bounty Films.
Six, Tom, dir. *The Human Centipede III (Final Sequence)*. 2015; Six Entertainment Company.
Soler, Julián, dir. *El castillo de los monstrous* [Castle of the Monsters]. 1958; Columbia Pictures.
Sommers, Stephen, dir. *Van Helsing*. 2004; Universal Pictures.
Spielberg, Steven, dir. *Jaws*. 1975; Universal Pictures.
Strock, Herbert L., dir. *I was a Teenage Frankenstein*. 1957; Santa Rose Productions.
Tappe, Holger, dir. *Monster Family*. 2017; Ambient Entertainment.
Tartakovsky, Genndy, dir. *Hotel Transylvania*. 2012; Sony Pictures.
Tartakovsky, Genndy, dir. *Hotel Transylvania 2*. 2015; Sony Pictures.
Tartakovsky, Genndy, dir. *Hotel Transylvania 3: Summer Vacation*. 2018; Sony Pictures.
Taylor, Don, dir. *Escape from the Planet of the Apes*. 1971; 20th Century Fox.
Thompson, D. Lee, dir. *Battle for the Planet of the Apes*. 1973; 20th Century Fox.
Thompson, David, dir. *Francis Bacon: Paintings, 1944–1962*. 1963; BBC.
Tourneur, Jacques, dir. *I Walked with a Zombie*. 1943; RKO Radio Pictures.
Tully, Montgomery, dir. *The Terrornauts*. 1967; Amicus Productions.
Ulmer, Edgar G., dir. *The Black Cat*. 1934; Universal Pictures.
Wagener, Paul and Carl Boese, dirs. *The Golem: How He Came into the World*. 1920; PAGU.
Waggner, George, dir. *Man-made Monster*. 1941; Universal Pictures.
Waggner, George, dir. *The Wolf Man*. 1941; Universal Pictures.
Walker, Stuart, dir. *The Werewolf of London*. 1935; Universal Pictures.
Wan, James, dir. *Saw*. 2004; Lions Gate Films.
Waters, John, dir. *Pink Flamingos*. 1972; New Line Cinema.

Wegener, Paul, and Carl Boese, dirs. *Der Golem*. 1920; UFA (Universum-Film).
Weir, Peter, dir. *The Last Wave*. 1977; United Artists.
Welles, Mel, dir. *Lady Frankenstein*. 1971; Condor International Films.
Wellman, William, dir. *The Story of GI Joe*. 1947; United Artists.
Whale, James, dir. *Frankenstein*. 1931; Universal Pictures.
Whale, James, dir. *The Invisible Man*. 1933; Universal Pictures.
Whale, James, dir. *The Bride of Frankenstein*. 1935; Universal Pictures
Wiene, Robert, dir. *The Cabinet of Dr. Caligari*. 1920; Decla-Bioscop.
Winckler, William, dir. *Frankenstein vs The Creature from Blood Cove*. 2005; William Winckler Productions.
Wise, Robert, dir. *The Haunting*. 1963; Metro-Goldwyn-Mayer.
Zinneman, Fred, dir. *The Nun's Story*. 1959; Warner Brothers.

Index

Page numbers in italics represent illustrations.

Abbott and Costello Meet Frankenstein
  (film) 36–7
abjection. *See also* Frankenstein's monster
  and agency 220, 230
  and defiance 138, 140 n.33, 140
  male self-procreation 96
  monsters as 133–4 n.5
  as threats 214, 215
  wraiths embodiment of 217, 223
adaptations 30, 101 n.15, 101. *See also various Frankenstein* adaptations
adaptation studies 114–18
Adorno, Theodor 152
  Composing for the Films 156, 168
Afro-Futurism, defined 118–19, 129
Afro-Futurism and Frankenstein
  Frankenstein adaptations 118–20
  mad scientists and 119, 123–6
  organ music 121–5
  rap 123–5
  zombie music of Monk 121–2
Agrippa 23–4
alchemy
  and birth/procreation 87–8, 92, 95–7
  courage and 102–3
  defined 98
  vs. electricity in lab 90
  overview 23–4, 91–2
  patriarchal alchemy 92–3, 95–7
  and Rosicrucians 25–6
  Shelley's publishing house 22
Alien (film) 169
allegory. *See also* women as monsters
  of allegory 207, 209, 211–12
  defined 198, 201
  distaste for 201, 206
  Get Out 208
  history of horror 199
  The Human Centipede 205–7
  as monstrous 202

  in porn 205
  Salò, or the 120 Days of Sodom 201–2
  in simple horror 199–201
  unconsumable films 208 n.34, 208, 212
  Us 208–9, 209 n.39, 210–11, 211 n.48
  as validation 200
Allegory: The Theory of a Symbolic Mode (Fletcher) 201
Anabelle (character) 220–2
androgyny 26
anxiety 126–9, 150, 215
Applebaum, Louis 158–9, 166–7
archaeology 195
Arley 80, 82, 83
Armitage, Missy (character) 177–80, 183, 184
Armitage, Rose (character) 173–7, 180, 183, 184
assimilation/brainwashing 178–80
atonality. *See also* twelve-tone method
  and agitated emotions 163, 171
  "James Dean sound" 162
  as otherness 150
  risks of 155
  as sound of horror 151–5

"Bad Luck Brian" meme 203
Baldick, Christopher, *In Frankenstein's Shadow* 116–17
Baron-Wilson, Margaret Harries 79, 82
Barthes, Roland 201–2, 205
BDSM 204–5. *See also* sex/violence
Begleitmusik zu einer Lichtspielszene (Schoenberg) 153–4
Bentley's Standard Novels 22, 65
Bernard, James 164–5
bestiaries 215–16. *See also The Witcher 3: Wild Hunt*
birdsong 67–8

birth/procreation
    and alchemy   24–6
    death from   12
    illegitimate   11 n.6, 11, 12, 26
    as male pseudoscience   87–91, 93–7, 106
    the Monster   9–10, 21, 31, 86–7 (see also self-procreation)
    theatricality (see self-procreation)
    women extracted from   90–3
Blake, William   16
Blanco, Mykki   146–8
The Bloody Brood (film)   167
Boyle, Danny   85–8, 96
Bradley, Scott   157–8
Bride of Frankenstein (film)   24, 32, 35 n.18, 66, 76
brides
    bride of the Monster   9–10, 29, 32, 93
    wraiths in *The Witcher*   216, *217*, 219
Briefer, Dick   50, 50 n.17
Brown, Norman O.   206, 207
Browne, Max   20
bruxae   227–8, *228*
Byron (Lord)   10–12

Canadian hip house   124, 128–9
Case, Sue-Ellen, "Tracking the Vampire"   136–7, 139
Castelnuovo-Tedesco, Mario   *161*, 169–70
The Cat That Hated People (cartoon)   158
censorship   100, 111, 205
Champion (opera)   138–9
Chaney, Lon, Jr.   32, 33, 39
The Chemical Wedding of Christian Rosencreutz (Andreae)   25
Chevalier, William   16
cinema
    adaptations   30, 101 n.15, 101–2
    and comic images   50
    early sound   49
    as fragmented   31, 42
    Monster as filmed event   52–3
    Monster's birth   87
    and morality   100
    restorations   99–100
    and Shelley's story   28–9, 31, 46, 49

special effects   104–5, *105*, 110, 159
techniques to show inner states   106 n.35, 106–7 (see also music; sound)
voyeurism   107
white women on screen   184
Clairmont, Claire   11, 12
Clinton, George   118–19, 122, 126
clones. See Us
The Cobweb (film)   162
colonization   178, 189–92, 196–7
comedy   20, 72–3, 81
comics
    ages of   45 n.2
    and cinema images   50
    Comics Code   50 n.16
    framing   57 n.29, 57–62
    iconic representations   43
    linear/concrescent serialization   43–4, 48–9, 56–8
    Luhmann's theory   54–5
    repetition/innovation   43–4, 46 n.7, 51–3, 55–6, 60
    retcon   56 n.26, 56
    speculation   55–6, 56 nn.25–6
    text and image   54–5, 62–3
coming out   141–3
composers lineage   *161*
Composing for the Films (Eisler and Adorno)   156, 168
confusion of Frankenstein and Monster name   28, 45–6, 120
Cooke, Thomas Potter (T. P.)   18, 65–6, 74 n.56, 75–7
coprophagia   204–5
corpse experiments   77
couplings   54–5
Cowper, William   79, 82
Creed, Barbara   215, 226
Cunningham, John William   80, 82, 83
curses   190–2, 196–7

dark power   138–9
Dawley, J. Searle. See *Frankenstein* (1910)
Day of the Beast (film)   96–7
Deadmau5   127–8
"Deep Lez I Statement" (Mitchell)   143–4

DeLacey family (characters)   68–70, 75–6, 78–81
De Natura Rerum (Paracelsus)   24
Denson, Shane   43–63 n.11
Der Tunnel (film)   90–1
Detective Comics #135, 52 n.18
Deutsch, Didier C.   94
disidentification   137 n.19, 137, 138–40, 141 n.40, 146
dissonance. *See* atonality; twelve-tone method
Divine   134, 140
Donnelly, K. J.   27–42
doppelgängers. *See* Us
Dracula   34–7, 39, 120. *See also* vampires
Dracula vs. Frankenstein (1971) (film)   38–9
Dracula vs. Frankenstein/Assignment Terror (1970) (film)   38
Dracula vs. Frankenstein/Dracula, Prisoner of Frankenstein (1972) (film)   39
Drake family (characters). *See The Four Skulls of Jonathan Drake*
drive-in cinemas   37

Earth-616   47, 50, 58
East of Eden (film)   161–2
Ecstasy/MDMA   125–6
Edison Studios   111. *See also Frankenstein* (1910)
Eisler, Hanns   155–6, *161*
  Composing for the Films   156, 168
electricity   24, 89–92
electronic dance music (EDM)   125–9
Elizabeth (character)
  Monster romance   12–13
  Victor romance   60, 93–7, 103, 109, 111, 112
  emotional blankness   142–3
erotic artwork   21–2. *See also* homoeroticism
The Evil of Frankenstein (film)   94–5
excremental vision   206 n.30, 206
expressionism   152–4

Faust   18–19, *19*, 23, 26
Faust (1825) (play)   18

feces consumption. *See The Human Centipede*
femme fatales   223–9, *224–8*
Ferreira, Seabra   92
figure/ground   27–8
Fletcher, Angus, *Allegory: The Theory of a Symbolic Mode*   201
Florescu, Radu   29
The Fly (1986) (film)   200
The Four Skulls of Jonathan Drake (film)   189–97
Frankel, Benjamin   *161*, 165
Frankenphemes   117–18, 123–4. *See also* Monster Mash films
Frankenstein (1910) (film)   *105*, *109*
  censoring novel   100, 111–13
  as centering Monster   29
  Cooke echoing   66
  keyholes   107 n.39, *107*
  overview   98
  psychological horror   105–6, 106 n.34
  reflections   107–9
  restoration of   99–100
  special effects   104, 111
  Victor as God-like   103
Frankenstein (1931) (film)
  as centering Monster   29
  and Cook performance   66
  electricity   89–90
  Karloff copyright   28 n.5
  and Schoenberg   154
  sound in   31 n.14, 49
Frankenstein (1974) (play)   85–6, 90
Frankenstein (2011) (play)   85–8, 96
Frankenstein (opera)   *234*
Frankenstein (Shelley). *See* Shelley, Mary Wollstonecraft
Frankenstein, el vampiro y compañía (film)   37
Frankenstein, or the Demon of Switzerland (play)   64–5
Frankenstein, Victor (character), and
  alchemy   24–6
  as ambiguous with Monster   46, 106, 108–9, 111
  apathy to women/natural reproduction   94–7
  destroying female monster   9–10

as divorced from Monster 40
feminization of 26
"Frankenstein" as the Monster 28,
  45–6, 120
as God-like 103
happy ending in 1910 film 103, 109,
  112
homoeroticism with Monster 13–16,
  17, 20
incest 11
laboratory 17–20, 17, 23, 24, 26,
  88–90
in Monster Mash films 36
psychological horror 106
Silver Surfer #7 (comic) 52
sound/silence reflecting character 74
staking Dracula 39
Frankenstein Conquers the World
  (film) 38
Frankenstein: Day of the Beast (film) 90
Frankenstein Meets the Wolf Man
  (film) 32–3, 35–6, 51
Frankenstein novel and popular culture
  creation scene in films 87
  creation scene in plays 86
  Detective Comics #135, 52 n.18
  Frankenstein (1910) 100–4
  Frankenstein (1931) 49
  Frankenstein (2011) 85
  Hollywood films 28–9, 31
  The Monster of Frankenstein 58
  overview 46
  technology 31
  theatricality 97
  Victor Frankenstein 94
  The X-Men #40, 51–2
Frankenstein or the Model Man (play) 89
Frankenstein's monster (Monster)
  (character). *See also various films*
  as ambiguous with Victor 46, 106,
    108–9, 111
  as articulate 85–6
  as automaton/android 41–2, 52
  beautiful body 13, *14*
  creation as filmed event 52–3
  creation of (*see* birth/procreation; self-
    procreation)
  death drive 35–6, 51
  desire for mate 9
  as diegetic/nondiegetic 49, 51, 53,
    56 n.26, 61–2
  as divorced from creator 40
  feminization of 26
  as fragmented 31, 41–2
  framing in comics 58–62
  as friendly 37
  goodness of 39, 68
  as hipster 38
  history in DC Comics 45 n.3, 47 n.10
  history in Marvel Comics 45–7
  Holst's features and 18
  homoeroticism with Victor 13–16,
    20
  identity as relational 27–8, 41
  known as "Frankenstein" 28, 45–6,
    120
  in *Marvel Comics Database* 46–7
  as mascot 40 n.28
  music/sound reflecting character 67–
    70
  as mute 33, 49, 62, 84
  as neglected child 9, 12, 19, 68 n.25,
    69 n.27, 69
  seeing own erection 17, 20
  as self-reflexive 49 (*see also* comics)
  as serial figure/character 48–50, 53,
    55–6, 61–2
  size of 24
  snatching music 75–6
  as social 30
  as stock character 30–1, 37, 39
    (*see also* comics; Monster Mash
    films)
  as streamlined 36, 41
  television versions 40 n.29
  and transgender rage 138
  trick effects in *Frankenstein*
    (1910) 104, *105*, 110, 111
  as ugly 13, 73
  Universal Pictures' derivative 29–30,
    51–3
  and vampires 34–7, 39, 41, 120
Frankenstein: The True Story (TV
  show) 95–6
Freedman, Harry 167
free love 11

Freud (film)   169
Fuseli, Henry   16, 18
   The Rosicrucian Cavern   25, 26

games   203, 229–31. *See also* video games; *The Witcher 3: Wild Hunt*
Gardner, Ray (character)   181–2
George IV (king of England)   21
Geralt (character). *See The Witcher 3: Wild Hunt*
Get Out (film)   172–81, 207–8
The Ghost of Frankenstein (film)   32–3, 35 n.18, 66
Godwin, William   11, 12, 23–4
Gold, Ernest   163–4
Goldsmith, Jerry   168–70
Gooding, Frederick W, Jr.   172–85
good *vs.* evil
   Dracula *vs.* the Monster   39
   Shelley's *Frankenstein*   103
   in Victor   106–8, 111, 112
   Wolf Man *vs.* the Monster   39
gothic aesthetic
   comedy   81
   Deadmau5   127
   Holst illustrations   17–18
   "The Initiation" (song)   148
   music and sound in novels   67
   Presumption, or the Fate of Frankenstein   72, 77–8, 81, 83–4
   "Vampires" (song)   142
   women and marriage   219–20
gothic theaters   65–6

Halloween (film)   199
Hammer Film Productions   37, 49 n.14, 49, 164–5
Hands Across America   209–10, 211 n.48, 211
Harmonielehre (Schoenberg)   151
Harris, Bertha   135
Henrique   82
Higney, John   64–84
Hollywood's Third Rail   173–6, 184
Holst, Theodor von   16–21
   Faust in his Study   19
   Frankenstein   17, 20, 23, 26

homoeroticism
   Byron and Polidori   10–11
   Der Tunnel   90–1
   Holst illustration   17, *20*
   Lagerquist illustrations   13, *14*
   Ward illustrations   13–14, *15*
homophobia. *See also* queerness embracing monstrosity
   disidentification   137–9, 141 n.40, 146
   double pressures   142–3
   lesbian monstrosity   135, 144–5, 226
   monstrous signifiers   133–4
homosexual panic   15–16, 20
homunculi   24, 25, 92
horror
   allegory and history of   199
   allegory in simple horror   199–201
   and atonality   151–5
   Frankenstein (1910) avoiding   111–13
   and Indigenous peoples   186–7
   paranoid   194
   psychological horror   105–6, 106 n.34
   secure   194, 196
   and twelve-tone method   160
House of Dracula (film)   33–4, 35, 36 n.19, 36
House of Frankenstein (film)   33–6, 38
The Human Centipede (film)   202–5, *204*, 206, 207, 209
Humphrey, Daniel   198–212
hunchbacks   34, 35
Hutcheon, Linda   100–2, 115–17

iconflation   120–1, 125
illegitimate children   11 n.6, 11, 12, 26
illness   221–2
"Imago" (Nieto)   134
incest   11–12
Indigenous peoples
   in *Frankenstein*   187
   history in horror   186–7
   in "An Introduction to the American Horror Film"   187–8
   as monstrosity   189, 192, 195
   and repression   188–9
   and Sasquatch   145–6
   as vanishing   196–7

In Frankenstein's Shadow (Baldick) 116–17
"The Initiation" (song) 147–8
insincerity/manipulation. *See* women as monsters
interracial mixing 173–6, 184
intertextuality 116–17. *See also* Monster Mash films
"An Introduction to the American Horror Film" (Wood) 187–9

Jackson, Michael 122–3
Jenkins, Philip 126
Jivaro people. *See The Four Skulls of Jonathan Drake*

Karloff, Boris 28 n.5, 29–30, 32, 51–3
Klock, Geoff 45 n.3
Koepnick, Lutz 90–1
Kool Keith 122, 126

laboratory
  and alchemy 23, 90
  astrology in 26
  electricity 24, 89–92
  as gothic 17–20, *17, 19–20* , 89
  theatricality 88–90, 93
Lady Frankenstein (film) 40
Lady Sasquatch (Mitchell) 144–6
Lagerquist, Carl 13, *14*
La maldición de Frankenstein (film) 90
language 49
The Last Laugh (play) 89–90
Leeder, Murray 186–97
Leigh, Augusta 11
Le manoir du diable (film) 105
lesbians as monsters 135, 144–5, 226. *See also* queerness embracing monstrosity; women as monsters
"Let Your Backbone Slide" (song) 123–5
Loiselle, André 85–97
Longworth, Karina 202–3
Lowe, Chris 141–3
Lugosi, Bela 32, 33
Luhmann, Niklas 54–5, 57–8
Luko, Alexis 1–5
Lutyens, Elisabeth *161*, 165
lynchings 174

McCutcheon, Mark A. 114–29
  The Medium Is the Monster 31
McLuhan, Marshall 27–8, 114
mad scientists 119, 123–6. *See also* az; *The Human Centipede*
Maestro Fresh Wes 123–5
The Man and the Monster (play) 89
marginality. *See* abjection; comics
marriage
  alchemy gold and silver 24–5
  gothic aesthetic 219–20
  women as monsters 216–17, 219–20
marriage/romance
  Elizabeth and Monster 12–13
  Victor and Elizabeth 60, 93–7, 103, 109, 111, 112
Marvel Comics. *See* comics
The Mary Shelley pub 28
Mary Shelley's Frankenstein (film) 95, 115
masculinity 87–91, 94–7
The Mask (film) 166–7
Mayer, Ruth 48 n.11
Meglis, Constantine *234*
melodrama 71–3, 73 n.50, 76–7
Milner, Henry 88–9
misogyny 214–16, 223, 227
Mitchell, Allyson 143–6
Moers, Ellen 11
Monáe, Janelle 119
Monk, Thelonious 121–3
the Monster. *See* Frankenstein's monster
Monster Mash films
  Abbott and Costello Meet Frankenstein 36–7
  actors playing the Monster 32–3
  brains 35
  characters meeting themselves 33, 34, 120
  defined 30
  Dracula vs. Frankenstein/Assignment Terror 38, 39
  as fragmented 31, 39, 41–2
  House of Dracula 33–4, 35, 36 n.19, 36
  House of Frankenstein 33–6, 38
  Japanese films 38
  Mexican films 37 n.24, 37

the Monster and Universal   29–30
the Monster at conclusions   35
parallel universes   36
parodied   40 n.27
The Monster of Frankenstein (comic series)   43, 56–62
The Monster of Frankenstein #3 (comic)   43
Monsters Unleashed (comic series)   61, 62 n.32
monster theory   190
monstrosity. *See also* lesbian monstrosity; queerness embracing monstrosity; women as monsters
   of allegory   202
   of assimilation/brainwashing   179–80
   curing in *House of Dracula*   35
   of free love   11
   illness as   221–2
   as Indigeneity   189, 192, 195
   as murder justification   217–18
   as Otherness   189–90, 213–15
   Otherness as   189–90, 213–15
   signifiers oppressing queer people   133–4
   technology as   114, 126–8
moral psychology   98 n.1, 98, 100–1, 106–8, 111
Mulvey-Roberts, Marie   9–16
music
   1930's films overview   154–5
   1940's films overview   155–60
   1950's films overview   161–5
   1960s films overview   165–9
   adaption practices   117
   armonicas   77
   Blanco   146–8
   Bride of Frankenstein   93
   consonances/dissonances   151–2 (*see also* atonality; twelve-tone method)
   electric dance music (EDM)   125–8
   Frankenstein (1910)   109–10
   guitar/synthesizer   123
   House of Dracula   36 n.19
   live   126–8
   Monster snatching   75–6
   organs   121–5, 127
   Pet Shop Boys   141–3

   from play to screen   67
   rap   123–5
   reflecting Monster's character   67–70, 76–8
   reusing   31 n.15, 34, 39, 169
   sampling/sequencing   115–17, 126
   tempo   124
   theater types   71–2
   theatricality   88
   Universal reusing   31 n.15, 34
   Universal's aversion to   154–5
   zombie music   121–2
"My Words to Victor Frankenstein..." Stryker   138, 139

negrophobia   173–4
Neumeyer, David   154, 162
New Faces Come Back (documentary)   159
niceness   183, 184
Nieto, Tristan Alice   134
North, John (character)   101

Otherness
   atonality   150
   exclusion   139
   as monstrosity   189–90, 213–15
   native culture   145
   and repression   188
   and violence   218 (*see also* violence, dehumanizing)
   women as   214

Paracelsus   92
   De Natura Rerum   24
parallel universes   33, 36, 56–7, 57 n.28. *See also* comics; Monster Mash films
paranoid horror   194
Pasolini, Pier Paolo   201, 208 n.34, 212
patriarchal alchemy   92–3, 95–7
patriarchy   177 n.5, 180 n.11, 180, 182–4, 214–15. *See also* misogyny
Peake, Richard Brinsley   64, 79–80. *See also Presumption, or the Fate of Frankenstein*
pederasty   11
Peele, Jordan. *See Get Out*; *Us*

Perry, Lee "Scratch"   118–19, 123
Pet Shop Boys   141–3
phalluses
    blades   218–19
    drills in *Der Tunnel*   91
    Holst illustrations   19–21
    sirens   225–6
    voices as weapons   229
    Ward illustrations   14, *15*
    Young Frankenstein   12–13
Picart, Caroline Joan   28
The Picture of Dorian Gray (Wilde)   139
Pindar, Peter (John Wolcot)   79, 82, 83
Pink Flamingos (film)   134
plague maiden   220–2, *221*
Planet of the Apes (film)   168–9
plausibility   200
Polidori, John   10
    "The Vampyre"   10–11, 120
popular culture, evolution of   44
pornography   21–2, 22 n.46, 26, 200–5
poverty   209–10, 211 n.48
Presumption, or the Fate of Frankenstein (play)
    and *Frankenstein* (1910)   66
    hoax of   16
    music   67, 70–3, 75–8, 81 n.80
    poetry   82–3
    popularity of   64–5
    Shelley's reaction to   64, 84
    silence   74
    songs   67, 70–1, 78–84, 81 n.80
    sound   72–3
psychological horror   105 n.31, 105–6
"Puttin' on the Dog" (cartoon)   157–8, *158*

The Quartermass Xperiment (film)   164–5
queer as term   137
queerness embracing monstrosity
    Blanco two faces   147
    Lady Sasquatch   144–6
    mantle of evil   136–40
    Otherness as exclusion   139
    Tabitha (character)   134–5
    Urselin   135

"Vampires" (song)   141–3
Waters's films   134

race. *See Get Out*; *Us*
race mixing   173–6, 184, 192–3
racism   145. *See also Get Out*; *Us*
rape
    Frankenstein (2011)   10
    Monster of Elizabeth   96–7
    of Victor   13, *14*
    The Witcher 3: Wild Hunt   219 n.24, 219, 223, 225
Rathburn, Eldon   *161*, 167
raves   125–6
repetition/innovation   43–4, 46 n.7, 51–3, 55–6, 60, 117
repression   187–8
reused footage   35 n.18
reused music   31 n.15, 34, 39, 169
reused texts   82
Rieger, James   24
Rigby, Mair   14–16
Rochberg, George   170, 171
Rosencreutz, Christian   25–6
Rosenman, Leonard   161–2, *161*
Rózsa, Miklós   *161*, 167–8

Salgueiro, Maria Aline   92
Salò, or the 120 Days of Sodom (film)   201–2, 205, 212
Salter, Hans   159–60, *161*
sasquatches   144–6
Schaeffer, Myron   166–7
Schoenberg, Arnold   151–3, 156, 157, *161*, 170
    Begleitmusik zu einer Lichtspielszene   153–4
science fiction. *See* Afro-Futurism
scopophilia   107–8
Scott, Grant F.   *14*
Scott, Ridley   169
Searle, Humphrey   *161*, 163
secure horror   194, 196
Sedgwick, Eve Kosofsky   15
self-procreation
    alchemy as   92
    distancing from domesticity   96
    and German cinema   90–1

monsters as women   215
    as patriarchal domination   94
    and theatricality   87–90, 93, 97
self-reflection
    Afro-Futurism   124
    Frankenstein (1910)   107
    serial Frankenstein's monsters   49, 52–3, 59
    Shelley's *Frankenstein*   49
    technology   118
serials. *See also* comics; twelve-tone method
    characters *vs.* figures   48 n.11, 48–9, 58, 61–2
    as lacking center   44
    and mediality   54–6, 57 n.29, 57–8
    Monster Mash films as   34
sexual deviancy   16. *See also* homoeroticism; homosexual panic
sexuality as evil   216
sex/violence   203, 218–19, 219 n.24, 227. *See also* torture-porn
Shelley, Mary Wollstonecraft. *See also Frankenstein* novel and popular culture
    Frankenstein as modern myth   116–18
    Frankenstein Bentley's Standard Novels   22, 65
    and Holst   22
    idea for novel   10
    illegitimate children   11 n.6, 11
    on invention   4
    Mathilda   11
    monstrosity of the nursery   11–12
    music/sound in novel   67–70, 78
    and *Presumption* play sound/music   67
    publishing *Frankenstein*   22, 64
    science in *Frankenstein*   77, 102–3
Shelley, Percy   11, 22, 101
shrunken heads. *See* tsantsas
Silver Surfer #7 (comic)   52–5
sirens   224–7, 225–6, 228–9
Six, Tom. *See The Human Centipede*
slasher films   199–200
slavery   178–9
Society for the Suppression of Vice   21

sodomy trials/executions   15–16
Son of Frankenstein (film)   32, 66
Soul (film)   181–2
sound
    Bride of Frankenstein   94
    Frankenstein (1931)   31, 49
    Frankenstein (2011)   86–7
    Frankenstein Meets the Wolf Man   33
    from play to screen   67
    reflecting Monster's character   67–8, 70, 77–8
    reflecting Victor's character   74
    women as monsters   228–9
Stang, Sarah   213–31
Stryker, Susan, "My Words to Victor Frankenstein…"   138, 139
substrate/form   54–5
subterranean tunnels   210–11
succubi   223–4, 224, 227
Sun Ra   118–19
suspense   178, 181
Swift, Jonathan   206 n.30, 206

technology
    Black secret technology   123
    Frankenphemes   117–18, 123–4
    as monstrosity   114, 126–8
    redefined by Frankenstein scenario   31
Tennant, Neil   141–3
theater regulations   65–6
theatricality   87–90, 93, 97
"Thriller" (song)   122–3
Tom and Jerry cartoon   157–8, *158*
torture-porn   200–4
Towns, Ethan   98–113
"Tracking the Vampire" (Case)   136–7, 139
transgender people   138, 139, 146–8
transvestitism   26
tsantsas   190, 192, 193, 195–6
twelve-tone method. *See also* atonality
    1940's films overview   155–60
    1950's films overview   161–5
    1960's films overview   165–9
    and comedy   157–8
    decline of   170, 171
    and drama   158–9
    East of Eden   161–2

Eisler 155–6
  fear of risk in 1930s 155
  and horror 160
  and radioactivity 164
22 (character) 181–2
Twitchell, James 30

Underground Railroad 210, 211
Universal Pictures. *See also Frankenstein* (1931); Monster Mash films
  film music 154–5
  Karloff as Monster 28 n.5, 29–30, 32, 51–3
  organ music 121
  overview 32
  reuse at 31 n.15, 31–2, 34
Urselin, Barbara 134–5, *136*
Us (film) 208–10, 209 n.39, *211*

vampires 120, 136–7, 141–3, 218, 227–8, 228. *See also* Dracula
"Vampires" (song) 141–3
"The Vampyre" (Polidori) 10–11, 120
Victor Frankenstein (film) 94
video games 214, 217–18, 230–1 n.47, 231. *See also* games; *The Witcher 3: Wild Hunt*
violence, dehumanizing 216–18
violence/sex 203, 218–19, 219 n.24, 227. *See also* BDSM; torture-porn

Wainewright, Thomas 21
Ward, Lynd 13–14, *15*
Washington, Chris (character) 173–80, 182, 184
Waters, John 134, 140
Watson, John and Charlotte 71, 81–2
Waxman, Franz 93–4
werewolves 135. *See also* Wolf Man
Whale, James. *See Frankenstein* (1931)
What If...? (comic series) 56 n.25
Whitesell, Lloyd 133–49
white supremacy/privilege 174, 176–7, 177 n.5, 180 n.11, 180, 182–5
white women. *See Get Out*

Wierzbicki, James 67, 110
Wilde, Oscar, *The Picture of Dorian Gray* 139
Williams, Allison 176, 184–5
witch doctors 191
The Witcher 3: Wild Hunt (video game)
  broken hearts and vengeful brides 216–23, *217–23*
  femme fatales 223–8
  overview 214, 215
  rape 219 n.24, 219
Wolcot, John (Peter Pindar) 79, 82, 83
Wolf Man 33, 35–6, 38, 39. *See also* werewolves
Wollstonecraft, Mary 12
women 19, 24
women as monsters. *See also* lesbian monstrosity
  agency 220
  deception 218
  fear 213–14
  femme fatales 223–9, *224–8*
  male anxieties 215, 229
  murder justification 217–18
  punishment 213–14
  sexuality as evil 216 (*see also femme fatales*)
  sounds of 228–9
  tragic marriage experiences 216–17, 219–20
  transgression 214–15, 230
  wraiths 216–19, *217–19*
Wood, Robin, "An Introduction to the American Horror Film" (Wood) 187–9
wraiths 216–19, *217–19*
Wright, James K. 1–5, 150–71

The X-Men #40 (comic) 51–5

Young Frankenstein (film) 12–13

zombies 134–5, 194, 195, 217
Zurich, Emil (character) 191–5
Zutai (character) 191–4

www.ingramcontent.com/pod-product-compliance
Lightning Source LLC
Chambersburg PA
CBHW052219300426
44115CB00011B/1747